W9-CBA-837

Francis A. Drexel
LIBRARY

Harvard Business School

Core Collection

1998

SAINT JOSEPH'S UNIVERSITY

The Marketing
Information
Revolution

REF

The Marketing Information Revolution

Edited by

ROBERT C. BLATTBERG
RASHI GLAZER
JOHN D.C. LITTLE

HF
5415.125
. M36C
1994

ST. JOSEPH'S UNIVERSITY

3 9353 00294 8840

Harvard Business School Press
Boston, Massachusetts

Copyright © 1994 by the President and Fellows of Harvard College
All rights reserved
Printed in the United States of America
98 97 96 95 94   5 4 3 2 1

Library of Congress Cataloging-in-Publication Data

The marketing information revolution / edited by Robert C. Blattberg,
    Rashi Glazer, John D.C. Little.
        p. cm.
    Includes bibliographic references and index.
    ISBN 0-87584-329-8 (alk. paper)
    1. Marketing—Data processing.   I.   Blattberg, Robert C., 1942–
    . II. Glazer, Rashi.   III. Little, John D.C.
    HF5415.125.M366   1994
    658.8′00285—dc20   93-15849
                                                         CIP

The paper used in this publication meets the requirements of the American National Standard for
Permanence of Paper for Printed Library Materials Z39.49-1984.

CONTENTS

v

INTRODUCTION

Robert C. Blattberg, Rashi Glazer, and John D.C. Little

FOR MORE THAN A GENERATION, futurists and other leading-edge pundits across many fields have predicted the onset of an "information age" in which information or knowledge replaces matter and energy as the primary resource of society. Among the most important developments of the past few years is the widespread, if belated, recognition that this prediction has finally come true. Notions of a "post-industrial" society, a "knowledge economy," and an "information revolution" are now commonplace, routinely invoked to explain a host of seemingly unrelated issues in a variety of disciplines.

As is true of all social institutions, business in general and marketing in particular are the beneficiaries of their own revolution. Almost all phases of marketing activity and thought, as well as the nature of the marketing function itself, are fundamentally being changed by the emergence of an information-based society. At the same time, most of the transformations have been "invisible," or at least without the conscious participation of the individuals and organizations involved. Now, however, there is a proliferation of new information-processing technologies being woven into the social fabric—unprecedented in both speed and scope of penetration—that is forcing explicit consideration of these transformations and rendering the invisible "visible."

This book is a collection of papers organized to discuss the impact of the information revolution on marketing theory and practice. Most of the papers were initially presented at a *Marketing Science Institute* conference, which brought together leading academics and practitioners working in different aspects of "information management" but whose activities have yet to be integrated within a common framework. The goal of the book is to provide that framework.

WHY A "REVOLUTION"?

There is nothing new about the concept of "information," or about collecting, analyzing, modeling, and using it as the basis of decision making. Marketing has always been primarily a function of information and information processing. The sophisticated use of marketing research began in the 1930s with innovators like A.C. Nielsen and continued to flourish into the 1990s. Why, then, is there a revolution?

Revolutions occur when the process of continuous change results in a discontinuity; or when a series of incremental, quantitative changes become qualitative. For decades, advances in the various components of information processing and transmission (data collection, analysis, and so forth) have been proceeding continuously, often independently, in more-or-less evolutionary fashion. Now, however, the cumulative effects of the simultaneous changes in the individual components have converged and resulted in a fundamental discontinuity—a qualitative change in the capacity to collect, store, process, and transmit information. Hence, a revolution.

In large measure, of course, this convergence has been driven by the technological convergence of the historically separated functions of information processing (i.e., computing) and information transmission (i.e., telecommunications). In this sense, the study of the marketing information revolution is the study of the role of information technology in marketing. The adoption of telecommunication and computer technology has resulted in dramatic increases in both the speed with which information is transmitted and in the amount of information that can be stored and processed in a given unit of time. It is, however, the product of these increases in transmission speed and processing capacity for creating new types of information organizations that form the heart of the revolution. As such, it is the information itself, and not the technology, that is the focus of concern.

This focus is reflected in the concept of the *information value chain* and in the related distinction between a cost-driven and value-driven approach to information and information management. Thus, cost-driven firms are oriented toward the recovery of costs associated with investments in the information technology infrastructure. Perhaps not surprisingly, the few studies that exist on the payoffs associated with investments in information technology conclude that the costs are almost never economically justified. By contrast, value-driven firms recognize technology as merely an "enabler" and focus on the use of information itself as the source of competitive advantage. The theme of this book is that the survivors of the marketing information revolution will be those organizations that recognize that technology is an enabler which will transform the firm into a truly customer-driven organization.

THE INFORMATION VALUE CHAIN

The concept of the information value chain is the organizing principle of this book. The information value chain contains five elements — data transmission and collection, data management, interpreted data ("information"), models, and decision support systems. Figure I-1 shows the information value chain schematically. In general, the chapters in this book are organized around the information value chain.

Data Transmission and Collection

The first stage in the information value chain is the *collection and transmission of data.* Indeed, the information revolution began with the use of technology to capture, store, and transmit raw data. Today, there are many forms of data capture, storage, and transmission. POS data are collected, stored, and transmitted from retail stores using electronic POS terminals. Electronic purchase diaries record all purchases of a household within and across outlet types and use electronic POS systems to collect and transmit the data. Customer purchase histories, captured and maintained on computer systems, have long served the direct marketing industry. Sales forces are now armed with laptop computers to record purchases, provide customers with the availability of specific SKUs, and track invoice and other relevant data required on a sales call. Hand-held computers are used to collect causal data such as whether an item is displayed at a specific drug store; these data are then transmitted to company headquarters. "Video carts," which provide consumers with information

FIGURE I-1
Information Value Chain

DATA COLLECTION AND TRANSMISSION	DATA MANAGEMENT	DATA INTERPRETATION: INFORMATION	MODELS	DECISION SUPPORT SYSTEMS
· Customer Files	· DB2	· DIS-Metaphor	· Time-Varying	· "SalesPartner"
· Causal Data	· Oracle	· CoverStory	· Mass Produced	· "AdExpert"
· POS	· Paradox	· Graphical	· Robust	· Models vs.
· Diary Panels		Information	· Adaptable	Managers
· Inventory		Presentations		· Adaptations to
Availability		· Summary		Managerial Inputs
		Statistics		

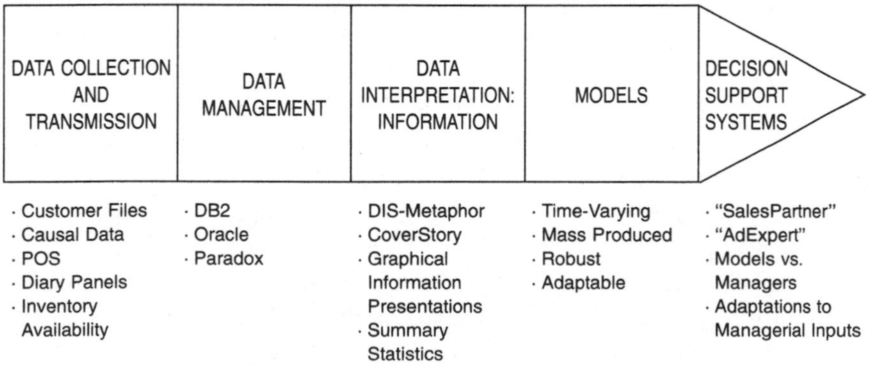

about specific products in grocery, drug, and mass merchandising chains, also capture information about how the customer shops at the store. As videotext systems (e.g., Prodigy) grow, purchase histories and causal data can be collected as a by-product of the customer's order. In business-to-business marketing companies such as Baxter/American Hospital Supplies use computer systems so their customers can order directly from them. The raw data about customer behavior are automatically captured by the computer system.

It is clear that capture of raw data has changed significantly from the days in which A.C. Nielsen sent auditors into retail stores once every two months to determine item sales or a salesperson transmitted an order through the mail. Computers and telecommunications have lowered the costs of collection and transmission of purchase and causal data. This transformation has led the way for the marketing information revolution. Chapters 2 and 3 are devoted to data collection systems. Ing and Mitchell (Chapter 2) focus on store-level data, while Deighton, Peppers, and Rogers (Chapter 3) concentrate on household-level data.

Data Management

As is increasingly becoming apparent, the quantity of raw data has begun to overwhelm users—both because of the sheer volume as well as the speed of capture. Once data have been collected and transmitted, the next stage in the information value chain is data management. Without a mechanism to *manage* the data, it will be useless. Many firms collect raw data, but very few have determined how to process and manage them so that they have value to the end-user. An example is the retailing industry, where great amounts of electronic POS data are routinely created. Yet, very few firms actually use the data; in part, because they cannot transform them into useful and succinct reports. Even if data are captured, they are maintained only for a relatively short period of time because of the cost and complexity of keeping vast quantities of data on-line. Therefore, processing data into a form that will allow it to be maintained and, more important, easily accessed by users is a critical step in turning data into meaningful information.

Computer tools, with the generic name of database managers, have been developed over the past two decades so that databases can be maintained efficiently. Commonly used database managers are DB2 for mainframes, Oracle for minicomputers, and Paradox and Dbase3 on PCs. Computerized database managers are now an integral component of the information value chain and much has been written about them elsewhere. In this volume, Ing (Chapter 4) describes current database management technology with an eye toward how it will change in the future and the implications for the marketing information revolution.

Interpreted Data—"Information"

For most observers, "information" is raw data that have been interpreted into a form meaningful to the user. The third stage in the information value chain is *data interpretation*. While database management tools such as DB2 can help organize and access the information, ultimately the real value from data comes from the ability to interpret them. Several different types of approaches have been developed to analyze raw data into user-meaningful forms. One class of early methods is embodied in the Metaphor Company's Data Interpretation System (DIS), now being marketed by IBM. DIS allows the user to take raw data, structure them in a relational database and then process them through various reporting, graphing, and tabling procedures. By allowing the user to process the raw data through various fundamental analysis tools, it was believed that the user would begin to capture key "learnings" from the data. The problem has been that systems such as DIS have been both data as well as labor intensive and managers rarely have time to use them to peruse databases. This has led to the need for managers to hire analysts to help interpret the data. Thus, DIS has become a fast and efficient method of creating tables, reports, and graphs for analysts, but is not a tool managers will use. Ing (Chapter 4) discusses DIS.

An alternative set of tools are expert systems, which analyze the data through the use of models or exception-reporting systems and then communicate the findings through textual information as opposed to reports and graphs. By developing heuristics to determine what is "news" in the data, these systems are able to do the searching for managers and provide interpretation of the events in the data. Schmitz (Chapter 5) discusses two examples of this approach, CoverStory and SalesPartner. The importance of these systems and others like them is that they take large databases and interpret the results by highlighting key data and events so managers can focus on the most relevant problems and opportunities. While these systems are still in their infancy, they have the promise to demonstrate efficient ways to search large databases.

McCann (Chapter 6) presents an alternative system which uses graphical presentational tools to simplify the information a manager receives so that it can easily be digested and understood. He argues that through the use of computer technology it may be possible to create a much more elaborate graphical or even animated delivery system, which combines reporting and interpretation so that the manager can receive the information in a form that is easy to comprehend and then act upon it.

Models

The next stage in the information value chain is *information modeling*. Statistical modeling of data has often been thought of as an advanced tool that few companies used or needed. Ironically, with the explosion of databases, this is no longer true. In the future, it may well be that the only way managers will realistically be able to summarize data is through key statistics that allow them to understand and interpret the environment in which they work. Historically, commonly used statistics in business are market share, sales growth, and penetration ratios and category and brand-development indices. More recently, more sophisticated statistical measures such as price elasticities, cannibalization measures, and feature and display multipliers are being used. By using statistical models, vast quantities of data can be reduced to relatively simple equations which can then be used for decision making. In retailing, tools such as price simulators and promotional design simulators rely heavily on models to determine what impact a decision has on sales and profits. Without models, managers rely on their judgment which may not lead to the most profitable decisions.

Little (Chapter 7) discusses the use of models to capture the effects of price and promotional variables on individual household behavior. Blattberg, Kim, and Ye (Chapter 8) address the development of automated large-scale models which will be necessary if the mega-databases that now exist in many industries are to be used effectively for decision support systems or in expert-based reporting systems.

Decision Support Systems

The goal of each stage of the information value chain is to add value to data. Ultimately, data and information are only valuable to the extent that they improve decision making. In recent years, a fifth stage in the information value chain has been identified—the *decision support system* (DSS). For many users, it has become apparent that, for the value of data to be maximized, it is desirable to enter the information into a decision support system so that managers can use the information to make decisions. There are a number of ways this can be accomplished and they are the concern of several chapters in this volume.

Burke (Chapter 9) describes the use of an expert system to help advertising executives make decisions. The relevant information is entered through rules and the output is a series of advertising copy recommendations. Mohan and Holstein (Chapter 10) describe the current state of DSS in industrial products companies and discuss some of the inhibitors to the growth of DSS in the industrial sector. Hoch (Chapter 11) addresses the issue of the form of a decision support system, focusing in particular on the relationship between models and human decision makers. Should a manager's intuition be included in the DSS? His answer is that a combination of models and managers is optimal and therefore it is clear that the manager's intuition needs to be incorporated in order to create a successful DSS.

IMPLEMENTATION AND THE FUTURE

The notion of an information value chain has emerged as a useful framework for organizing a wide range of issues associated with information technology and information management. There are, however, other topics that fall somewhat outside the value chain framework per se, but that are nevertheless crucial to a full appreciation of the impact of the marketing information revolution on business thought and practice. Several chapters in this volume are devoted to these topics.

While it is clear that software, hardware, and telecommunication technology is driving the rapidly changing marketing environment, the ability to utilize this technology is far behind. Part of the reason is lack of knowledge of the capabilities of information technology and part the organizational structure of the firm. Until the firm learns how to adapt, the potential advances in improved decision making available through better use of information will not occur. Day and Glazer (Chapter 12) discuss this extremely difficult and important issue.

Among the most far-reaching consequences of the marketing information revolution are those associated with the legal and ethical issues raised by the ability to collect, store, and process information on a scale unprecedented in human history. Ultimately, the degree to which the market information revolution "succeeds" will depend not only on marketplace activities but also on the decisions made by the society at large through its political and legal institutions. The interactions among business, legal, and political decision making with respect to the use of information and information technology are discussed by Bloom, Adler, and Milne (Chapter 13).

Paralleling the widespread social adoption of computers and telecommunications has been the globalization of business. While a thorough treatment of the international aspects of the marketing information revolution is beyond the scope of this book, the discussion would not be complete without an attempt to understand what is happening in this area outside the United States. In this regard, Katahira and Yagi (Chapter 14) describe the state of the art of marketing information technologies in Japan. Their chapter offers an interesting perspective on the issue of whether cultural factors and differences in customer behavior shape the particular ways in which information technologies for marketing are adopted by an economy.

Finally, the rest of the chapters in the book are bracketed by two general discussions which attempt to offer glimpses into the future. Blattberg and Glazer (Chapter 1) look into the future and discuss how information technology will change the role of marketing decision making within the firm. Specifically, they follow marketing through its stages of evolution and address how it will change based upon the information revolution. They describe a world in which customers communicate their needs through expert systems which transform the customer's language to the firm's product design language. They predict that customization of products will become more prevalent and describe the role of firm as assembling products from components produced by different manufacturers. This view of the firm and the role of marketing is far different from the current one in which products are produced and then sold. In their world, products are sold and then produced. This shift is made possible by information technology.

In a related vein, but from a different perspective, Haeckel (Chapter 15) concludes the volume by making predictions, some provocative, about what we are likely to see in a world dominated by information technology. Focusing on the notion of "information intensity" with respect to both the overall environment and individual organizations, he gives several examples and discusses how the future will change as firms catch up to information technology. Of perhaps greatest interest to both marketing practitioners and academics is his belief that, as firms struggle to align their information technology strategy with their overall business strategy, it is the discipline of marketing that will provide the "missing link" in the alignment process.

1

MARKETING IN THE INFORMATION REVOLUTION

Robert C. Blattberg and Rashi Glazer

IN THE PAST DECADE, *business rediscovered the customer. Building "market-driven," or "customer-focused" organizations became the rallying point for both competitive strategy and internal efforts at firm restructuring and "re-engineering." In an important sense, this renewed emphasis on customers, after several decades in which other concerns predominated, represents nothing more than the fulfillment of the age-old marketing concept which was supposed to guide company behavior—find out what people want and give it to them! However, what has become clear only in hindsight is that the marketing concept has been more of an ideal than a reality for most organizations, and that being truly customer focused is not possible if the organization is not, first, information intensive. In other words, the rediscovery of the customer is a by-product—perhaps the most important one—of the onset of the information revolution.*

In this introductory chapter, Blattberg and Glazer begin by tracing the role of marketing—and of marketing information—within the historical evolution of markets. They conclude that what is being called the "marketing information revolution" is really the fifth stage in an evolutionary process, one characterized by "decentralized products in decentralized markets." In such an environment, the key competitive question is, Who "controls" the customer? The authors suggest that the organization succeeding in customer control is not necessarily the one able to manufacture or produce the best products, but the one that becomes a "systems integrator" and, through information management, helps customers simplify their buying process. Within this framework, the chapter then describes the specific implications of the information revolution on the tactical elements comprising the marketing mix (product development, pricing, channels management, and marketing communications).

9

THE REVOLUTION IN CONTEXT: MARKETING ENTERS A NEW ERA

In this introductory chapter, we suggest ways the information revolution will likely transform the firm and the marketing function within it. (For related work in this area see Blattberg and Deighton 1990; Glazer 1991, 1993; Pine 1992.) How the information revolution will transform marketing is perhaps best understood in an historical context—i.e., by tracing the evolution of the market and highlighting the role of marketing activity during the various phases of the evolutionary process. An admittedly stylized and by-no-means complete review of market development identifies four such historical stages (as summarized in Figure 1-1):

1. *Pre-Market Stage*—what is often referred to as a "Robinson Crusoe" economy, characterized by self-sufficiency on the part of individuals and/or small social groups and the lack of meaningful levels of exchange. By definition, as an activity "marketing" does not exist in this phase.

2. *Undifferentiated "Products" in Decentralized Markets*—the beginnings of specialized "production"—and hence, the distinction between "firms" and "consumers"—and the emergence of opportunities for

FIGURE 1-1
Role of Marketing in Phases of Market Development

Market Phase	Role of Marketing
Pre-Market Stage "Robinson Crusoe"	
Undifferentiated Products/ Decentralized Markets	Marketing identifies buyers and sellers
Undifferentiated Products/ Centralized Markets	Efficient distribution; price set by market; beginning of advertising to generate awareness/primary demand
Differentiated Products/ Centralized Markets	Efficient distribution of specialized markets; target marketing based on customer needs; brand advertising
Differentiated Products/ Decentralized Markets	Shift from one-way communication to two-way; marketing manages information flows between firm and customers

exchange in which "buyers" and "sellers" seek each other out. Within such a structure, the role of marketing is to facilitate the exchange process by helping buyers and sellers identify each other.

3. *Undifferentiated Products in Centralized Markets*—the formalization and institutionalization of exchange through efficient distribution (i.e., the centralized market) and price mechanisms. Here, marketing—in addition to activities associated with the distribution function—serves to inform buyers about the existence of sellers *and* their products (i.e., "advertising"), thus generating "primary" demand and leading to *inter*commodity competition.

4. *Differentiated Products in Centralized Markets*—the present situation (at least until recently), in which the identification of heterogeneity in buyers' tastes leads to the development of "brands" or *intra*commodity (i e , within a product "category") competition and the generation of "secondary" demand. The role of marketing is to manage competitive strategy, through "segmentation" and "positioning"—i.e., target marketing based on market research to identify customer needs, efficient distribution to targeted markets, brand-level advertising, and so forth.

The driving force throughout the evolution of markets and marketing activity has been *efficiency*: specialization of economic agents into producers and consumers and the development of centralized markets to facilitate the exchange process and the delivery of goods and services from producers to consumers. Whereas the discovery of diverse consumer tastes leads to product differentiation and thus a degree of market fragmentation, the focus is still on the efficiencies that come with market centralization—now in the form of *segments*, or homogeneous subgroups within a larger population.

In the course of market evolution and the development of evermore sophisticated marketing activity, information plays an increasingly important role; but, in the service of specialization and greater efficiency, the patterns of information flow between producers and consumers is also increasingly *sequential*. Competitive advantage goes to those that do the best job of managing the sequence of these information flows. Thus, in the contemporary situation characterized by Phase 4, the successful marketer is one that first, collects information from consumers about their needs and preferences; second, uses the information collected to design products and services that meet these needs; third, communicates to consumers the existence of the products, and so forth. Although both firms and consumers send and receive information, the process is characterized by a series of essentially one-way communication, separated sufficiently in time to preclude truly meaningful feedback—i.e., information that can change the nature of the original signal. Thus, the hallmark of success for the traditional firm has been, first, to find the one right thing to do (the problem of "strategic effectiveness") and, next, to continue to do it for as long as possible (strategic "efficiency").

The proliferation of information-processing technology—the creation of the information infrastructure—has fundamentally altered the possibilities inherent in the patterns of information flow. The dramatic increases in which ever-greater amounts of information can be processed and transmitted in ever-shorter intervals of time mean that the sequences of one-way communication are giving way to opportunities for meaningful two-way communication or the simultaneous flow of information between firms and consumers. The result is the emergence of a new phase in the evolution of markets and marketing:

5. *Differentiated Products in Decentralized Markets*—the consequence of the information revolution, in which the firm can identify *individual* buyers who continually provide it with information about their needs and preferences, thus enabling the firm to develop and provide *specific* products for them. In this environment, the role of marketing is to manage the simultaneous flows of information—or the *relationships*—between the firm and its customers.

There are several dramatic implications of the emergence of this fifth phase in the history of markets and marketing. First, in comparison with the preceding phase, the notion of segmentation loses a good deal of its theoretical and practical importance. This is what is meant by "differentiated products in *decentralized* markets." If information management allows every customer to have a unique relationship with the firm, then each customer effectively becomes a segment, and the concept of dividing up the market into homogeneous subgroups becomes obsolete. Furthermore, most competitive strategies and marketing mix decisions are developed for and conducted at the segment level, and therefore we should expect to see profound changes in the nature of marketing strategy and marketing mix decisions as well.

Beyond this, however, because the creation and delivery of goods and services is now a function of the continual two-way information flows between firm and consumer, the customer is now an *active participant, a partner in the production process.* This represents a reversal of the historical trend characterizing the first four phases of market evolution wherein economic agents increasingly specialized into firms and consumers. Although the reversal does not represent a return to a "Robinson Crusoe" world—because the information age is distinguished by economic and social *interdependence*—it nevertheless signals the emergence of greater levels of consumer self-sufficiency. Consequently, as customers begin to take on many of the firm's traditional functions, perhaps the most interesting implication is that the information revolution forces a redefinition of the firm as an ongoing economic entity.

What does this mean? Historically, the firm designed products with some customer input and then offered them to the market. Now, the customer designs the product and the firm assembles it. Traditionally, the firm provided information to the customer through advertising and other communication vehicles. Now, the customer searches through computerized third-party information sources and decides which information to use. In the past, the customer bought through traditional channels of distribution that provided various customer-service functions; now the customer uses computer technology to find the relevant product or service to buy. As in the Robinson Crusoe economy, the customer provides many "production" functions, but now information technology serves as the enabler—since matching customer need with available offerings becomes far more efficient when the customer and the firm interact directly in real time.

This is not to suggest that firms will "disappear"—only that it will become increasingly difficult for a given organization to identify and maintain a differentiating source of value-added for its products and services for which it is entitled to receive above-average returns, or "rents." In the remainder of this chapter, we suggest that those firms that are able to achieve sustainable marketing advantage in the information age are those that do the best job of "controlling the customer."

WHO CONTROLS THE CUSTOMER?

As noted above, one of the most important manifestations of the information revolution in marketing has been a shift away from one-way toward two-way communication, where the customer, as well as the firm, provides information that is the basis of product design and delivery. It is critical to understand how this two-way communication process allows the firm to create and maintain *relationships* with its customers. Controlling the customer in light of the information revolution is largely a matter of managing these relationships so that the firm (1) continually learns about customer needs and (2) can tailor its products and marketing programs to meet those needs.

To begin, using examples of two prominent companies, we compare two types of firms. One, through the availability of information, has the ability to manage, or control, the relationship between the customer and the firm directly. The other must work through a marketing intermediary, or distribution system. It loses control because it does not have direct contact with the customer. We then discuss the skills required to match customer needs to the production and operations systems of the firm.

Maytag versus Spiegel

Maytag is one of the leading firms in the home appliance market. Maytag's success is due, in large part, to a thorough understanding of customer needs, often the result of conventional approaches such as marketing research, which result in a steady stream of high-quality products and a loyal group of customers. At the same time, Maytag sells through traditional home appliance dealer networks. Maytag therefore has very little *direct contact* with its end-users. Its customer chain, i.e., all of the agents involved in the sale of a product, includes dealers as well as consumers. It is the dealers who have direct contact—i.e., are responsible for the information flows—with the consumer and hence direct control over the end-user. In this regard, it is noteworthy that Maytag dealers are not usually exclusive and often have other home appliance lines. The lack of control over the consumer was not a critical issue during the segmentation-oriented mass marketing era (Phase 4) when products were mass-produced to drive down costs. Indeed, in the interests of production and marketing efficiency, letting someone else— a marketing intermediary—take over the responsibilities for customer contact was strategically appropriate. Today, however, such a strategy may be a serious liability.

Spiegel offers an interesting contrast to Maytag. Most of its marketing is direct to the consumer through catalogs and other direct-response vehicles. Spiegel acquires merchandise from manufacturers such as Liz Claiborne or specifies products to be manufactured (private label). It is a conduit between the manufacturer and the consumer. Through its position in the distribution system, Spiegel has direct access to the consumer and is able to obtain detailed customer information, which it can then use to design and select products to sell. Spiegel controls the consumer. It does not need to rely on others for the gathering and processing of information to understand the needs of its consumer base.

In a sense, Maytag and Spiegel represent ends of a continuum with respect to the nature of the relationship between the producer (or service provider) and the end-user. There are, of course, many types of structural arrangements between a company and its channels, each of which involves a different level of customer control. Whereas historically the differential structural arrangements characterizing channels have co-existed and have been equally viable, the information revolution would appear to put a premium on direct contact with the consumer. This is because, in the next several decades, the ability to produce customized products that meet the specific needs of *individual* consumers—as opposed to target segments—will be critical to differentiation and the creation of a sustainable competitive advantage. The ability to acquire consumers cost-effectively and retain them by marketing additional products and services to them will determine the economic viability of the firm. In such an environment, detailed consumer knowledge is critical to success.

Of course, in our somewhat stylized example, Maytag's dealers are endowed exclusively with managing customer information flows. In reality, Maytag, like other leading manufacturers, is beginning to capture and process customer information *for and by itself*. However, if our assertion is correct, and if firms like Maytag do not gain control over their consumers, will they "fail"? Our answer is no in the short run, but, potentially, yes in the long run. Just as production systems changed in the 1950s and through the 1980s and U.S. firms lost their advantage as mass producers, so will firms that continue to mass-market, even at the level of target segments, without understanding the specific needs of the customers, slowly lose their advantage. How might this happen?

Suppose Maytag continues to design and produce several varieties of appliances that meet the needs of the average consumer in particular segments. A competitor decides to innovate by changing its marketing and production methods and sets up a system in which the individual consumer specifies the type of appliance desired and the appliance is then produced to the user's exact specifications. Will the consumer prefer a custom-built appliance or a generic appliance without the key features the consumer desires? The answer, of course, depends on the cost differential between custom and generic appliances; but if the costs and quality are essentially equivalent—as developments in flexible manufacturing are suggesting they will be—then the customer will desire the custom-built product. This innovation will then allow Maytag's competitor to change the rules of the game and capture increasingly significant parts of the market.

The challenge that Maytag and other manufacturers selling through distribution channels must face will be to directly access information from consumers. The ability to do so will become the most important element in the marketing process.

First-Time versus Repeat Buyers

A window into the future is provided by the experience of direct marketers today. Direct marketing firms have learned that the likelihood of purchase by a repeat buyer is much greater than that by a randomly mailed household who has never been a customer. Once an individual or firm becomes a customer, the direct marketer begins to collect information to manage the relationship. For example, the direct marketing firm can identify the products already being bought and can determine the customer's response to specific promotions. "Profiling" allows firms to learn more about the consumers' interests and products or services desired. Firms can better target customer needs.

For too many firms today, the scenario just described is not possible because the customer is *not identified*. The customer may make multiple purchases, but the firm does not have the ability to tailor its products, services, and marketing activity to the customer. Only through self-selection does the customer repeat purchase from a mass marketer. Tailoring the product or service does not exist. The consumer will repeat purchase because the product or service offers good value, not because it meets his or her *specific* needs.

First-time buyers exemplify the problem that follows from lack of customer information. Direct marketing firms often send out "lead-generating" mail pieces so that the customer self-selects. In other words, because it is difficult to design specific products for first-time customers, firms will cast a "broad net" to find them. Direct marketers then begin to tailor their promotions to the customer. By the third purchase, the direct marketing company is able to develop a sophisticated direct marketing program in which the customer has implicitly identified the products or services that he or she is interested in purchasing and the firm has tailored its offerings to the customer. However, the process is not truly interactive because the customer does not directly "specify" the desired product or service he or she wants. The information revolution will require firms to be more than "direct marketers"—i.e., to go beyond customer identification to the process of *customerization,* or partnering with the customer in designing, developing, and delivering products to meet the customer's *specific* needs.

SKILLS REQUIRED TO CONTROL THE CUSTOMER

As suggested, controlling the customer is critical for long-term competitive success. This involves, first, customer identification and, next, customerization. To accomplish the latter firms need to (1) develop products through modular production methods; (2) provide techniques to simplify customer decision making, so that specific needs can be met without the consumer thinking of him or herself as a production technician; and (3) redefine its role from manufacturer to systems integrator.

Modular Product Design

To meet individualized user needs efficiently, the firm must be able to create *modular* products or services which allow the user to then participate in the development of the specific product using a menu of options. For example, in purchasing a washing machine, consumers want numerous options—capacity, placement of doors, style, color, and so on. The role of the producer firm is to assemble these components quickly and at low cost so that the consumer can have the product or service desired at a reasonable price. This is similar to having options, but the number and types of options are much greater.

Why is modularization important in controlling the customer? For the firm to provide the range of products or services that customers want, it must have as many options as possible. This means that the component product or service attributes need to be developed so they can be combined into a final product that meets the specific needs of the consumer. Without that capability the firm is merely a mass marketer and has no specific relationship with the customer; the product or service is generic. Customers can become loyal to a specific brand or product in a competitive market in which all firms are providing generic products. However, as firms begin to provide modular products efficiently, so that customization costs are low, customers begin to get the products they want. They then develop a stronger relationship with the firm relative to mass producers. However, it is critical that the customization costs are low; otherwise, the customer may be willing to select a product that is mass-produced because the price differential is too large.

Simplifying the Consumer's Decision Process

As the product or service becomes customized, the consumer faces serious problems in trying to specify the product or service he or she desires. For example, if the average person were asked to design a customized life insurance policy, it would be very difficult, because he or she does not know what the options are or cannot easily specify what the options mean. It will be necessary for the firm to develop interactive information-processing systems so that the consumer can identify his or her needs and then have the product or service designed to meet these needs.

Working with consumers to design customized products will mean giving customers a battery of questions or actually allowing them to test different products or services and having their implicit "utility" function determined. For example, a person buying insurance could be asked about risk, income, estate planning, and the trade-off between present and future financial position. The life insurance product would then be designed based on the information provided. This function is now being performed by the financial planner or the life insurance agent; but the products sold are generic and the marketing task is to try to have the preexisting product array fit the customer, rather than to try to design a specific product. The firm needs to create a procedure—embodied in an expert system perhaps—that, first, allows the customer to enter specific desired characteristics and trade-offs and, then, designs the product. If the product costs too much, the consumer can look at related options to reduce it. However, questioning the consumer must be done in lay terms and the expert system must convert the information into a product (e.g., insurance policy) that meet the needs of the consumer.

The Firm as a Systems Integrator

In the information age, successful firms will be *systems integrators*. A systems integrator takes components from other producers, or a set of products produced by the firm and other producers, and combines them to create a system—*which is the product*. The most common example is the industrial firm such as a computer hardware producer (the "computerless

computer company") that takes components from a number of manufacturers and combines them into a finished product—a system—which
may have some proprietary software as the basis for its uniqueness. The
skill of the systems integrator is to match the customers' needs with
available components in the market.

To help understand the concept of a systems integrator, the "restaurant"
provides a useful model. The restaurant buys raw materials from various
sources (products) and then combines them through recipes to produce
the final "system" (the meal). The restaurant provides a menu, which is
simply a listing of component products; though typically, the menu has
a structure or "theme" (French, Italian, etc.) which simplifies consumer
decision making and makes it *easier for the customer to determine which
"system" the restaurant is producing.*

Suppose that a restaurant had a list of ingredients that could be made
into meals and the customer, rather than ordering from a menu, pre-
ordered the day before, say, through an interactive computer program.
Furthermore, assume that the "delivery time" was designated and the
customer was charged in advance, so that production without payment
would not occur. The restaurant would be able to create special meals
and still "mass produce"—through *modularization*—since many of the
inputs such as sauces and other elements would still be efficiently produced in "batches." Customers would gain flexibility because they could
specify individual meals to be served at specific times. For example, the
restaurant offers souffles and the customer specifies the particular type
in advance. The restaurant could order the relevant products to provide
the specific souffle, but the "batch" processing factors—having a cook
who knows how to make souffles, eggs and other ingredients—could all
be available, with minor variations depending upon the customer's needs.
The right entree ingredients would be ordered and there would be no
left-over product "in inventory."

In the process just described, what is the value-added of the restaurant?
The systems integrator's value-added are (1) the skills to know about the
availability of components, (2) the know-how to combine them, and
(3) the determination of which customers want a specific system. The
restaurant's skills are specifying the structure or theme of the meal—i.e.,
the menu (French, Italian, etc.)—identifying expert systems integrators
(chefs), and providing information to the market explaining its unique
product offerings. Similarly, the general systems integrator must have
expertise in identifying the type of components available in the market
and in combining components in unique ways that provide value-added.

The systems integrator must also provide a "positioning" for the product or service and information to the customer, so that the customer can understand the value-added of the firm. In the value-added chain of supplier–firm–customer, the real value comes from the function of systems integration, because this is where the product or service is tailored to meet the customer's specific needs. Note, further, that for the customer who buys from the systems integrator, the identities ("brands") of the components that go into the system are unimportant, just as the diner at a restaurant pays little attention to the brand names of the ingredients. What *is* important is the name of the restaurant, i.e., the identity and reputation of the systems integrator!

Among those industries that apply the systems integration concept are brokerage firms such as Merrill Lynch or PaineWebber, that provide their customers with financial management services. Historically, this has meant trading stocks or bonds and managing the customer's portfolio. However, with the growth of mutual funds and other financial instruments, the customer can now buy pre-packaged financial products. What is the role of the broker in the new environment? The customer wants financial management services in which the broker (or the financial consultant) can offer systems integration. The customer wants to be able to specify certain financial goals and have the systems integrator provide the relevant products at the "right price." What does the systems integrator offer the customer? First, knowledge of products in the market. There are thousands of financial products available. The typical customer cannot know all of the options. Second, translating the customer's needs and desires into specific financial goals and objectives. Third, developing the expertise to *match* available products with the needs and desires of the customers. Customers could, theoretically, perform these functions, but it is very difficult to do so.

The Role of Artificial Intelligence and Expert Systems

Because a critical element of the value-added associated with being a systems integrator is matching user needs with products and services, it is necessary to manage this information effectively. The critical node in the process is *translating* user needs into product information—i.e., problem solving. Ultimately, if products are systems, systems integrators are problem solvers. In the case of financial services, customers indicate preference for risk, give a financial profile, and state financial goals and other relevant data so the broker can determine the type of portfolio that would best meet their needs. It would appear that some type of expert system or artificial intelligence (AI) is required to translate this complex information into a portfolio recommendation that can be implemented by the financial services firm. The financial consultant, being human, may not be able to *translate correctly*—because of the complexity of the information. The expertise required is equivalent to a highly complex engineering function in which the goals are well delineated but the means to achieve the goals offer many possible combinations. Computer systems are capable of iterating across alternatives to see if the recommended system (i.e., portfolio) meets the customer's goals. Unfortunately, most financial consultants are incapable of managing the customer and financial market information adequately.

The concept of the AI and expert systems is based on the need to create a translation mechanism between the user's needs—which are not stated in the language of production systems—and the available components (i.e., to translate between "features" and "benefits"). For example, when a customer buys an automobile, he or she indicates desires in styling, ride, handling, acceleration, and special features such as stereo systems, power seats, and windows. The engineer must translate these feature-based data into the product the customer wants. The key to being a successful systems integrator is the ability to learn what the customer wants and then translate this into the design of the product.

Customer inputs can be specific. For example, an automobile manufacturer can collect inputs by creating simulated cars with different features so that customers can indicate preferences. The simulator could take measurements about the seat, ride, handling, stereo system, and so forth, which could then be translated into the suspension system, the interior of the car, and other features. Expert or AI systems could then translate the inputs into a car design. The design could again be tested with a simulator until the customer decides that it meets his or her needs. The car could then be produced from the modular components available at the production site.

Other forms of market and customer research may still be needed. Expert or AI systems may not be able to create genuinely new products or services such as a Sony Walkman. Rather, they will be used to translate consumer wants into customized products and services. *Customer translation programs* must become sufficiently sophisticated so that customer wants can be interpreted in such a way as to recognize that a new product or service is required, and what type of configuration this represents. Only then will expert or AI systems be used for designing truly new products or services.

Manufacturers versus Systems Integrators

In many markets today it may be difficult to understand how the manufacturer could be a systems integrator and why the customer will need systems integration. Many customers may not be willing to pay for systems integration because they have determined that within a category, the average product is close enough to meet their needs and the cost of systems integration is too high to overcome the benefits of customization. For example, will a consumer nondurable goods manufacturer such as Procter & Gamble become a systems integrator? The consumer is able to buy the system components to "produce" clean clothing by first buying a washer and dryer and then buying detergents. Of course, there are laundry services providing a completely integrated system to the customer, though not customized, which allows the individual to have clean clothes at a higher price. However, customization is extremely expensive and the customer can provide the systems integration function at a relatively low cost. In this situation, Procter & Gamble does not have an incentive to be a systems integrator.

In looking at the systems integration function, the customer performs the task when the information required to complete it is readily available and the cost of integration is high relative to the benefits. There are often mixed situations in which the customer provides some of the systems integrator's functions. For example, to produce meals, the customer, at restaurants that are systems integrators, takes components (food, spices, etc.) and combines them. At other times, the customer decides to produce at home and acquires the components to do so. The systems integration occurs at home. Not in every case will it make sense for the household to acquire products and services through systems integrators.

However, whereas one may argue that the cost of systems integration is still too high to be feasible in some industries, information technology is clearly changing the value of the systems integrator. In the Chicago area, for example, a service called Peapod is being offered in which the customer can buy grocery products through an on-line computerized system. The system currently allows the customer to specify his or her shopping list and then modify it when actually placing the order. Suppose that Peapod had a function in which the customer specified *menus* rather than individual products. Daily menus could be selected along with the number of people being served. The system would then specify the items and recipes and would select the best available brands based on quality and price. The manufacturer would then no longer control the customer. The customer could override the items and select specific brands, but most likely he or she would not. The manufacturer would face the same problem in selling branded products to restaurants and institutions, because the end-user does not know what the raw materials are. Borden's cheese cannot be identified by the end-user, forcing Borden to compete with smaller producers that offer comparable quality at lower prices. Thus, even if it appears that systems integration may not be feasible today, emerging developments in information technology may make it possible for consumers and users to specify end products and the system will indicate the raw materials. In this world, manufacturers lose their power to be systems integrators.

IMPLICATIONS FOR THE MARKETING MIX

The skills required to control the customer—modular product design, simplification of consumer decision making, and systems integration—fundamentally redefine marketing strategy in the information revolution. In this section we hypothesize how the information revolution will recast the marketing function through changes in the marketing mix: product development, pricing, promotions, distribution, and advertising.

New Product Development

Product development will become a combination of technical expertise and acquisition of existing components and products, and new product organization will develop expertise in understanding its value-added to the customer. This means that researching customer needs and creating an affinity between the customer and the firm will become central to new product success. At present, product development is highly concentrated on designing new products. As information technology becomes more important, the designers need to understand how to acquire (or produce) new products that are *consistent with the relationship* the firm has with the customer. For example, should Maytag enter other segments of the appliance business because it has a very strong franchise in laundry products (washers and dryers) and in dishwashers? The answer depends upon how it analyzes its business. If the customer believes that Maytag's product line franchise extends to other products such as refrigerators, then it is clear they can enter this segment. Maytag may choose to acquire a manufacturer and put its brand name on its product (assuming it meets Maytag's quality standards).

How does information enter into this decision? Maytag has little direct knowledge of or relationship with its customers. Suppose that, rather than producing appliances, Maytag also managed the whole appliance relationship—which includes servicing and providing customers with relevant information on their appliances. The firm could then determine "how" refrigerators or stoves and ovens were viewed as kitchen appliances. What specific services should be combined with providing the appliance? How does the firm create a strong long-term relationship with the customer? What other information should it provide? Should it create modules to replace existing parts (an after-market) as better technology becomes available? Complete information concerning customer appliance purchasing and behavior would make it easier to answer these questions. The firm could shift the new product development function from one based almost exclusively on product design to one focused on relationship management.

Pricing

Pricing is the mechanism by which a product's value is determined—a reflection of the amount that a customer will pay for the product. In commodity, stock, and bond markets prices are determined by the bid and ask price system. Some consumers receive a "surplus" because they perceive they are receiving greater utility than they are forgoing by paying the price asked. The reason is that pricing is not individually based. There is no ability to "price discriminate," to charge each customer a different price for the same product. From the firm's perspective, optimal pricing would be to use price discrimination. The product is priced according to its demand curve. For example, customer A may be willing to pay $1,000 for Lotus 1-2-3 but customer B would only pay $200. If the firm can charge only one price, it charges $1,000; but if it could charge each customer differently, its revenue would increase to $1,200. Because the marginal cost of Lotus is low, e.g., $50, it is optimal to be able to charge customer B $200 because total profits increase.

Customer databases make it more likely that firms can price discriminate. An example is the statistical software market. Through licensing mechanisms, such firms as SPSS and SAS can charge customers prices based on specific characteristics. For example, suppose that telecommunication firms are willing to pay significantly more for statistical software than firms in heavy manufacturing. By analyzing demand across different types of customers, the statistical software producers can determine that the demand curves are different. Those with heavy demand that have certain usage patterns pay significantly different amounts than those with other patterns.

Beyond this, however, information technology allows firms to price by using an exchange similar to commodity exchanges. Airlines, with their "yield management" systems, are the leaders in using this pricing mechanism—which is effectively an auction. Ultimately, other service providers and even product manufacturers should be expected to set up a bid-ask price system in which products are essentially auctioned. An auto manufacturer that produces with short lead times could price as a function of demand. If demand is high, prices are high. As demand drops, prices drop. At present, products are produced, *then* priced. In the auction market buyers bid before the product is produced.

Information technology and management are, of course, critical to the bid-ask system of pricing. Customers on a network in which prices are listed can "bid" for products. If demand is low, the "ask" price can be reduced and the market clears. The firm can charge each customer his or her bid price, or it can only clear certain orders. The procedure is similar to a stock exchange.

Although it may appear that bid-ask pricing is too "avant garde," it solves many problems of production. It reduces costly overruns, decreases the need for after-sale markdowns, and reduces excess inventories. When customers can order directly from the manufacturer and have the product shipped directly, logistical costs and excess dealer's inventories are greatly reduced. Pricing is "instantaneous," and the customer need not negotiate with a salesperson. The firm can then decide if it wants to sell at the given price. Prices for future delivery versus immediate delivery can also vary depending upon cost savings. This production system more closely mirrors demand and reduces inefficiencies in the system.

Promotions

If pricing is based on an electronic exchange auction mechanism, then promotions become options or futures contracts. The seller offers the buyer a futures contract in which the opportunity to buy the product at a specified price is *actually a way to induce the customer to purchase.* Today, in effect, a promotion is an adjustment to the regular price— which adjusts the "spot market" without changing the list price. If there are overstocks, promotions are used to adjust the price. If pricing moves away from list pricing, then a promotion will not be an adjustment to the list price. Rather, it will be a way for the seller (manufacturer or retailer) to guarantee a future price to the customer. By receiving a lower price, the customer guarantees a purchase. The seller can produce based on these guarantees. The buyer can transfer his or her contract to other buyers. A market will then be developed in which buyers of products can resell them in the marketplace for a profit without taking delivery.

Information technology will make product transfers possible. For example, if a customer wants to buy an automobile, a manufacturer might offer a futures contract for the product at a specified price. The customer can purchase the contract and then resell the product at a later date. This guarantees a future sale, and the manufacturer will reduce the price for this guarantee because production costs can be managed more efficiently. If the customer wants to buy in the spot market, the price may be higher or lower depending upon demand and supply.

This view of promotions is the opposite of promotional practices today in which promotions are actually price reductions. For example, in apparel and other fashion goods, the manufacturer produces, ships, and then learns whether or not the goods are sold. If customers could place orders prior to receipt of goods and the firm could then produce to demand, costs would be reduced in the system. Electronic catalogs, along with just-in-time flexible manufacturing production, will allow manufacturers to begin to produce to demand. To motivate customers to order early (thus reducing costs), the firm can offer an inducement (futures contract) to convince them to buy early. The incentive now is to buy late because prices always drop. The customer wants to be in the spot market, not the futures market, which causes manufacturers to have large overstocks and to constantly mark down prices. Consumers learn to wait to buy, resulting in even larger markdowns. But by restructuring pricing and promotion activities as a consequence of the information revolution, manufacturers can realize significant gains in production and marketing efficiency for a wide range of product and service markets. Those that take the lead should enjoy the advantages that come from pioneering new rules of the game within their industries.

Channels of Distribution

As noted above, a key issue emerging in the information age is, Who controls the customer? Because they provide many key functions that involve direct customer contact (such as locations for storage of products or selling agents who can reach customers effectively), a firm's traditional channels of distribution are well positioned to compete for ultimate control of the customer. However, in the information age, a new type of firm will emerge—a "customer information firm" (CIF). These firms will collect information from customers and transmit it directly or indirectly to manufacturers. Customers will order from the CIFs and manufacturers will provide products to them. They will be the nexus of the customer relationship.

Whether the customer information firm of the future will be the manufacturer or distributor of today—or an entirely new entity—is an open question. The closest analogy to the CIF is the retailer. The retailer makes it efficient for the customer to shop; its stores can contain as many as 50,000 items from hundreds of manufacturers. The CIF can serve the same function, except that the customer purchases via computer technology and the information about the transaction is captured and processed so that it can be used to design one-on-one product, price, and promotion offerings. Furthermore, the CIF will not necessarily carry products in a warehouse but will drop ship to the customer whenever it is economically efficient. Inventories, to the extent they will still exist, will reside only in one location, the manufacturer's warehouse. However, as production is linked more closely with demand (aided by pricing and promotion acting as futures markets), the manufacturer will be able to produce after the order is received, thus reducing finished goods inventory carrying costs to zero—just-in-time at the consumer level.

Thus, the channel of distribution in the future will be focused less on product flows and the efficient logistical management of products and more on information management. The emerging "retailers" are likely to be firms that manage—not simply products—but information, for both consumers and producers.

Advertising

Perhaps the greatest casualty of the information revolution will be advertising. As noted, the essence of the revolution is the shift from one-way to two-way communication. Firms that base their strategy on using information to manage customer relations will, quite naturally, rely less on talking "to" or "at" customers through traditional advertising media and more on using information technology to establish "dialogues" with consumers.

Beyond this, however, mass-market (or segment-based) advertising is highly unfocused. It reaches millions of noncustomers and the messages are untargeted, resulting in high advertising costs and questionable sales effects. On the other hand, direct marketers are able to manage their advertising budgets and communication messages in a more sophisticated manner—because they have detailed customer information. They are able to direct their advertising based on actual *customer behavior*. For example, if a Spiegel customer buys accessories, she receives catalogs and other information about accessories; if she does not buy lamps or linens, she does not receive home furnishing catalogs. The customer's actual behavior determines the types of communications received, not the demographics or other inferential customer characteristic data. The shift toward advertising driven by customer behavior is significant. In an era when mass distribution and mass production were the philosophy of the firm, mass advertising made sense, because customerization was not the goal of marketing. Rather, it was low cost per thousand to reach and sell the customer. In an era in which differentiation and customerization will be the goal of marketing, firms will need to design and develop advertising strategies consistent with targeting and specialized messages. Advertising will be based on addressability and customer behavior, not mass communications.

To become a focused advertiser, firms will need to collect behavioral data about the customer. Once a household or firm becomes a customer, then detailed behavioral information can be used to target and design communications. For example, the direct marketing industry has learned that recency, frequency, and "monetary" (RFM) are very good predictors of actual buying behavior. Customers who spend heavily and who buy often are the ones most likely to buy in the future. It is surprising that so few firms focus on these customers, instead devoting significant resources to acquiring new customers. RFM is an excellent predictor of buyers, but is not used extensively to direct advertising spending.

Product affinity is also a good predictor of future buying behavior. Someone who buys an appliance from Sears is likely to be a good prospect for another appliance from Sears. This means that an existing customer is the best prospect for the firm's products. One might argue that if someone buys an appliance, he or she is not a good prospect for another appliance, but data show that he or she is still a better prospect than a noncustomer who has the "correct" demographics. For clothing and other frequently purchased products, current buyers of the line are clearly the best customers. The firm should focus its advertising on these segments of the market. Advertising, to be effective, is going to need to be based on actual behavior, not inferential data such as demographics or psychographic lifestyles. Clearly, detailed customer information files and the management of information are going to be crucial to this effort.

SUMMARY

We have suggested that one of the main consequences of the marketing information revolution will be a new phase in market development and marketing activity—one characterized by differentiated products in decentralized markets and a shift from one-way to two-way information flows between producers and consumers. In such an environment, many of the traditional historical distinctions between producers and consumers as specialized economic agents break down, as customers begin to take on more of the functions of the firm and participate in the creation of products and services. The role of marketing becomes that of managing the relationships between the firm and its customers—each of whom is now seen not as part of a larger segment, but as an individual market. Competitive advantage goes to those firms that best manage these relationships, in effect controlling the customer through direct contact and the continual exchange of information. The strategic skills required to control the customer revolve around modular product development, the ability to simplify the customer's decision-making process, and systems integration. These strategic initiatives, in turn, have profound implications for tactical changes at the level of marketing-mix decisions such as pricing, promotion, and advertising. The subsequent chapters in this volume build on this theme and explore in greater detail the mechanics of how successful firms use customer-based information along the various stages of the information value chain.

REFERENCES

Blattberg, Robert C., and John Deighton (1991). "Interactive Marketing: Exploiting the Age of Addressability." *Sloan Management Review*, 5–14.

Glazer, Rashi (1993). "Measuring the Value of Information: The Information-Intensive Information." *IBM Systems Journal*, 32, 99–110.

——— (1991). "Marketing in an Information-Intensive Environment: Strategic Implications of Knowledge as an Asset." *Journal of Marketing*, 55, 1–19.

Pine, B. Joseph II (1992). *Mass Customization*. Boston: Harvard Business School Press.

2

POINT-OF-SALE DATA IN CONSUMER GOODS MARKETING: TRANSFORMING THE ART OF MARKETING INTO THE SCIENCE OF MARKETING

David Ing and Andrew A. Mitchell

ONE OF THE MAJOR INNOVATIONS *that has led to the information revolution is electronic point-of-sale (POS) data collected through optical scanners. As academics and practitioners begin to look at these data it becomes apparent that POS data will drastically change how marketing and logistics are conducted. However, to utilize these data effectively requires a major financial commitment. Unfortunately, many retailers and manufacturers have not made this commitment and hence cannot take full advantage of the information contained in the data. Some argue that companies that recognize its importance and thus organize their operations and systems to use it are at a strategic advantage; and, conversely, not being able to access and utilize electronic POS data puts a company at a strategic disadvantage. At the very least, over the next ten years, organizations that do not utilize electronic POS data at the tactical level to manage distribution and determine the effectiveness of their marketing programs will be less efficient economically and will be vulnerable to more efficient, lower-cost producers.*

This chapter begins by describing different sources of electronic POS data. The authors then discuss many of the uses of the data while providing a typology of decisions for which electronic POS data are best suited. The chapter ends with a discussion of some current issues surrounding the most effective uses of electronic POS data. By the end of the chapter the reader will be far more knowledgeable about the uses and potential of electronic POS data. This should translate into an ability to design a strategy for accessing and utilizing these data and thus transforming them into information.

INTRODUCTION

During the 1980s, there was a dramatic increase in the installation of systems that capture point-of-sale (POS) data by retailers. The increase of installations was greatest in the supermarket segment, after the adoption of an industry standard for bar coding (i.e., the universal product code) by the consumer packaged goods manufacturers. The reported benefits from this adoption of standards has led to similar standards by vendors of other lines of consumer goods (e.g., apparel) carried by department stores and mass merchandisers. The initial impetus for retailers to install sophisticated POS systems was to decrease the time required to record the item purchased by customers, and to improve the accuracy of prices charged at checkout. Both manufacturers and retailers believed, however, that even greater benefits might be realized when the POS data were analyzed, and applied to improve the effectiveness and efficiency of marketing activities logistics.

Prior to the general availability of POS data, marketing was usually considered to be an art. One reason for this view was that measures of market performance were available only at very aggregate levels, temporally and geographically. This made it difficult to assess the effect of specific marketing events (e.g., price promotions) which might have occurred for a brief period of time (e.g., one week) in a particular retail chain. Consequently, successful marketing was attributed to the intuitive understanding of consumer tastes, and the creativity of media advertising. The availability of weekly POS data at the household, store, account, and market level, when coupled with measures of causal variables (e.g., store displays), provides the opportunity to obtain precise measures of the effect of different marketing events. However, in order to take advantage of the availability of these data, firms must take a more scientific approach to marketing, and an appropriate commitment of resources.

The decision to commit the resources necessary to effectively use these data, however, has proven to be neither simple nor obvious for most companies. Although the cost to retain POS data as an electronic by-product of transactional systems is low, the resources required to store and analyze these data are significant. In addition, attributing improvements in bottom-line profitability to the direct application of these data has proven difficult.

The purpose of this chapter is to discuss the form and content of POS data available to marketers, how these data supplement and replace other forms of marketing data, and issues that have arisen in their effective managerial use. In the first two sections, we discuss the data as generated from transactions, and as applied in the two-stage channel structure which is common in consumer goods marketing. In the third section, a learning curve of expertise in the science of marketing is introduced. The following four sections review some leading-edge applications. The chapter concludes with an outlook on the future for POS data.

POS DATA AND TRANSACTION CYCLES

In order to better understand the impact that point-of-sale data have had, the consumer goods marketing process may be described as a number of cycles of transactions. Figure 2-1 depicts a two-stage distribution channel as four cycles: product marketing, manufacturing/distribution, retail, and purchase/consumption.

The leftmost two cycles are the primary concern of the manufacturer. The marketing function focuses on the outer "Product Marketing Cycle": a product is produced, and a marketing program consisting of advertising and promotion is designed to support it. Consumer advertising builds product awareness, knowledge, and preference; promotions are sponsored to induce brand switching or purchase acceleration. For this cycle, data which report on the success of inducing customers to purchase particular brands are of primary interest. The time spent on these activities is called "Product to Consumer."

In the "Manufacturing/Distribution" cycle (inner left) products flow through manufacturers' warehouses to the retailer's (or wholesaler's) distribution center. The quantity and price of inventory transferred are captured for accounting purposes, and are frequently made accessible to the sales force to service customers. These activities of the manufacturer/retailer dyad are called, colloquially, "Product to Shelf."

The retailer is primarily concerned with the "Retail Cycle" (inner center). In this cycle, merchandise processing activities, such as breaking down case lots, marking or ticketing, and/or redistribution to individual stores are performed. Customer purchases are recorded at the point-of-sale, and the record of these transactions is summarized and stored by retailers. In general, retailers are primarily interested in using POS data to design merchandising programs and product assortments which will be successful in attracting consumers to their store(s). These activities may be described as "Shelf to Consumer."

The consumer, in the "Purchase/Consumption Cycle" (inner right), makes a number of decisions which lead up to the point-of-sale. These

FIGURE 2-1
Transaction Cycles in Consumer Goods Marketing

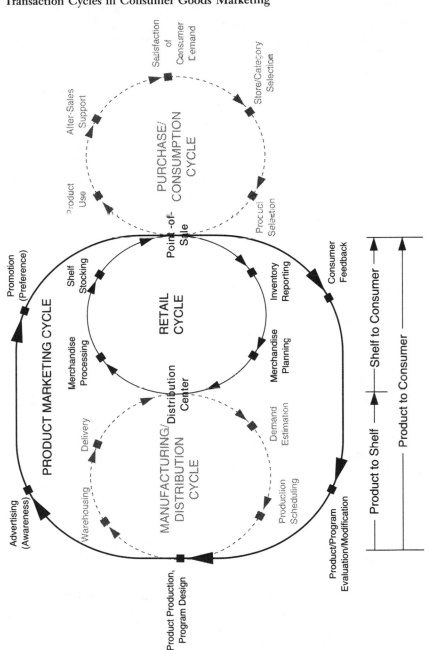

include which store to visit on a particular shopping trip and the brands or products to be purchased. With products that are not immediately consumable, some after-sales support, in the form of additional services offered by the retailer or manufacturer, may contribute to final satisfaction or dissatisfaction with the product.

The point-of-sale is but one point in the many cycles depicted in Figure 2-1, but is perhaps the most important for marketers. Since this is the point at which consumer demand is reflected most clearly, it drives the speed at which all of the other cycles turn. It is valuable not only in the retail cycle, but could be used to greatly increase the efficiency of product marketing and manufacturing/distribution. POS data, are, however, proprietary to the retailer, and have only recently become cost-effective to capture and analyze, through information technology. The next section will discuss the many forms in which marketers view POS data, some alternative data sources, and the orientations of manufacturers and retailers.

POS DATA, AS APPLIED BY MARKETERS

POS data originate in the checkout lane or cash register of the retailer, but this is not the form in which marketers view or use it. Figure 2-2 illustrates the flow of data inside retailers, through market research firms, and to manufacturers. In addition, some other related marketing data sources are shown.

In the retail store, POS transactions are commonly recorded at an electronic terminal, in the natural process of selling, tendering, and settling the consumer's purchases. At the very least, the sale of a particular item is recorded; other information such as the price paid, the type of tender, the use of a coupon, or the basket of goods purchased in the same transaction could easily be made available. Most POS systems are now based on programmable PC-based platforms, enabling current item prices to be stored online and looked up when the SKU number (stock-keeping unit) or bar code is read from an input device (e.g., numeric key pad or laser scanner). The raw stream of data is continuously processed locally by the POS system to accumulate counts such as cash balance and item movement totals. Retailers offering credit card programs link to their proprietary credit card databases to exchange dollar amount data, at the department level, for customer billing.

Item movement totals are closed, and summarized after some period of time (e.g., hours or days) into item movement databases residing on

FIGURE 2-2
Transactions and Data Sources in Consumer Goods Marketing

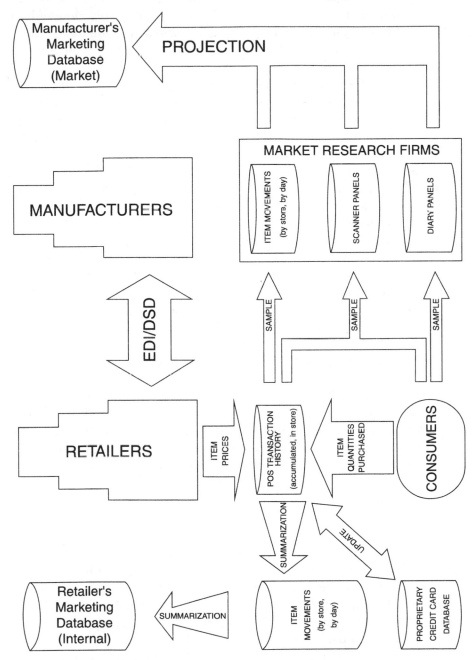

an in-store processor (ISP) and/or the head office mainframe. In contrast to the real-time accumulations maintained at the POS, these systems balance sales and inventories in batches (e.g., at the daily close of business). Data in these systems are valued primarily for audit and control functions, and are archived offline when the accounting period is closed (e.g., at month-end).

Whereas the item movement database provides item-level data for accounting purposes, the retail marketing database provides item-level data for merchandisers and buyers. Generally, these latter databases retain one or two years of sales histories, consolidated by departments or categories across all stores, aggregated on a weekly or monthly basis. In some cases, the history may be available store by store, for comparisons and trending, and may include store causal data (e.g., price and display) which allows the analysis of promotions.

Market research firms obtain POS data by installing devices, in a sample of stores, to passively "listen on the store loop" between the POS terminals at checkout stations and the POS computer. A microcomputer accumulates the transactions and forwards them to a central site for consolidation into a market item tracking database. This database is generally organized by product category, and is used to calculate weekly sales, market share, price, display, and advertising information on an all-category volume basis. Agreements to capture data on consumer packaged goods from supermarkets are most common, either with a payment of fees and/or an agreement to deliver market information to the retailer. Although alternative retail channels (e.g., mass merchandisers or warehouse clubs) have been increasing their share of packaged goods sales, little progress has been made in establishing agreements with them. General merchandise channels (i.e., department or specialty stores) usually do not participate in reporting lower-volume products (e..g, apparel or hard goods) to market research firms.

Related Data Sources

Consumer panels augment item movement data with household purchase information, collected by one of two methods. Scanner panels are comprised of households clustered around specific supermarkets that record POS data. At checkout panel members present a scannable card which links the household to item purchases. Diary panels rely on panel members to keep their own records. The chore of maintaining handwritten diaries has been relieved by some market research firms providing a scanning "wand" to each respondent. After returning home from a shopping trip, purchases are recorded by scanning the bar codes on each item, and then keying in details on the quantity purchased, the price paid, the retail outlet where the purchase was made, and which member of the household made the purchase.

Each type of panel has both advantages and disadvantages. Scanner panels limit panel members to specific geographic regions, and purchases are recorded only in participating stores. The data may be augmented by having panel members keep purchase receipts from nonparticipating stores. Electronic capture at the POS, however, allows prices to be recorded accurately, and the small selection of stores can be monitored for display and store advertising information at a relatively low cost. In addition, if the households are located in cities with cable television, exposure to television commercials can be monitored electronically. Consequently, both purchase data and television advertising data can be recorded for each household, creating "single-source data."[1]

The panel diary methodology is not limited to households in specific geographic regions, and provides a means for recording purchases from all retail outlets. For product categories distributed widely through a variety of retail channels (e.g., nylon stockings), this method provides a better measure of actual household purchases. Disadvantages include data entry by the consumer rather than by a trained cashier, so that price information may not be recorded accurately. In addition, it is difficult to monitor display and store advertising inexpensively, since the households are generally dispersed geographically.

Item movements between the manufacturer and retailer may also be captured, as shown in Figure 2-2, through one of two forms of transaction communication. With direct store delivery (DSD), hand-held terminals can be used by route salespersons to capture item deliveries and consumer take-away electronically at the store level.[2] These data are transmitted overnight to the head office, and provide counts close to actual consumer sales by retail outlet. Additional measures, such as estimated sales of

---

[1]See David J. Curry, "Single-Source Systems: Retail Management Present and Future," *Journal of Retailing*, Spring 1989, pp. 1–20.

[2]Common examples of programmable hand-held terminals used in industry are manufactured by Telxon, MSI, and Norand. Route salespersons visiting each retail store can acknowledge the deliveries, issue invoices immediately, and even record more detailed information such as returns of stale products. Terminals are plugged into a "docking station" overnight, so that the batteries may be recharged, the day's deliveries and data transmitted to the head office, and the next day's orders loaded.

competing products, may be recorded using the same technology, but these efforts would be the result of corporate initiatives rather than industry standards. Because of the large investment in delivery trucks and route salespersons, DSD is used primarily by manufacturers of perishable products.

Item movement data within more traditional channels of distribution may be captured from electronic data interchange (EDI) communications between organizations concerning orders, confirmations, and invoices. In the most advanced operations, advanced shipping notices may be used by retail warehouse staffs to schedule manpower and dock assignment for arriving trucks. If integrated into centralized systems accessible to the marketing function, valuable information tracking the expected delivery dates of new merchandise can be provided to the retailer's merchandisers and sales personnel.

For organizations accustomed to acquiring information about markets primarily from marketing research (e.g., survey research), POS data sources require different attitudes to working with data. The former acquire information on variables believed to mediate consumers' responses to marketing programs, and are executed as discrete, fixed-cost projects. POS data are, in contrast, an electronic by-product which are captured at a low incremental cost, matching the continuous stream of transactions. POS data do provide a direct measure of consumer response, but do not directly link those results to mediating marketing variables. A large investment in information technology is required to effectively use these data on an ongoing basis.

Orientations Toward POS Data

Since retailers own the POS systems where the transaction data are captured, their opportunities to use the data are limited only by the amount of resource they commit. Consumer goods manufacturers, on the other hand, do not have direct access to these data, and rely primarily on marketing research firms, such as A.C. Nielsen, to supply them. These firms provide clearinghouse functions such as data cleaning, validation, and projection of their sample up to an account, market, and/or national levels.

The different orientations of manufacturers and retailers are summarized in Table 2-1. The first and most obvious difference is the interest of manufacturers toward individual brands. Retailers are more concerned

TABLE 2-1
Orientations of Manufacturers and Retailers

Manufacturers	*Retailers*
Brands	Product Categories, Stores
Time Series	Cross-sectional
Analytical Solutions	Workable Solutions
Active Marketers	Passive Marketers

with the profitability of the entire product category and, more generally, the performance of each store.

Manufacturers are more interested in their data as a time series, where performance is compared to that in previous quarters, or years. This may be attributed to the importance of maintaining efficiency in the "production pipeline," by operating factories at full or near-to-full capacity. Retailers, on the other hand, have a cross-sectional orientation. They look at the breadth of items in stock at a given period in time. This reflects the costs of holding inventory, and a requirement to respond quickly to fashion trends or the price promotions of competitors.

Manufacturers have seen the benefits in finding analytical solutions to their marketing questions. With the large costs associated with advertising and promotion, and low rates of new product success, more accurate estimates of consumers' responses improve the probability and size of return on investments. The benchmark by which they determine their performance is, in comparison to their peers, in terms of market shares. Retailers, with a much shorter time horizon and little patience for an elaborate search for an optimal solution, want an immediate "workable" one. A first-order approximation using a simple rule of thumb is a large improvement over a decision made with little information.

Finally, retailers have historically been passive marketers. It is the manufacturers that have actively developed products and communicated to the consumer through media advertising. Retailers traditionally select the assortment of goods from manufacturers which they believe will be the most attractive to customers.

The marketing information revolution is, however, changing the orientations of manufacturers and retailers, and the relationship between them. Access to electronic POS data has the potential to greatly increase the power of retailers, and to turn them into active marketers. With these data, retailers are able to assess the profitability of individual SKUs, categories, and promotions. Armed with this information, retailers are less willing to be led by manufacturers, and more likely to request (or demand) specific promotions and products based on their own strategies. These changes have forced consumer goods manufacturers to broaden the impact of promotions from just their own brands, to conform with the retailer's perspective on profitability of the entire product category.

EXPERTISE WITH POS DATA: THE LEARNING CURVE

The amount of POS data generated at the retail level is immense. A single store may generate around 50,000 transactions per day. These transactions may involve 25,000 to 30,000 SKUs for a supermarket, and up to 1.5 million SKUs for a department store. In either segment, the typical size of a retail marketing database with weekly movements, SKU by store, will be on the order of 12 to 16 gigabytes. Consumer goods manufacturers typically have fewer brands and regions, but many more causal variables. Market research firms may provide databases on 5,000 items for 50 markets, over a two-year weekly history.

These large databases create two issues. First, online access of stored data requires a considerable investment in hardware, software, and data processing staff. Second, and of direct concern to marketers, is the amount of managerial time and effort required to obtain an understanding of the data. A consumer packaged goods brand manager in the United States now has the opportunity (and burden) to examine 2 million new numbers each week.[3] In order to effectively use POS data for decision making, firms must ascend a learning curve requiring increasing expertise. This learning curve (Figure 2-3) contains five stages of development.

The first stage, data assembly, requires the development of systems to

FIGURE 2-3
Stages of Sophistication with POS Data

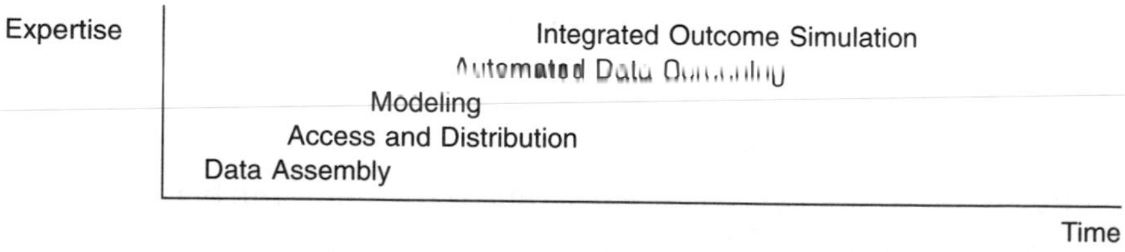

Expertise

Integrated Outcome Simulation
Automated Data Overviewing
Modeling
Access and Distribution
Data Assembly

Time

[3]John H. McCann, John P. Gallagher, William G. Lahti, and Justin Hill, *The Generation and Management of Marketing Insights: Conceptual Foundations and a Computer Approach* (in press, 1993).

acquire reliable POS data, to be organized and integrated with other relevant data (e.g., causal information) into marketing databases. Cashiers at the POS must be trained and monitored to ensure that the data entry and scanning procedures are followed. The detailed data from each checkout must be "cleaned," summarized, transmitted from the store to a central computer, and validated to clean up such mistakes. The immediacy of the data is important for decision making, and must be prepared for online access. These tasks are performed internally by retailers, and by market research firms on behalf of manufacturers.

Although accessing online data may be simple for the IS professional, the second stage empowers the marketers themselves, by putting systems into place that will allow them to independently access the data they require. Data access and distribution systems permit less sophisticated users to quickly query the database, interactively, from the comfort of their offices.[4] The flexibility to build a subset or summary of data is important in transforming the volumes of data into manageable sets of information for review. It is important that the data be presented in contexts that facilitate decision making. These may be cross-sectional views (e.g., market shares) or time series views (e.g., changes in sales trends). Simple market status reports can give the marketers an indication of the health of their business.

The stage at which marketing may first be called a science is the third: modeling. This step formalizes the marketer's concepts about relationships between marketing variables and their effects through quantitative analyses. Establishing a correlation between two variables (e.g., volume increasing as prices decrease) may be relatively simple, but more complete decompositions of effects (e.g., volume effects attributed to price cuts, in-store displays, and flyer advertisements) require the use of multivariate statistical techniques such as multiple regression analysis. The use of these techniques, however, requires an appropriate level of sophistication in the user, since they may be easily misapplied. Quantitative methods may also be applied to customer purchase datasets and to cluster consumer groups based on behavior. These different groups may then be targeted for different offers or promotions.

As noted, considerable managerial time is required to obtain an understanding of POS data. The major emphasis at the stage that follows,

---

[4]Examples of commercially available products providing this function are the Metaphor Data Interpretation System (DIS) and IRI Express.

automated data screening, is the automatic analyses and structuring of these data to facilitate their use by decision makers. This may occur by automatically summarizing the data or by identifying exceptions. An example of a system designed for the former purpose is "CoverStory."[5] This system is based on the metaphor of a "marketing newspaper," which reports on what has occurred in a market during a particular time period. As an example, important sales and market share changes for different brands and sizes are summarized for a market, along with the list of promotional activities that may have caused them. Like a newspaper, this approach makes the information easier to browse, by highlighting the most important facts.

An extension of the above approach shifts the information orientation of the presentation to an action orientation. Discovery of poor performance in a marketing program should naturally lead to the suggestion of some remedial actions to correct the cause.[6] Continuing the example above, if poor brand sales are attributed primarily to a share decline at only one chain of stores, special recommendations could be made to those sales representatives.

In the store, systems at this level may be used as automated "detectives" to sift through data at the transaction level to uncover theft. More sophisticated systems in department stores might provide early identification of categories which are selling well for quick reordering, or items selling poorly for additional merchandising effort. Screening out items within a "nominal" range around plan, or within a comparable range to other stores in the chain, would greatly reduce the amount of data requiring inspection by the marketer.

At the fifth, and highest, stage of the learning curve are systems that perform integrated outcome simulation tasks. These systems close the loop on the planning process, by extending and combining the multiple automated recommendations from lower-level applications. These are integrated into alternative marketing programs with expectations of particular outcomes, which the marketing decision maker may review. Lower-level systems focus on solving individual problems rather than on integrating the knowledge within the organization to determine an overall result. What would be the effect of following through with a recommendation, not only for an individual marketer, but for the company as a whole?

---

[5] John D. Schmitz, Gordon D. Armstrong, and John D.C. Little, "CoverStory—Automated News Finding in Marketing," *Interfaces*, vol. 20, 1990, pp. 29–38.
[6] McCann et al., *The Generation and Management of Marketing Insights*.

For manufacturers, these systems would use the quantitative models developed at the third level to allow brand managers to estimate the sales, market share, and profit which would be obtained with different marketing plans. Retailers might use these systems to plan the merchandising strategy for the next season. The emphasis with these systems is not to fix a problem of a previously created strategic plan, but to assist in the creation of a new, improved plan.

The next four sections will each review applications of POS data in the transaction cycles framework outlined at the outset of this chapter. These will illustrate the level of sophistication which has been demonstrated in companies working at the state of the art.

PRODUCT MARKETING APPLICATIONS WITH POS DATA

The product marketing cycle involves two functions from the manufacturer: brand management and the field sales force.

Brand Management

The earliest and most intensive analysts of marketing data have historically been brand managers in consumer packaged-goods manufacturers. They have combed the data to identify market opportunities, to assess the impact of marketing programs of their own and competing brands, and to develop marketing programs and strategies. In the 1980s, bimonthly projections of brand shares by region were replaced by weekly estimates by market (i.e., major metropolitan areas), or even by account. This "data explosion" has raised some issues in the management and delivery of data from market research firms.

The weekly frequency of refreshes has created technical difficulties in data delivery. Market research firms have traditionally duplicated copies of their databases to be sent to consumer goods manufacturers, but a weekly turnaround results in their comparison to "tape factories." As an alternative, the databank approach has allowed A.C. Nielsen to centrally maintain its database, while giving the marketing analyst at the manufacturer an easy method of remote online access. In contrast to simple communications packages which slowly download a full "cube" of data onto the microcomputer, the databank uses metaphor data interpretation system to quickly access "slices" of data. Analysts are able to create customer groupings (e.g., "our coffee brands") as ad hoc subsets, and analyze them with PC-based tools to identify sales and market share changes within a market, or to estimate the effects of a particular promotion. This approach cleanly separates the data management function at the market research firm from the client's data analysis function. Over 100 gigabytes of data are currently available in 500 databases.[7]

A number of manufacturers have been experimenting with micromarketing at the store level. However, because they do not have direct access to store-level data, they have relied on geodemographic data[8] to determine the characteristics of the population within the trading area of a retail store. Knowledge of differences in sales or response to promotions by demographics allows the manufacturer to tailor products, advertising, and promotion at the store level.[9]

Some manufacturers are entering into partnership with retail chains, to experiment in micromarketing at a store level.[10] Multiple data sources are used to compare consumer purchasing patterns in store locales against their estimated potential profiles. POS data across categories and stores are used to create an "historical purchase behavior" of products selected from the store's existing assortments. The "shopper group purchase potential" identifies potential product purchases consistent across five shopper profiles.[11] These programs have generally been used by the sales forces of manufacturers to increase their product differentiation in the marketplace.

Sales Force

The manufacturer's sales force is responsible primarily for ensuring that retailers provide the appropriate amount of support for their products. This includes an appropriate assortment of products, a fair allocation of shelf space, and suitable level of promotional support. Most manufacturers deliver their products only to the retailer's distribution center, so it is difficult for them to assess their positions relative to competitors at a

---

Personal communication with Laura Reeves, Metaphor Computer Systems.

[8]Geodemographic data and access software may be synthesized from government census data, combined with market surveys. Some firms that provide this service are CACI, Claritas, Donnelley, Equifax, and CompuSearch.

[9]Zachary Schiller, "Stalking the New Consumer," *Business Week*, August 28, 1989, pp. 54–62.

[10]Major sessions on the micromerchandising approach were featured at the Food Marketing Institute meetings in Chicago, in May 1989 and May 1990. The final report was prepared by Willard Bishop Consulting Ltd. for the Food Marketing Institute, "Micro-Merchandising: Targeted Consumer and Category Merchandising," Food Marketing Institute, 1991.

[11]As examples, Full-Margin shoppers showed relatively little response to price cuts or coupons, whereas Mini-Baskets were retirees who would shop frequently and would be more responsive to promotions.

particular retailer. In addition, since accurate measures of consumer demand in the stores are unavailable, the manufacturer must bear the extra cost of higher safety stocks in its warehouse.

Manufacturers supporting a direct store delivery (DSD) method of distribution have a path around some of these disadvantages.[12] With a delivery cycle ranging from a few days to several weeks, DSD data do not have the frequency of POS data. However, the manufacturer can frequently obtain a good estimate of consumer sales of its products, and a rough estimate of sales of competing products, store by store.

Unfortunately, most commercially available "sales force automation" packages emphasize personal productivity applications (e.g., paperless expense statements or electronic mail) on laptop computers. Other systems provide the sales force with inventory information, and/or sales by account.[13]

In order for a sales representative to be most effective on customer calls, he or she should have (1) access to information not available to a single retailer (e.g., performance comparisons versus the market), and (2) better and/or timelier presentations of in-depth analyses of sales and profits, by promotion and by shelf space position.

The ultimate vision for the sales force may be a system which creates a tailored, professional sales presentation for each call upon a retailer. One prototype, called the "I Want Knowledge Base,"[14] was developed by the Duke University Marketing Workbench Project. This system provides more than just data or information, and creates sales visuals, complete with a script to justify increased promotional support from a retailer. Another system, called "SalesPartner," analyzes POS data to identify sales opportunities, and then organizes the data for a sales presentation.[15]

Most consumer packaged-goods manufacturers today are trying to manage the data and make them available to managers. This is the second stage of the learning curve. The more advanced consumer packaged-goods companies are modeling the effects of promotion, beginning on the third stage of the learning curve. Data suppliers, on the other hand, are well established at the third stage of the learning curve, developing procedures

---

[12]Frito-Lay is a much-cited leader in DSD. See Jeremy Main, "Computers of the World, Unite!," *Fortune*, September 24, 1990, pp. 115–122; and *The Wall Street Journal*, January 30, 1990.

[13]Alan J. Ryan, "Report from the Field: Toss Out the Scissors," *Computerworld*, May 21, 1990, p. 100.

[14]McCann et al., *The Generation and Management of Marketing Insights*.

[15]Peter Guadagni, "Artificial Intelligence and Scanner Data," paper presented at the TIMS College on Marketing Special Interest Conference on "New Directions in Scanner Research," 1990.

for measuring market response to causal variables. Both IRI and A.C. Nielsen provide estimates of changes in sales due to price changes, in-store displays, and advertised specials. Both also have procedures for measuring the profitability of promotions, based on estimates of "baseline sales" (i.e., sales that would have occurred in the absence of promotional activity).

RETAIL APPLICATIONS WITH POS DATA

The key to effectively managing the retail cycle is the estimation of demand. This is required to determine the appropriate product assortment and to manage inventory in the store and at the retail distribution center. POS data are critically important for all of these decisions. For buying, two strategies are conventionally used by retailers: replenishment for "staple" items with a recurring seasonal profile; and merchandise planning, for fashion items or highly promoted categories.

Replenishment is a common methodology, where item-by-item forecasts can be mathematically extrapolated from their sales history. In the high-turnover, highly promoted environment of grocery products, this methodology is known as computer-aided ordering (CAO). In 1990, only 14% of supermarket chains and wholesalers were using CAO, and 29% were planning to do so. The 57% that were not planning any form of CAO had issues primarily in the reliability of their scanned data.[16] Although the final approval for ordering may still rest with the buyer, much of the ordering procedure for many grocery and mass-merchandised products can be delegated to software programs at the headquarters level.[17]

A number of retailers have experimented with the use of electronic POS data for inventory control and ordering at the store level. In order for these systems to work properly, a high degree of accuracy must be achieved in recording POS data, and in forecasting demand under normal and promotional conditions at the SKU level. Wegman's, a supermarket chain in western New York state, has developed a system that accurately forecasts demand at the SKU level for automatic ordering under normal conditions. It has, however, experienced difficulty in forecasting demand when promotions are in effect.[18]

---

[16]Deloitte & Touche, Supermarket/Wholesaler Advanced Merchandising Technology Survey 1990, in Warren Thayer, "Computer-Aided Ordering Is Ready . . . Should You Care?," *Progressive Grocer*, March 1991, pp. 81–86.

[17]IBM's Inforem software, used for "Inventory Replenishment," is an example of a mathematically based approach.

[18]Danny Wegman, speech at the Food Marketing Institute conference, 1992.

In a replenishment environment, the buyer generally plays an important role in negotiating prices and quantities with vendors. This is especially true with trade promotions. The buyer must decide which promotions to accept, how much should be ordered on promotion, and how to merchandise the promotion. Access to electronic POS data and the ability to evaluate the effects of previous promotions on sales and profitability of the promoted item and the product category are very useful to the buyer in making these decisions.

Merchandise planning is conducted by buyers in categories where items change frequently and/or in environments where demand is difficult to forecast. Here, the personal judgment of a buyer may be required, since demand, prices, and style change frequently (e.g., in fashion apparel, where inventory is manufactured and distributed up to four seasons per year). In these cases, it is frequently difficult to make accurate estimates of demand when orders must be placed six to nine months prior to delivery. In many cases, the distribution of sales by size and color vary considerably among styles of products. Unfortunately, for buyers, "retail is detail," and some person must take responsibility for each item on each shelf in each store.

It is not uncommon for a fashion buyer in a major chain to have responsibility for 20,000 SKUs, with a requirement to place orders each season (two or four times per year) for each item. With seasonal fashion items, the buyer may be able to order only once. Poor decisions result in either lost sales opportunities or markdowns to clear out unpopular items.

Because it is frequently difficult to accurately forecast demand for fashion items, a number of retailers have used electronic POS data from key stores for early identification of sales patterns of seasonal fashion products. Fast-moving items are quickly identified and additional production is ordered. Similarly, slow movers are also identified, and special promotions are initiated to clear these items out early in the season.

Merchandise planning covers a broad range of applications, such as vendor management,[19] store distribution planning,[20] and assortment planning.[21] Sales and profitability comparisons of items, both within and

---

[19]The Buyer's Workbench project was based on Metaphor Data Interpretation System (DIS). Private communications with Richard Goulet and Kelvin Cantafio, Canadian Tire Corporation.

[20]CLAS was the runner-up to the RITA (Retail Innovation Technology Award) in 1990. See "K mart Tackles Distribution with CLAS."

[21]Stephanie Spring, presentation at the IBM Retail Executive Conference, April 1991. *Chain Store Age Executive*, October 1990.

between stores, can be used for a number of decisions: items to be added or deleted; which items to be promoted; how an item should be promoted; and within or between category shelf allocation. If there are considerable differences in performance among retail stores, then a store-by-store analysis may greatly increase the effectiveness of marketing programs.

The shift from the art of marketing to the science of marketing will require retailers to strike a balance between the two approaches. Replenishment software may be purchased and operated by less sophisticated staff, but requires at least basic Stage 3 (modeling) skills. There are aspects of buying and merchandising (e.g., a fashion sense) that cannot be captured in models, but buyer's estimates are likely to be enhanced with some basic quantitative measures, supplemented by personal judgment.[22] Since retailers are both buyers and sellers in the marketplace, their negotiation skills can have a major impact on their bottom line. On the other hand, the ability to understand quantitative relationships in the marketplace adds a degree of precision to the retailer's knowledge.

MANUFACTURING/DISTRIBUTION APPLICATIONS WITH POS DATA

Product distribution by a manufacturer is not a function where the role of POS data is obvious. Scanner data, as reported by market research firms, do not provide store-level detail, so manufacturers have traditionally used shipments as a rough estimate for distribution. Because products are generally delivered to retail distribution centers manufacturers are not privileged to have store-level POS data, which greatly inhibits their ability to forecast demand accurately. This has provided an impetus to consumer goods manufacturers to approach retailers with proposals for strategic alliances.

Although these strategic alliances vary in form and substance, they are based on motives beyond the application of electronic data interchange (i.e., the reduction of transaction costs of printing, mailing, and then rekeying forms for orders, invoices, and payments). If only EDI is implemented, the dynamics of two-stage marketing still remain: the retailer creates a marketing program independently of the manufacturer,

---

[22]Robert C. Blattberg and Stephen J. Hoch, "Database Models and Managerial Intuition: 50% Model + 50% Manager," *Management Science*, August 1990, pp. 887–899.

and both parties may attempt to gain in negotiations at the expense of the other.

As an alternative to the confrontational postures between buyer and seller during negotiations, some suppliers have suggested alliances where both parties to the transaction will benefit. Rather than having the retailer periodically place an order when the inventory is stocked out, an agreement can be made in advance that the manufacturer should automatically send out product to the retailer, based on POS data shared directly.

In apparel, this process is called quick response.[23] Domestic soft-good vendors adopted this approach in the early 1980s, to counteract the threat of imported goods. Merchandise was being produced at a lower cost in the Far East, and so U.S. manufacturers had to find a method to compete. Adopting just-in-time production techniques would reduce their costs, but they would still be out of line with imports. In order to add value to their product, the domestic manufacturers guaranteed just-in-time marketing and distribution services to the retailers, taking advantage of their proximity to the market, and guaranteed better service levels to the retailers. Instead of committing to a large inventory of merchandise imported from the Far East, retailers could choose to maintain a lower level of inventory, and have it replenished rapidly from nearby manufacturers.

In consumer packaged goods, similar partnerships began to emerge only at the close of the 1980s. For manufacturers dealing with supermarkets, the challenge was the eroding value of their brands to retailers. High slotting allowances were being paid to introduce new brands on the shelf; forward buying ensured that retailers were stocking up with product at low margins; the diversion of goods meant that prices encouraging local promotion were spread nationally; and the administration required to support promotions was increasing. Managers at Procter & Gamble estimated that 25% of salesperson time and 30% of brand management time were being spent in designing, implementing, and overseeing promotions. In the food industry, manufacturer and distributor costs from trade promotion amount to an estimated 2.5% of retail sales.[24]

The pioneering partnership in this industry segment was between

---

[23]Some examples of QR are cited in "Special Report: QR," *Chain Store Age Executive*, March 1991.

[24]Robert D. Buzzel, John A. Quelch, and Walter J. Salmon, 'The Costly Bargain of Trade Promotion," *Harvard Business Review*, March–April 1990, pp. 141–149.

Procter & Gamble and Wal-Mart in 1988. In a demonstration of commitment, 12 managers were moved from Cincinnati to Bentonville, Arkansas, to support the Wal-Mart account. Diapers, a category turning 52 times per year, was chosen as the first experiment, where POS data from Wal-Mart's satellite network was transmitted to P&G headquarters for analysis. After three months, diapers turns had improved to 104 times, and service levels had risen from 91% to 99.6%.[25] Based on this success, P&G has assigned more than 120 teams to various customers in the United States, some sharing their POS data in a similar fashion.[26]

In order to obtain the cost savings necessary to make strategic alliances successful, accurate forecasting systems need to be developed. This requires firms to be at Stage 3 (modeling) of the learning curve.

PURCHASE/CONSUMPTION APPLICATIONS WITH POS DATA

Although manufacturers have used POS data to influence consumer segments to prefer their brands, the use of POS data by both manufacturers and retailers to target individual consumers is a recent concept.

In the battle to retain a loyal consumer base, both manufacturers and retailers have been implementing relationship-marketing programs, in the form of frequent shopper, or customer loyalty campaigns. These programs have been especially prevalent as the size of retail stores has grown, and fewer personal services are provided to consumers. Relationship-marketing activities mark a changed attitude in the industry, harkening to a simpler time, when customers were individually known by the local merchant. As an extension of micromarketing, information technology is being used as a method of enhancing the shopping experience, and tailoring product offerings and marketing programs through the recognition of individual tastes.

Relationship-marketing programs can be executed at two levels. The first is an operational/transactional level in stores, either by sales staff or at the POS. The second is a tactical level, through the use of customer purchase histories to design marketing programs targeted at specific households. Because modern POS systems are programmable the first level is relatively easy to implement. Consumers are readily recognized by their

———

[25]Lou Pritchett presentation at the Retail Executive Forum, IBM Canada Ltd., Markham, September 1990.

[26]Barnaby J. Feder, "Moving the Pampers Faster Cuts Everyone's Costs," *New York Times*, July 14, 1991, pp. B1, B5, B6.

frequent-shopper identification number. Marketing programs can be designed that give immediate discounts to consumers at the point-of-purchase, or record dollar purchases as points, accumulated for a later reward. In 1991, 12% of 17,000 chain stores and 3% of 14,000 independent grocers offered some sort of electronic marketing programs. The implementation of rewards, however, has changed: the "instant gratification" of electronic coupons appears to be winning over points clubs.[27] In upstate New York, the Wegmans' Shopper Club offers electronic coupons on up to 60 designated items per week. Data are collected on the demographics and buying patterns of its customers, and shared with the manufacturers who underwrite the costs of the program.[28]

The second level of these programs, the tactical level, represents a greater challenge. As a contrast to the samples of the shopping population drawn in a traditional consumer panel diary, market baskets collected at the POS can provide practically a complete survey of the retailer's client base. The disadvantage of these data are that they only provide information about a household's purchase at a single retailer, instead of purchases for all retailers. If the particular household does not buy certain products from a particular retailer, that retailer will not know if the household purchases elsewhere, or simply does not purchase these products.

A successfully executed marketing program may expect 70% of shoppers in a store as participants.[29] Many pioneers have not executed on the tactical aspects of their relationship-marketing programs, and have achieved competitive advantage solely through the early operational implementation of the programs.[30] Much as many retailers have had faith in the implicit value of POS item-movement data, there is a similar belief in frequent shopper data. These benefits, however, may accrue only to the first few retailers who implement such a program, and may be lost if more innovative programs are offered by competitors.

The true value of a relationship-marketing program is not to provide electronic discounts to all consumers, but to influence individual behaviors in a manner that will prove profitable. This, however, requires Stage 3 (modeling) activities to form market segments for targeting.

---

[27]Deloitte & Touche survey.

[28]N.R. Kleinfield, "Targeting the Grocery Shopper," *New York Times*, May 26, 1991.

[29]Paul Walters, "Winning in the Zellers Zone," presentation at the Retail Council of Canada meetings, October 1991.

[30]Kenneth R. Whightman, "The Marriage of Retail Marketing and Information Systems Technology: The Zellers Club Z Experience," *MIS Quarterly*, December 1990, pp. 358–366.

WHAT DOES THE FUTURE HOLD?

In this chapter, we have discussed current and potential uses of POS data for different types of decisions by retailers and consumer goods manufacturers. A learning curve for using POS data was presented, and the extent to which marketers have ascended it for different types of decisions has been reviewed. Currently, most retailers and packaged goods manufacturers have reached Stage 2 of the learning curve, by developing systems that permit access and distribution of the data to its marketing managers. Market research firms have been active in Stage 3 (modeling) projects for some time, and have started developing Stage 4 (automated data screening) systems to meet the demands of consumer packaged-goods manufacturers. In the following section we discuss the impact of changes in technology and the management focus required to take advantage of POS data.

Ever-Improving Information Technology

Over the next ten years it is estimated that computer performance/cost will improve by two orders of magnitude.[31] In the areas of managing POS data, this will have an impact in two ways. First, as the storage of large (and larger) volumes of data becomes more economical, it is inevitable that databases will grow in size and number. Second, as real-time processing becomes more rapid, complex analyses and presentations that will enhance the interpretability of the data are enabled. It is this latter trend that will make the greater difference to marketers.

Greater processing speed permits more sophisticated software to be developed, which allows a business professional to work with the computer through a more intuitive interface. Information supporting the decision environment may be more richly represented, and relationships within the data may be reduced to simpler, visual presentations. The complexity of large computer systems has resulted in a trend away from centralized, all-encompassing systems (i.e., "the" marketing system) toward more modular, interrelated applications (i.e., a "suite" of marketing applications). In this way, a specific domain of decisions can be supported with a smaller subset of data. As an example, many of the key decisions for media

---

[31]Robert I. Benjamin and John Blunt, "Critical IT Issues: The Next Ten Years," *Sloan Management Review*, Summer 1992, pp. 7–19.

planning[32] require different data from those required for promotional planning. This approach requires management not of a single system, but the coordination of a number of specialized applications which may access different views of the main database. A major challenge for developers will provide some consistency to users who must use and learn multiple applications.

Whereas the prices of computer hardware will continue to plummet, the underlying complexity of computer software will increase, with greater function and sophistication. Software development, however, is a labor-intensive activity, and business knowledge which gives it value is a scarce resource. Marketers have the option of choosing to make or to buy their own software. In-house development has proven to deliver competitive advantage (e.g., American Airlines' SABRE system), but requires a commitment of resources to be at the leading edge of technology. The componentization of software makes the purchase of off-the-shelf software a possibility, but the cost of development must be borne by the number of clients over whom the software is distributed. Applications that are of interest to only a few clients are necessarily more expensive per unit, as there is but a small number of customers over which the software development costs can be distributed.[33]

An alternative approach to exploiting information technology has been to substitute raw computing power for expertise which must be built into the software. "Smart" systems based on technologies such as neural networks have proven to be effective on problems that may be defined as "pattern-matching'" applications. The software is "trained" to recognize a pattern, and then allowed to search the database to find similar patterns. Although this is a "black box" approach, where the relationship between input variables and output variables is not explicitly identified, it appears to be promising on large databases.

As computers become increasingly ubiquitous, software will continue to be enhanced to become customized to the business problems of each individual at hand. Computer systems have reached a stage where less effort is placed on building a system than on ensuring that it will be used.

---

[32]Andrew A. Mitchell describes such a system for media planning. "The Development of a Knowledge-Based Media Planning System," in W. Gaul and M. Schader (eds.), *Data, Expert Knowledge and Decision* (New York: Springer-Verlag, 1988), pp. 67–79.

[33]David Liddle (Metaphor Computer Systems, 1990) coined the description of a "software development sandbar" to depict the economics of developing niche application software.

Corporate Focus on Exploiting Information Technology

In order for POS data to achieve their full potential in marketing, a change in the attitudes within all levels of the corporation must occur.

First, corporations must take a more analytical posture toward marketing questions. In the past, there has been a reluctance toward the hard quantification of the benefits of marketing activities. This has led higher management in some companies to think of the marketing function as an expenditure where the financial returns are unclear.

Electronic POS data can play a role in changing these attitudes if marketing managers change the way in which they think about marketing problems. A more analytical orientation attempts to more precisely calculate the expected marginal return for each specific marketing expenditure.

To statistically derive the impact of specific marketing activities, a basic requirement is a considerable amount of variance within the causal variables (e.g., price) and little collinearity between the causal variables (e.g., display and advertising). Where these conditions have not been met, carefully controlled market experiments, or a program of systematically varying the critical variables, should be conducted.[34]

Increased quantification in the marketing function may be inevitable, since one general trend from management has been the increased accountability of bottom-line results, from a strategy perspective, down to a customer-by-customer review. POS data provide an impartial "scorecard" which can draw attention to triumphs and failures.

A second change, to improve the development of more effective systems for using POS data, is a closer coordination between marketing and management information systems functions which has been lacking in many corporations. This coordination can be accomplished by forming teams with skills in marketing, database analysis, and statistics. If these cross-functional teams are empowered to deliver results without the escalation to higher authorities for arbitration, resources within the company may be rechanneled for greater effectiveness. Approaches such as the strategic alignment model align business and information technology strategies, with an integrated strategic-management process.[35]

---

[34]Mitchell, "The Development of a Knowledge-Based Media Planning System."

[35]John C. Henderson and N. Venkatraman, "Understanding Strategic Alignment," *Business Quarterly*, Winter 1991, pp. 72–78.

This model has successfully been applied by Sears Canada Inc. in its understanding of the information requirements in its catalog business.[36]

A strategy to exploit POS data for competitive advantage is a large undertaking, and requires a first step. Projects need to be prioritized to identify the "low-hanging fruit" to be picked. Bounds for each should be clearly defined so that progress and early results can be publicized. To accelerate through an initial peak of workload, outside resources such as consultants may provide additional leverage to the internal team. Climbing the first few steps of the learning curve will point the way to more advanced projects.

Finally, corporations must do more than simply apply technology to their current business practices. This has proven not to improve productivity. Instead, changes must be made across the organization. The organizational structure of most corporations was designed in the "Age of Paper," prior to the advent of electronic communications and documentation.[37] The original decomposition of corporate activities into departments has resulted in some operating at cross purposes to others, at the detriment of managerial decision making.

Effectively managing the corporation to achieve these objectives is very difficult. People resist change. They are very hesitant to change how they make decisions and to adopt new technology. As the firm moves up the learning curve, changes required increase dramatically.

The movement from Stage 1 (data assembly) to Stage 2 (access and distribution) requires investments primarily in computer hardware and software. The greatest challenge for managers, at this point, is learning the basics of working with software, and coping with the huge increase in the amount of available data. These systems provide summaries of the data, and quick-and-easy answers to ad hoc data queries.

Movement above Stage 2, however, requires major changes in the expertise within the corporation, and the way in which managers approach marketing problems. In the past, the marketing function has not been held responsible for hard cost-justification of its activities. To effectively move to Stage 3 (modeling), marketing managers must be prepared to

---

[36]G. Joseph Reddington, "Using Technology in the Catalogue Business," *Business Quarterly*, Spring 1991, pp. 87–92.

[37]Michael Hammer, "Reengineer Work: Don't Automate, Obliterate," *Harvard Business Review*, July–August 1990, pp. 104–112.

think more precisely about the expected marginal returns for specific marketing expenditures.

Stage 4 (automated data screening) and Stage 5 (integrated outcome simulation) are even more difficult to reach. First, since it is difficult to hire one person with expertise bridging the disciplines of database management, artificial intelligence, statistics, econometrics, and operations research, firms instead hire a number of individuals to form a team. Unfortunately, these technical people often lack the understanding of the business problem, and marketers with the knowledge find it difficult to articulate their technical requirements. Second, specifying the relationships between marketing variables and sales is not straightforward. Considerable skill is required to estimate statistical models to obtain "correct" parameter estimates.

Consumer packaged-goods manufacturers that have demonstrated a long tradition of conducting market research activities may find the transition to scientific approaches to marketing with POS data somewhat easier. The major adjustment, on their part, will be the adapting from project-by-project (e.g., survey-based) marketing research to the continuous flow of POS data. For retailers, the impediments to developing these systems are far greater than for consumer goods manufacturers. To accept marketing as a science, they must accept analytical methods, develop an appreciation for marketing research, and plan with a longer horizon.

CONCLUSIONS

Eventually, all retailers and consumer goods manufacturers will climb the learning curve in their use of POS data. Whereas this will move marketing more toward being a science, it will not completely eliminate the art of marketing. In the art of music, keyboard synthesizers and digital sequencers can be used as surrogates of brass or string sections, but this does not necessarily diminish the creative element of the composition. Modern technology can give the composer a direct degree of control that is unmatched by an ensemble of journeymen musicians, along with an ability to create sounds that do not exist in nature. Technology enriches the artistry of leading-edge musicians and their creativity flourishes. Marketers are now facing similar changes. The science of marketing is a discipline that has only begun to develop, and it can change the business world as we have known it. As anyone who has ever attempted to learn a new musical instrument will affirm, expertise does not come without years of practice. In marketing, the most successful will be those who are able to uncover the art in the science

3

CONSUMER TRANSACTION DATABASES: PRESENT STATUS AND PROSPECTS

John Deighton, Don Peppers, and Martha Rogers

MANY ARTICLES ON THE MARKETING INFORMATION REVOLUTION *concentrate on the use of point-of-sale (POS) data. However, these databases have been commercially available only for the past ten years. By contrast, the true pioneers of the marketing information revolution were companies that began constructing customer transaction databases in the 1940s and 1950s. Reader's Digest, Old American Insurance, USAA, Time-Life, and many other direct marketing firms have been innovators in the use of "customer information files." More recently, Citicorp POS tried to create a massive database of all consumer purchases in grocery stores so that manufacturers could use the information to market interactively to their customers. Retailers such as Neiman Marcus have created frequent user cards. The airlines, over the past ten years, have recognized the power of information collected through their frequent flyer programs.*

This chapter reviews the power and potential of customer databases with a focus on the use of these databases as a new marketing medium. As the chapter states: "When a marketer has access to a census database, recording transactions of both customers and noncustomers, marketing takes on a fundamentally new character. In place of broadcast marketing, which disseminates messages and products widely but not precisely, programs can now be directly addressable. They go to only those customers or prospects whose past behavior suggests they are receptive."

Rather than use information technology to improve decision making or logistics (as was the focus of Chapter 2), the authors emphasize the use of information technology to help manage customer relationships. One issue not discussed in depth in this chapter is the necessity to marry "high-powered analytical tools" with specialized interactive marketing communication techniques. For broadcast media, this marriage was unnecessary.

Market research and statistical modeling are important "enablers" in creating interactive communications.

As one reads this chapter, it becomes clear that interactive communications will push the boundaries of privacy and confidentiality concerns. An interesting question which one should consider while reading this chapter is, What happens if stricter privacy laws are instituted within the United States and other Western countries? Chapter 13 addresses some of these issues in more detail.

INTRODUCTION

The adoption of scanner technology in supermarkets (see Chapter 2) transformed the practice of packaged goods marketing. This innovation let firms know, moment by moment, how their products and competitors' products were performing. The topic of this chapter is the next phase of the information revolution, one with implications far wider than packaged goods marketing. It refers to the construction of *customer transaction databases* to marry a customer's name and address to a record of every transaction between that customer and one or more firms. Examples of customer transaction databases are credit card holder purchase records and airline frequent flyer accumulations.

Some transaction databases are quite primitive, such as when a trader keeps track of each customer's credit purchases in an accounts receivable ledger. Even these simple databases are useful, however. They can distinguish prime customers from less important customers, detect transaction patterns that forewarn that a customer may be about to defect to another supplier, or build a profile of good customers to define new business prospects.

More sophisticated databases pool data across competitors. They allow firms to compute market shares and calculate measures of an individual's loyalty. An example is the supermarket scanner panel. Here shoppers agree to have all their supermarket purchases scanned and recorded against their names. This database unites a comprehensive record of each shopper's transactions with a demographic profile of the shopper. It is, however, a sample and not a census database. Developments discussed in this chapter promise to turn scanner panels into full census databases. When this happens, not only will the panels offer better-quality market research information, but the database will potentially be a communication medium.

Even more sophisticated databases keep track of how a customer uses a product or service, and intervene if they discover something going wrong. For example, some credit card issuers monitor card usage and alert the customer if they notice a pattern that might indicate a stolen card. Some auto manufacturers monitor dealership repair records to detect whether individual car buyers are experiencing an abnormal pattern of repairs. Manufacturers of industrial equipment that transmits data over phone lines can monitor the data flow to learn how intensively their equipment is being used. Here the customer is hard-wired to the manufacturer. Marketers observe customer satisfaction grow or fade just as if the user and the product were still in the factory.

We will review the power and potential of this new technology. When a marketer has access to a census database, recording the transactions of both customers and noncustomers, marketing takes on a fundamentally new character. In place of *broadcast* marketing, which disseminates messages and products widely but not precisely, programs can now be *directly addressable*. They go to only those customers or prospects whose past behavior suggests they are receptive. The potential of a transaction database is not fully realized, however, until marketing becomes *interactive*. By interactive we mean that a marketer's message can be modified to take account of what the customer has said or done at an earlier point in the relationship. At its most sophisticated, then, a transaction database is a record of the conversations between a firm and each of its customers, in which the firm's offering evolves as the dialogue unfolds. The promise of transaction databases, in summary, is the power to build relationships in mass markets one customer at a time, using electronic means to tailor communications to fit the needs of each individual customer.

TECHNOLOGY FOR RELATIONSHIP MANAGEMENT

Whether electronic or personal, relationship management follows a sequence:

1. *Prospecting* for leads to potential new customers, or opportunities for cross-selling new products to existing customers;
2. *Qualification* of leads to decide whom to pursue;
3. *Conversion* of leads into customers;
4. *Retention* programs to try to keep customers loyal; and
5. *Reacquisition* programs to try to retrieve customers who have defected.

Customer transaction databases allow some degree of electronic management of each of these stages of the customer chain. For example:

Prospecting can use look-alike modeling of customers. Marketers extract the demographics and behavior of key customers from the database and use them to build statistical models to predict the conversion probabilities of new prospects. For example, L.L. Bean Inc. can profile the geodemographics of its most valuable customers. It can send its new prospect catalog to names on mailing lists that conform to that profile.

Cross-selling prospects can be similarly profiled. For example, a credit card issuer identifies heavy restaurant users from its cardholder database. It then looks for cardholders whose usage profile is similar except that restaurant use is low. These cardholders, it speculates, may be using a competing card to charge restaurant meals. They become prime targets for joint promotions with specific restaurants to encourage visits and use of the card. Citicorp plans to make this kind of prospecting data available to marketers generally by selling access to its files on its 21-million credit card customers. Database members can be asked to supply referrals. Frequent flyer programs grew rapidly in their early years because airlines asked members to identify likely prospects for membership solicitation.

Finally, conventional advertising media can be used to persuade interested prospects to identify themselves, so that they can be invited into a continuing relationship. For example, Warner-Lambert Co. invited the public to phone an 800 number to find out the pollen count in their vicinity. Those who responded became a transaction-based mailing list, and were sent coupons for Benadryl.

Qualification of leads, the process of deciding whether or not to invest resources in forging a relationship, also uses look-alike modeling to forecast relationship value. Usually it has some preliminary transaction data at its disposal to drive the model. Some database marketers let a prospect become a customer for a probationary period before committing themselves to the terms of business, to build up a transaction history. Catalog marketer Spiegel uses rates of purchase during an initial period to decide how many catalogs to mail, and the kind of catalog to mail, in the subsequent period. American Express uses a charge cardholder's early transaction history to set the credit terms it later extends.

Conversion may mean different things in different industries, but generally it means shifting a customer's frequency of purchase of commitment to a single supplier. What does it take to convert a customer? Frequent shopper programs at supermarkets, such as APT's Vision 1000 program, offer clues to conversion from the patterns in shoppers' transaction histories. Coca-Cola, for example, can find audiences ripe for conversion to Diet Coke. It can look for sugared Pepsi users whose transaction histories hint at concern for their weight in their choices in other product categories (category conversion). It can look for heavy Diet Pepsi users who have begun to sample other brands (brand conversion). It can target light Diet Coke users to increase their consumption (brand development). Each of these audiences needs a different conversion program tailored to its particular susceptibility.

Retention marketing is the goal behind the construction of many transaction databases. The term generally refers to direct communication to a firm's established customers, to build loyalty and inoculate against competitors' appeals. Three forms of retention marketing are common:

Frequent user programs offer direct incentives for heavy use to customers. For example, Waldenbooks, a book retailer, invites its best customers to join a club. It then tracks their purchases and sends them newsletters tailored to their individual reading preferences, and offers discounts based on volume purchases. American Multi-Cinema formed the Movie-Watcher club. It offers incentives for frequent cinema attendance and tries to shift demand to times of the week when its theaters are underused. Fotomat issues a Preferred Customer Card to bring customers back to Fotomat for film processing in exchange for discounts and incentives. Cruise lines offer distress merchandise (undersold cruises) to heavy users who can be counted on to respond quickly.

Affinity clubs have a more subtle objective. Like broadcast advertising, they aim to enhance and nurture the sense of satisfaction customers receive from using a brand. Clubs for Lego and Nintendo have been popular with children. They deliver information about contests and tips on product use, they recognize high-performance users, and they are a vehicle for selective coupon promotion. CPC International Inc. sends its *Health Watch* newsletter to dieticians and home economists to promote Mazola Oil. RJ Reynolds owns a database with the names of millions of smokers who have requested free samples. Kraft-General Foods manages several clubs. One extends brand advertising by inviting children to join the Kraft Cheese & Macaroni Club. It publishes a quarterly magazine, *What's Hot*, for children. Its Crystal Light brand of powdered soft drink maintains a LightStyle Club for young adults. In support of the Nine Lives cat food brand, it launched *The Morris Report*, a full-color quarterly magazine designed to build brand loyalty. It sends the magazine to consumers and to small animal veterinarians for their waiting rooms.

Carnation has created Friskies Buffet Cat Club, complete with membership card. Hormel's Kid's Kitchen Club promotes shelf-stable entrees to children. The club sends children a newsletter and a Kidalogue, a catalog of items available with Kid's Kitchen proofs-of-purchase.

A *defector program* uses statistical modeling to identify the profiles of customers likely to defect to competitors, so that preemptive action can be taken. Firms with comprehensive transaction databases, such as credit card issuers and other "membership" organizations, can install these programs at little incremental cost. One long-distance telephone company, for example, continuously monitors the number of subscribers in each of its market zones who switch to other carriers. If the rate of defection to a competitor in a zone exceeds chance levels, it assumes a local competitor is attacking and launches its own defensive response.

In summary, technology now exists to manage relationships—initiate them, nurture them, and defend them—on the scale of mass marketing but with the flexibility of individual marketing. In a word, this is the technology of *addressability* (Blattberg and Deighton 1991; Kotler 1989). It goes beyond simple direct marketing to the extent that it is interactive. By this we mean that the marketer differentiates among households so that different homes receive different messages. Consistent with the conventions of good conversation, the message respects its audiences' uniqueness. The Benadryl campaign discussed earlier was simple direct marketing. To become interactive, Warner-Lambert might have gleaned information from questions to the inbound callers, such as duration and severity of allergy symptoms or the results of past treatments, and modified its outbound communications in the light of this information.

THE LIFETIME VALUE OF A RELATIONSHIP

In orthodox accounting systems, customers show up in a firm's financial statements as a line in the income statement, the sum of all the revenue they have contributed that year. When the accounting system is geared to track the impact of individual customers, it becomes tempting to think not only of the annual revenue attributable to a customer, but of the customer's asset value. That is how other assets are treated: if a firm owns an income-producing asset, perhaps an office building, it accounts for the asset both on the income statement, recording the rents received in the past year, and on the balance sheet at cost or market value. Market value is appraised as the net present value of the cash the asset will generate for the rest of its economic life, discounted at a rate established by the market for comparable cash flows. Can a customer relationship be appraised in the same way?

Sewell and Brown (1990) claim that a first-time buyer of a new Cadillac automobile will, over the course of his or her lifetime, spend $322,000 with the dealership. This revenue flows from a variety of transactions: car sales, routine servicing, repairs and parts, and accessories. Some are more certain than others, and some have a higher gross profit than others. But if the dealership keeps a transaction history on each of its customers, it is a relatively simple exercise in actuarial statistics to estimate the probabilities of each cash receipt from the historical data and then to capitalize the flow. For the average dealership, let us assume the calculation yields a lifetime value (LTV) for a first-time Cadillac buyer of $40,000. A well-run dealership, able to keep its customers happy and loyal, might be able to appraise its first-time Cadillac buyer as an asset worth $70,000. Assuming 200 first-time Cadillac sales a year, the average dealership has a customer equity of $8 million, compared to $14 million for the well-run dealership. That difference, $6 million, becomes a precise estimate of the impact of good marketing on the market value of the well-run dealership. It becomes a measure by which the management of the dealership can be judged. It is a more dependable measure than annual profits, which can be manipulated by short-term promotional tactics that boost sales but deplete the stock of customer LTV.

As a second example, consider how a marketer of personal computer software can compute the value of an addressable customer. When a customer buys a spreadsheet package and sends in the warranty registration card, the customer becomes addressable and the firm can attempt periodically to sell upgrades to him or her by direct mail. Assume that 30% of addressable customers buy the upgrade compared to 5% for owners of the package who have not returned their warranty cards and who must be reached by broadcast media. Assume the upgrade sale generates a gross profit of $100. Assume the firm's transaction database shows that a user of the spreadsheet has a life of six years, in which time two upgrades will be issued. Then the LTV of an addressable customer is $(30\% \times \$100 \times 2) = \$60$. The LTV of a broadcast customer is $(5\% \times \$100 \times 2) = \$10$. Thus, the value to the firm of each warranty card they can persuade a customer to return, or, to express it differently, the value of capturing an address, is $50.

In this example, there are a number of ways to manage the software firm so as to enhance its customer equity (the sum of its LTVs). It could offer more to each customer—if its product portfolio were larger, it would be better placed to capitalize on the relationship. It could increase the life of its customers beyond six years. It could improve the yield rate for its direct mail solicitations, perhaps by making the upgrades more useful to customers. It could offer an incentive that would increase the number of warranty cards returned. Note that the sum of the firm's LTVs is the metric by which the firm can decide whether the benefit of achieving any of these changes exceeds the cost. In that sense, maximizing customer equity is a powerful criterion for judging business performance.

THE ECONOMICS OF ELECTRONIC RELATIONSHIP MANAGEMENT

There is a sizable cost to running a transaction database, and broadcast communication is the default option against which directly addressable communication must be compared. Gains from more efficient delivery of messages, or more effective customized messages, must be enough to offset the system's cost.

What features of an industry make customer transaction databases economically attractive? An answer to this question can be inferred from the order in which industries have adopted the innovation. The cost of maintaining a data file has declined steeply in recent years, so that the order of adoption suggests how fixed benefits have offset declining costs.

Airlines were probably the first industry to incur the cost of setting up databases for no reason other than marketing advantage. The frequent flyer program of American Airlines was the pioneer. Catalog marketers and supermarkets followed later, with frequent shopper programs. At the tail of the distribution are marketers of infrequently purchased consumer durables such as white goods that generally show little interest in these programs.

We discuss here factors that dispose an industry to use database marketing. The first is the lifetime value of a customer address in that industry. As we have discussed, a customer's LTV is the annual incremental profit attributable to the customer (usually the product of the margin on each transaction and the frequency of repeat purchase for the customer's buying life, plus referral profits) discounted at a rate to reflect the riskiness of the cash flow. The higher the LTV of an industry's typical customer, the higher will be the returns to investment in database marketing. A loyal takeout pizza consumer might represent a $1,000 asset to a pizza chain, justifying perhaps a computer system to record the fastest way to get to a customer's home and what toppings the customer likes. An affluent young buyer of a luxury car might be a $60,000 asset, enough to justify a number of relationship-building initiatives. On the other hand, the most loyal buyer of laundry bleach is unlikely to be worth more than $100 in LTV. Unless the marketer of the bleach can deepen the relationship by extending the product or service portfolio quite considerably, this relationship is better managed with broadcast media than with the help of an addressable database. It is worth emphasizing, however, that the LTV of a customer is not a function of product characteristics. It depends on the firm's skill in leveraging its access to its customers.

Second is the cost of acquisition of an address. This is the sum of the marketing costs to acquire the customer, and the incremental cost (if any) to obtain the address. Cost of customer acquisition is obviously high for an involving product such as an automobile, and lower for inexpensive consumer nondurables. Some industries, including credit card issuers, telephone utilities, and magazine publishers, need the customer's address to deliver service. For these industries, the cost of address acquisition is no more than the routine cost of winning the business. For others, such as supermarkets, some incentive may be necessary to compensate the customer for supplying an address. In still other cases, a distributor owns the address and may have a substantial disincentive to share the address for fear of losing the customer. For example, a travel agent may try to block a vacation cruise line from obtaining direct access to its client. The HBO cable television network is blocked by cable suppliers from learning the names of its subscribers. The cost of circumventing these blocks can be very high. In turn, the cost of customer and address acquisition diminishes the attractiveness of database construction.

Third is the cost of alternative programs to build brand loyalty. When loyalty is difficult to create in any other way, the firm is more likely to incur the cost of setting up and managing a database. When the customer must incur costs to switch out of a relationship, as in a doctor patient relationship or as a telephone subscriber or bank customer, the cost of retention is low. Less investment in relationship-building is needed than, for example, when the product is an airline ticket.

So-called badge products and services, those with the power to confer status on their users, are another way to command loyalty. These products have less need to incur the costs of database marketing. A prestige liquor brand would be less likely to need a frequency program, for example, than a less well-known brand.

Next is the incremental cost of communicating with members of the database. The bank faces low retention costs, but it also experiences low incremental communication costs because it writes to its customers monthly in the normal course of business. A supermarket, on the other hand, must absorb the full cost of a mail program if it chooses that medium to deliver incentives.

Next we identify the cost of file management as a factor inhibiting the use of database marketing. The economies of scale in file management seem to follow a U profile. Costs fall initially as scale increases, but, given current limitations of computing technology, when scale becomes very large, costs rise rapidly. National databases are limited in the amount of data they can store and the cost and time it takes to identify patterns in the data. A national database of supermarket purchases, for example, would soon exhaust the capacity of the largest data storage system.

Finally the returns to database construction are higher when the opportunities for differentiation are greatest. When consumer tastes are not highly differentiated, as, for example, in utilitarian product categories like detergents and toothpastes, the power to address customers individually is of little value. When tastes are highly differentiable, addressability is valuable because it can be used to customize offerings. In financial services markets, for example, in categories such as life insurance or portfolio investing, it is very useful to be able to tailor the offering to a specific address.

THE ECONOMICS ILLUSTRATED: THREE CASES IN THE EVOLUTION OF TRANSACTION DATABASES

In the section that follows we shall illustrate our thesis, describing the economic factors that favor or discourage the construction of customer transaction databases. The first two cases describe unsuccessful applications, and contrast usefully with the third. In the interest of comparability, each example is drawn from the packaged goods industry. This is not to suggest that services and business marketing domains are not as important or more important areas of application.

Quaker Direct

Among packaged goods marketers, the Quaker Oats Company ranks about 30th in advertising expenditures, but fourth in coupon distribution. In 1990, Quaker was concerned about the cost of coupon delivery, by newspaper and by syndicated services such as Carol Wright and Select & Save. Furthermore, redemption rates by shoppers were declining. The challenge was to reduce Quaker's cost per coupon redeemed.

Quaker's solution was to build its own targeted coupon delivery system. Quaker estimated that about 26 million U.S. homes used coupons. They were to be the target for Quaker Direct. The objectives were to win market share from competitors and to reward current users. Quaker hoped to transform merely habitual behavior into brand loyalty, building brand equity for the Quaker name. Quaker Direct began to be seen as much more than a low-cost coupon delivery system. Like advertising, its larger task was to add perceived value to Quaker's stable of brands. The company saw it as part of a shift from *brand* marketing to *household* marketing. In brand marketing, single-brand programs were designed to address the needs of customer segments. In household marketing, a program involving multiple brands would be addressed to the needs of a single family.

Quaker's first step would be to mail a 100-question survey to a list of prospect households. Quaker felt that those who responded were "promotionally responsive" and likely to use coupons. In the second step, a household's survey responses would be used to assemble and send it coupons. Each home received a customized package based on its profile in the questionnaire. Families without dogs did not receive coupons for Kibbles & Bits, for example. Those who reported eating Post Raisin Bran may have received a coupon for Raisin Life. The response rate was four times that of mass-distributed, free-standing inserts in Sunday newspapers (FSIs). Each coupon was bar coded to identify the recipient and the product. In the third step, therefore, Quaker would build a database that recorded each household's redemptions. Subsequent coupon mailings would take account of the pattern of earlier redemptions to decide which brands to promote and what size incentive to offer. The plan was to estimate household price elasticities, so that variable value coupons could be issued, their face values set at a level to maximize the household's contribution. Face values could be as low as zero. If the coded data showed that a household often used a particular Quaker brand, it might be offered zero-dollar coupons for that brand. These coupons earned credit in a larger promotion to reward loyalty and discourage use of competitors' coupons.

The program began with the distribution of a questionnaire to 50 million households in Select & Save coupon mailings. In September 1990, Quaker mailed coupons for ten of its own brands and six noncompetitive brands to the 18 million households who had responded to the survey. The cooperative effort reduced the cost per brand. To promote the coupon drop, Quaker tied in with CBS Television's fall season's programming promotion. In later mailings Quaker tied in with Paramount Home Video and a Chevrolet giveaway. Epsilon/American Express supplied the technology to manage the database. It housed the files and analyzed the data. Computerized Marketing Technologies (CMT) of New York shared the cost of the original questionnaire mailing and managed data entry. CMT shared profits by selling space to brands that were not in competition with Quaker.

Quaker Direct was an heroic but ultimately unsuccessful experiment. In the first quarter of 1991, Quaker abandoned the program. Quaker has offered no explanation for the termination, but it may relate to costs. Quaker was dependent on printing, delivery, and redemption of paper coupons, and at the mercy of a manually delivered mail system. Although response rates were higher than those of coupons delivered as inserts in Sunday newspapers, delivery costs must have been much higher. Typically coupons delivered by newspaper insert cost $7.00 per thousand, whereas direct mail delivery of bundles of coupons might cost ten times that amount. Costs per delivered coupon were apparently uncompetitive. Furthermore, by structuring the program as a proprietary system, Quaker had to spread costs across noncompeting brands. This was too narrow a base to support its costs.

Reward America

Citicorp POS Information Services is a division of the Citicorp banking group, formed in 1984 to give the group a stake in the information gathering and marketing industry.

In October 1989, the division launched a program called Reward America in 27 supermarket stores. It invited customers of the stores to join a *frequent shopper program*. Those who agreed were sent a membership card with a magnetic encrypted panel, and were told to show it each time they paid for groceries. In this way the store tracked their purchases. Members earned points toward bonuses by buying specified brands. A monthly newsletter let them know how many points they had earned and how many points they needed to receive cash or product incentives. The program earned revenue from three sources. First, it sold information to 25 manufacturers, including Procter & Gamble, Campbell Soup, Ralston Purina, and Kraft-General Foods. Second, it sold manufacturers *access* to the member customers for promotional purposes. A cereal manufacturer could target a promotion at consumers of a rival brand. Buyers of a single copy of a magazine could be sent an offer to subscribe. Third, it sold information to retailers. Retailers could study patterns of buying across product categories for insights into micromerchandising, store layout, and category pricing.

The program expanded rapidly in 1990 to more than 200 stores, but in November 1990, it was abruptly scaled back. A report in *The Wall Street Journal* attributed the setback to several causes. Fewer retailers had adopted the program than had been expected. They expressed unhappiness at having to pay for data generated in their own stores. They contended that the program benefited manufacturers more than retailers because it influenced brand shares more than category volumes. Consumers were said to find the incentives were too long deferred to be appealing, and shopper participation apparently fell off. Manufacturers claimed that the program promised much more data analysis than it delivered, perhaps because the volume of data generated by the system exceeded the capacities of the division to interpret it. Executives of the division had speculated that a database of ten million shoppers would be necessary before the program was a viable medium for communicating with consumers. At the time of the scaling back it claimed about two million members. Finally, the setback occurred at a time when the bank as a whole was reporting poor results. Nevertheless, Citicorp did not abandon the program. It cut back the division's budget from $125 million in 1990 to $65 million in 1991, and terminated only 174 of the division's staff of 444. It seems reasonable to interpret the experience of Reward America not as an indictment of the idea of addressable supermarket databases, but as a reflection on a particular method of implementation.

Vision Value Club

Procter & Gamble in 1987 faced the same problem that the Quaker Oats Company had recognized: the declining efficiency of cents-off coupon promotions. In discussions with CheckRobot, Inc., the idea of a frequent supermarket shopper program took shape. The two firms joined forces with A.C. Nielsen Company, Schlumberger Technologies, PNC Corporation, and GTE Interactive Services to offer it to supermarkets and other consumer goods marketers. (Customers include Campbell Soup, Del Monte, General Goods USA, Kraft, McNeil Consumer Products, Oscar Mayer, and Ralston Purina.)

They incorporated as Advanced Promotion Technologies (APT) of

Deerfield Beach, Florida. Its goal was to establish a national network in retail stores to deliver a broad array of marketing services to consumers. APT markets the *Vision 1000 System,* a paperless promotion delivery system for supermarkets. Vision uses an electronic medium, a smart card the size and shape of a credit card, that contains a 256K microchip to record purchases and entitlements. Vision can be enhanced with a frequent shopper program, the *Vision Value Club.* This program rewards customers for certain shopping patterns with points that can be redeemed for catalog merchandise. Each time a Vision Value Club member goes through the checkout line at a participating store, points accrue on the membership card. As the points are stored on the card and not a particular store's computer, the customer can get credit at *any* participating club store. APT first tested the system in two Big Bear grocery stores in Columbus, Ohio, in 1988, and in April 1990, expanded to all 69 of the chain's Ohio and West Virginia stores.

Customers who enter an APT store see a kiosk with shopping lists and pictured specials of the month's promotions at the store's entrance. When they reach the cash register, they see a color video monitor that runs 10-second animated messages from video disk. Some of these messages are triggered by the scanning of purchases the customer has just made. At the checkout, the cashier scans the shopper's card. The shopper's current point balance appears on the video monitor. As the cashier scans the customer's order, the customer sees the point balance increase on the screen whenever a promoted item passes by the scanner. (Promoted items are flagged on the shelves with shelf talkers.) Points are exchangeable for goods listed in a catalog offering jewelry, audio and video equipment, appliances, cookware, and other items. The promotion program changes monthly, providing manufacturers with the opportunity to switch or add items. Although no competing brands in the same product category are promoted in a given month, those manufacturers that do not renew may be displaced. Brand managers apply to APT for slots in its calendar most advantageous to their brands, just as they buy space and time in other media. During checkout, the screen alerts shoppers to instant savings on products. It provides information about in-store specials, prints redeemable coupons and recipes, and displays the last five items scanned by the cashier. An animated register tape on the video monitor shows prices and descriptions of each item purchased.

The video messages are interactive. Customers can "Touch Here" on the monitor screen for a coupon, a free recipe, or the next message. The screen offers shoppers promotions whenever the checkout operator scans a promoted product's UPC code. If a competitor's product is scanned, a manufacturer has the option of responding immediately with a coupon on its own product. Because the system is card-based, shoppers can accumulate credits with multiple purchases over many shopping trips at different stores. It compares favorably to a paper-based rebate offer. A paper rebate must be pulled from the shelf, taken home, and mailed in with proof-of-purchase, a procedure that delays gratification for weeks. The card stores the customer's demographic information so that the system can send offers to particular customers. For example, the smart card makes it possible for a young family to receive a disposable-diaper offer that will not be seen by a shopper without small children. Someone buying diet soda may get a coupon for a low-calorie frozen entree based on the inference that the shopper is calorie-conscious. Retailers pay part of the cost to install the equipment. APT pays for a local service and marketing staff to assist retailers, and recovers these costs from manufacturers that bear the system cost. They pay for coupons and credits issued, and a fee to APT for inclusion in the month's program, and for the laserdisk production of their messages. The retailer owns the data, which links the shoppers, demographically defined, with their purchase histories and shopping habits.

PROSPECTS FOR THE TRANSACTION DATABASE INDUSTRY

Transaction databases are a new *communication medium*, challenging television and print as ways to reach customers. They are also new *information vendors*, competing with market research suppliers. They generate volumes of behavioral data that can be used to track and evaluate how well marketing programs are working. In the markets where they are used, this power to evaluate performance will transform marketing into a more accountable discipline.

Each of the three programs described above began as an information medium, inspired by the search for a better way to distribute promotions. Each program built an addressable communication medium, one that could persuade as well as offer incentives. Whether the content of the message was an incentive or a personalized appeal, its impact was likely to be greater than one that was merely broadcast. Cost, however, was a problem. The cases suggest that when the medium was paper-based, and depended on the mail system for execution, the benefits of tailoring did not offset the costs. APT solved the problem with electronic display and receipt of information.

Consequently, each program discovered that it could increase its economic viability by becoming an information vendor. Quaker had less opportunity than the others to sell data because it sought to assemble proprietary data. Quaker restricted its market for information to non-competing firms. It could not capture all of the proceeds of information vending in its market. Citicorp POS and APT, by contrast, were *information intermediator* programs, located between the generator and the user of the information. They sold data interpretations, and the ability to access addressable customers, to the highest bidder, much as a publication sells the audience it has created. They sold access to customers, not their identities, so that the buyer remained dependent on the intermediator to continue the relationship. Citicorp pooled retailer information to sell to manufacturers. APT sold retailer information back to retailers. Its data were useful to the manager of a store or the regional manager of a chain even if not comprehensive enough to appeal to national manufacturers. The APT program may have been successful just because it thrived on a limited scale. As information vendors, these programs depended on their ability to pool data across retail chains and across manufacturers, to function as data clearinghouses.

It is important not to overstate the importance of information vending at this time. To show that an addressable medium can survive and flourish without selling information, consider the case of Catalina Marketing. This firm is simply a communications medium for promotions, with no information clearinghouse capability. It dispenses coupons to shoppers at the supermarket checkout register, using only knowledge of the goods a shopper has bought on that trip to decide the brand to be promoted and the size of the incentive. Yet it has been successful, operating in 4,100 stores in 26 regional markets since its inception in 1985. In 1991, 180 manufacturers used the Catalina service, generating revenues of $48 million for the company (Petersen 1991).

Given the success of Catalina, the relative success of APT's Vision 1000, and Citicorp's difficulties, it seems reasonable to conclude that, at this stage in the information revolution, supermarket transaction databases are more valued as communication media than as information vendors. They are little more than ways to target promotions. They lack the analytical sophistication and perhaps the sheer computing power to extract strategic information from cross-brand and cross-retailer transaction histories. These, however, are solvable problems.

Information intermediation has emerged as a source of competitive advantage in the credit card industry. The American Express Green and Gold cards commanded higher than average merchant discounts because they are information intermediators to their clients. They analyze customers' charging behavior with a merchant and its competitors, and then design information and promotion programs for that merchant. An individual service establishment (e.g., a hotel property) can designate up to ten firms as competitors and then ask for a report that compares its customers' spending behavior to the profile of the average of these competitors.

In the example just described there is an obvious limit to the value of the information supplied to vendors. A vendor sees only the behavior of those customers who charge with a particular credit card. To put together a complete picture of the market for, say, hotel or car rental services it would be necessary to pool the data of all credit card issuers. Such a transaction database would fill a void in industries that today have no reliable aggregate market information, let alone information at the disaggregate customer level. Industries in which most transactions are charged to a credit card would have a resource at least as useful as supermarket scanner panels. It would be comparable to the national transaction database conceived of by Citicorp POS. Yet, apparently, no credit card issuer sees advantage in cooperating with other card issuers to form an *information pool*. Because they combine the role of information intermediary with that of a user of that information for their own account (unlike Nielsen, IRI, or Citicorp POS), they see more value in information asymmetry than in information parity. The customers for this information, however, may decide that the value of total information is greater than exclusive rights to a part of the total picture. If that is so, it is reasonable to expect that, with the support of these customers, an organization will emerge to intercept communications between vendors and credit card issuers. This organization will be able to build a pooled national transaction database at least in selected industries.

We can make this argument general, and claim that the mixed information broker/user firm (of which credit card issuers are an example) is a transitional form in the history of information technology. In the early stages of the revolution, the user generates marketable information as a by-product of running its primary business, and makes a market in it. Eventually, however, it comes to overvalue private data, and creates an opportunity for a pure-form information intermediator, with no mixed motives, to enter the market. A test of this prediction is unfolding in upstate New York. A supermarket chain, Price Chopper, is building a transaction database system similar to those of Reward America and the Vision Value Club, but restricted to the customers of its chain. As an information user, Price Chopper is denying itself the competitive information it could have by joining a pool. In return, it has exclusive use of its private transaction data. As an information broker, Price Chopper plans to sell to manufacturers the ability to reach customers who buy specific products. Our prediction is that Price Chopper's go it-alone program may be viable in the short term, given the immature state-of-the-market in supermarket transaction databases today. In the long run the firm will suffer from the absence of competitive information. As a vendor of information, its clients will prefer to buy from sources that sell comprehensive regional audiences pooled across supermarkets.

The history of credit rating services can be read in this light. Credit evaluation began as a private activity, performed by department stores as a source of competitive advantage. The advantage was weak, however, and the benefits of creating information parity were great. Consequently, third-party credit rating firms emerged to pool the information of each participant. Today three firms exist to rate individual household credit: TRW, Trans Union, and Equifax. They maintain what are effectively three credit transaction databases covering every household in the United States. Opportunities to sell analyses of these databases extend far beyond the original user market of banks and granters of loans.

Airline frequent flyer programs, on the other hand, have very little incentive to pool. The value of private information to an airline is great, and the value of pooled information is quite low. Nevertheless, we assert, pooled information has a market value and an information intermediary may yet emerge even in this industry. Perhaps American Express's Membership Miles program, which grants rewards for airline flights on any of seven airlines, marks the beginning of the end of airline-controlled frequency programs. If card issuers, or more pointedly travel agents, controlled frequency programs for air travel, the ability of these programs to sustain brand loyalty would be lost. Market power made possible by frequency programs would pass to distributors as it has done in the grocery industry.

This experience may be repeated in other industries. At least in the short term, industries that develop transaction databases may discover that they weaken the power of brands and strengthen the power of distribution channels. They may help retailers more than they help manufacturers because retailers are more decentralized. APT, for example, can accumulate information useful to a particular local retailer more easily and cheaply than it can assemble data on a scale broad enough to help a manufacturer.

In summary, the future of media is linked to addressability and information vending. The most successful database programs are likely to be those that are

- paperless communication media, not dependent on a postal service;
- able to receive, interpret, and analyze responses rapidly and at low cost;
- free to assemble an information pool across competing products;
- able to function as information intermediaries, selling comprehensive market census data; and
- able to break even at less-than-nationwide scale, serving regional or local niches.

PRIVACY AND CONSUMER HARASSMENT

Early in 1991, Lotus Development Corporation and Equifax announced a joint venture to sell a set of compact disks for the personal computer containing data on almost every household in the country. The 30,000 protests they received against the dissemination of this data led Lotus to withdraw the Marketplace program. Curiously, the information represented by Marketplace is still generally available to businesses. Large companies can buy it direct from Equifax, and similar databases are available online from competitors. The launch of Marketplace meant that, for the first time, small businesses with a personal computer and a compact disk reader could use this information. Nevertheless, the public opposition to the publishing of these data in so accessible a form showed the depth of concern for privacy.

Consumers leave behind them a trail wherever they go. Being born, applying for a driver's license, a passport, a home mortgage loan, or a social security number, submitting a tax return, redeeming a coupon, shopping from home, using a credit card, entering a sweepstakes, giving birth or dying, each of these is an event that can be accessed by marketers. Consumers have begun to notice that their lives are thus exposed. They object to this loss of privacy for at least two reasons.

First, the very idea of so much information being available to marketers is upsetting even if the injury is not apparent. Equifax studied whether consumers could be reassured. They explained to consumers the potential benefits of a program such as Marketplace: more targeted marketing, less junk mail, fewer people offended by unwanted and irrelevant ads or products, even saving resources by not printing unwanted ads. They concluded that when consumers saw what was in it for them, their objections faded. However, the cost of reframing would be great.

Second, consumers link the availability of data to the blizzard of commercial messages that has become a part of modern life. Many high-income or high-response households receive over 50 pounds of direct mail a year, excluding catalogs. Unsolicited outbound telemarketing has become a particular cause for resentment toward the direct marketing industry. The movement to curb markets in transaction data appears as a defense against the shrill commercialization of private life.

Several legislative solutions to these issues of privacy have been proposed. One possibility is that marketers that sell names and addresses be required to notify a consumer each time they sell information about the consumer to another marketer. Such a requirement would place a very onerous burden on the marketer. The effect would be to substantially reduce the use of product lists. Ultimately, it would reduce the options available to consumers. If such a full-disclosure law applied to government agencies, it would likely have an adverse effect on compiled lists. However, it would have no effect on syndicated services such as Carol Wright and Select & Save that make explicit bargains with consumers to trade information for benefits.

Any information intermediary could make such a bargain just as these syndicated couponing services do. In return for yielding up rights to one's transaction history records, a consumer could be promised coupons, samples, or even money. The term *consensual database* is used to describe data assembled in this way. Equifax, a large credit-reporting service and information intermediary, recently launched a consensual database under the brand name Equifax Buyer's Market. Most frequency programs are consensual because members are rewarded for participation with free merchandise and other benefits. Whereas legislation designed to protect privacy may in the future specify the terms of disclosure required for consumer participants, it is unlikely that it will restrict consensual services. For that reason, some have predicted that, within a decade or less, consensual databases will be the principal form of database in widespread use for marketing purposes (Westin 1992).

CONCLUSION

We have identified several evolving patterns in the use of customer transaction databases.

First, there is increasing interest in addressable, rather than broadcast, communication. As it becomes progressively cheaper to store names and addresses in machine readable form, addressable media will become more cost competitive with broadcast media as ways to transmit both persuasion and incentives to consumers.

Second, many firms are experimenting with interactivity. Addressable media make possible programs of communication in which messages become progressively more differentiated from one another and tailored to the self-expressed interests of their audiences. These experiments are easy to read. The manipulated variables can be linked directly to the behavior of the addressed households, certainly more so than in broadcast advertising environments. So interactive marketers learn quickly, and adapt faster than competitors who are not interactive.

Third, information intermediaries are emerging in several industries and there is reason to think they will appear in other industries. These new firms, free of the narrow interests of those who generate information and those who use it for their own account, can build the new addressable media *and* make markets in interpretations of the pooled information these media generate.

Information intermediaries will put competitors close to parity with respect to data so that the scarce resource will not be information itself, but creativity in the uses to which the data are put. In the short run, information pooling will help distributors more than manufacturers because retailers can use local area data while manufacturers want aggregated pictures. In the long run, manufacturers will realize that information intermediaries are the enemies of brand equity. Their challenge will be to use private transaction databases in tandem with the pooled databases to create brand-specific customer value.

Finally, consumers today fear the information revolution. They resent the proliferation of direct communications. The revolution can be stalled, if not defeated, if this sentiment begins to influence political decision making.

REFERENCES

Blattberg, Robert C. and John Deighton (1991). "Interactive Marketing: Exploiting the Age of Addressability." *Sloan Management Review*, 5–14.

Bleakley, Fred R. (1991). "Citicorp's Folly? How a Terrific Idea for Grocery Marketing Missed the Targets." *The Wall Street Journal*, April 3, B1.

Brown, Paul B. (1990). "Paper Trail." *Inc.*, August, 113–114.

Kotler, Philip (1989). "From Mass Marketing to Mass Customization." *Planning Review*, September–October, 10–48.

Petersen, Laurie (1991). "The Checkout Kings." *Adweek's Marketing Week*. October, 22–23.

Sewell, Carl and Paul Brown (1990). *Customers for Life: How to Turn That One-Time Buyer into a Lifetime Customer.* New York: Doubleday/Currency.

Westin, Alan (1992). "Consumer Privacy Protection: Ten Predictions." *Mobius*, February, 5–11.

4

THE EVOLUTION OF DECISION SUPPORT SYSTEMS AND DATABASES IN CONSUMER GOODS MARKETING

David Ing

THE CONCEPT OF *marketing decision support systems (MDSS) is now over two decades old. Early emphasis was on developing statistical models to guide managerial decision making, but over the past decade the focus has shifted to both computer hardware and software technology. Whereas technology is critical because of the massive databases being analyzed, as MDSSs mature the emphasis must shift back to helping managers make decisions. Technology must be a means toward an end. The problem is that those versed in DSS and, more specifically, MDSS will be hard pressed to find systems that help managers improve decisions.*

This chapter provides a history and definition of marketing decision support systems. The author discusses new technology such as graphical user interface and other interesting access-and-delivery systems on the horizon and then emphasizes the need to have statistical models "drive" MDSSs. He ends his chapter with the following question: "In closing, given the change in computer technology over the previous decade, should we prepare for another radical shift in the MDSS environment in the next decade?"

Specialists who manage marketing information technology will need to know the answer to this question. After studying this chapter, the reader will be in a much better position to make a prediction.

A number of other chapters in this volume focus on how information must be formatted to make it more useful for managers. Schmitz's chapter discusses the use of expert systems that report information to managers in the form of a "newspaper"; Hoch discusses how managers interact with models and shows that decisions are actually improved when models and managers "interact"; and McCann presents new concepts on how to communicate results to managers. Related to the presentation of information is the need to process it so that it leads directly to making a decision. Blattberg, Kim, and Ye discuss the need to mass-produce models so that they can be used as the basis of an MDSS. Little also addresses this issue but for customer panels. Thus, many of the later chapters in this volume focus on the issues that Ing discusses here in Chapter 4.

INTRODUCTION

The transactional efficiency of delivering goods to the consumer has been aided by the falling cost of computing through the 1980s. PC-based point of sale (POS) systems are standard, improving customer service through speedier checkout times and better inventory estimates in stores. Manufacturers routinely use hand-held terminals to record shipments made to distribution centers or directly onto the retail floor. Operational-level systems can mechanically perform tasks such as replenishment (i.e., automated item-level reordering) but often do not fully capture the dynamics of today's changing markets. At the tactical level, retail buyers and manufacturers' brand managers struggle to distill macro trends from the multitude of marketing activities that simultaneously occur. The frequency and number of promotions have skyrocketed; competitive positions change with the rapid introduction and withdrawal of new products; consumer segments are constantly being redefined and remapped. "Overnight ratings," "ad hoc analysis," and the "zero-sum game" for market share set the stage for "instant answers" and compression of the planning cycle. In this environment, marketing decision support systems (MDSSs) need to be more than the eyes and ears of the marketplace; they must provide the marketing intelligence on which future actions may be based.

The capability for "conversational" dialogues with 1970s time-sharing mainframe systems created a vision that business professionals, without the assistance of a programmer, might be able to view and manipulate corporate data through the use of a decision support system (DSS). This chapter will review some early concepts of MDSSs, first with a view inside the "black box," and then from a "support system" perspective, contrasted to other interactive computer systems. Some examples of MDSSs commercially available today are then reviewed in these contexts. Key information technologies that comprise MDSSs are then discussed, followed by some ideas on the roles of managers in the development of these systems within the organization.

CONCEPTS: WHAT IS INSIDE AN MDSS?

Little, an early (1979) proponent of marketing decision support systems, defined one as a

> coordinated collection of data, systems, tools and techniques with support software and hardware by which an organization gathers and interprets relevant information from business and environment and turns it into a basis for marketing action.[1]

To learn about the business environment, the marketing manager would interact with a black box which would have four components (Figure 4-1):

Databank: This would encompass quantitative marketing variables (e.g., sales, advertising, promotion, and price) from internal sources, as well as competitive performance and news reports from external sources. "Soft" information from newspapers and from members of the organization would also be included. Marketers might not be satisfied by existing accounting systems, which are oriented toward processing transactions.

Models: These are the manager's conceptions of "how the world works." Using the numerical data stored in the data bank, various hypotheses could be tested and developed into explicit computational representations to aid planning and decision making.

Statistics: This is the process of relating models to data. Although sophistical mathematical techniques are included, the most frequent operations are simple techniques such as grouping, aggregation, taking ratios, picking exceptions, or tabulating summaries.

Optimization: With an objective of improving the performance of the organization, techniques could range from simple operations (e.g., ranking alternatives) to the more formal (e.g., operations research).

As an alternative to the meetings, studies, and reports where marketers exchange ideas on the data and methodologies, an interactive Q/A process with the MDSS would permit an electronic method of communicating about analyses.[2]

When Little's article was published, marketing was still perceived very

---

[1]John D.C. Little, "Decision Support Systems for Marketing Managers," *Journal of Marketing*, vol. 43, Summer 1979, p. 11.

[2]Abridged from Little, "Decision Support Systems for Marketing Managers," pp. 9–11.

FIGURE 4-1
A Black Box Definition of MDSSs

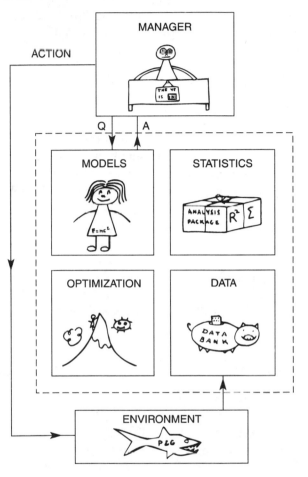

Source: John D.C. Little, "Decision Support Systems for Marketing Managers," *Journal of Marketing*, vol. 43, Summer 1979.

much as an art. Little saw an intermediary problem-solving role for the marketing scientist, to make sense of the numerous data and measures available. Trained in marketing, statistical methods, and database systems, these intermediaries would create quantitative models which could be exercised by novices. Market status reporting (e.g., What is our market share?) would be transformed into market response reporting (e.g., Are our promotions as effective as expected?). For the 1980s, Little predicted an increase in magnitude in the amount of marketing data used (i.e., the "POS Data Explosion"), matched by a similar increase in computer power available for analysis. Unfortunately, a shortage of marketing scientists (which, arguably, has continued into the 1990s) was also predicted because of the scarcity of individuals developing this mix of skills.

As a black box definition, Little outlines some ideas of what is inside the MDSS, but doesn't describe the working details of the software components in action. The average marketer can enter questions and receive answers, but probably does not understand how the data, models, statistics, and optimization function together to produce the result. In this context, the contents of the black box are solely the responsibility of the marketing scientist, who embodies his or her skills and expertise into software. This view reflects the programming tools of the 1970s, of fourth-generation and procedural languages, but such a view would not be inconsistent with approaches based in knowledge-based systems. The revolution in information technology that has occurred over the past decade should not lead us, however, to constrain our definition of MDSSs to the technology available but to look to the requirements of the marketer. To expand our understanding of an MDSS to a more abstract level, the nature of the marketing questions to be answered and the role of the user in the human/computer conversation are discussed in the next section.

CONCEPTS: HOW DOES A DSS "SUPPORT" DECISIONS?

Traditional marketing reporting systems often present choices for information much like meals are presented on a restaurant menu. By selecting a choice, the marketer can request a recipe that reproduces a predictable result. Unfortunately, alternatives not appearing on the menu cannot be requested, even if the ingredients are readily available in the kitchen. Some marketers, faced with a limited selection, may be prepared to move to the buffet table where they can take a personal hand in creating their own results. Reporting systems follow the metaphor of step by step recipes. Decision support systems, however, enable the user to be flexible in choosing ingredients and to combine them according to the needs of the moment. The judgment of the marketer can contribute to the final result, and experience is gained with additional iterations through the process. Little's definition of an MDSS does not reflect the dynamism suggested in this metaphor: the final result obtained through the Q/A process is the same, whether it is generated by a novice or a master.

To satisfy the requirements for a number of classes of users, Keen suggested a "Modest Proposal" for the generic design of DSS software.[3] The system would be accessible to the novice or executive/casual user (e.g., a manager who only runs pre-written programs); and to the expert (e.g., a marketing analyst able to customize existing programs to solve problems); as well as to the programmer (e.g., a technical professional able to produce efficient code, and "bulletproof" against user errors). In the era of character-based interfaces which prevailed at that time, these requirements presented a tall order. The APL[4] computer language, however, demonstrated a number of features desirable for DSSs: an interactive operating environment, and an ability to tailor "functions" which seamlessly extend operations that already exist in the language.[5] An APL programmer can create conversational routines that accept fixed values (e.g., 1, 2, 3) from the novice as readily as a personal program (e.g., MYPROGRAM) that returns some values as created by the expert. Providing the features of portability (i.e., the same user interface on multiple hardware platforms) and a standard library of routines, APL was an early "end-user programming" alternative to procedural languages such as FORTRAN or COBOL.

As interactive, online systems became more common, Keen refined the definition of DSSs to differentiate their use from simpler query-and-reporting applications.

> The label "Support System" is meaningful only in situations where the "final" system must emerge through an adaptive process of design and usage. This process may be needed for a variety of reasons:
>
> **"Semi-Structured" Tasks:** The designer or user cannot provide functional specifications, or is unwilling to do so. [Structured tasks can be automated or routinized, thus replacing judgement, while unstructured ones entirely

---

[3]Keen suggested that natural language processing would be the ultimate user interface, but this branch of artificial intelligence was (and still is) underdeveloped. See Peter G.W. Keen, "Interactive Computer Systems for Managers: A Modest Proposal," *Sloan Management Review*, Fall 1976, pp. 1–17.

[4]APL was invented as a mathematical shorthand by Kenneth Iverson while at Harvard and implemented as an interactive programming language on IBM time-sharing systems in the 1960s. The language is still popular, where its strengths in rapid application development and the manipulation of multidimensional arrays are needed, although most novices are likely to prefer the more visual representations of data, as in spreadsheets. See Doris Appleby, "APL," *Byte*, December 1991, pp. 141–146; a special edition on the 25th anniversary of APL, *IBM Systems Journal*, vol. 3, no. 4, 1991; and Kenneth E. Iverson, *A Programming Language* (New York: John Wiley, 1962).

[5]In contrast, fourth-generation languages (4GLs) typically have functions and a syntax that are different from the compiled language in which they are built. As an example, linked lists (as pointers) are a basic feature of the C programming language, but a 4GL written in C is unlikely to provide such a construct.

involve judgement and defy computerization. Semi-structured tasks permit a synthesis of human judgement and the computer's capabilities.]

Adaptive Design: Users do not know what they want, and the designers do not understand what they need or can accept. [Traditional systems development projects follow a life cycle with end user requirements clearly defined through analysis and specification phases, in advance of any application coding. A "final" system is released to end users only after exhaustive testing. In contrast, a DSS follows a "middle-out" process, where an initial system is implemented quickly, and then gradually firmed-up, modified and evolved.]

Conceptual Evolution: User's concepts of the task or decision situation will be shaped by the DSS. The system stimulates user learning and new insights, which in turn stimulate new uses and the need for new functions in the system. The difficulty in pre-specifying how a DSS will be used is reflected through this learning process, as its structure evolves in response.

Structural Evolution: Intended users of the system have sufficient autonomy to handle the task in a variety of ways, or differ in the way they think to a degree that prevents standardization. [Since there is no "standard" or "right" method to reach a decision, the computer interface must support personalization, and a flexibility for the user to shape the system.][6]

Transactional reporting systems often provide information similar to that required by marketers, but they differ in the degree of structure. Accounting, as an example, is based on relatively clear structure for classification, e.g., assets as cash, inventory, or plant and equipment. Marketing structures, on the other hand, may be based on overlapping and shifting views of the marketplace. Products may be classified by fuzzy definitions such as product characteristics (e.g., regular or family size), by category (e.g., gourmet food), or by price ranges (e.g., budget or premium). Consumers may be segmented by demographic characteristics (e.g., senior citizens), lifestyles (e.g., baby boomers), or geographic location. Because it is impossible (and impractical) to reduce the data into every conceivable cluster imaginable, marketers are often provided with detailed, disaggregated data, which can be reaggregated when needed.

The volumes of data now available make the creation of aggregates and summaries unmanageable without the assistance of IS (information systems) professionals. Unfortunately, the marketing process compounds

---

[6]Abridged/adapted from Peter G.W. Keen, "Decision Support Systems: A Research Perspective," Center for Information Systems Research #54, Sloan Working Paper #1117–80, March 1980, pp. 6–11.

the above vagaries of classification with trade-offs between conflicting objectives (e.g., market share and profitability) so that it is often difficult to specify exact information requirements in advance. This semistructured decision-making environment does not suit the traditional methodology of project management for software development. The shorter (weekly) planning cycle associated with marketing data is too short to create a project plan, or to ensure the quality of execution. In addition, the resources of a programmer and/or the computer are not best utilized by creating a multitude of "ad hoc reports" that may be irrelevant in the following week. The role that the traditional IS organization can play with decision support is limited: it can install the software and provide basic technical assistance, but it is the marketing scientists who must combine marketing and computer skills to create a true MDSS.

Little's definition of an MDSS is not incompatible with Keen's view of a DSS, except in one area: the degree to which the black box is "closed." Keen's "adaptive process of design and usage" would suggest that an MDSS initially structured by a marketing scientist should be sufficiently "open" such that its shape could be adjusted to personal tastes and/or needs. Beyond merely adjusting some input parameters through a Q/A interface, the marketer should at least have some flexibility to make some cosmetic changes (e.g., changing decimal places) and perform simple logic modifications at will. Although a marketing scientist is valuable in implementing the more technical aspects of the MDSS, introducing him or her as an intermediary can intrude on the marketer's conceptual evolution during the adaptive design process. At a high level, Little's vision of a marketing decision support system is appealing, but its black box structure is too much of an artifact of the menu-based, compiled programs of the late 1970s. Marketers today are much more comfortable with the concept of "personal computing" and are skeptical of computer programs they do not understand. An ideal marketing decision support system would blend the black box's internal structure with flexibility for structural evolution.

MDSSs IN PRACTICE — TWO EXAMPLES

To bring the definitions of MDSSs to life, two very different approaches to satisfying the needs of marketing managers will be described in this section. The first, CoverStory, designed specifically to meet an information need of consumer packaged-goods marketers, more closely follows the spirit of Little's vision for an MDSS. The second, the Metaphor Data

Interpretation System, is used by marketers across many industry segments and stands truer to Keen's vision. The examples are compared to the definitions of MDSS above, and their strengths and limitations are highlighted.

CoverStory[7] was conceived as a solution to the "scanner data explosion" in grocery products, where marketers accustomed to brand-level regional aggregates are overloaded with a multitude of marketing measures at the UPC level by geographic market. The increased volume of data available for analysis has not been matched by a similar increase in the manpower to review it; in fact, most marketing staffs have been downsized since the late 1980s. The challenge to "summarize what is important in this data" was answered by an approach that automates the creation of a summary memorandum describing key events in the database.

The procedure follows four steps. First, marketing models quantifying the impact of marketing variables (i.e., distribution, price, display, features, and price cuts) are created. Products and markets are then aggregated into clusters, and ranked to draw attention to the "top few" of interest, by share or volume change. The most noteworthy products and markets are decomposed for further analysis, and the top associated factor changes are scored and ranked. Finally, an English-language presentation constructed with sentence templates is filled out and published through a word processing package.

The CoverStory module is but one part of a larger MDSS, but it reflects a general approach to reducing the large volume of scanner data. Following Little's definition of an MDSS, CoverStory's greatest strengths are its model and optimization components. Marketing models quantify an expected outcome from marketing activities by which actual results may be benchmarked. Optimization is a simple ranking of the variances from expectations, drawing the most significant to the immediate attention of the reader.

Completing Little's definition, the data bank of UPC-level scanner data is obvious in its volume, as are the summary statistics of clustered product markets. The sophistication of the CoverStory procedure, however, removes the Q/A flavor of an interactive conversation, with written reports instead generated in a batch. Although it is practical to deliver the reports electronically on a computer screen, printing hard-copy reports

[7]John D. Schmitz, Gordon D. Armstrong, and John D.C. Little, "CoverStory—Automated News Finding in Marketing," *Interfaces*, vol. 20, no. 6, November–December 1990, pp. 29–38.

may be for either of two reasons. The first might be technical: because the data are not updated in real time, running all product markets as a single overnight "batch" is less resource intensive than computing the many online requests for each product market, one at a time, while the marketer waits. The second is based on the way in which marketers have become accustomed to looking at data: even if brand managers were able to view an electronic form of the same report more rapidly on a computer screen, many would still prefer to print the report on paper, and then physically file it away.

The orientation of CoverStory toward reporting and away from a "purer" decision support system is reflected in Keen's definition. CoverStory routinizes the semistructured task of reviewing marketing data into a standardized presentation. Adaptation of the design for other purposes would require that advanced end-users be able to pull out specific submodules to be combined with alternative procedures. Further structural evolution of this system, however, is likely beyond the capabilities of an end-user and calls for the skills of a professional programmer. CoverStory emphasizes its primary strength in supporting the conceptual evolution of the marketer's decision environment, while de-emphasizing the other functions of the MDSS. By introducing a "top-down," "exception-based" methodology to reviewing scanner data, the attention of the marketer is focused where his or her decisions will have the greatest impact.

In contrast to CoverStory's narrowly defined problem domain, Metaphor Data Interpretation System (DIS) is a platform that is more consistent with Keen's definition. In comparison to some PC software which have appended graphical-user interfaces onto older character-based products, DIS was designed as an object-based interface which would simplify workgroup access to large-scale databases and manipulation of the data. Relational tables are graphically depicted through a Workstation Tools Data Dictionary, assisting marketers in the creation of complex queries to one or many databases. A Tool-to-Tool Communications facility transfers data from one tool (e.g., a query to a mainframe database) to another (e.g., a plot) through a few clicks of the mouse, and application capsules may be assembled by connecting the tools together, as arrows between icons (Figure 4-2). DIS has been used not only by brand managers for the analysis of scanner data but also by retailers for internal point-of-sale and inventory movements and by insurance companies for targeting clients.

Unlike the "application-orientation" common in most computer envi-

FIGURE 4-2   DIS Application Capsule

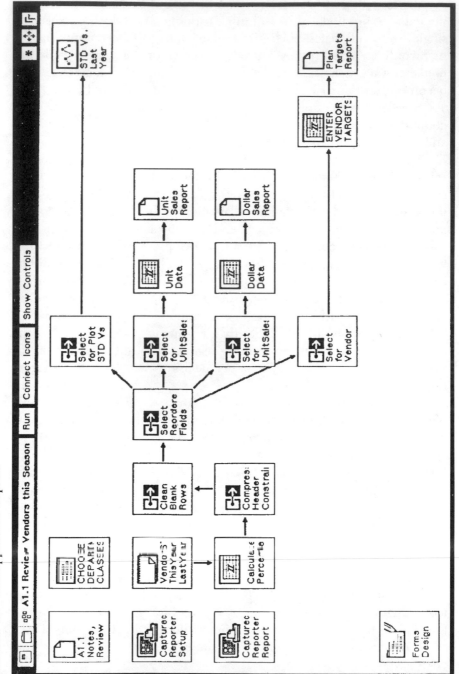

ronments to date, DIS is architected as programs and data modularized into "objects," providing an environment where applications are developed by linking icons together.[8] Consistent with Keen's definition, DIS can support a semistructured task/solution process by offering a large set of tools which appears as icons to be connected together as the user works through a problem. As an interactive system, development can follow an adaptive design process. Options within each tool can be selected or modified, and data may be directed in whichever way the icons are visually connected. Conceptual evolution can occur as the marketer incrementally adds tools to manipulate the data as needed. Finally, programs are normally not "compiled" or "locked," so that end-users are encouraged to evolve the structure of applications.

DIS is a popular MDSS among consumer goods manufacturers. A.C. Nielsen offers a Databank[9] service for selected consumer goods manufacturers, providing remote access to over 100 gigabytes of data in 500 databases, with tailored groupings of products and markets for each company. The system is often used for the promotional analysis of events with the consumer (e.g., coupons) or the trade (e.g., allowances and incentives) and for competitive analysis. Manufacturers providing direct store delivery (DSD) can review their sales volumes and analyze distribution patterns of product from the warehouse to the stores.[10] Retailers have adopted DIS for category analysis and assortment planning to ensure that the sizes, flavors, or colors demanded by consumers are being purchased and stocked. Vendor performance on delivery and profitability are tracked. Recently there has been interest in using DIS to generate customer profiles and to target offers to segments of the customer base.[11]

DIS has the potential to fulfill Little's definition of an MDSS, but the components he describes are not all immediately "ready-to-use" when the system is delivered. Simple statistics and optimization procedures are easy to build in the DIS environment, and an interactive Q/A process is native. In situations where a marketing data bank does not already exist, however, one must be designed and implemented, often based on the

---

[8]DIS is described as an object-based environment, as it demonstrates many of the features of object-oriented technology. For an easy description of this area, refer to David A. Taylor, *Object-Oriented Technology: A Manager's Guide* (Reading, Mass.: Addison-Wesley, 1990).

[9]Personal communication with Laura Reeves, Metaphor Computer Systems, Chicago.

[10]These applications are discussed in more detail in a "Value Assessment Study of the Consumer Packaged Goods Industry," conducted for Metaphor Computer Systems.

[11]Many of these themes are discussed in "Value Assessment Study of the Retail Industry," conducted by Ernst & Young for Metaphor Computer Systems.

summarized accounting and transactional records.[12] The greatest variability in DIS implementations, however, is the sophistication of models available to the marketer. In some companies, where a backlog of requests to the MIS department has left marketers starved for data, DIS becomes merely a substitute reporting system which relieves the programming bottleneck. In these cases, marketers can become overwhelmed by a new volume of reports that merely relate "what happened" rather than follow models that explain "how the world works."

When a company has no experience with marketing models, the semistructured nature of MDSSs can make the initial specification of an application suite on DIS onerous. A project to develop models for proprietary internal data sources requires special focus to ensure that applications are constructed and readily available for marketers. One approach was to introduce a "Marketing Toolkit" by first creating a blueprint of the application suite needed by marketers and then constructing "proof-of-concept" applications in DIS used to demonstrate the "look-and-feel" and purpose of marketing models.[13] Although constructing the full "Marketing Toolkit" was expected to take some time, the training to raise the level of organizational learning about marketing models could be conducted in parallel.

The above two examples illustrate the current state-of-the-art in MDSSs. A balance must be established between structure, as demonstrated with the rich models built into CoverStory, and flexibility, as demonstrated in the assembly of tools in DIS. This is achieved through the appropriate design in suitable information technologies as well as management commitment to a vision of developing MDSSs. The next section addresses the first issue by discussing the emerging information technologies on which MDSSs will be based in the near future. The chapter concludes with a discussion of the managerial role in the development of MDSSs.

MDSSs IN PRACTICE   KEY INFORMATION TECHNOLOGIES

The combination of Little's definition with that of Keen creates three basic requirements for information technologies of an MDSS: a wide

---

[12]Databases to support tactical decision making are designed differently from those optimized for transactions. See William H. Inmon, "The Atomic Database: Building the Perfect Beast," *Enterprise Systems Journal*, November 1990, pp. 62–87.

[13]David Ing and Ray R. Serpkenci, "Designing a Retail Marketing Decision-Support Toolkit," paper presented at the TIMS Marketing Science Conference, March 12, 1993.

variety of data should be readily accessible to the marketer; the exchange of ideas, data, and methodologies should be supported between marketers through the system; and the system and its shape should be responsive to the user. Three technologies are key in providing an appropriate environment for decision making: data repositories which retain and share news on the marketing world; workgroup networks which support the exchange of information between and within marketing teams; and user interfaces which can electronically extend the problem-solving capabilities of marketers. The combination of these three technologies provide the foundation for a corporate MDSS platform.

Data repositories were simpler to maintain in the 1970s era of mainframe computing, when all access and technical support were provided centrally on a few large machines. Personal computing and decentralized processing have resulted in data being stored in many places, and in many different structures. One symptom of poor data management is the downloading of data to personal spreadsheets for reformatting and manipulation, not only by single individuals but by entire workgroups. The solution to this unproductive activity is not to increase the speed at which personal computers can reformat data but to provide improved access methods so that the data can arrive at the marketer's desk in a more manageable form.

The current standard for multi-user marketing databases is the relational model.[14] Although relational databases are often adopted first for their benefits in improving programmer productivity, marketers can benefit greatly from the flexibility through which data can be selected. Instead of having data structure designed for one specific application (e.g., favoring access by product category rather than geographic regions), the relational model advocates a methodology of data modeling and "normalization" to define multiple, two-dimensional tables. When the data from multiple tables are required, the tables are "joined" to create a new two-dimensional view (Figure 4-3).

Queries to relational databases are constructed with structured query language (SQL), an English-like computer standard. Many software products now offer a graphical depiction or prompted interface to simplify specification of the query, some with a data dictionary to translate requests into SQL. In contrast to alternative database models based on keys, the "nonnavigational" orientation of SQL means that the user specifies the

---

[14] IBM DB2 and Oracle are two examples of popular products.

FIGURE 4-3
Star-Join Query

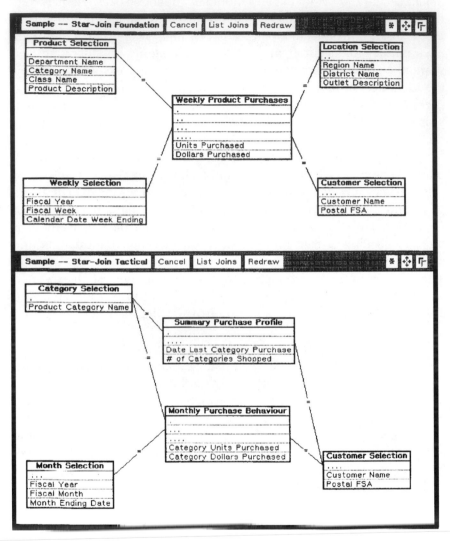

characteristics of the data to be selected, rather than the physical path by which the search should be conducted. Further, a "logical view" (e.g., a weekly accumulation) may be created by the database administrator as an abstraction of the true physical records (e.g., actual day-by-day transactions) and be similarly queried using SQL. Advances in distributed relational databases now enable queries to a local database to be forwarded on to a remote database when the data are not available on the local machine.

Relational databases are well suited to the structural evolution required of MDSSs. Instead of having to reorganize a database for each new view required, multiple tables may be joined in manners originally unforeseen. Although some new technologies such as object-oriented databases[15] may better handle complex datatypes (e.g., images of printer advertising), it is likely that the bulk of marketing data available (e.g., point-of-sale unit and dollar movements and inventory) will remain in relational tables. Improvements in the management of the ever-increasing volume (i.e., terabytes) of data will come as the result of both incremental insight on how to use the data and simpler methods of depicting the structure of data to end-users.

The second key technology, workgroup networks, currently appears in marketing organizations as computer hardware that has often not been fully exploited by software. A bare-bones implementation is characterized by a network adapter card installed in a personal computer so that the user sees virtual disks (e.g., an H: drive, when there is physically only one C: drive on the immediate machine) from which programs and data may be copied. More sophisticated workgroup software conceals the physical location of the data and programs and represents other computers as extensions of the marketer's own. In an environment of structural evolution, it is important not only to be able to access the same data as co-workers but also to tap into the models and methods which compose the expanding knowledge base of the organization.

The simplest software environments to implement are peer-to-peer architectures, where all computers on the network are similar in hardware and operating system configuration. Common functions include share printers, access to site-licensed software packages, and simple mail facilities. These are an electronic alternative to the "sneaker-net," where data and programs are replicated on diskettes and then physically carried to another machine for copying. More advanced workgroup functions include electronic conferencing, as repositories to exchange knowledge,

---

[15]Object-oriented databases are currently in use for CAD/CAM and multimedia applications. For a deeper comparison of the relational and object-oriented structures see Christopher M. Stone and David Hentschel, "Database Wars Revisited," *Byte*, October 1990, pp. 233–242; Herb Edelstein, "Relational vs. Object-Oriented," DBMS, vol. 4, no. 2, November 1991, pp. 68–79; or Won Kim, "Object-Oriented Database Systems: Strengths and Weaknesses," *Journal of Object-Oriented Programming*, vol. 4, no. 4, July–August 1991, pp. 21–29.

and workflow processing, to ensure the execution of interdependent tasks. In a team of marketers, an MDSS should assist the individual and also enhance communications within a group.

Client-server architectures enable more sophisticated "program-to-program" communications between a client machine (e.g., a personal computer requester) and a centrally maintained server (often a system of a different platform, e.g., a minicomputer or mainframe). Advanced client-server programs can transparently extend the personal computer so that external databases, communications to remote systems, and/or mail from other locations seamlessly appear to be part of the user's personal system. "Cooperative processing" between the two computers balances tasks to each's strengths, coordinated through short synchronizing messages. Commonly, the graphical user interface is the Q/A front end in the personal computer client, and computationally intensive routines or access to large volumes of data are managed by the server. In client-server decision support systems, marketers are often responsible for assembly of their own models and optimization routines on the client systems, whereas the IS departments manage the data and statistics in the servers.

The third key technology, user interfaces (and graphical user interfaces—GUIs[16]—in particular), has changed the face of computing. For users, mass-marketed, shrink-wrapped packages such as spreadsheets provide a capability to personally perform simple calculations and formatting. More involved procedures, as might be experienced in developing marketing models, however, often test the bounds of capabilities for which the package was designed. The traditional path for growth, custom application development, is undesirable for MDSSs. A second alternative, combining several specialized packages together, is difficult in most GUIs. A "cut-and-paste" or "clipboard" approach visually copies data from one software package to another, but it often loses the richer attributes of the data (e.g., numbers that add up), causing users to think about datatypes (e.g., numeric, text, or graphic) rather than the meaning of the data themselves.

The popularity of GUIs is driving some uniformity in the "look" of software, but the "application-orientation" of packages from different vendors can give each a slightly different "feel." As feature upon feature is added to each package, users may solve problems by using the software they know best rather than choosing the most appropriate method. In a

---

[16]The Apple Macintosh environment and Microsoft Windows (on top of PC-DOS) are popular examples of GUIs. Third-party software developers build their application software products to work on top of these environments.

semistructured environment such as an MDSS, the risk may be best expressed by the maxim, "When the only tool you have is a hammer, every problem looks like a nail." The recent trend in software development has been to create environments where packages focus on their primary strengths and may be more simply "snapped together" as the user desires.

Object-oriented user interfaces (OOUIs) provide a more consistent foundation for packages by establishing a user's conceptual model of metaphors (e.g., a file drawer) and implementing an object model with appropriate behaviors (e.g., dragging another object onto a file drawer).[17] Some software environments currently offer "macro" facilities which can capture keystrokes and replay them by rote,[18] but these approaches have not proved robust for "industrial-strength" applications. The next generation of operating systems, currently in development, will provide object-oriented characteristics which will enable nonprogrammers to "encapsulate" their procedures and visually "link" objects on their screens.[19] Specialized routines (as demonstrated by the functionality of CoverStory) may eventually be purchased as "components"[20] which may be simply connected together to other components which have already been assembled. In this environment, marketers will have a greater facility to control the structural evolution of their models, without having to write programming lines of code.

These three technologies have each evolved independently, but it is the combination of the three that provides an environment suitable for an MDSS. Data repositories based on multiple relational tables give marketers the flexibility they need to rejoin normalized data structures

---

[17]Abridged from David E. Liddle, "What Makes a Desktop Different," working paper, Metaphor Computer Systems, September 25, 1989.

[18]The "Agent" in the Hewlett-Packard New Wave environment creates "scripts" of keystrokes and mouse clicks for later invocation. New Wave is designed as an application environment for Microsoft Windows GUI, which is, in turn, based on the MS-DOS operating system. See John R. Rymer, "Unraveling the New Wave Confusion," *Patricia Seybold's Office Computing Report*, vol. 14, no. 9, September 1991, pp. 3–14.

[19]"Application Capsules" in the Metaphor Data Interpretation System have been used to direct data from one object to another (e.g., query from a relational database, to a spreadsheet, to a text tool) since the mid-1980s. More recently, Apple has implemented a slightly different concept with the "Publish/Subscribe" feature in their System 7.0. See Patricia B. Seybold, "Metaphor Computer Systems: A Quiet Revolution," *Patricia Seybold's Office Computing Report*, vol. 11, no. 8, August 1988; and Tom Thompson and Owen Linderholm, "Seven's a Success," *Byte*, June 1991, pp. 42–48.

[20]Charles Irby graciously provided me with an unpublished "Constellation Technical Overview White Paper," in which Patriot Partners (founded by the IBM Corporation and Metaphor Computer Systems in 1990) described the development of an application environment where "Component" software would be interconnected by "Protocols." This mission was superseded by the formation of the Taligent partnership between IBM and Apple Computer Inc.

in the manner required at the moment. Workgroup networks enable the data to be physically located on any machine within or outside the marketing team and facilitate the communication of marketing knowledge and models in addition to the data. Object-oriented user interfaces are the "glue" with which the marketer can assemble components of data and programs into marketing models. This environment provides a foundation for adaptive design, conceptual evolution, and structural evolution, as described by Keen. Although it is possible to use these technologies to create a black box, as defined by Little, they present opportunities to provide a more open environment, where the marketing manager has better access to and understanding of the marketing scientist's thinking.

Clearly, adoption of these advances in information technology does not occur without strong leadership and vision. The next section discusses the management role in the evolution of marketing decision support systems.

MANAGEMENT'S ROLE IN THE DEVELOPMENT OF MDSSs

The concept of marketing decision support systems is now over a decade old. What challenges face the marketer of the 1990s? Four areas that require some focus can be suggested: (1) positioning expectations for MDSSs, in comparison to other technologies, (2) development of "model bases" to capture "organizational knowledge," (3) improved distribution of the knowledge in the MDSS, and (4) the ongoing renewal of MDSSs.

Although many computer-based technologies have been loosely called MDSSs, it is important to position MDSSs neither too low nor too high in their capabilities. An MDSS may be used as report generator, just as a bicycle may be used as a delivery vehicle — it may be simple to use for small tasks, but it may not be well suited for industrial-strength jobs. MDSSs are unlikely to replace large, production computer systems optimized for efficiency on routinized transactions. At the other extreme, there is some controversy over how much "intelligence" can be built into an MDSS. To the novice computer user, there may appear to be little difference between one black box called a "decision support system" and another called an "expert system." Once the input data and algorithms are in place, is it a small task to replace human judgment? By Keen's definition, this change would require the complete structuring of a semi-structured problem, and closing opportunities for adaptive design, conceptual evolution, and structural evolution. Such a system, incorporating human judgment, would then be called a knowledge-based system (KBS) rather than a decision support system. Unfortunately, the software development process for knowledge engineering leaves little room for the marketer to incorporate his or her learnings, once the system is in production. Today's KBS shells are designed to create complete production systems and do not interface well with other operating environments. In the emerging, object-oriented world (perhaps in the beginning of the next millennium), it will be a challenge to see whether or not the "knowledge bases" and "inference engines" can be "componentized" to work with other software functions.

In the more immediate future, how then can MDSSs "grow" in their contribution to the business? Much as a "marketing database" has become a standard within many companies, a "marketing model base" must be developed. The most analytical marketers reviewing marketing data are skilled in identifying important events in the marketing data and focus their analyses to support actionable decisions. Models are developed in their heads and applied with experience. In order to improve the skills of the less-sophisticated marketers, some of these procedures must be captured in the MDSS software. Who should take responsibility for populating the model base? Unfortunately, marketers with day-to-day responsibilities do not usually capture the process of "adaptive design" in the software.

The supply of ready-to-hire marketing scientists is likely to remain below the level of demand, so, for the near future, cross-training the current work force may be the only reasonable option to obtain the desired combination of skills. Marketers with computing skills and programmers with a business sense are obvious choices, although both usually require development of their use of statistics. The type of system used by these "experts" is also an area of controversy: given the greater analytical requirement and understanding of the marketing scientists, should they have an "advanced" system, while "novices" are given a "simple" system? With the increased popularity of object-oriented user interfaces over the next few years, it will become more common to encapsulate complex analyses, so that an "average" marketer will not have to see what is "under the covers," unless he or she wishes to do so. In the new generation of componentialized software, the marketing scientist will build components that the average marketer can snap in to an analysis, giving some flexibility in shaping the DSS. Companies that choose not to migrate from the previous generation of software, however, are likely to retain separate levels of sophistication for the expert and for the novice.

The distribution of marketing models as software components can simply be performed electronically, as local area networks (LANs) have become more common. "Public File Drawers" are shared resources accessible to the workgroup as a natural extension of their own desktop. It is not the physical distribution of marketing models that presents the challenge, however, but the view of organizational knowledge as a corporate resource. Keen makes a distinction between

> **Personal Support Systems (PSS),** for use by individuals in tasks that involve no interdependencies, so that the user can indeed make a decision;
>
> **Group Support Systems (GSS),** for tasks with "pooled" interdependencies that thus require substantial face-to-face discussion and communication; [and]
>
> **Organizational Support Systems (OSS),** for tasks involving "sequential" interdependencies.
>
> A PSS may thus support a manager's own budget *decision*, a GSS support the budget *negotiation*, and an OSS support the organizational budget *process*.[21]

Marketers dissatisfied with their computer support may have originally turned to personal computers as PSSs, but the need for individual marketers to share a centrally managed database signals the infrastructure of an OSS. The era of personal computing is coming to a close, and the trend toward downsizing corporate staffs and flattened marketing organizations[22] calls for improved teamwork through the sharing of methods and knowledge.

By the very definition of MDSSs, ongoing renewal of the databases and model bases is required to support decisions in the changing marketplace. If a problem becomes sufficiently structured, it should be considered for recoding in a traditional computer language with greater execution efficiency. New data sources are likely to become available, and methods of analyzing existing data are sure to improve. The role of individuals with responsibility to support and maintain the marketing knowledge through all of these changes is unclear in many organizations. The natural turnover of employees not only results in a loss of organizational knowledge but also presents a learning challenge as new marketers

---

[21]Keen, "Decision Support Systems," pp. 5–6.

[22]See George Low, "Conference Summary: Conference on Sales Promotions from the Consumer, Manufacturer and Retailer Perspectives," Marketing Science Institute Report #92–103, February 1992.

must follow in the footsteps of those preceding them. In order to consciously capture and retain organizational knowledge, a role for a marketing methods librarian may arise.

In closing, given the change in computer technology over the previous decade, should we prepare for another radical shift in the MDSS environment in the next decade? Although many might point to the shift of platform from the personal computer to the scientific workstation as the next trend, this is unlikely to have a great impact on MDSS users. The advent of the graphical user interface on a client/server architecture means that, to the average marketer, the MDSS will "look" the same. The ability to link componentized software will modularize the applications created by marketing scientists. Programmers may have to adjust to object-oriented technology, but this will probably be hidden from the marketers. In the next phase of evolution of marketing decision support systems, the emphasis will not be on technology but on the building models that will assist marketers in making better decisions.

5

EXPERT SYSTEMS FOR SCANNER DATA IN PRACTICE

John Schmitz

TECHNOLOGY, PARTICULARLY in the area of expert systems, is just beginning to be used in marketing to help managers transform data into information and, more important, into decision-making tools. One of the most interesting applications is CoverStory, which scans through marketing databases to determine key changes of importance to the marketing manager and sales force. It then produces an English text document describing the information identified in the data. For a typical consumer products firm with 70 sales territories, 5 key competitors, and 20 high-volume SKUs in the category, the ability to peruse the 7,000 series of information each week is almost impossible. CoverStory, using an expert system in combination with statistical models, can search through large databases quickly and efficiently and then select "news" (abnormal events) to report to the manager. This use of technology allows the manager or salesperson to concentrate on actions related to the findings of the data search, rather than devote an inordinate amount of time to searching through the data for "news."

SalesPartner is an important advance beyond CoverStory because it takes the information and then transforms it into a system designed to be the analytical assistant to a sales representative. SalesPartner assembles the quantitative analysis needed to support the sales representative in asking for shelf space or merchandising support for the brand or item.

When looking at CoverStory and SalesPartner, we quickly recognize that expert systems are moving into a new realm in which the decision domains are "fuzzy" and the quantity of data enormous. The ability to sort through and transform all of these data and then translate the results into recommended decisions is a major leap forward. As managers are confronted with the information explosion in industry after industry, the template created by SalesPartner and CoverStory shows a key new direction in trying to harness the power of market information.

INTRODUCTION

Information Resources Inc. (IRI) distributes consumer purchase and merchandising data from food, drug, and mass merchandising stores. The company also produces software that retrieves and analyzes this data and performs similar retrieval and analytical tasks for financial data. In developing and applying these ideas we find a need for more automation of the data analysis task, previously assigned to human analysts. The two main reasons for this need are that the databases to be analyzed are getting bigger and more complex, and that there is a small number of people available to the analytical task and they are being given more work to do. To meet this need, we have developed automated data analysis algorithms and software. CoverStory (Schmitz et al. 1990) is used for analysis of marketing data. SalesPartner, described here, is a tactical sales support system which helps a sales representative identify sales trends and opportunities and then assemble a fact-based sales proposition for the customer and a retail outlet for the product.

Both systems start with the same general goals of identifying noteworthy events in the database then tracking through the causes of these events. A basic strategy of hierarchical decomposition coupled with exception ranking and trend identification is used in both systems. SalesPartner, depending on very specific data measures, continues by searching for product comparisons which a sales representative can use to convince a retailer to switch shelf space or merchandising support from a competitor to his or her own product.

The Database Setting and the Task

InfoScan is a data collection system developed by Information Resources. InfoScan measures consumer purchases of products at the individual item level as identified by the industry's universal product code (UPC). InfoScan contains data collected from a nationally representative sample of over 2,500 scanner-equipped stores covering major metropolitan markets and many smaller cities. Similar samples are used for drugstores and mass merchandising outlets such as Kmart and Wal-Mart. Retail stores provide basic volume, market share, distribution, and price information. InfoScan also contains a variety of measures collected by in-store and in-market observation of merchandising and promotional activities. These include retailer advertising in newspapers and flyers, in-store displays, and coupon distribution. Most of the measures contain several levels of coding; for example, newspaper ads are coded A, B, or C, according to their prominence. In addition, the InfoScan database provides access to individual household purchase data collected from approximately 70,000 households across 27 market areas.

A typical InfoScan database. An example syndicated database contains several hundred million numbers covering 100 data measures, 10,000 products, 125 time periods (weeks, four-week periods, quarters, and so forth), and 50 to 200 markets and chains. It is augmented with tens of millions of new numbers every four weeks. Finding important events in this body of data is a big job.

The job of analysis. A market or brand analyst must use a database like InfoScan for many purposes. One of these is problem identification. The analyst must find those products, markets, and measures of market performance that signal problems or opportunities. In the mass of data, the analyst must somehow rank these problems and opportunities and communicate them to appropriate decision makers.

COVERSTORY: DESCRIPTION, MECHANISMS, AND TECHNIQUES

CoverStory is an expert system developed to automate the exception-finding problem in marketing databases. The goal for CoverStory is to provide a cover memo, like the one a marketing analyst writes, to describe key events that are reflected in the database—especially in its newest numbers. This section of the paper describes the basic series of decomposition steps embodied in the CoverStory strategy, and the linearization and ranking processes used in CoverStory to decide what facts are most worth mentioning. A sample CoverStory memorandum is shown in Figure 5-1.

Flow of Analysis and Decomposition

The central idea in CoverStory is that we will analyze the behavior of an aggregate product in an aggregate market by a series of decompositions or disaggregations. An aggregate product is a product that includes more than one UPC. The UPC is the bar code marked on a package and is the lowest level of product detail available in a scanner database. An example of an aggregate product is Chock Full 'O Nuts Coffee. It consists of many different sizes, package types, and grinds. An example

FIGURE 5-1
CoverStory Sales Review: Secret Apdo, NY

To:	Director of Marketing
From:	CoverStory
Date:	October 15, 1992

Subject: SECRET APDO Summary for Four Weeks Ending August 2, 1992 in New York—FOOD—Evaluating Ounce Share of Category vs Year Ago

SECRET APDO's ounce share of DEODORANT/ANTIPERSPIRANTS in New York—FOOD was 10.1 share points for the four weeks ending 8/2/92. This is a decrease of −2.3 share points from a year earlier but up +0.9 from last period (4 Week Ending Jul 5, 92). This reflects volume sales of 412.5 thousand Equivalent Units—down 24.0 percent since last year.

SECRET APDO's ounce share is 10.1— down −2.3 share points from the same period last year.

Price rose over the past year from 2.62 dollars to 2.72. Display activity and featuring fell during the year. The largest decline was in featuring which went down by −17 points of ACV to 50 points of ACV. Unsupported price cuts (57 points) and distribution (100 percent of ACV) remained at about the same level as a year earlier.

DEODORANT/ANTIPERSPIRANTS volume in New York—FOOD (currently 4.1 million Equivalent Units) declined −6.5% from last year and declined −4.9% from the prior period.

DEODORANT/ANTIPERSPIRANTS volume in total US (currently 61.7 million Equivalent Units) declined −1.0% from a year earlier. New York − FOOD represents 6.6 percent of DEODORANT/ANTIPERSPIRANTS volume in the US. This has decreased by −0.4 percentage points since last year.

Components of SECRET APDO

Among components of SECRET APDO, losses occurred for:

SECRET AROSPRY APDO: down −1.2 share points from last year to 4.0 pts (but up +0.3 since last period)

SECRET ROLLON APDO: down −1.0 to 1.8 pts (but up +0.1 since last period)

SECRET STK APDO: down −0.2 to 4.2 pts (but up +0.6 since last period)

SECRET STK APDO's ounce share decrease happened even though there was also a fall in price of −5.4% vs yr ago. **SECRET ROLLON APDO's** decrease is associated with a rise in price of +17.1% versus a year ago and a fall in featuring of −39.6 points of ACV versus a year ago and a decrease in display activity of −15.4 ACV points versus a year ago. **SECRET AROSPRY APDO's** decrease follows an increase in price of +13.2% since last year and a decrease in featuring of −48.2 points of ACV versus a year ago.

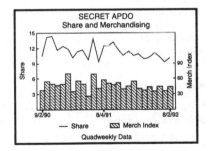

SECRET APDO
Share and Merchandising

Competitor Summary

Among SECRET APDO's major competitors, the principal gainers are:

BAN FRESH DRY APDO: up +0.3 share points from last year to 0.3 pts (but down −0.1 since last period)

ARRID XTRA DRY APDO: up +0.2 to 7.9 pts

OLD SPICE APDO: up +0.1 to 0.6 pts

FIGURE 5-1
(continued)

Losses occurred for:

XTRA DRY APDO: down −0.8 to 4.8 pts (but up +1.5 since last period)

SURE APDO: down −0.6 to 7.6 pts (but up +0.5 since last period)

BRUT 33 APDO: down −0.3 to 2.8 pts (but up +0.3 since last period)

BAN APDO: down −0.3 to 5.6 pts

ARRID APDO: down −0.1 to 0.2 pts

Those with small ounce share changes from a year ago were:

ARRXD GLD ON APDO: unchanged from a year earlier but up +0.1 share points since last period to 0.2 pts

OLD SPICE APDO's ounce share increase happened even though there was also a rise in price of +9.8% since last year. **BAN FRESH DRY APDO's** increase is associated with a rise in distribution of +79.8 percent of ACV versus a year ago. **ARRID APDO's** decrease coincides with a fall in distribution of −6.7 percent of ACV since last year. **ARRXD GLD ON APDO's** decrease coincides with an increase in price of +9.0% versus a year ago and a decrease in distribution of −5.4 percent of ACV since last year. **BRUT 33 APDO's** decrease occurred despite a fall in price of −8.7% vs yr ago.

Key Account Highlights

SECRET APDO showed significant gains relative to a year ago in:

NEW YORK—GRAND UNION: up +1.6 share points from last year to 13.6 pts. This is related to an increase in featuring of +100.0 points of ACV since last year and a decrease in price of −10.2% vs yr ago and a rise in unsupported price cuts of +70.8 points vs yr ago.

but posted declines in:

NEW YORK—A & P: down −4.9 to 9.6 pts. This follows an increase in price of +34.9% since last year and a fall in featuring of −100.0 points of ACV versus a year ago and a decrease in unsupported price cuts of -92.1 points since last year.

NEW YORK—PATHMARK: down −4.0 to 8.2 pts (but up +0.7 since last period). This coincides with a decrease in display activity of −29.3 ACV points vs yr ago but occured in spite of a fall in price of −4.9% vs yr ago.

Among competitors to SECRET APDO, major regional changes occurred as follows:

NEW YORK—A & P: SURE APDO is up +0.8 share points since last year. **BAN APDO** is up +0.4 share points. **ARRID XTRA DRY APDO** fell −0.6 share points. **XTRA DRY APDO** is up +0.9 share points. This is related to a rise in featuring of +82.5 points of ACV versus a year ago. **BRUT 33 APDO** fell −0.7 share points.

NEW YORK—GRAND UNION: OLD SPICE APDO is up +1.3 share points. This coincides with an increase in featuring of +100.0 points of ACV vs yr ago and an increase in distribution of +9.3 percent of ACV since **SURE APDO** fell −1.2 share points. This is related to a decrease in featuring of −100.0 points of ACV versus a year ago and an increase in price of +10.7% vs yr ago. **BAN APDO** fell −0.5 share points. **BAN FRESH DRY APDO** is up +0.5 share points. This is associated with an increase in distribution of +100.0 percent of ACV versus a year ago. **ARRID XTRA DRY APDO** fell −0.7 share points. This is related to a rise in price of +15.9% versus a year ago. **XTRA DRY APDO** fell −2.5 share points. This may be partly attributable to a fall in featuring of −33.0 points of ACV vs yr ago and an increase in price of +4.2% since last year. **BRUT 33 APDO** is up +0.6 share points.

NEW YORK—PATHMARK: SURE APDO fell −1.9 share points. This happened even though there was also an increase in featuring of +46.8 points of ACV since last year and a decrease in price of −16.4% **BAN APDO** fell −2.6 share points. This may be partly attributable to a rise in price of +16.9% vs yr ago. **XTRA DRY APDO** fell −1.3 share points. This may be partly attributable to a decrease in display activity of −82.2 ACV points since last year but occurred in spite of a fall in price.

of an aggregate market is the United States, which can be disaggregated into regions or individual cities and then into grocery chains within markets.

In doing decomposition, CoverStory follows a style observed in the analytical marketing reports used in many companies. Analysis proceeds by answering the following questions: (1) What is going on overall in the aggregate product for the aggregate market? (2) What changes does this reflect in the components of the aggregate product? (3) What is happening to competitive products? CoverStory performs each of these steps in turn. Within each section of the analysis, CoverStory follows a standard series of steps:

Rank the components (markets or products or market/product combinations) by some criteria.

Select the most noteworthy few markets or products or combinations for mention and for further analysis.

Calculate causal factor changes for these top few markets, products, or combinations. Causal factor changes are distribution, price, and merchandising changes.

Rank these causal factor changes (more on this later) then select the top few causal changes to include in the report.

The need to select the top few items from different lists is dictated by the size of the scanner database. The number of events that can be mentioned is enormous. Without strictly limiting the amount of information in a report, we find that the news drowns in the detail.

Ranking the products or markets. We nearly always rank component products or component markets by share or volume change. When we are looking at size groups within an aggregate product, for example, and we are analyzing share changes, size group ranks will be based on share changes.

Selecting the top few products or markets. The top few are the few that are the most noteworthy. We calculate which component products or markets are furthest away from average and retain these extremes for mention. This usually leads CoverStory to pick winners and losers. In some cases, however, when most of the products and markets are behaving in similar fashion, CoverStory will select only the top winners or only significant losers. This approach has been very effective and it closely mimics the way human market analysts select individual segments of a product line or individual markets for mention.

Calculating causal factor changes. When CoverStory points out share or volume changes, it also tries to mention possible causes of these share or volume changes. To do so, we calculate the amount of change in marketing support for each of the marketing factors that affects the product. For example, a share change in one size in Boston may have been partially caused by distribution, price, display, advertising, or price-cut activity.

Ranking causal factor changes. CoverStory can generate a large number of explanatory, causal factor changes when it decomposes aggregate product and market behavior into components. If there are 10 product components, 50 markets, and 8 causal factors being screened, there are 4,000 causal changes that are candidates for mention. Trimming this down to a small number for inclusion in the CoverStory report requires a ranking procedure. The procedure chosen is similar in spirit to the evaluation functions used in evaluating positions in game-playing programs (Barr and Feigenbaum 1981). We calculate a score for each of the causal measure changes. The score reflects the market in which the change occurred, which causal factor changed, and the magnitude of the change. Symbolically:

$$\text{Score} = \text{Change} * \text{Factor weight} * \text{Market weight}$$

Change is the amount of change in the causal factor and is either a percentage change or raw change depending on the factor. Factor weight is different for each of the marketing factors such as distribution, price, displays, featuring, and price cuts. These factor weights are intended, informally speaking, to make different marketing changes have the same score if their impact on sales is the same. We initialize factor weights based on regression analysis done outside of CoverStory based on logit models of the type described in Guadagni and Little (1983). Market weight is a term that makes it more likely that an event in a large market will be mentioned than an event in a small market. CoverStory originally used market size, but we found this was too strong. Only events from New York, Chicago, and Los Angeles were mentioned. We have softened the impact of market size by using the square root of market size as the market weight. Motivation for use of the square root of market size comes from the concept of a ladder of re-expressions as described in Mosteller and Tukey (1977). The square root is a relatively gentle monotonic transformation and has, thus far, proved adequate to our needs.

This scoring method yields a ranked list of causal factor changes, where such a change can be described in terms of

- What happened? (e.g., price went up by 20%)
- Where did it happen? (e.g., in the southeastern region)
- What product did it happen to? (e.g., the 32 oz bottle)

The events that CoverStory describes are the ones that rank highest using this scoring mechanism.

CoverStory is now in use by several companies. They have found the main value of the system to be its ability to automate the exception-finding task which has been at the heart of one of the brand analysts' job.

THE DEVELOPMENT OF SALESPARTNER

CoverStory is an analytically oriented system. It can be used by many audiences to answer questions about what is going on in a market. Some of those audiences have more specialized needs. SalesPartner is an adaptation and extension of CoverStory, which is meant specifically for sales representatives in a consumer packaged goods company. It tunes reporting and exception finding to the needs of this audience.

Definition of SalesPartner

SalesPartner, written at Information Resources originally in 1989–1990, is an expert system designed to support the tactical sales function for consumer packaged goods. It is the analytical assistant to a sales representative.

For illustration in this discussion, we will talk about a sales agent trying to increase Tide sales at a large Boston supermarket chain, Stop & Shop.

In an encounter between the sales representative for Tide and the buyer for Stop & Shop, the sales representative is trying to convince the buyer to do something to support Tide sales. The following are the kinds of actions the sales agent wants to encourage:

Putting a product on the grocery shelf. For example, putting a new package size of Tide on the shelf.
Giving more shelf space or better shelf space to the product.
Putting up a Tide display.

Including Tide in a feature ad. In Boston, major food chains run large circulars in the Sunday newspaper and a second full-page ad on Thursday.
Cutting the shelf price of Tide.

In recommending these actions, the Tide sales agent is competing for a limited amount of total support the retailer is willing to give to all products combined. A traditional-format grocery store has 20,000–25,000 different items on its shelves. It can't fit many more than that. For a particular size in a particular product category, the number of stocked items may be very limited. And in local, well-stocked grocery stores there are 40 different 13 to 16 oz packages of ground coffee. There are about six brands and variants on package type, caffeinated versus decaffeinated, grind type, and so on.

The number of items on special display in Boston grocery stores averages 500–600. There aren't enough special locations to put more than that on display. The feature circular has enough space to run a limited number of advertisements. A recent circular run by one of the major Boston chains mentioned about 400 products.

Given this limited amount of total available space for products and product merchandising, the Tide sales agent has to convince the Stop & Shop buyer to take support away from some other product in order to give it to Tide.

The traditional approach to this problem has been classic person-to-person selling. Establish personal rapport and trust, weave a web of favors and counterfavors, apply pressure when appropriate, and offer trade incentives to encourage retail support. To the extent that quantitative analysis or arguments played a role, they relied on use of broad market aggregate numbers.

SalesPartner encourages more fact-based selling. SalesPartner locates data to support a sales presentation like "If you put up a display for Tide instead of your house label, you will sell an extra two thousand pounds of laundry detergent," or "At a price of $5.99 rather than $7.99, your dollar sales will be 43% higher."

To make the argument, SalesPartner uses the retailer's own historical data.

SalesPartner's Goals

SalesPartner has three goals. First, it tries to give the sales representative a picture of what is going on in a retail chain. This is in the form of reviews which are closely patterned after CoverStory. Second, it ranks opportunities for selling more product or for increasing profits. Third, it develops a fact-based argument for supporting a particular product.

SalesPartner contains separate mechanisms for analyzing item placement on the shelf (slotting), for display support, for feature support, and for general price reduction. Under development are arguments for specific price points and specific amounts of shelf space.

SalesPartner's Relation to Prior Systems

SalesPartner grew out of research and development done on CoverStory. The orientation and target audience for SalesPartner is sales representatives more than market researchers.

APEX (Odcttc and Berkman 1990) has a broadly similar goal in selling financial services to individuals. Related systems are ADSTRAT (Gatignon and Burke 1991) for designing advertising and advertising campaigns, the Promotion Advisor and DEALMAKER (McCann and Gallagher 1990), and the New Item Evaluation System and Weekly Merchandising Planning Systems (McCann and Gallagher 1991).

Back-Office Expertise

SalesPartner works specifically with InfoScan data. To fully understand SalesPartner, you need to understand something of the data on which it is based. Much of the expertise of SalesPartner resides in the back-office systems that provide the InfoScan data. Cooper and Nakanishi (1988) have a good general description of scanner data collection so only a brief summary is included here.

There are two principal streams of raw data into the InfoScan data collection system:

Store movement files contain data on what products moved in each store. In essence, each record contains five elements; a store number, a week number, a UPC code, a unit price for that week, and the number of units sold.

Causal data collection files contain data collected on in-store conditions. Each record contains a store number, week number, UPC code, and set of flags showing what merchandising conditions (displays and features) were in effect for that UPC in that store.

From these raw data files we calculate some auxiliary, inferred measures, described below.

Baselines. First we calculate a baseline of sales. The baseline is an estimate of what sales would have been in the absence of promotional activity. The details of the algorithm are complex and proprietary but the core idea is straightforward:

Figure out whether or not promotional activity is taking place.
If no promotion is taking place, use raw sales as the baseline.
If promotion is taking place, use an average of recent baseline sales in the store as an estimate of baseline sales.

The complexity arises in accounting for seasonality, missing data, and outliers. Outliers, periods when sales are very high with no recorded promotional activity, may indicate an error in the raw data which needs correction.

Baseline sales, by its nature, is a relatively smooth series. It rises or falls, usually slowly, in response to distribution, long-term price shifts, media advertising, new product introduction, and changes in consumer taste.

Lift factors. From the baseline of sales, we can calculate lift factors for different promotional conditions. A lift factor is the percentage increase in sales expected under promotional conditions. For example, if you expect coffee sales to rise from 1,000 pounds to 4,000 pounds when you put up a display, the display lift factor is 300%. There is enormous variation between brands and categories and between outlets in lift factors. To give an idea of what lift factors may be, representative values for grocery products may be 50–100% lift from a feature advertisement, 200% from a display, and 300–500% from a display supported by a feature ad. Sometimes, however, the lift from features will be larger than the lift from displays. McCann and Gallagher (1991) describe the concept of lift factors in some detail.

As in baseline calculations, the idea behind the algorithm is simple yet the details are complicated. In essence, the lift factor for a particular promotion type (say, display) can be calculated for any week in which displays took place as

100 * Incremental Sales Due to Display / Base Sales

Incremental sales due to display are total sales in a display period less base sales. For small, lightly merchandised products these lift factors can be wildly variable. For large, established brands, the volatility is less.

A problem particular to lift factor calculation is that the merchandising week does not always coincide with the data reporting week. We may get product movement reported on the basis of a week that spans Sunday through Saturday whereas the store merchandising cycle is organized from Wednesday through Tuesday. Back-office systems accommodate this by, in essence, moving incremental volume to coincide with the merchandising week.

InfoScan contains separate lift factors for displays, feature ads, display supported by feature ads, and shelf-price reduction unsupported by either feature advertisements or displays.

In any particular case, the lift factor depends on the depth of the price reduction that accompanies the merchandising event. InfoScan can calculate these separate lift factors; but, because of data storage considerations, we almost always perform analysis based on average price lift factors.

A particular difficulty in both baseline and lift factor calculation is that of special package types, a problem also mentioned by McCann and Gallagher (1990). Special packs are different UPC codes that represent essentially the same product. This event occurs when there is seasonal packaging, bonus packs, buy-one-get-one-free, and so forth. When we calculate baselines and lift factors for special pack products we have to aggregate them carefully into a single SKU.

Cannibalization. Many of the analyses in SalesPartner hinge on the effect of a merchandising action on total category sales or profitability. For example, we can make a strong argument for a display of Tide if we can provide evidence that Tide displays increase overall detergent sales in the store. In order to calculate these measures, we need to know not only the effect of merchandising on our sales but also the cannibalization effect our brand has on the rest of the category. Cannibalization is a complex phenomenon which relates to who buys a product which is being promoted. The sources of volume can be classified as follows:

People who would have bought the product without promotion.
People who buy more of the product because of the promotion.
People who change the timing of purchases and stock up when a promotion occurs.
People who switch from another store to your store because of a promotion.
People who switch from one brand to another because of the promotion.

This last category is what we try to measure when we model cannibalization. If all the sales are cannibalized (in this sense), then a promotion will have no net effect on total category sales in the store. Promotions will only switch around the brand composition within the category. If, however, there is no brand cannibalization, then promotions can have a profound effect on weekly sales of a category as well as the individually promoted products within it.

We summarize cannibalization in a coefficient which is defined as a percentage of a brand's incremental sales which are incremental to the category.

For example, if powdered Tide has a display yielding 4,000 pounds of incremental sales, and if total category sales were 3,000 pounds in excess of normal, then 1,000 pounds of the Tide sales were cannibalizing other brands in the category. Three thousand pounds were incremental to the category. For Tide, therefore, the percentage of incremental sales that are incremental to the category would be 75%.

Calculating cannibalization coefficients requires estimation of models that relate category sales to individual brand promotional activity. This is done as part of SalesPartner setup. Estimating these models requires calculating and assessing a large number of regression models. In SalesPartner, it is necessary to carry this through with substantial attention to statistical detail. The statistical details can be daunting. SalesPartner has mechanisms to account for data problems such as outliers and autocorrelation issues.

For very small brands and for brands with severe data problems, SalesPartner interpolates cannibalization coefficients from the estimated brands. In doing so, we have to take brand size into account. A priori, a large brand will cannibalize less than a small brand. At an extreme, if a brand accounts for 100% of the category sales, there aren't any other brands to cannibalize from. All of its incremental sales will be incremental to the category because it is the category.

Structure of a SalesPartner Database

From the InfoScan set of available data, we construct the subset needed to support the sales analysis activity. You can accurately think of the database as being a set of about 35 cubes of data, each containing a different measure, plus a large number of formulas based on these cubes.

Each cube of data is organized by three dimensions:

A *product* dimension shows category totals, manufacturer and brand totals, size/flavor/packtype totals, SKUs, and so forth organized into a hierarchy very much like an outline. Category is the most aggregate, then type, then manufacturer within type, brand within manufacturer, and so on. A typical SalesPartner database has 5,000–10,000 products in the product dimension.

A *market* dimension usually contains the entire United States, a few regions, InfoScan markets within the regions (like Boston or Chicago), then chains within the markets. The number of distinct geographical entities in a database will normally be between 50 and 200.

A *time* dimension containing weeks and aggregates of individual weeks.

The structure of the product and market dimensions is important to SalesPartner's functionality. It supports the drill-down, search, and aggregation which SalesPartner does.

In the product dimension, we identify several important levels in the hierarchy.

The category or type level on which share calculations should be based.
The manufacturer level.
The brand level.
The promoted product level. This is the level in the hierarchy (often flavor or size) that is normally the focus of a display or feature campaign.
The SKU is the lowest level on which we do analysis. The SKU may be the same as a UPC but in many cases it is an aggregate of UPCs because of special packs or a very fine level of flavor detail.

Constructing a SalesPartner database involves setting up not only the data but also this meta-data describing products and markets and their relationship with one another. The meta-data are important in guiding the analysis. We need to know what level in the product hierarchy is the *promoted product* level so we can know the level at which to put together arguments for promotions. To construct sensible arguments for slotting products, we need to know what an *SKU* is because stores only stock SKUs.

SalesPartner Mechanisms — Reviews

The first purpose of SalesPartner is to give the sales representative insights into what is going on in the market or account for his or her product. SalesPartner does this through a series of reviews. A typical review page is shown in Figure 5-1.

A review page contains a set of reports and graphs along with a bullet point summary relating to a particular topic. For example, SalesPartner could display information about base and incremental volume for Secret in New York.

The structure of an individual review is very much like CoverStory. It contains highlights from the data based on a set of rules about how to judge importance and based on meta-data about the decomposition of products into components and competitors.

The review pages in SalesPartner answer several questions:

- What merchandising support is a product getting and how effective is it? This ranks and reports lift factors and measures like percent of stores featuring a product.
- How is a product (and its competitors and components) doing on base and incremental volume?
- What are the most important causal factors behind these changes in base and incremental volume?

The reviews in SalesPartner can be seen as specialized CoverStory reports.

SalesPartner Mechanisms—Sales Presentation Development

The *punch line* in SalesPartner is not insight into market mechanisms but, rather, selling more product. To do this, SalesPartner provides very structured quantitative input into a sales presentation. As an example, the underlying argument in the presentation might be something like:

> You should give a week of feature advertising to Secret APDO. A week of feature ads increases category sales by 17,900 ounces. To get space for this feature ad, take it away from any of the following brands which you have featured in the past and for which support is less effective.

> Ban Fresh (week of feature only increased category sales by 300 ounces)
> Old Spice (similar low category incremental effect)

The particulars of the sales presentation used will vary with the market, the brand, and the chain, but the thrust is the same. Define the action you want the retailer to take, find some things the retailer has done in the past which were less effective, and point out the comparisons.

The resulting report would display information supporting a request for feature support of a particular product in a particular chain—say,

Secret ADPO at Ralph's in Los Angeles. According to the data, a week of feature support for Secret has historically increased deodorant category sales volume by 17,900 ounces. The report would show several other brands which have historically yielded much smaller incremental category sales.

Once the back-office expertise has been applied to the database, and once the meta-data in the database has been established, these sales presentations can be seen as being large search processes. Over the historical period selected, SalesPartner identifies product merchandising strategies actually used by the retailer which did the retailer less good than the strategy we are trying to convince the retailer to use.

SalesPartner—Distribution and Substitution Analysis

SalesPartner also contains logic for constructing arguments for putting your product on the shelf at a retailer. For example, the Tide sales representative may try to convince the Stop & Shop buyer to put a new SKU—47 oz Lemon Scent powder—on the shelf.

The sales representative can simply try to make a case for the new product. Alternatively, to account for the scarcity of shelf space, he or she may try to argue for replacing an existing SKU, a competing product, with the new Tide product.

To support an argument for replacing one (currently stocked) product with another (currently unstocked) product, SalesPartner gathers facts from the database that show benefits to the retailer. As an example, we will show how an argument will be put together by SalesPartner for putting 47 oz Lemon Scent on the shelf at Stop & Shop.

The argument assembled in SalesPartner revolves around comparing movement of 47 oz Lemon Scent at other retailers in the market to all of the reasonably competitive products that are currently carried. SalesPartner identifies currently stocked items that are slow movers and highlights them. Suppose 47 oz Lemon Scent sells at a rate of 10 pounds for every million dollars of ACV in the rest of the Boston market but is not carried at Stop & Shop in Boston. Suppose further that Stop & Shop does carry detergents A, B, and C, all of which are in the same general size (about 3 pounds) as 47 oz Lemon Scent. If they move at Stop & Shop at rates of 2, 4, and 12 pounds per million dollars of ACV, respectively, SalesPartner would highlight the first two as candidates for de-listing.

SalesPartner states the sales presentation, as with sales presentations for merchandising support, in terms stressing the gain to the retailer. If you, the retailer, replace detergent A with 47 oz Lemon Scent, you will sell so many extra cases of detergent every week.

SalesPartner—Summary

SalesPartner incorporates several sources of expertise in an effort to make a very large, marketing database operationally useful to a technically unsophisticated audience.

The sources of expertise we have identified are as follows:

Back-office calculation of baselines and lift factors.
Calculation of cannibalization effects.
Large-scale searches through historical databases to find changes of retail behavior which are beneficial both to the retailer and to the manufacturer.

We have tried to remain focused on the task of the sales representative—selling product through the retail channel and knowing what to sell. This has led us to take an eclectic development approach which incorporates expert systems technology, large-scale database management, and data presentation.

SalesPartner is now in use at a great many manufacturers.

CONCLUSIONS

Experience with CoverStory, SalesPartner, and other experimental and developmental systems has taught us two important lessons:

The expertise is in the knowledge. This is a reiteration of lessons reported by Davis (Davis and Lenat 1982). Neither SalesPartner nor CoverStory gets its power from deep and complex reasoning mechanisms. Instead, they work by applying robust, relatively straightforward algorithms to rich, underlying databases. The underlying data contains raw numbers, statistically derived lift and response factors, product and market hierarchies, and so forth. The underlying data, when appropriately navigated, contains useful, operational information.

Systems have to become operational to be used. Some of our experiments have been received poorly. CoverStory and, especially, SalesPartner have been well accepted because they help real people solve real problems. CoverStory automates the task of producing summary memos of recent market events. SalesPartner helps sales representatives sell their products.

It has taken a great deal of effort to craft SalesPartner and CoverStory. We have, at times, tried to create tool kits for making this process easier. Our goal has been to make it possible for end-users to create their own expert systems. So far, we have not been able to do this. Thus far, it is still necessary for professional programmers and knowledge engineers to put together these systems. This is frustrating because it limits the resources we can apply to the myriad of opportunities for this type of system.

The great rush of integrated marketing data contains an enormous potential for improving the analytical quality of sales and marketing efforts for consumer packaged goods. Through systems like CoverStory and SalesPartner, we are starting to see how to tap this potential.

REFERENCES

Barr, Avron, and Edward A. Feigenbaum, eds. *Handbook of Artificial Intelligence*. Los Altos, Calif.: William Kaufman, 1981.

Cooper, Lee G., and Masao Nakanishi. *Market-Share Analysis*. Boston: Kluwer Academic Publishers, 1988.

Davis, Randall, and Douglas B. Lenat. *Knowledge-Based Systems in Artificial Intelligence*. New York: McGraw-Hill, 1982.

Gatignon, Hubert, and Raymond R. Burke. *ADSTRAT: An Advertising Decision Support System*. San Francisco: Scientific Press, 1991.

Guadagni, Peter M., and John D.C. Little. "A Logit Model of Brand Choice Calibrated on Scanner Data." *Marketing Science*, vol. 2, no. 3 (Summer, 1983), 203–238.

McCann, John M., and John P. Gallagher. *Expert Systems for Scanner Data Environments*. Boston: Kluwer Academic Publishers, 1990.

———. *Databases and Knowledge Systems in Merchandising*. New York: Van Nostrand Reinhold, 1991.

Mosteller. Frederick, Andrew F. Siegel, Edward Trapido, and Cleo Youtz. "Fitting Straight Lines by Eye." In *Exploring Data Tables, Trends, and Shapes*, eds. David C. Hoaglin, Frederick Mosteller, and John W. Tukey. New York: John Wiley, 1985.

Mosteller, Frederick, and John W. Tukey. *Data Analysis and Regression*. Reading, Mass.: Addison-Wesley, 1977.

Odette, Louis L., and L.J. Berkman. "Expert Systems in Sales and Marketing." In *Expert Systems for Business and Management*, ed. Jay Liebowitz. Englewood Cliffs, N.J.: Yourdon Press, 1990.

Schmitz, John, Gordon O. Armstrong, and John D.C. Little. "CoverStory— Automated News Finding in Marketing." *Interfaces*, vol. 20, no. 6 (November–December, 1990), 29–38.

6

GENERATING, MANAGING, AND COMMUNICATING INSIGHTS

John M. McCann

AS NOTED THROUGHOUT *the earlier chapters in this volume, the vast quantities of data that are being generated by the new technologies pose serious problems to managers' ability to access information. These problems include the actual quality of the data, the capability of developing enough models required to use the data, and the ability to transform the models into systems and forms usable for managers. Among the most promising approaches to solving these problems is the* expert system, *which represents the next stage in the evolution of the marketing decision support system.*

This chapter provides a framework for thinking about the development of expert systems in a marketing context. After discussing the historical evolution of marketing information systems over the past few decades, and how these systems are likely to evolve over the next few years, the author proposes a new marketing "discipline"—that of marketing informatics. *The term is designed to describe the integration of traditional marketing information systems with a range of new information technologies (including data, text, video, and so forth) as well as information-management procedures.*

The chapter illustrates the marketing informatics concept with some examples from the consumer packaged-goods industry. Of particular interest is the use of graphical and audio/video information to help managers interpret data better. One notable idea is that of a "multimedia marketing plan"—which harnesses the full power of computer technology to move beyond just number and text processing in order to help managers make decisions based on more "realistic" models of the marketplace. Finally, the chapter concludes with a discussion of the implications of the "marketing informatics" approach for both research and marketing education.

Readers of this chapter are likely to find many of its ideas provocative, yet at the same time reflective of the managerial environment that is likely to emerge as a consequence of the marketing information revolution.

INTRODUCTION

This chapter describes the current state of computer use in marketing and makes projections about future paths. Examples from the consumer packaged goods industry are used to illustrate the concepts and to project the use of computerized data by marketing and sales managers. It is divided into two parts. The first describes how applied marketing systems have evolved over the past 20 years, and will likely evolve in the next few years, based upon the prototype systems now in place. The focus is on the generation, communication, and management of insights. The second part of the chapter describes some other computing approaches and discusses how they might be implemented in marketing. This section ends with a call for a new marketing discipline: marketing informatics.

THE EVOLUTION OF APPLIED MARKETING SYSTEMS

This section provides a brief overview of the evolution of marketing systems over the past three decades. This evolution follows the DIIP model: data to information to insights to programs.

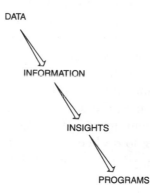

DATA

INFORMATION

INSIGHTS

PROGRAMS

This model is based upon the idea that the primary job of marketing managers is the design and execution of marketing programs. Before the marketing manager can design marketing programs, he or she must understand market situations, and this understanding is obtained via insights. But in order to have insights, the manager must have information. And, before he or she can have information, there must be data. Marketing computer applications and systems have changed in terms of their focus on the different elements. Early systems focused on the data-to-information links, and more recent systems move to the next level: the information-to-insights link. The remainder of this section takes the reader through this evolution.

Data on Paper

The first attempt to computerize marketing data was with data processing systems, such as those that were prevalent in the 1950s and 1960s in most corporations. These systems were usually written in the COBOL language to run on the early mainframes in batch mode. Standard reports containing rows and columns of numbers printed on large-format paper would be produced on a periodic basis and distributed to anyone in the firm who had a need for the data. The name "data processing" was a good description of the purpose of the systems: they took in raw data and processed it into a more meaningful form. They typically summarized the data by time period and/or geographical region and product line.

These types of systems are still in use in some firms, although on a limited basis because of the large volume of data. It is simply not practical to produce printed reports of all the possible views of the data that are needed by different people within the firm. A conversation with a marketing research manager in the mid-1980s illustrated the problem. The firm had a data library in a small room, and it had just switched from purchasing store audit data to buying scanner data. The manager said that the printed scanner data were delivered by truck to the firm's loading dock, where they had to be handled by a forklift truck. It completely filled the small library. About the time the data were moved into the library and organized, a new shipment arrived. The manager's comment: "I don't know what we are going to do because we are drowning in these data and our data processing systems cannot deal with it."

Data in Computer

Management information systems (MIS) came into vogue in the 1970s with the advent of time-sharing computer systems. The earlier data-processing systems only operated in the sequential, batch mode, which meant that only one program or "job" could be processed at one time. Operators would sequence the jobs in terms of a priority system and process them one after the other. Time-sharing systems allowed multiple jobs to run at once, thus permitting many people to use the same computer at the same time. One outcome of this technology was the ability to place marketing data in a file or database and then to allow different users to gain access to the data in the same time frame. A brand manager could work at a computer terminal and request a brand topline report at the same time that a sales planning analyst was using another terminal to produce an account review report.

Such information systems opened a new door for marketing managers because it allowed them to get the information when they needed it in the form that they needed. However, the early systems did not live up to this promise because they had restricted capabilities because of the lack of computing skills by marketing managers and analysts. These systems tended to allow the managers to produce and print a limited number of standard reports; for instance, brand topline, region topline, brand trend, region trend, brand opportunity matrix, region opportunity matrix, and so forth. Managers would use a terminal to select the desired report type, enter several parameters that specified the brand, styles, flavors, time periods, and regions. Some time later, a screen full of numbers would appear on the manager's terminal. Such systems were the dominant ones in use by marketing managers in the mid-1980s.[1]

The latter part of the 1980s saw an evolution in the power and ease of use of management information systems, along with emergence of two clear market leaders: the Express System with its Dataserver front-end, and the Metaphor system which has been acquired and rewritten as the Data Interpretation System. Ease of use was dramatically improved from earlier systems via the Dataserver's use of flexible pop-up menus and the iconic interface employed in the Data Interpretation System. These systems allow marketing managers to start using the system after a short training period, and provide a large degree of freedom in the types of reports that can be generated. It is common for firms to identify more than 100 report types that they can generate as needed.

By the early 1990s, almost all consumer packaged-goods firms have acquired and made use of one of these two systems. Most brand groups could and would make use of these systems to produce standard reports as needed, and to do periodic ad hoc analyses. It was quite uncommon for a firm to develop its own marketing information system; firms would buy a system rather than make one.

---

[1]John McCann, *The Marketing Workbench* (Homewood, Ill.: Dow Jones-Irwin, 1986).

Knowledge in Computer

The advent of the large databases has created a data overload problem in which managers and analysts cannot perform the required analysis. Several knowledge-based systems have been developed, usually in proto-type form, for dealing with this problem. The basic idea behind most of these models is to program the knowledge-based system to perform one or more tasks normally performed by a manager or an analyst. Two such systems are available commercially. The CoverStory[2] employs a drilling approach, similar to that found in a manual Executive Information System, to uncover and report exceptions in the data. A similar approach is taken in the SPOTLIGHT[3] system from A.C. Nielsen.

These commercial systems have implemented the ideas and concepts that appeared in several prototype systems. Rangaswamy et al.[4] developed INFER, a system that analyzes scanner data. Alpar[5] used traditional knowledge engineering techniques to build a knowledge-based model of a marketing manager's problem-solving behavior. Bayer and Harter[6] went one step further: they interviewed Nielsen account managers and discerned three models for analyzing scanner data: miner, manager, and researcher. McCann et al.[7] report on an analysis by composition approach to composing a marketing report. In this approach, termed the Brand Manager's Assistant, the manager views existing documents on a computer screen. When the manager views a section of a report that he or she would like to have written for his or her situation, the manager instructs the system to rewrite that section for the situation. McCann and Gallagher[8] report on a series of knowledge-based system prototypes for analyzing and applying marketing data.

[2]John D. Schmitz, Gordon D. Armstrong, and John D. Little, "CoverStory—Automated News Finding in Marketing," *Interfaces*, 20, 6 (November–December 1990), pp. 29–38.

[3]Tej Anand and Gary Kahn, "SPOTLIGHT: A Data Explanation System," paper submitted to IEEE Conference on AI for Applications, 1992.

[4]Arvind Rangaswamy, Barri A. Harter, and Leonard M. Lodish, "INFER: An Expert System for Automatic Analysis of Scanner Data," *International Journal of Research in Marketing*, 8, 1 (April 1991), pp. 29–40.

[5]Paul Alpar, "Knowledge-Based Modeling of Marketing Managers' Problem-Solving Behavior," *International Journal of Research in Marketing*, 8, 1 (April 1991), pp. 5–16.

[6]J. Bayer and R. Harter, " 'Miner', 'Manager,' and 'Researcher': Three Models of Analysis of Scanner Data," *International Journal of Research in Marketing*, 8, 1 (April 1991), pp. 17–28.

[7]John M. McCann, William Lahti, and Justin Hill, "The Brand Manager's Assistant: A Knowledge-Based System Approach to Brand Management," *International Journal of Research in Marketing*, 8, 1 (April 1991), pp. 51–74.

[8]John M. McCann and John P. Gallagher, *Expert Systems for Scanner Data Environments: The Marketing Workbench Laboratory Experience* (Boston: Kluwer Academic Publishers, 1990).

The goal of these systems is to write a story that uses the data to explain what has happened to a brand in one or more markets. An extension of this approach would be to prepare a sales presentation for use by sales managers. Figure 6–1 contains an example of the type of presentation that such a system could prepare.

This knowledge-based system has examined data about the performance of two brands (Grinders Choice and Magic Bean) in a retail account (Safeway). Based upon this analysis, it has concluded that the brand under study (Grinders Choice) does not deserve additional merchandising support in the form of displays or advertising features. A sales representative who is preparing for a sales call on Safeway could have used the system to produce this sheet of paper. If the sales representative was also going to call on other accounts, then he or she could produce other sheets of paper applicable to these accounts.

The system's conclusion could be termed an insight, and the system could be said to have generated the insight that Safeway was not a likely candidate for increased feature or display support.

FIGURE 6-1
Safeway Promotional Support
(from 88-01-09 to 89-01-28)

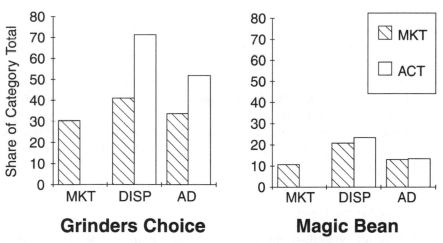

Safeway provides strong support for Grinders Choice promotions both in its displays and its ads. Safeway gave Grinders Choice 71% of all its coffee displays and 52% of all its coffee ads. Thanks for supporting our profitable partnership!

Grinders Choice is important to Gotham City retailers. It has a 30% share of category sales in this market. In this area Grinders Choice sells 2.8 times more volume than Magic Bean. Magic Bean only gets a 11% share of the market.

Knowledge in a Loop

Systems that tell a story about a market or prepare a sales presentation could be run as needed, or they could be run automatically for all relevant cases.

```
DO
    FOR ALL MARKETS
    FOR ALL ACCOUNTS
    FOR ALL BRANDS
    FOR ALL SIZES
    FOR ALL FLAVORS
    RUN KNOWLEDGE-BASED SYSTEM
END DO
```

That is, the knowledge system could be treated as a traditional data-processing system that ran in a batch mode, with the results distributed to interested parties. An application such as CoverStory or the I Want system could be run for all items in all accounts in all markets, and the resulting pages distributed to the marketing and sales managers who need to have the results.

The result of executing the I Want system in this loop would be insights about feature and display opportunities for all brand items in all accounts in all markets. This exhaustive set of insights makes possible another system, one that summarizes the insights for senior managers. Figure 6-2 is an example of the output of a knowledge-based system that takes insights as its input and produces a summary.

This type of report could be prepared for managers at different levels in the organization: district sales managers, regional managers, vice presidents, brand managers, and so forth.

Putting the knowledge system in a loop allows the firm to obtain common insights for all its items in all of its markets. The implications of this approach are explored below.

Insights on Paper

The result of putting the knowledge in a loop is a stack of paper, perhaps one sheet for each item in each account in each market, along with various summary sheets. If there are five accounts in each of 60 markets, and if the marketing manager's brand has 50 variants (sizes, flavors, and so forth), then the stack could contain 15,000 pages.

If the purpose of the analysis were to distribute the relevant pages to

FIGURE 6-2
Merchandising Support Opportunities for Ivory from National Perspective
(from 01–09–88 to 01–28–89)

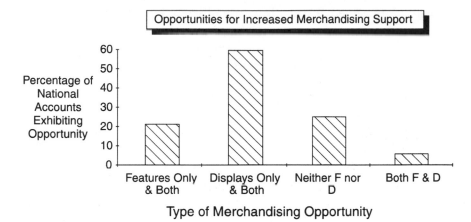

Note: This graph presents a national summary of merchandising support opportunities in 52 accounts for Ivory. Each account has been classified by the likelihood of gaining increased support for Feature Ads, Displays, Both, or Neither. In this graph, the Displays Only & Both column combines accounts with opportunities to expand Displays Only plus Both Features & Displays. As such, it reflects the total number of accounts where there are opportunities to expand Feature Ad support.

It can be seen that 60% of these accounts provide an opportunity for expanded Display support. From this view, it may be suitable to seek additional Display support through a program of increased case allowances.

There appears to be only a moderate opportunity from the national perspective for programs that emphasize increased Feature support. 21% of all accounts provide this type of opportunity.

It may be appropriate to assess the degree to which this opportunity for increased Display support is due to a single competing brand which is oversupported in these accounts. If there is such a brand, it may provide a target for your sales effort.

the appropriate sales representative, then the size of the pile would not be an issue because it would never land on a manager's desk. But what about the brand manager who wants to have an overview of feature display opportunities? In this case, another knowledge-based system could be written that summarizes the display and feature opportunities.

Insights in Computer

Just as data were placed online with management information systems, textual and graphical insights can also be placed in a computer so that managers can retrieve them upon demand. One such system has been built, the *Marketing Insight Center.* It organizes the output of knowledge-based systems so that marketing managers can browse pages of insights and follow logical links among the pages in a hypertext system. This browsing is possible because of the use of semantic networks to describe market and product structures. Semantic networks are knowledge representation schemes involving nodes and links (arcs or arrows) between nodes. The nodes represent objects or concepts and the links represent relations between nodes. The links are directed and labeled; thus, a semantic network is a directed graph. In print, the nodes are usually represented by circles or boxes and the links are drawn as arrows between the circles as in Figure 6-3, which is an example of a small segment of a semantic network.

These nodes and links allow one to capture knowledge about the relationships in markets and product categories. For instance, the semantic network in Figure 6-3 knows the Quad Cities is a market, that Chain56 is in Quad Cities, that 87481 is an item, and this item is carried in Chain56. Given such a model, software can be developed for extracting information about any of the nodes of the network and for following these links to locate related information and insights. For instance, if one were examining a printout about item 87481, the network would allow the user to quickly move from the item to the markets in which it is carried. Extensions of this simple network would then allow the user

FIGURE 6-3
Segment of Semantic Network

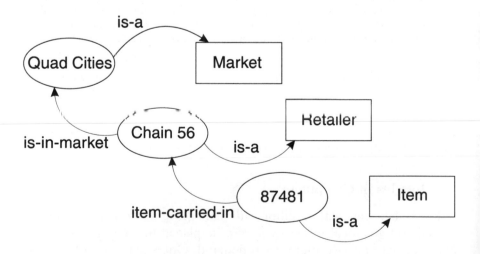

to determine what other items are carried in that market, or what other markets carry item 87481.

The Marketing Insight Center implements a large semantic network that allows the user to navigate around the system to find reports of interest. The outputs from systems such as I Want and Marketing Opportunity Inspector are stored in, and accessible from, this network. After reading one report, the links in the semantic network allow the user to easily locate other reports that are related in one of many ways to the retrieved report.

Insights in Newspaper

Given a large number of insights, yet another knowledge-based system could be developed that composes and publishes a newspaper. Perhaps the *Grinders Choice Daily*. This newspaper could publish all the news that has been produced by insight generation systems, plus stories from news wires and those produced manually. Such a system would meet Alan Kay's definition of a computer agent:

> An agent would be a "soft robot" living and doing its business within the computer's world. . . . A persistent "go-fer" that for 24 hours a day looks for things it knows a user is interested in and presents them as a personal magazine.[9]

This agent would search through the documents in the Marketing Insight Center and find the ones it knows a manager is interested in. It would assemble segments of these documents into a personal newsletter that it could then mail to the manager. Such a newsletter could be prepared for all interested managers in the firm.

Discussion

This first part of the chapter has described an evolution of marketing systems. The early period of marketing use of computerized data is characterized by the data being in the computer and information produced on paper by a data processing system. The next step was a management information system that permits the marketing manager to retrieve the data on demand. Both approaches result in rows and columns of

---

[9]Alan Kay, "Computer Software," *Scientific American* (September 1984).

data, or what is commonly called *information*. Managers used their own intelligence, their knowledge about marketing, and data analysis to interpret this information. The results of this interpretation could be termed *insights*. Managers generated insights by examining information. As the databases increase in size, it becomes problematic for managers to apply their knowledge to produce the insights—there is simply too much data.

Knowledge systems have been developed to capture and apply the marketing and data analysis knowledge of marketing managers and analysts. These systems generate the insights that managers could produce using information systems if they had the time and/or knowledge. Another phrase for these knowledge systems is *insight generation systems*, which is a more descriptive term of the task performed by the knowledge-based systems. The output of the insight generation systems is paper, or an image of the paper in the computer. Additional systems, termed *insight management systems,* can be built for managing these images. The forthcoming book *The Generation and Management of Marketing Insights*[10] provides a detailed discussion of these new types of marketing systems.

The most important aspect of the evolution of marketing systems is that they are getting more intelligent. This intelligence is being achieved by moving the marketing manager farther down the information-value chain. This movement is made possible by capturing and computerizing knowledge of (1) the data, (2) the conversion of the data into information, and (3) the conversion of the information into insights. The computer adds value by converting data into information, and information into insights. The manager adds value by converting the insights into decisions.

MARKETING INFORMATICS: EXPANDING THE COMPUTATIONAL MODELS

The first section described an evolution that has taken place in the types of computing applications used by marketing managers in generating, managing, and communicating insights. However, there are other ways to generate insights, and other computing approaches for insight generation. This section describes other types of systems, other models, that either have been used or are on the horizon.

This evolution of marketing systems has gone beyond management

---

[10]John M. McCann, John P. Gallagher, William G. Lahti, and Justin Hill, *The Generation and Management of Marketing Insights* (forthcoming).

information systems to include developments in the field of artificial intelligence such as knowledge-based systems and semantic networks. This means that the use of computers in marketing is broadening beyond the traditional *management information system* model. This approach has brought us data processing systems, information systems, database systems, decision support systems, and executive information systems. These have been mainstay technologies in the evolution of marketing systems. But new technology areas are on the horizon that will augment these traditional approaches to marketing systems. The first step was to look to the field of artificial intelligence for guidance in the application of expert system technologies to marketing, as well as semantic network and case-based reasoning methods. These are now in prototype and production systems.

The next step is to look at the computational science, graphics, scientific visualization, and data visualization fields for help in getting value from the ever-expanding marketing databases. These fields are light-years ahead of marketing in terms of the sizes of their databases. For instance, an upcoming space probe will generate trillions of bytes of data every week.[11] This database is much larger than marketing databases, and the developments in these areas should offer strong potential for marketing applications.

To aid the field of marketing in moving beyond management information systems to encompass many diverse technologies, we need a term or phrase that describes the destination of our journey. Perhaps we could borrow a term from another discipline, one that has taken a similar journey: medicine. Because of the large number of instruments used to diagnose a patient, medicine has experienced a data explosion which has led to considerable research into the use and management of information, and has spawned the term *medical informatics.*[12]

Marketing could adopt and adapt this phrase to describe the various technologies and approaches one might use to gain insights from marketing data. The result would be *marketing informatics.* This field would encompass both the existing technologies that have been implemented in various marketing systems and new developments in other technology areas. Figure 6-4 depicts these technologies.

---

[11]R.L. Peskin, S.S. Wallther, A.M. Froncioni, and T.I. Boubez, "Interactive Quantitative Visualization," *IBM Journal of Research and Development*, 35, 1/2 (January–March 1991), pp. 205–226.

[12]Marsden S. Blois, *Information and Medicine: The Nature of Medical Descriptions* (Berkeley: University of California Press, 1984), p. 234.

FIGURE 6-4
New and Emerging Technologies

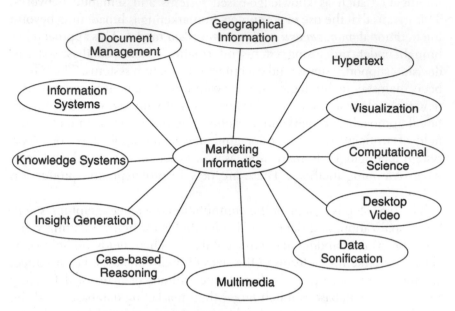

The remainder of this section discusses the new and emerging technologies shown in this figure.

Document Management Systems

The common characteristic of most of the existing knowledge-based systems is that they tell a story or write a presentation, and these stories and presentations are sent to, or composed in, a word processor. Thus they are textual material, usually a *compound document* containing text and graphs. These documents can be printed and they can be stored in the computer, either in their original form as a word processor document or in a print image form. This computer storage leads to a need to access the documents in an intelligent manner, and systems that attempt to meet this need are termed *document management systems*.

Hypertext Systems

One approach to an intelligent document management system is the Marketing Insight Center, a PC-based prototype system for managing the output of knowledge-based systems. However, the system is not limited to computer-generated reports; it could handle any document in computer-readable form. It utilizes a semantic network to build linkages among the elements of a marketing manager's world: brands, sizes, flavors, retailers, coupons, and so forth. This network generates a cascading menu system that the manager can use to navigate through the information space to find one or more documents of interest. After reading these documents, the manager can use the linkages to find related documents. Such movement around documents is a type of hypertext that is based upon the underlying semantic network.

Case-based Reasoning Systems

An area of artificial intelligence that is devoted to assisting people in solving problems is case-based reasoning:

> A case-based reasoner solves new problems by adapting solutions that were used to solve old problems.[13]

Case-based reasoning is sometimes referred to as analogical reasoning—reasoning about a current problem by (1) finding an analogous situation, (2) extracting the relevant elements from that situation, and (3) applying these elements to the current problem. Burke has developed a system for applying marketing research results from past studies of advertising effectiveness to help predict the effectiveness of a current advertisement.[14] McCann, Hill, and McCullough[15] have used a similar approach to develop a prototype system that builds a promotion plan based upon past promotion plans.

This approach to marketing systems holds promise because it provides a way for the firm to bring what it has learned in the past to bear on present situations. Day has articulated the need for this type of system:

> Organizations without practical mechanisms to "remember" what worked and why have to repeat the failures and rediscover their success formulas

---

[13]C.K. Riesbeck and R.C. Schank, *Inside Case-Based Reasoning* (Hillside, N.J.: Lawrence Erlbaum, 1989).

[14]Raymond R. Burke, "Reasoning with Empirical Marketing Knowledge," *International Journal of Research in Marketing*, 8 (1991), p. 75ff.

[15]John M. McCann, Justin Hill, and Don McCullough, "The Application of Marketing Experiences via Case-Based Reasoning," Working Paper, Fuqua School of Business, Duke University, October 1991.

over and over again. Memory mechanisms are needed to ensure that useful lessons are captured, conserved, and can be readily retrieved when needed.[16]

The technologies of case-based reasoning provide such a mechanism.

Geographical Information Systems

Geographical information systems (GIS) are a rapidly growing area for computing applications due to wide-spread geographical data, along with high-speed workstations with large, high-resolution monitors. The importance of this approach to computing and information display was enhanced in 1988 when the National Science Foundation established the National Center for Geographical Information and Analysis.[17] These growing capabilities are bringing the GIS into business applications. A further boost is coming from the Census Bureau through the development of the Topographically Integrated Geographic Encoding and Referencing (TIGER) System Line Files.

TIGER is the digital map of the entire United States that is being used by almost all data and GIS vendors. It is important in marketing because it allows one to plot customers on a map based upon their address. It is allowing retailers and manufacturers to better understand the dynamic nature of micromarkets, as evidenced in the following example application:

> Retailers can record the dynamics of markets, take advantage of customer segmentation methodologies or combine them to develop comprehensive market strategies. For instance, trade areas tracked over time record the changing competitive nature of a dynamic market, including competitor locations, sizes and effectiveness.[18]

This type of activity by the retailers is causing manufacturers to place similar interests in micromarketing, and thus in GIS. These developments have led one GIS vendor, Tactics International Limited, to offer the Trade Dimensions' Supermarket Database on 30,000 supermarkets for

---

[16]George S. Day, "Learning about Markets," *Marketing Science Institute Report* 91–117, June 1991, p. 8.

[17]Rita Shoor, "Plotting a New Course with New-Generation GIS," *Computer Graphics Review* (November 1989), pp. 18–26.

[18]Andy Moncla and Lee McConnell, "TIGER Helps Retailers Address Marketing Issues," *GIS World* (October 1991), pp. 80–81.

use with its GIS package Tactician. This database and other marketing databases that contain geographical location information facilitate the move from mass marketing to local or micromarketing, as is happening at one retailer: "Chains like Lucky are developing systems to target specific shoppers in specific neighborhoods as the mass market is dying."[19]

Computational Science

A new computing model emerged during the 1980s, primarily in the academic research community: computational science. Prior to this time, the dominant scientific models were experimental science and theoretical science.

> We have seen the emergence of an entirely new paradigm for doing science: in addition to experimental science (where nature is probed and tested), and theoretical science (where an attempt is made to understand and codify nature), we have computational science where the computer—as a stand-in for nature—is probed and tested. Without computational science, for example, we would have little understanding of the interiors of stars and planets. It's difficult to perform an experiment on the sun, but easy to do so on a computer model of it.[20]

Computational science involves the use of supercomputers to repeatedly solve a mathematical representation of a physical entity, such as a planet, the solar system, an ocean, a tornado, and so forth.

> The primary goal of computational science, a flourishing area in scientific research, is not merely to simulate the optical appearance of reality, but to simulate models that precisely and completely describe real physical systems. Computational science is directly linked to the supercomputer revolution.[21]

There was an early tradition among some in the marketing academic community to apply similar ideas and concepts that are now being practiced in the computational science community. Amstutz developed a

---

[19]Dick Fredericksen, Senior Vice President, Statewide Marketing, Luck Stores, quoted in Elliot Zwiebach, "Neighborhood Marketing Ahead for Large Chains," *Supermarket News*, March 5, 1990, p. 6.

[20]Brand Fortner, "Scientific Visualization on the Macintosh," *SciTech Quarterly*, 2d Quarter, 1991, p. 6.

[21]Donna J. Cox, "The Art of Scientific Visualization," *Academic Computing*, March 1990, p. 21.

very detailed model for use in marketing; he succinctly describes the purpose of his model in the first sentence of his book:

> This book was written to present elements of an organized behavioral theory of market interactions and to suggest an approach to management based on the use of microanalytic computer simulations of interactions within the marketing environment. It focuses on the development and implementation of behavioral models and system configurations designed to provide a formal quantitative structure within which management problems involving the environment external to the firm can be defined and analyzed.[22]

This micromodeling approach was ahead of its time, if for no other reason than the lack of good data on the microunits and the computing costs associated with the simulations of the large number of decision-making units that are modeled in the system. The new scanner and scanner panel data, couponing data, inventory data, and other related databases, along with the dramatic decrease in computing costs, make this computational science approach much more feasible today. In fact, dropping computing costs and networked computers has made computational science possible, along with advances in the area of scientific visualization.

Data Visualization Systems

Data from computational science models and marketing measuring instruments need to be analyzed, and an increasingly common approach is to move the data to high-speed, graphic workstations where they are plotted and graphed in ways that allow scientists to use their visual senses and cognitive powers to gain a new understanding of the entity under study. The need to visualize the masses of simulated data (as well as large databases generated from cameras and sensing instruments on spaceships such as *Voyager*) has led to new software called scientific visualization systems.

> The goal of scientific visualization is to give researchers the ability not only to view pictorial representations of their data as they are generated

---

[22]Arnold E. Amstutz, *Computer Simulation of Competitive Market Response* (Cambridge, Mass.: MIT Press, 1967), p. 1.

but to promote insight into the meaning of the data by allowing researchers to modify the computational process as it is occurring.[23]

Although these systems were initially developed for use in the physical sciences, recent arguments have been made for a broader view, one that would recognize many more data forms than are currently utilized by the scientific visualization community. In fact, some of the scientific visualization software has found its way into the business community, initially in visualizing financial data.[24] It is only a matter of time before they are moved to the problem of viewing, and thus understanding, marketing data. Perhaps the phrase "data visualization" will replace the more restrictive "scientific visualization."

With this new phrase as a guide, one begins to encounter a stream of research and computer tools that can be potentially useful in marketing. One such stream is dynamic graphical methods, which has been defined as "the direct manipulation of the elements of a graph on a computer screen."[25] This direct manipulation of the graph is then quickly followed by virtually instantaneous changes in the graph. The purpose of such manipulation is to discover and/or formulate hypotheses about the structure of multivariate data. Developers of one such system, VISUAL/Pxpl, describe their work as taking a "guided tour" of a multidimensional data space, with the goal of "visualizing the structure of high-dimensional space by encoding the structure as movement and changing the brightness in three-dimensional space."[26] In this way, six-dimensional space can be visualized on a flat computer screen. Other researchers refer to a "grand tour"[27] of multivariate data. From this type of work has emerged the notion of a *visualization pipeline:* a well-defined method and mechanisms for data access and management of the visualization processes.[28] This pipeline allows the user to control the flow of data and promotes rapid exploration. When data visualization is coupled with mathematical modeling, researchers have formed another phrase, computational steering,

[23]Craig Mundie, "Interacting with the Tiny and the Immense," *Byte* (April 1989), p. 279.

[24]Barbara Robertson, "Biz Viz," *Computer Graphics World* (September 1991), pp. 45–50.

[25]William S. Cleveland and Marylyn E. McGill, *Dynamic Graphics for Statistics* (Belmont, Calif.: Wadsworth, 1988), p. xi.

[26]F.W. Young and P. Rheingans, "Visualizing Structure in High-Dimensional Multivariate Data," *IBM Journal of Research and Development*, 35, 1/2 (January–March 1991), p. 97.

[27]D. Asimov, "The Grand Tour: A Tool for Viewing Multidimensional Data," *SIAM Journal of Scientific and Statistical Computation*, 6 (1985), pp. 128–143.

[28]L.A. Treinish and C. Goettsche, "Correlative Visualization Techniques for Multidimensional Data," *IBM Journal of Research and Development*, 35, 1/2 (January–March 1991), pp. 184–192.

to denote the process one uses to build a model of the underlying phenomena.

Explorations of visualization techniques were conducted as part of a category review or exploration project in the Marketing Workbench Laboratory.[29] The goal was to find graphical representations that would allow the manager to view and understand the structure and performance of a product category. Figure 6-5 shows one visual representation of the detergent category, broken down by sizes and then by manufacturers. We refer to a hierarchical view of a product category like this as a product structure tree.

Figure 6-6 is a view of a window holding a color-coded representation of the same tree. Besides showing the structural composition of the detergent category, the matrix of rectangles represents the following information: (1) share of category units is indicated by the relative width of rectangles; (2) the performance of an item or group of items relative to

FIGURE 6-5

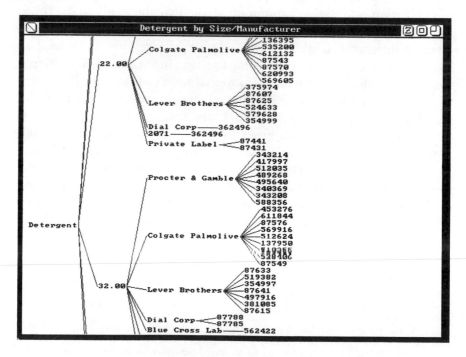

---

[29]McCann, Gallagher, Lahti, and Hill, *The Generation and Management of Marketing Insights.*

FIGURE 6-6

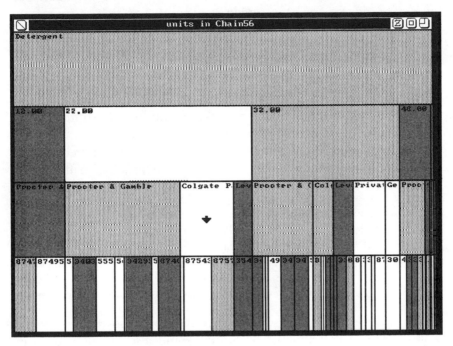

the market is shown with color, in which white is above average, black is below average, and gray is neutral; and (3) the trend for share is indicated by the shape of the cursor, in which an up-arrow indicates a positive trend and a down-arrow indicates a negative trend. (*Note*: Normally a wide variety of colors are used to code information in addition to that which is presented in this screen, but for the purpose of this paper, the color spectrum has been limited to white, gray, and black. Therefore, some useful information has been lost.)

Figure 6–6 is a composite view of the category in a particular location. Through the use of spatial relationships and color, we convey two very useful pieces of information simultaneously: (1) how a group of items is doing at a particular location and (2) how that group of items is doing with respect to the rest of the markets. In other words, a sense of how a set of items is doing and an indication of whether or not it could be doing better is provided. This *colorful hierarchy* shows that 22 oz items and specifically, 22 oz Colgate Palmolive items, are doing much better in Chain56 than in the rest of the market.

The manager can interact with this screen by moving the cursor from rectangle to rectangle, i.e., from one product grouping to another. As the cursor moves across the screen, it may change from an up-arrow, denoting a positive trend in the variable that is represented by the triangle, to a down-arrow that denotes a negative trend. This two-position cursor could be expanded to all 12 positions of a clock to denote gradations in trend. And trend is only one variable that could be represented via the cursor.

Although the shape of the cursor allows one to add a third variable to the original two-variable representation, other mechanisms are available for expanding the width of the communication channel between the data and the human brain. Research is progressing in the use of sound to scientific visualizations via the sonification of data.

> Sonification relies on sound that is driven directly by the scientific data set used to drive the graphics. The idea is to use sound as an additional "channel" beyond the visual, for carrying information to the human brain, while perhaps cashing in on synergies of combined aural and visual perception. . . . Data might be mapped to frequency, volume, attack and decay rates, duration, timbre, reverberation, brightness, or stereo placement.[30]

Any of these sound representations could accompany the cursor as it moves over the colorful matrix. Sound could also be used to "play" marketing data in the background of a marketing manager's office. When something interesting is detected in the sound data, the manager could turn to the computer screen to view graphical and/or numerical representations of the same data.

Multimedia Systems

Multimedia systems involve the marriage of the computer with other forms of communication: audio, music, animation, and video.

> The interface is what it's all about—multimedia means adding video, audio, music, animation, and other media to enhance the computer's ability to communicate. It's a merger of the computer's information processing power with television's communication power to create a new medium greater than the sum of the parts.[31]

---

[30]Wes Iversen, "The Sound of Science," *Computer Graphics World* (January 1992), p. 56.
[31]Nick Arnett, "Dawn of a New Age," *Computer Graphics World* (August 1989), p. 35.

Although this concept has been around for a few years, it has not had a major impact in business except in education and training. Recent research into the use of computers in education is showing that multimedia tools can be used to enhance the learning process, but in ways that are different than expected. The traditional model for multimedia computers in education is for the instructor to develop or purchase a multimedia package on a particular topic, and to then use the package as a substitute for a textbook. The new approach: students do not use someone else's multimedia system, they develop their own.[32] This approach may have a major impact on the way computers are used in education, and in a similar way, on the practice of marketing.

This use of multimedia as a communications technology for individuals treats it in a manner similar to the way people use computer spreadsheet and word-processing packages: as tools for performing a task and producing an end result.

> Such use of one of two models of multimedia authoring:
>
> - User-centered: the producer is also the consumer is also the producer.
> - Traditional: there are a few producers and many consumers.
>
> The user-centered model, with the producer as consumer, draws parallels with the use of personal computers in general and desktop publishing in particular. The enormous power of the tools means that previous consumers of newsletters, flyers, or typeset pages suddenly become producers of their own typeset pages. The user-centered model predicts that consumers of sound and motion video will take up their own recorders and camcorders and produce music and home videos. Although not necessarily of the highest professional quality, these productions will be good enough for most purposes, will become very popular, and will certainly provide a new outlet for the creative talents of many current personal computer users.[33]

This vision of user-centered multimedia authoring could come true in the field of marketing. One avenue: a *Multimedia Marketing Plan.* Marketing managers and their support organizations (e.g., advertising agencies, promotion houses, marketing research firms) will use multimedia tools to prepare a marketing plan. The marketing plan is then much

---

[32]Elliot Soloway, "How the Nintendo Generation Learns," *Communications of the ACM* (September 1991), p. 23.

[33]Jack Grimes and Mike Potel, "Guest Editors' Introduction: Multimedia—It's Actually Useful!," *IEEE Computer Graphics and Applications* (July 1991), p. 25.

more realistic. It is not a static paper description of the firm's efforts for the next year, but a version of the actual thing. It can be used to simulate the execution of the plan, and as a presentation and selling tool within the organization. For instance, it could contain an animation of the television executions. Or even a "home video" version of the executions. It could contain pictures of in-store events, coupons, and so forth. And it could grow and become more realistic over time as professional executions of the elements of the plan become available.

Multimedia offers great potential for extending the computer into all aspects of marketing. Consider the recent comments of one who follows this technology:

> The PC has been relegated to the arenas of number crunching, word processing, and data analysis too long. Numbers and text are the easy stuff but account for only a small part of our real lives. For the PC to fully function as an extension of our minds, it must be made to capture, store, process, and render any type of data used in human communications. This includes video images and sound.[34]

This statement is very germane to marketing. Numbers are only a small part of the objects in a marketing manager's world. Images are much more important. Brand image is, in fact, the number one responsibility of a brand manager. His or her job is to develop a brand image, implant it in the firm's mind, implant it in the customers' minds, implant it in the consumers' minds, and protect it from attack by competitors. To do this, a marketing manager works with other images—advertisements, packages, promotions, and so forth.

McCann identified the Four-D roles of brand management:[35]

Detective: scanning the environment to identify problems and opportunities;

Designer: designing marketing events, programs, and plans for solving the problems and capturing the opportunities;

Decision Influencer: selling the plan vertically in the organization by influencing the decisions of senior managers to allocate resources to the manager's plan; and

Diplomat: selling the plan horizontally in the organization to other depart-

---

[34]Charles Petzold, "Beyond the Beep: The Coming of Mulitmedia Windows," *PC Magazine,* October 29, 1991, p. 403.

[35]John M. McCann, *The Marketing Workbench* (Homewood, Ill.: Dow Jones-Irwin, 1986).

ments and individuals who must execute one or more elements of the plan.

Today's installed systems such as DIS and Dataserver are aimed at the detective role. Multimedia technology may provide a path to expand the use of computers beyond numbers and static words and into the other three roles: designer, decision influencer, and diplomat. Multimedia could be used to capture, represent, and simulate the marketing plan and thus will provide a means to communicate the insights that were generated via the use of other computer applications. Today, the plan usually exists in one of two written forms: a formal report or a presentation "deck." These are very static forms that have only been slightly impacted by computers. In almost all instances, computers are background or preparation tools. They are used to extract and format data, to do statistical analysis, to prepare budgets and pro forma statements, to do simple "what if" analysis, to generate graphs, and to type the report or deck. Once the report is prepared, the computer leaves the scene; is no longer part of the action. Can multimedia tools be used to keep the computer at "center stage" throughout the year?

The computer plays a very limited role in the creative aspects of marketing; those aspects of marketing that tend to deal with images; images of brands, stores, customers, cities, lifestyles, coupons, packages, advertisements, and all aspects of the daily lives of consumers of the product category. Up until now, computers were not well suited for this creative aspect of marketing and thus were not used in the most important parts of a marketing manager's work. Consider the comments of a Procter & Gamble brand manager: "Generally speaking, most of my time is spent on the development and execution of marketing plans and strategies. . . . The challenge is to deliver marketing plans and strategies—that's where you win, competitively speaking."[36]

The following breakdown is an estimate of the amount of time that each member of a brand group spends working with numbers:

Assistant Brand Manager	80%
Associate Brand Manager	40%
Brand Manager	20%

---

[36]Ron Doornick, Brand Manager of Pampers disposable diapers, in *Procter & Gamble: The House That Ivory Built,* by the editors of *Advertising Age* (Lincolnwood, Ill.: NTC Business Books, 1989), pp. 119–121.

This means that the senior people on the brand are not good candidates for using today's computers in most of their work. Only the new members of the brand groups, the new MBAs, make much use of DIS and other existing tools. Brand managers use other tools, usually ones that do not involve a computer. This fact is illustrated by another quote from the P&G brand manager: "Planning is critical in brand management; therefore, we try to use planning tools like project lists." Surely the computer can do better than a project list.

Communicating is a key aspect of a marketing manager's life that could be enhanced by multimedia; communicating with customers, consumers, suppliers, managers, the sales force, and others in the organization.

> Do *you* need multimedia? For example, if you make formal presentations in business, you've probably been getting along nicely with flip charts, overhead transparencies, and attractively bound reports—why change now? The most compelling reason is that when you use older methods, chances are, most of your audience isn't absorbing as much information as they should, and some may not be paying attention. The longer the presentation, the more people you will lose. And the more information you present, the less the audience absorbs because you can't hold their interest. It's not your fault, and your audience isn't stupid or lazy; it has more to do with the way people are built. They see in color, focus on motion, and hear keenly. These are not incidental properties of the human machine. They are traits that originally kept us from being devoured, and they are now central to how we take in and process information. Multimedia is, in part, about presenting information through more than one of the senses. Multisensory presentations speed and improve understanding, and they can hold an audience's attention.[37]

Multimedia thus offers the potential for enhancing the communication of the insights generated from marketing data by other types of systems. A key component of this enhanced communication capability is the marriage of two dominant technologies: computers and television.

Desktop Video

Related to, and an integral part of, the multimedia advances is the desktop video. The trend to higher and higher quality and functionality in home video technology is allowing quasi-professionals (called *procon-*

---

[37]Tom Yager, "Information's Hidden Dimensions," *Byte* (December 1991), p. 154.

sumers) to develop fairly good video material. One technology that is driving the use of desktop video in advertising is computer animation software. The FCB/Leber Katz advertising agency is using this technology to produce comps (rough ad layouts) and animated storyboards at much lower costs and much faster than previously possible.[38] Another agency is using desktop video technology to produce actual commercials.[39]

Desktop video is made possible by advancements in hardware and software that bring video technology to the computer. One of the leading breakthroughs is the Video Toaster, a plug-in card and software package that transforms the Amigo computer into an easy-to-use, multipurpose video application.[40] This package, which costs less than $5,000 and can be coupled to IBM personal computers, provides the capabilities of dedicated video production equipment that cost close to $100,000. These types of systems are becoming available because of advancements in computer chips that digitize and process video signals, along with software and hardware standards. For instance, IBM and Intel have defined a set of standard methods and an architecture for building desktop multimedia and video applications. The resulting Advio-Video Kernel promises to enhance the development communities' ability to develop technologies and applications that run on a wide array of platforms.[41] Such developments are leading to a new model for desktop multimedia: the video production studio.

IMPLICATIONS FOR RESEARCH AND EDUCATION

This chapter has (1) described an evolution of applied marketing systems, (2) introduced a new phrase, marketing informatics, for pulling together the application of computer and video technology in marketing, and (3) described some emerging technology areas that could become a part of marketing informatics. If a segment of the marketing academic community agrees that these are viable ways to view marketing systems, what are the implications for research and education in marketing?

To gain insights into the research needs, it is informative to look at

[38]Carol S. Holzberg, "Comps and Animatics: FCB/Leber Katz," *Desktop Communications* (March–April 1990), p. 32.

[39]Carol S. Holzberg, "Quick Videos: Farago Advertising," *Desktop Communications* (March–April 1990), p. 34.

[40]John Spofford, "NewTek's Toaster Slices Costs," *TV Technology* (March 1991), pp. 48–49.

[41]John W. Donovan, "Intel/IBM's Audio-Video Kernel," *Byte* (December 1991), pp. 177–186.

an analogous situation: marketing research. For instance, if one were to get a copy of the 1966 edition of *Research for Marketing Decisions* by Green and Tull,[42] one would see that it described research methodologies that are now common in the field of marketing research. At the same time, one would realize that a lot of the examples and applications of these techniques that were described in the text were taken from other fields such as psychology and statistics. Subsequent editions of the text contained higher and higher percentages of examples from actual marketing research, until today's edition is entirely devoted to applications from the field of marketing. These changes were possible because researchers in the marketing academic community devoted considerable interest in exploring the use of tools and techniques from other disciplines in the field of marketing research.

For instance, quantitative psychology gave us conjoint measurement, which is now one of our most widely used marketing research techniques. Probability theory gave us beta binomial and logit models, and thus laid the foundation for hundreds of studies of consumer choice. Developments in econometrics yielded our tradition in response functions, and economics gave us agency theory which is leading to new insights into areas such as sales management.

The common thread in all of these areas is that marketing academics explored analytical technologies from other disciplines, and these explorations led to important advances in the application of the techniques in marketing and marketing research. A similar approach is needed with the emerging computer and video technologies. Creative minds need to explore the use in marketing of the various tools and technologies that have been identified in this paper. It is through this exploration that we will advance the ability of marketing managers to move beyond data and information into the insightful design of competitive marketing programs.

In addition to technology-oriented research, effort needs to be applied to understanding the organizational implications of intelligent marketing systems. Consider a system that (1) identifies display, feature, and price opportunities for each account in each market, and (2) suggests the best tactic for capturing the opportunities in each account. If this system were placed in a loop, it would identify opportunities for all accounts in all markets. When these systems produce reports, they are sent to managers.

---

[42]Paul E. Green and Donald S. Tull, *Research for Marketing Decisions* (Englewood Cliffs, N.J.: Prentice-Hall, 1966).

Their arrival on the desks of a lot of managers at the same point in time has an interesting effect. The reports provide a focus and a means for the organization to easily attack the problems and opportunities identified in the reports. No work was done by anyone in the organization prior to the reports' arrival. All of a sudden a large number of problems have been identified and solutions proposed. All of this is suddenly known to every person who is touched by the situation. This results in a situation where the organization can easily decide to solve the problems or capture the opportunities identified in the reports.

An article by James March provides insights into this situation. March explains the garbage-can theory of decision making.

> It is argued that any decision process involves a collection of individuals and groups that is simultaneously involved in other things. . . . Individuals attend to some things and, thus, do not attend to others. The attention devoted to a particular decision by a particular potential participant depends on alternative claims to attention. . . . Such ideas have been generalized to deal with flows of solutions and problems, as well as participants in what has come to be called a garbage-can decision process. In a garbage-can process, it is assumed that there are exogenous, time-dependent arrivals of choice opportunities, problems, solutions, and decisions makers.[43]

This is a view of dis-organization; a view of an organization as a collection of busy people, all attending to their own agendas. When something new arrives, all of the involved parties must focus on it. If it has not been completely analyzed or understood, then they must each decide how much time to allocate to it. This might explain the slow nature of the decision-making process in organizations. An insight generation system tends to cut through the time-dependent arrival of choice opportunities, problems, solutions, and decision makers. It serves to make all decision makers simultaneously aware of the problems and solutions. It focuses everyone on the same problem at the same point in time, and in a way that makes it easy for them to accept the recommendations of the system. Given that a solution is attached to the problem, it is easy to focus on the problem and participate in the decision to move forward. This fits with another of March's observations about decision makers: *Indeed, they often do not recognize a "problem" until they have a solution.*[44] If solutions

---

[43]James G. March, "How Decisions Happen in Organizations," *Human-Computer Interaction*, 6 (1991), p. 109.
[44]Ibid., p. 112.

are included in the same documents that identify problems, it is easier for managers to accept the problem and its analysis. Once they accept it, they can then go back to the other activities that are competing for their time.

The need for new and innovative organizational structures are being recognized. For instance, one observer recently predicted that traditional marketing research departments will disappear, to be replaced by a new corporate unit headed by a chief information officer. The business academic community has the knowledge and background to research these developments. Models like the garbage-can model need to be explored as means of describing and/or optimizing marketing organizations.

From an educational perspective, it is important that future marketing and marketing research managers know how to be leaders in a marketing informatics environment. Our educational programs need to be broadened so that students understand marketing data, how to convert it to information, and how to build insight generation systems. Recent advances in personal computer technologies are making it possible for business professionals such as marketing researchers to use spreadsheets and word processors to construct an insight generation system. In fact, all of the technologies described in this chapter are suitable for use by marketing researchers. A stumbling block is the lack of educational programs that focus on marketing informatics.

This field of marketing informatics needs to be nurtured and brought alive by the marketing academic community, with funds supplied by the users and suppliers of the technologies. Research programs need to be developed in each of the areas of marketing informatics that explore how these technologies and concepts can be used to further and enhance the practice of marketing. The ultimate aim of these programs would be the generation, communication, and management of marketing insights.

These developments are necessary because of the need for marketing systems to become the center of market-driven inquiry.

> Organizations that are well educated about their markets stand out in their ability to rapidly sense and act on events in volatile and fragmenting markets. They have an ability to learn what makes them better equipped to anticipate how their markets will respond to actions designed to retain or attract customers or thwart competitors. . . . The learning process must include the ability of managers to absorb what is going on in the environment into their mental model of how the market behaves, share the new understanding with members of the management team, and then act decisively. Firms need to learn how to enhance this learning

competency, for otherwise their ability to compete will be severely compromised.[45]

The goal of the continual evolution of marketing systems should be to enhance the ability of the firm to learn, to "know what it knows," and to effectively communicate its knowledge and plans to others.

---

[45]G. Day, "Learning about Markets," p. 1.

7

MODELING MARKET RESPONSE IN LARGE CUSTOMER PANELS

John D.C. Little

SINCE THE 1940s, consumer diary panels have been collected by research firms such as Marketing Research Corporation of America and newspapers including the Chicago Tribune and the Milwaukee Sentinel. In the 1960s, AdTel was started to combine advertising viewing with diary panel data on consumer purchases. The consumer purchase data were collected through paper diaries which were laborious and which may have led to significant reporting errors. In the 1980s, Information Resources innovated with the use of computerized scanners to collect panel data so that the process would be much less obtrusive and less time consuming. When a household member visits the store, purchases are automatically recorded—simply by use of a card with a unique number to identify the purchaser. The pharmaceutical industry has also adopted customer panels, as have the textile, toy, electronics, and restaurant industries.

An alternative to diary panels is a complete census of purchases made by customers. In Chapter 3, Deighton, Peppers, and Rogers discuss these types of data and their uses. In all cases, whether the data are a complete census or a sample (customer panel), the need to develop market response models is critical because the information must be summarized to capture key effects. For example, direct marketing companies summarize individual customer purchase histories using a relatively simplistic system based on "RFM" (recency, frequency, monetary). Whereas the concept of recency (When did I last buy?), frequency (How much have I bought?), and monetary (How much have I spent?) may seem fundamental, it has been shown to be an excellent predictor of future behavior and reflects the power of behavioral (what the customer actually does) versus survey or demographic data.

This chapter addresses more sophisticated modeling issues and concentrates on predicting market response, which allows the manager to evaluate the effects of specific marketing activities on customer behavior. The statisti-

cal procedures are evolving rapidly in both the academic world and "the real world." As rapidly as the modeling procedures are changing, so are the issues that are being addressed. These include advertising, promotions, pricing, store switching, brand loyalty, and brand equity. Understanding these issues is fundamental for managers designing marketing strategies, tactics, and annual marketing plans. The chapter also discusses how the results of the market response models can be translated into decision models so that managers can set marketing policies. This is a critical area which is likely to become the focal point of future research by both academics and practioners.

INTRODUCTION

The information revolution has produced a cornucopia of new data for understanding customer response to products, services, and their marketing mixes. This has driven changes in marketing strategy and tactics. One manufacturer of power transformers has used its customer data to model its best combination of price, warranty, and product characteristics. Implementation of the results produced striking gains in market share. Consumer packaged-goods manufacturers regularly test new products, advertising strategies, and other marketing innovations in special laboratory markets containing thousands of households who have volunteered to have their purchase histories electronically tracked. Analysis of such household data has brought new understanding of the relative importance of price reductions, special displays, and newspaper features and has led manufacturers to reallocate their marketing dollars. If your household is one of the 70% in the United States that uses cents-off coupons, you may have noticed that expiration dates for redeeming coupons have become shorter in the past year or two. This is because the analysis of purchase histories of 60,000 regularly monitored households shows that people who hold their coupons for a long time produce few incremental sales.

For the most part, the data underlying these applications come as a spinoff of companies' transaction operations with customers. This is happening in the back rooms of banks, credit card firms, and mail order houses. Marketers also combine such transaction data with specially collected supplementary information. This is the case with the point-of-sale data from grocery purchases and pharmaceutical prescriptions.

Individual customer data, coupled with mathematical models and analysis, offer the promise of new understanding of customer behavior and therefore increased efficiency for delivering products and services that meet people's needs.

Such customer data contrast sharply with traditional aggregate market data. Although the analysis of aggregate data has certainly yielded sales response information, it tends to be weak in diagnostics; that is, it does not tell who in the population responds to which marketing activities and why. Individual customer information frequently offers such insight.

We distinguish between two types of customer data. One is *census* data—complete files of all customers, e.g., all depositors at a bank, all physicians in the United States, or all customers of an automobile dealership. The other is a *panel* data—samples, often large ones, of target populations. Examples are a panel of physicians who report sales calls by pharmaceutical representatives, a panel of households who record their textile purchases in a diary, and, the most highly studied panels to date, households who identify themselves at supermarket checkouts so that their purchases can be tracked.

The first type, census data or customer files, is discussed by Deighton, Peppers, and Rogers in Chapter 3. Here we focus primarily on samples of customers, and our goal will be to extract information from them to assist in making marketing decisions. Although much of the published work has dealt with the large scanner panels of the consumer packaged-goods industry, the same techniques are excellent for targeting individual customers when complete customer files are available. Furthermore, many of the packaged goods models apply to other data-rich environments in which marketing inputs are known on a customer-by-customer basis. One good example is the pharmaceutical industry.

The chapter proceeds as follows: first we discuss the nature of the data being collected and how they are gathered. Then we introduce the concept of market response reporting and contrast it to conventional status reporting. Next is a discussion of approaches to customer response modeling. Finally, we describe several practical applications and suggest a research agenda of further opportunities.

The Data

Although large databases are emerging everywhere, the leading edge of published work on market response is to be found in consumer packaged goods. In this industry, today's rich databases are a spinoff of optical scanning of the bar codes on grocery products. Scanners first appeared in 1974, not long after grocery manufacturers and retailers set up the universal product code (UPC) for marking their products. The major goal of scanning was to save labor and speed checkout, but people quickly realized that the information collected would have great value in itself. Nevertheless, the growth of installations was slow and it was not until the mid-1980s that reliable national samples became possible. Such *store data*, from samples of 2,000–3,000 supermarkets, provide the raw numbers for the major national tracking services offered to grocery manufacturers by Information Resources, Inc. (IRI) and Nielsen Market Research (Nielsen).

Individual *household data* appeared even before the national store data because they were collected for market tests. In 1979, Information Resources introduced *laboratory markets*, in which all stores were equipped with scanners (in many cases by IRI), and voluntary panels of 3,000–4,000 households per market were recruited who identify themselves at checkout with an ID card. In these stores the cashier enters the household ID into the checkout terminal, whereupon the store computer segregates the purchases and accumulates them over time by household. The store computer also provides price and unit sales information for all products, not just those bought by the panel. In addition, IRI encodes store flyers, newspaper ads, and special displays in the stores. When members of the panel redeem coupons, the cashier puts them into a small plastic bag and labels it with the panelist's ID for subsequent entry into the database. The laboratory markets are chosen for their high cable-television penetration, and the panel households on the cable have specially modified television sets so that different groups of people can receive different commercials in test and control fashion. A subset of the TV sets are monitored every five seconds to determine the channel tuned in. Thus is created a remarkable testing laboratory for new products, television advertising, and other marketing activities in a service that IRI calls BehaviorScan. There are about six of these markets nationally. In addition, IRI collects most of the same information on a smaller scale in major cities.

Nielsen also has an extensive household panel but collects the data by home scanning. Households rescan the products with a hand scanner, or "wand," after returning home from shopping. This has the advantage of picking up purchases made at stores that do not have scanners. However, it fails to identify the competitive conditions of price and display at the store where the product was bought.

To summarize, in consumer packaged goods there is a customer panel database, currently containing more than 60,000 households, for which is known not just the individual purchases but also a remarkably complete picture of the marketing environment of each household. The data includes:

- purchases
- prices
- store flyers
- newspapers
- TV advertising
- displays
- coupons

The information in known not only for the product that is purchased but also for the brands that were *not* purchased, i.e., all the competitors. The availability of both company and competitive data at the point-of-sale offers a remarkable opportunity to understand what drives purchase behavior. Because all the marketing variables are collected for the same households as the purchases, the data are often referred to as *single-source*.

The pharmaceutical industry, although not as advanced in single-source data as consumer packaged goods, is beginning to have integrated data of high quality. The "customer" in this case is the physician, the person who writes the prescriptions and therefore has the most (but by no means all) influence on product choice. In this industry the most detailed source of purchase data is the pharmacy, where automation is leading to the capture in individual prescriptions by specific patient and doctor. This and data provided by other services, identifies:

- prescriptions
- details (sales calls on the doctor)
- direct mail advertising
- magazine advertising
- samples

Such information is available by therapeutic class and physician specialty. In some cases, for example, sales calls, competitive activity will be known only in aggregate, but a pharmaceutical company will know its own actions by individual physician.

MARKET RESPONSE

Traditional analysis of panel data has focused on issues such as brand and category penetration, brand share of household purchases, frequency of purchase, heavy and light usage, average purchase size, brand switching, and percentage of volume bought on various types of promotion. These are all important descriptive measures, valuable for understanding customer behavior. They describe *market status*. It is desirable to monitor them over time, looking for trends and changes.

However, from a decision-making point of view, we really want to know how such measures are affected by our marketing actions. This is *market response* information. For example, we want to know not only how many heavy and light users there are but also whether or not they respond differently to our merchandising or advertising.

MODELING APPROACHES

We can divide modeling approaches into *descriptive* and *prescriptive*. Descriptive models seek to uncover marketing phenomena and represent them in mathematical form. This is the classical task of science—to describe the world with fidelity and parsimony. Such models increase our understanding and help us make measurements that delineate our customers and markets. Prescriptive models, or *decision models*, are for solving problems. Although they must obviously describe the market, they must meet other criteria as well (Little 1970). They must be usable and understandable to their users. They should include the variables and phenomena that are vital for the problem at hand, but, just as important, they should leave out those that are not. Such a requirement for artful incompleteness is obvious to practicing management scientists but often not to academics and even businesspeople, a situation that sometimes causes difficulties in communication.

Within descriptive models we can break down the literature into work *with* and *without* marketing *decision variables*, i.e., controllable activities like price, promotion, and advertising. Although one might think such variables important for understanding customer behavior, a considerable body of academic work does not include them. Such models serve to summarize data in various ways. An important stream of descriptive models without marketing decision variables goes back to the 1950s and includes the work of Ehrenberg (1959, 1988), Chatfield, Ehrenberg, and Goodhardt (1966), Massy, Montgomery, and Morrison (1970), Morrison and Schmittlein (1981, 1988), Goodhardt, Ehrenberg, and Chatfield (1984), and others. These models have been widely used for analyzing household data, typically as collected by diary panels. The most common model is known as the negative binomial. This can be derived by making the statistical assumptions (1) that an individual customer has a constant probability over time for purchasing the product and (2) that the underlying purchase rates vary from customer to customer but the variation across rates can be described by a gamma probability distribution. Under these circumstances the number of purchases by a randomly chosen customer in the panel over a fixed time period is described by a negative binomial distribution. Empirical work shows excellent fits to the data.

A typical use of this model is to calibrate it on a four-week period and predict the distribution of purchases in the next four-week period. Deviations from prediction can often be attributed to changes in one's own or competitive marketing actions and can therefore provide measures of marketing effectiveness and stimulate ideas for improving performance.

Our primary focus here, however, will be on descriptive models containing marketing variables that a manager can control or at least influence. Such models offer immediate insight into marketing effectiveness and form the basis for making marketing mix decisions. Single-source data from scanner panels in the packaged goods industry has opened up dramatic new opportunities for such models because of the completeness of the description of the purchase environment. Furthermore, as a result of the broad availability of the data in the academic community, there has been a surge of published research. Other industries might take note.

The Multinomial Logit Choice Model

Because we are working at the individual customer level, we wish to model influences on the customer's choice of brand, product, or service, or, in the case of industrial goods, choice of supplier. By far the most widely used and successful choice model to date is the multinomial logit. This model calculates the probability that a specific customer will choose a particular product on a specific occasion. The technique has a long history in transportation research (Ben-Akiva and Lerman 1985), where it has been used to study people's choice of transportation mode (car, bus, subway, and so forth). An early application in marketing was Punj and Staelin's (1978) study of student choice of business schools. An outstanding success story in industrial marketing is told in Gensch, Aversa, and Moore (1990). We shall discuss these examples in our section on applications.

The multinomial logit was first used on scanner data by Guadagni and Little (1983). In scanner panel applications the logit calculates the probability that a particular household will purchase a specific brand and size on a given occasion. Typical explanatory variables include those listed earlier as available in scanner databases—price, display, newspaper advertising, store flyers, promotional price cuts, and coupons.

Demographic variables are also available for household scanner panels and are sometimes useful. However, Guadagni and Little discovered that a household's past purchase behavior could be summarized into much more powerful variables for explaining purchases than conventional demographics. These authors defined variables, which they called brand loyalty and size loyalty, that are weighed averages of past purchases of a household. Such variables have proved exceptionally effective in explaining differences of purchase behavior across households. This is because most households have strongly entrenched buying habits.

The logit model typically tracks sales and share of the household panel remarkably well. For example, Guadagni and Little drew 100 households at random from a scanner panel in Kansas City and used them to calibrate a multinomial logit model for regular ground coffee. A 26-week preperiod served to initialize variables and a 32-week calibration period to estimate the parameters of the multinomial logit. To test the quality of the model, they then drew an entirely new sample of 100 households and predicted the brand and size choices of these new households. Figure 7-1 shows a plot of predicted and actual share for the small size of Maxwell House coffee for these 100 households over a 52-week period. The agreement is very good. Not only is predicted share close to actual during the 32 weeks used for calibration but tracking is good in the last 20 weeks (starting in October), which represents an entirely new period.

Since the original paper appeared, there have been many extensions and improvements, addressing a variety of further questions. We describe some of these:

Category expansion. The basic multinomial logit predicts brand and size choice given that the household makes a purchase from the product category. Therefore, if marketing activity expands the category, this will not be reflected in the model. Guadagni and Little (1987) address this problem with a variant, the nested logit, that introduces shopping trips into the model. The model asks first: What is the probability that a household will buy within the product category on a particular trip? Then it asks: Given that a product is bought, what is the probability that

FIGURE 7-1
The tracking of small-size Maxwell House coffee in a new sample of 100 households shows that actual share falls almost entirely within the confidence band. Weeks to the right of the vertical line are beyond the period used to calibrate the model.

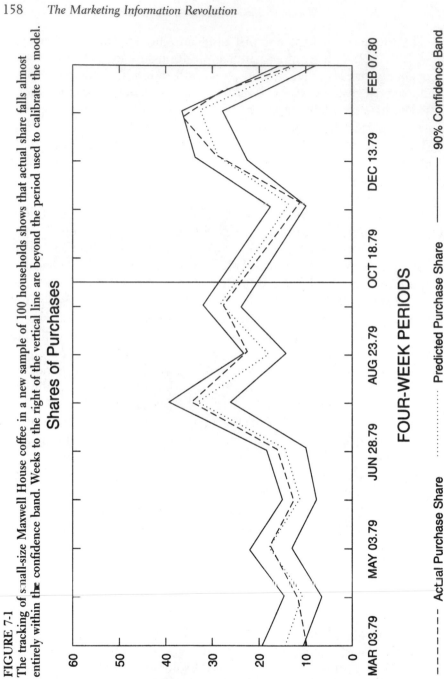

the customer will choose a particular brand and size? Gupta (1988) also models the quantity purchased but does not determine the size of the package chosen.

Inclusion of TV advertising. The direct measurement of the effect of media advertising on sales has remained an elusive but strongly sought goal. IRI's laboratory markets offer an experimental approach to doing this. This has proved effective for measuring advertising weight and copy effects on various products and has also yielded general insights (Levin 1991). However, a single test versus control measurement primarily tells that one treatment is better than another. Although this information is actionable, it occurs in a go/no-go format—do the one best thing. The results would be more useful if they were presented in a response model that could assist targeting and provide response information about interactions with other activities. Tellis (1988), using IRI data from Eau Claire, Wisconsin, has shown that advertising exposures can be successfully introduced into the logit formulation, suggesting that such response models are indeed possible. Developing them is an important task for future research.

Store switching. Retailers, as well as manufacturers, stand to benefit from customer data. A question of vital importance to them is: What marketing causes customers to switch stores? Lattin and Bucklin (1991) develop a nested logit model to study category-specific store competition among grocery retailers. The category on which they illustrate their work is liquid laundry detergents, using Neilsen data from Sioux Falls. They determine the effect of category price and promotional activity on both the household's choice of store and the quantity purchased in a given store. Such information, if generated across major store categories, can powerfully assist a retailer in setting merchandising strategy.

Segmentation by promotional sensitivity. Some customers are more sensitive to price and promotion than others. Bucklin and Gupta (1992) show how to use the multinomial and nested logit models, along with a way of identifying customer segments, to sort out groups of customers that respond to key marketing variables in different ways. Working with liquid laundry detergents, they find, for example, that many customers who switch brands based on price and promotion do not necessarily stockpile the products, whereas stockpilers are often not switching brands. This work, valuable to manufacturers and retailers seeking to understand the effects of their promotional activity, is a good example of adding market response information to standard panel analyses to provide a new decision-oriented thrust.

Household brand loyalty. As mentioned, Guadagni and Little (1983) introduced a measure of brand loyalty, which is the brand's share of a household's purchases with recent purchases weighted more than older ones. In their study, this variable played the dual role of explaining differences across households and the adjustment over time of a given household's product preference. However, it would be desirable to decompose these two phenomena. Fader and Lattin (1991) provide a method for doing this and show that it improves the quality and interpretability of the basic logit marketing mix model and provides a deeper understanding of customer preferences.

Other Choice Models

Techniques besides the multinomial logit hold promise for modeling panel data. An approach that makes fewer restrictive assumptions is the multinomial probit. This is a choice model based on the assumption of an underlying multivariate normal distribution. Currim (1982) shows that the probit has the advantage of greater flexibility than the logit for describing certain kinds of competitive interactions. However, the probit has the disadvantage that for the same number of products and variables it requires much more computation. As a result, much less exploration of marketing phenomena has been conducted using this technique. Another approach is to view the decisions of when and what to buy as a semi-Markov process (Vilcassim and Jain 1991; Hauser and Wisniewski 1982). This approach too has yet to be explored extensively and, like the probit, has computational requirements that increase rapidly with the number of products considered. Therefore, the applications we shall discuss below employ the multinomial logit.

PRACTICAL APPLICATIONS

Market response models at the customer level are increasingly working their way into managerial decision making. This is happening in two different, although often overlapping, ways. One is through *measurement models,* the other through *decision models.* Although almost any practical application of a model involves estimation of parameters and therefore measurement, we shall use the term *measurement model* when the primary goal is measurement of some marketing action, for example, a price elasticity or, in an illustration described below, the extra sales generated by a cents-off coupon. In such cases the measurement becomes separated from the model and is used by itself. By contrast, we use the term *decision model* to describe the situation in which a marketing mix model is calibrated on data (and possibly judgments) after which the whole model is used to examine and evaluate alternative scenarios, or courses of action, i.e., the model is used to ask "what if" questions. The most powerful applications often produce both stand-alone measurements and usable decision models.

Before turning to recent developments in the consumer packaged-goods arena, we report two fine applications that have nothing to do with packaged goods. An early application of the multinomial logit in marketing was Punj and Staelin's (1978) study of choice of school by applicants to MBA programs. In this case the data were specially collected for the study. Besides modeling the effects on choice of individual student characteristics (e.g., GMAT scores) and school characteristics (e.g., size of entering class), the model included variables under the school's control such as the offering of fellowships and loans. Out of the study came not only measurements of key influences on school choice but also the ability for a school administrator to analyze the effects of different student aid programs and other controllable variables.

A remarkably successful application of management science to industrial marketing strategy appears in Gensch, Aversa, and Moore (1990). These authors describe a choice model and market information system that helped ABB Electric increase its market share and become the dominant company in medium-power transformers in the North American electric utility market. The technical side of the work is reported in Gensch (1984). At the heart of the analysis is a multinomial logit model built on individual customer data. Important control variables of the model are price, quality, appearance, and warranty. Understanding customers, segmenting them, and using the model to make targeting, product design, and competitive bidding decisions led to strong company growth despite a declining total market.

Measurement

As an example of using logit models to make measurements in the consumer packaged-goods industry, we describe the evaluation of cents-off coupons. Coupons have grown in popularity as a marketing tool. According to data from NCH Promotional Services, 292 billion were distributed by U.S. marketers in 1991. Approximately 2.55% were redeemed (i.e., cashed in). The average face value was 54 cents per coupon, saving consumers about $4 billion. Retailers received $600 million in fees for handling the coupons, and the cost of distributing them was approximately $1.3 billion. Thus, the manufacturers are paying big dollars for coupons. But are these dollars profitable?

Prior to scanner panels manufacturers evaluated coupon effectiveness by counting the number of redemptions. This is inadequate because many of the customers who redeem coupons would buy the product anyway. Scanner panels have revealed much new information. Bawa and Shoemaker (1989) analyze a test versus control experiment run in IRI's BehaviorScan markets to determine incremental sales from a direct mail coupon. Because the authors have panel data, they are also able to determine that some market segments, for example, larger, more educated households who own their homes, tend to be more responsive than others. Such information is valuable for targeting promotional effort and essential to determining the overall profitability of the coupon drop. Here again we see the ability of customer data to add response information to conventional panel analysis.

However, test versus control experiments are relatively costly and time consuming. It would be desirable to determine the incremental sales produced by a coupon in an ongoing way from naturally collected data. Today this can routinely be done using a combination of household-level choice models and the panel records regularly collected from 60,000 households in 25 markets.

Here's how it works. A logit model is built to predict the purchase probability for each household in the panel. The calibration can be done over the year before the coupon drop. Then the model can project ahead to determine what the households would have purchased in the absence of the coupon. An example appears in Figure 7-2. The difference between actual and forecast sales, shaded in the figure, reveals the extra sales attributable to the coupon and becomes the basis of a report card for each coupon dropped. Once incremental sales are known, internal company records on product margins and the cost of producing, distributing, and redeeming the coupon serve to evaluate its profitability.

Decision Models

Customer data can also be used to build *decision models.* Brand-choice models like the multinomial logit have a rich potential as planning tools.

FIGURE 7-2
The shaded area, which is the difference between actual sales and predicted sales
without the coupon, measures the coupon's effectiveness at stimulating new purchases.

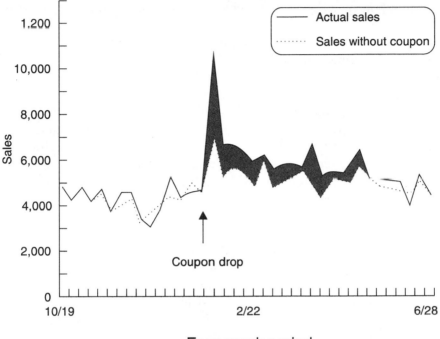

Four-week period

They are fully competitive, contain all the day-to-day elements of the
marketing mix as seen by the customer, and can be reliably calibrated
on scanner panel data. Coefficients estimated from the data tend to be
similar and stable from time period to time period and market to market
even as market shares and marketing activity change, thereby suggesting
that these parameters measure fundamental characteristics of the customer population.

However, the development of planning tools from household models
faces two major problems, *input transformation* and *output aggregation*.
By input transformation we mean: How can we convert managerial plans
into inputs for a household-level model? The difficulty arises because
the manufacturer sets a list price, but the household actually sees a shelf
price in a specific store in a specific week. The manufacturer designs
trade promotional programs with allowances per case, performance requirements for the trade, and timing over the year, whereas the household

sees particular features, displays, and price reductions in particular stores in specific weeks. The manufacturer designs a consumer promotion plan with coupons spaced out over the year with certain face values and distribution media. The household sees packets of coupon ads in the Sunday paper. And in the media advertising, the manufacturer will have a countrywide plan with chosen levels of GRPs directed at relevant target groups in various markets, probably arranged in flights and organized around particular dayparts. What the household receives, on the other hand, is advertising exposures on certain programs and days.

Provided that the input transformations can be made, our models of household response, principally the multinomial logit, are quite good and will predict for us the households' choices of products. However, then we encounter the second problem, output aggregation. This means taking the disaggregate choices and adding them up over many individual households and geographic regions to determine company performance measures such as sales and share.

We shall describe two approaches to handling input transformation and output aggregation. One is through *stochastic models*; the other, *natural scenarios*. A good example of stochastic modeling is the work of Wagner and Taudes (1986). Using an example based on a German diary panel, the authors built a comprehensive model of purchase timing and brand choice that incorporates the influence of marketing mix variables, seasonality, and trend. Certain assumptions are made about customer behavior. For example, they assume that the customer purchases are a Poisson process with a rate that varies over the population and is influenced by factors such as seasonality and the marketing mix. They carefully argue and support their model with data. The input transformation problem is handled by specifying aggregate control variables as directly influencing microparameters. It is assumed that the influences of the marketing mix are equal for all customers. Aggregation is done by analytic integration. The model is quite complete, although one property it lacks is purchase event feedback. In other words, the purchase of a particular brand does not have an influence on future purchases of that household, although most marketing managers would probably expect there to be one. Nevertheless, Wagner and Taudes present impressive results of tracking the shares of the products they have modeled.

Another good example of the stochastic modeling approach appears in Pedrick and Zufryden (1991). Their work focuses on the introduction of advertising into the decision model and on using the model results for setting media strategy with respect to reach and frequency.

The natural scenario is an alternative to stochastic models for handling input transformation and output aggregation. In this approach, one uses actual household histories as much as possible, thereby keeping the natural variation across the households in terms of their demographics and brand experiences, including loyalty, heterogeneity, and competitive conditions. Competitive conditions can, of course, be manipulated by the user in the same fashion as the marketing inputs for the target brand, but in many cases historical events are often a useful first approximation of what to expect in the future and avoid the effort of forecasting competitive action. In an application, the marketing manager specifies what he or she plans in terms of number of features and displays. Rules can be set for adding and deleting these events in the shoppers' environment over the evaluation period in response to increases or decreases in manufacturer trade promotions. The same goes for inserting or removing coupon drops and TV advertising. Simulation is done one household at a time and aggregation is the simple process of adding up the results over the household population of the database.

As an example in which the goal is to help allocate the marketing budget, we describe a study reported by Honnold, Brooks, and Little (1990). The application started with a laboratory market test in IRI's BehaviorScan facility. Levels of TV advertising and consumer promotion were experimentally varied and the results used to calibrate a nested logit model. As an indication of size and scope, the database contained two markets and 990 households, who, during the time period of the test, made 1,997 category purchases including 511 of the target product. These purchases were made in the course of 104,529 shopping trips. The database included information on distribution, features, display, coupons, other special events, and ad exposures.

The nested logit looks at brand choice as a two-step process. First, does the household buy a product in the category on the shopping trip? This is handled by the category purchase model. Then, if the household does buy within the category, what will be the brand and size selected? This is handled by the multinomial choice model. In commercial applications such as this, the models are large and inclusive. Table 7-1 lists the 24 variables used in the two submodels. Figure 7-3 portrays actual and predicted sales over the time period of the test for the product.

The model can now be used to evaluate marketing plans. We illustrate two. A *base plan* involves high TV advertising and three coupon drops. A *reallocation plan* employs low advertising and six coupons. To perform the evaluations, we must solve the two problems cited earlier, input

TABLE 7-1
Many variables have been uncovered that affect product choice. The commercial application of Honnold, Brooks, and Little (1990) models five brand sizes and uses the 24 variables shown here.

Brand-Choice Variables	Category-Choice Variables
advertising	category attractiveness
features (2 kinds)	nuggets inventory
displays (7 kinds)	propensity to buy nuggets
regular prices	spending on trip
price-cuts	advertising
manufacturer coupons	seasonality
brand loyalty	holidays
type loyalty (refrig/shelf stable)	alternative specific constants
target brand trial	
alternative specific constants	

transformation and output aggregation. In keeping with the natural scenario approach, except for the target brand, the households' decision environment of competitive activities, seasonality, and store characteristics is kept as in the historical record. Activity for the target brand is altered, e.g., coupon drops are added or removed, percentage of stores with displays increased or decreased, advertising exposures augmented or diminished, and so forth. Then the model determines household choices, which are added up to perform the output aggregation. Figure 7-4 shows simulated product sales under the base and reallocation plans. One can see the peaks introduced by the new coupon events. In this case it turns out that the reallocation plan generates a 17% increase in sales over the 52-week test period.

Abe (1991) has taken advertising modeling a step further and at the same time has retained the major features of the natural scenario approach. He calibrates a nested logit model on a BehaviorScan test in which advertising levels have been varied. Then he develops an input model that translates managerial plans, expressed as GRPs by daypart, into expected exposures for each household (determined from their actual TV watching histories), and goes on to calculate expected sales. In an illustrative example he shows that, for his product, a reallocation by daypart improves sales results.

A RESEARCH AGENDA

The above examples illustrate the methodologies available today and show that practical results can be obtained now. However, much work

FIGURE 7-3
The nested logit model shows an excellent fit between actual and predicted sales of the target brand.

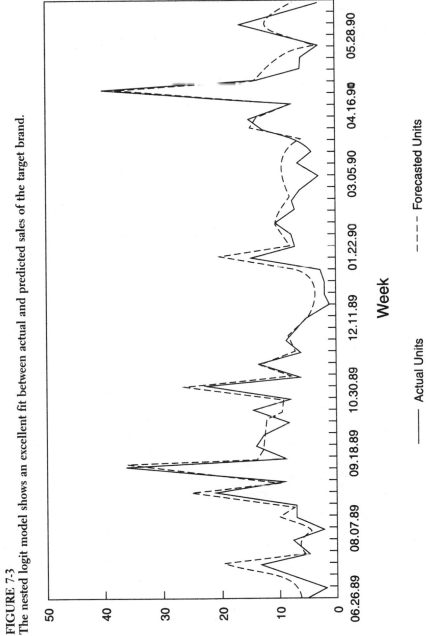

FIGURE 7-2
The nested logit model, used for marketing planning in the natural scenario method, compares the sales of the target brand under the base plan and a reallocation plan.

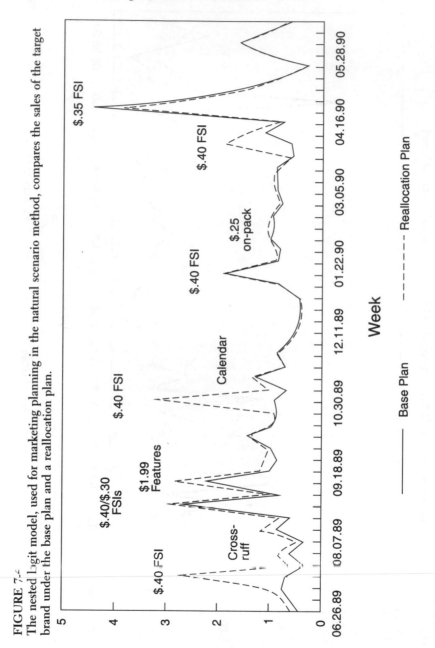

remains to be done. Here are several promising topics for a research agenda:

Choice modeling. Other techniques besides the multinomial logit should be investigated. The multinomial probit is in many ways the most flexible of choice models. Currim (1982) has shown some of its advantages. Perhaps recent advances in estimation techniques such as the method of simulated moments (McFadden, 1989) will make probit models viable for practical problems. The treatment of purchase timing by "hazard-function" modeling (Cox 1972) and semi-Markov models (Hauser and Wisniewski 1982) are beginning to be explored in scanner panel data (Jain and Vilcassim 1991 and Vilcassim and Jain 1991) and may prove fruitful. In a quite different direction, Currim and Schneider (1991) investigate a microapproach for describing consumer decision making. They develop a taxonomy of customer purchase strategies involving brand preferences, the promotional environment, and the household inventory policies. Household purchase histories are individually analyzed, classified, and clustered into groups. Although computationally intensive, their approach is a refreshingly different look at household purchase behavior. A related research direction is to explore the applicability neural network technology. Scanner panels contain many variables and large numbers of observations and so would appear to offer good opportunities for the strengths of neural nets in nonlinear estimation and pattern recognition.

Panel response. The task of expanding classic panel analysis of market status into a dynamic version that includes market response has hardly begun. So far we have choice models like the multinomial logit that incorporate price, merchandising, advertising, and other marketing control variables and that predict aggregate sales and market share very well. However, marketers want more detail. What is happening to penetration? Do heavy users respond differently from light users? What about frequency of purchase and average purchase size? The published literature reveals little testing of the models on such issues. But marketers need such information to reap the rewards of the big customer panel databases and their potential for understanding customer behavior. As part of this, there is a need to link behavioral theories into the models. Initial steps in this direction appear in Gurumurthy and Little (1989) and Hardie, Johnson, and Fader (1991), which investigate such issues as asymmetric response to price changes—customers react more negatively to price increases than they do positively to price decreases.

Decision models. The decision models of today are too much at the extremes: on the one hand, stochastic models with quite restrictive assumptions about customer behavior, and at the other, relatively cumbersome natural-scenario models. Especially, it would be desirable to make decision models directly usable by managers instead of depending on staff studies or consulting projects as they do now. This will require better input modeling, more efficient computational methods, and the development of appropriately easy-to-use interfaces. Some decision models might usefully be targeted at specific planning functions, e.g., the planning of advertising programs or of consumer promotion, whereas others will be needed that evaluate the whole marketing mix at once.

New industries. The methodologies originating in consumer packaged goods need to be adapted and amplified into other arenas. A candidate for early exploitation is pharmaceutical data. Furthermore, as has been demonstrated in the examples from school admissions and industrial customers, the models are by no means industry specific.

CONCLUSION

Customer-level information, particularly single-source data containing not only purchases but also marketing variables, is giving rise to new understanding of customer behavior and is leading to a new class of customer-level marketing mix models. These have produced practical commercial applications and will certainly lead to more. Many challenges remain in terms of fundamental research to be done in models, statistical methods and techniques to facilitate applying them to practical problems. Extensions to new arenas will further broaden the value of the methods.

REFERENCES

Abe, Makoto (1991). "A Marketing Mix Model Developed from Single-Source Data: A Semiparametric Approach." Ph.D. thesis, MIT, Cambridge, Mass.

Bawa, Kapil, and Robert W. Shoemaker (1989). "Analyzing Incremental Sales from a Direct Mail Coupon Promotion." *Journal of Marketing*, vol. 53 (July), pp. 66–78.

Ben-Akiva, M., and S.R. Lerman (1985). *Discrete Choice Analysis: Theory and Application to Travel Demand.* Cambridge, Mass: MIT Press.

Bucklin, Randolph E., and Sunil Gupta (1992). "Brand Choice, Purchase Incidence, and Segmentation: An Integrated Modeling Approach." *Journal of Marketing Research*, vol. 29, no. 2 (May), pp. 201–215.

Bucklin, Randolph E., and James M. Lattin (1992). "A Model of Product Category Competition among Grocery Retailers." *Journal of Retailing*, 68, 271–293.

Chatfield, C., A.S.C. Ehrenberg, and G.J. Goodhardt (1966). "Progress on a Simplified Model of Stationary Purchase Behavior." *Journal Royal Statistical Society A*, 129, 317–367.

Cox, D.R. (1972). "Regression Models and Life-Tables." *Journal Royal Statistical Society B*, 34, 187–200.

Currim, Imran S. (1982). "Predictive Testing of Consumer Choice Models Not Subject to Independence of Irrelevant Alternatives." *Journal of Marketing Research*, vol. 19 (May), pp. 208–222.

Currim, Imran S., and Linda G. Schneider (1991). "A Taxonomy of Consumer Purchase Strategies in a Promotion Intensive Environment." *Marketing Science*, vol. 10, no. 2 (Spring), pp. 91–110.

Ehrenberg, A.S.C. (1959). "The Pattern of Consumer Purchases." *Applied Statistics*, vol. 8, pp. 26–41.

——— (1988). *Repeat Buying*, 2d ed. New York: Oxford University Press.

Fader, Peter S., and James M. Lattin (1993). "Accounting for Heterogeneity and Nonstationarity in a Cross-Sectional Model of Consumer Purchase Behavior." *Marketing Science*, vol. 12, forthcoming.

Gensch, Dennis H. (1984). "Targeting the Switchable Industrial Customer." *Marketing Science*, vol. 3, no 1 (Winter), pp. 41–54.

Gensch, Dennis, Nicola Aversa, and Steven P. Moore (1990). "A Choice Modeling Marketing Information System That Enabled ABB Electric to Expand Its Market Share." *Interfaces*, vol. 20, no. 1 (January/February), pp. 6–25.

Goodhardt, G.J., A.S.C. Ehrenberg, and C. Chatfield (1984). "The Dirichlet: A Comprehensive Model of Buying Behavior." *Journal of the Royal Statistical Society*, A, 147, 621–655.

Guadagni, Peter M., and John D.C. Little (1983). "A Logit Model of Brand Choice Calibrated on Scanner Data." *Marketing Science*, vol. 2, no. 3 (Summer), pp. 203–238.

——— (1987). "When and What to Buy: A Nested Logit Model of Coffee Purchase." Sloan School of Management Working Paper 1919-87, MIT, Cambridge, Mass.

Gupta, Sunil (1988). "Impact of Sales Promotion on When, What, and How Much to Buy." *Journal of Marketing Research*, vol. 25, no. 4 (November), pp. 342–356.

Gurumurthy, K., and John D.C. Little (1989). "A Price Response Model Developed from Perceptual Theories." Sloan School of Management Working Paper 3038-89, MIT, Cambridge, Mass.

Hardie, Bruce G.S., Eric J. Johnson, and Peter S. Fader (1991). "Modeling Loss Aversion and Reference Dependence Effects on Brand Choice." Wharton Marketing Department Working Paper 91-025.

Hauser, John R., and Kenneth J. Wisniewski (1982). "Application, Predictive Test, and Strategy Implications for a Dynamic Model of Consumer Response." *Marketing Science*, vol. 1, no. 2 (Spring), pp. 143–179.

Honnold, Douglas J., Robert J. Brooks, and John D.C. Little (1990). "Logit for the Boardroom." Presentation at the 1990 Marketing Science Conference, University of Illinois, Champaign-Urbana, Ill.

Jain, Dipak C., and Naufel J. Vilcassim (1991). "Investigating Household Purchase Timing Decisions: A Conditional Hazard Function Approach." *Marketing Science*, vol. 10, no. 1 (Winter), pp. 1–23.

Levin, Gary (1991). "Tracing Ads' Impact." *Advertising Age*, November 4, 1991, p. 49.

Little, John D.C. (1970). "Models and Managers: The Concept of a Decision Calculus." *Management Science*, vol. 16, no. 8 (April), pp. B466–B485.

Massy, W.F., D.B. Montgomery, and D.G. Morrison (1970). *Stochastic Models of Buying Behavior*. Cambridge, Mass.: MIT Press.

McFadden, Daniel (1989). "A Method of Simulated Moments for Estimation of Discrete Response Models without Numerical Integration." *Econometrica*, vol. 57, no. 5 (September), pp. 995–1026.

Morrison, D.G., and D.C. Schmittlein (1981). "Predicting Future Random Events Based on Past Performance." *Management Science*, vol. 27, pp. 1006–1023.

———— (1988). "Generalizing the NBD Model for Customer Purchases: What Are the Implications and Is It Worth the Effort?" *Journal of Business and Economic Statistics*, vol. 6, pp. 145–160.

Pedrick, James H., and Fred S. Zufryden (1991). "Evaluating the Impact of Advertising Media Plans: A Model of Consumer Purchase Dynamics Using Single-Source Data." *Marketing Science*, vol. 10, no. 2 (Spring), pp. 111–130.

Punj, G.N., and R. Staelin (1978). "The Choice Process for Graduate Business Schools." *Journal of Marketing Research*, vol. 15, pp. 588–598.

Tellis, G.J. (1988). "Advertising Exposure, Loyalty, and Brand Purchase: A Two-Stage Model of Choice." *Journal of Marketing Research*, vol. 25, pp. 134–144.

Vilcassim, Naufel J., and Dipak C. Jain (1991). "Modeling Purchase-Timing and Brand-Switching Behavior Incorporating Explanatory Variables and Unobserved Heterogeneity." *Journal of Marketing Research*, vol. 28, no. 1 (February), pp. 29–41.

Wagner, Udo, and Alfred Taudes (1986). "A Multivariate Polya Model of Brand Choice and Purchase Incidence." *Marketing Science*, vol. 5, no. 3 (Summer), pp. 219–244.

8

LARGE-SCALE DATABASES: THE NEW MARKETING CHALLENGE

Robert C. Blattberg, Byung-Do Kim, and Jianming Ye

IN THEIR ATTEMPTS *to turn data into useful information, marketers are becoming increasingly overwhelmed by the exponential increase in the amount of data available. Even with rapid access, the ability to make actual marketplace decisions is constrained by managers' ability to process data into something meaningful in a timely fashion. As large-scale databases become the basis for the marketing decision support systems (MDSS) discussed in previous chapters, the need for both a general framework and specific techniques to analyze these data is becoming the new marketing challenge.*

This chapter presents such a framework—the idea of "mass-produced" models. Mass-produced models are statistical analyses of large databases where literally thousands of models are created for a single data set with little or no human intervention. The chapter begins by describing a typical application of MDSS to a large-scale database—the development of a "price simulator" for setting retail prices across many items in a product category. Next, the authors discuss the requirements necessary for models to be mass produced. Finally, the remainder of the chapter is devoted to an introduction to some specific statistical techniques for actually mass-producing models. This chapter should prove useful both for generalists searching for a framework within which to begin to approach the rather daunting task of how to analyze large-scale databases, and for technicians who have been charged with the task of actually producing models for marketplace decisions.

INTRODUCTION

The 1980s began the database revolution in marketing. Information Resources started producing electronic POS data at the beginning of the decade, followed by A.C. Nielsen and SAMI. Citicorp POS planned to build purchase histories for tens of millions of households, airlines have developed large frequent flyers databases, and NDL (National Demographics and Lifestyles) has compiled a database of 25 million households on lifestyle characteristics. Database marketing, born from direct marketing, is viewed as a new era in marketing by many because it combines detailed customer purchase behavior with one-on-one marketing techniques (see Chapter 3 this volume).

Databases offer tremendous promise to marketers, but many are overwhelmed by the quantity of data being produced. McCann and Gallagher (1990) provide the following table summarizing the magnitude of a typical database now available to a brand manager in a consumer packaged goods firm.

Data Volume by Type of Data

Type of Data	Size of Database (millions)
Store audit	1
Warehouse withdrawal	10
Market-level scanner	300
Chain-level scanner	500
Store-level scanner	10,000

McCann and Gallagher (1990) state (pp. 10–11):

> Consider a brand group that had been running its business with the old (bi-monthly) Nielsen data. They get 50,000 numbers every ninth week. Interviews with a number of these groups indicate that about five person-days would be devoted to analyzing these 50,000 numbers. This situation is not too bad: five days every ninth week.
>
> This same group operating with the market-level scanner data would receive two million numbers every week, a 40 times increase in the size of the data and a nine times increase in the frequency. Even if the group could become 40 times more efficient in their analysis, they would have to spend all the time analyzing the data.

They continue later on the same page:

> This data explosion means that the marketing managers have a difficult time capturing the opportunities in the data because of their sheer size. Data must be converted into information by applying marketing and analy-

sis knowledge. This knowledge application process may break down because of the size of the databases.

It has been commonly believed that systems such as Metaphor or DIS (data interpretation system),[1] which allow managers rapid access to data (see Chapter 4 this volume for a discussion of these systems), would make it possible for managers to transform raw marketing data into information to make better decisions. The problem is that rapid access to data, even if the manager can table or plot it, may not be enough. Going back to our consumer packaged-goods manager, suppose he or she has just obtained scanner data for one product category in each of 50 U.S. markets. Assume there are 100 relevant UPCs[2] and 100 weeks of data. The manager for just one product category—Procter & Gamble does business in approximately 100 categories—has 500,000 sales numbers to analyze, and there are usually five to ten causal measures associated with each sales statistic. It is impossible for this manager, even with DIS, to process these data efficiently.

More rapid data access, even if processed into information, does not translate into better decision making. As an analogy, consider the production of power from crude oil. Only through refinement can crude oil be transformed into gasoline, but, more important, only through sophisticated engines can it become power. Data are analogous to unrefined (crude) oil and Metaphor or DIS translates it into information (gasoline). But what is the engine that transforms information into power?

Continuing with our analogy, a statistical model[3] is the "engine" that transforms information into decisions. By taking marketing inputs, which are often summaries of raw data (hence information), and transforming them through a "model," information can then be used to directly make (or aid in making) decisions.

To help understand these issues we show how a retail pricing manager needs to use statistical models to make effective decisions from scanner

---

[1]DIS and its antecedent Metaphor are icon-driven systems which allow users to rapidly access and manipulate data from disparate sources. They provide graphics and report writing but do not offer sophisticated analytical tools to users.

[2]A UPC is the lowest reporting level provided by data vendors such as Nielsen. It is close to an SKU (stock-keeping unit) but is based on the universal product code (UPC), which serves as a unique identifier.

[3]Throughout this chapter, a model relates inputs (e.g., advertising) to outputs (e.g., sales). A statistical model uses some type of fitting procedure to estimate the unknown parameters of the model.

data. Suppose the data on price and quantity given in Table 8-1 were available. If one were to use a DIS, how would one interpret it? The manager would use DIS to plot the data. Figure 8-1 shows a plot of these data. Can the pricing manager make a decision? Unlikely. The manager might then compute the mean sales at each price point to see which maximizes profits. This helps, but is it optimal to price at $2.99 or $2.69, or, more important, should the price be set at a point other than the two

TABLE 8-1
Price and Quantity

Week	Sales (in units)	Price
1	1,056	$2.99
2	1,476	2.99
3	2,499	2.69
4	1,997	2.69
5	2,203	2.69
6	1,318	2.99

FIGURE 8-1
Price versus Sales

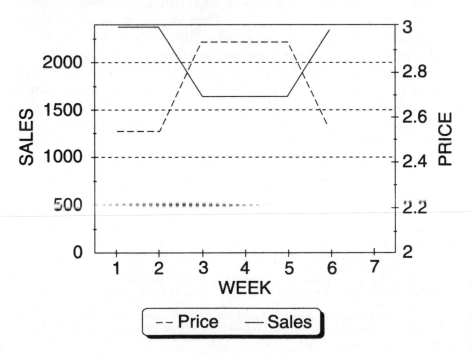

observed in the data? The manager must be able to develop a relationship between price and quantity in order to determine the optimal price.

To identify the relationship between price and sales, statistical estimation of the parameters of a mathematical model to relate price to quantity is used.[4] Using a log-log model[5] one can estimate a price elasticity for the data given in Table 8-1, which is (-5.3). This simple statistic in conjunction with a model allows the manager to determine the optimal price if the costs are known. For this example, and assuming a log-log model, if the cost of the item is \$2.00, the optimal price is $b/(b-1) \times c$ where b is the elasticity and c is the cost. For this example, the cost is 5.3; therefore the price is $5.3/4.3 \times \$2.00 = \$2.47$, which is clearly below the \$2.69 charged by the retailer. This example shows that simply tabling or plotting the data, the goal of DIS, is not enough for managers to make decisions. Some form of mathematical relationship between the input and the output is needed.

This issue is exacerbated when one recognizes that the pricing manager of a retail chain must make thousands of decisions every month. DIS or other sophisticated data-access tools, while beneficial, will not enable managers to use the information adequately to make decisions. The result is failure to harness a key resource, information.

What is needed to solve this dilemma? Mass production of models. Mass production of models means the ability to estimate the model's parameters using automated techniques so that each model that is estimated does not require a high "labor" content. Just as Henry Ford developed systems to produce automobiles en masse, models must also be produced en masse. If the U.S. auto industry or any other major U.S. industry in the 1990s relied solely on individual labor to build the product (not capital goods), the U.S. standard of living would be exceptionally low. Yet in building and estimating models we see a very high labor component and very little automation. The result—inefficient production. Whereas individually tailored products are usually better because they meet a specific need, their cost is very high and the number produced is too low. Mass production has led to widespread availability of products to a mass population. In building marketing models, the same principle

---

[4]We recognize that the amount of data in the example is limited and that the statistical estimation will not be highly reliable, but it will show the importance of models in transforming input data into recommended decisions.

[5]A log-log model is a model that is linear in the logs with dependent and independent variables logged. See equations 1–3 for examples of log-log models.

applies. By increasing the availability of models which are then used in a decision support system, marketing managers will be able to determine the marketing mix far more efficiently.

The remainder of this chapter discusses the requirements and methodological issues associated with mass-producing models. We will describe the unique problems model builders face and will offer some possible solutions when the number of models to be estimated shifts from ten to ten thousand. Specific issues that will be discussed are

- Models to Drive Decision Support Systems
- Mass-Producing Models
- Requirements for Mass-Produced Models to Be Used in Decision Support Systems
- Alternative Modeling Techniques Available to Produce Effective Mass-Produced Models

STATISTICAL MODELS AND DECISION SUPPORT SYSTEMS

Before discussing the general issue of mass-producing models, it is useful to discuss the use of models in decision support systems (DSS)[6] and why they enhance the use of large-scale databases. The types of statistical model that will be used here are designed to take a series of inputs and predict an outcome. For example, suppose a manager is responsible for setting price. If the manager knows the relationship between the input, price, and the output, sales, it is easy to determine the "optimal" price if costs are known. In the example given above, the mathematical relationship between price and sales was

$$S = a\,P^{-b} \tag{1}$$

where S is sales and P is price. Equation (1) allows the manager to evaluate different price levels to determine their impact on sales and profits. If a and b are known, then one can simply substitute them into the equation and determine the relationship between price and sales. In fact, equation (1) has an optimal price equals $b/(1-b) \times c$ where c is

---

[6]A decision support system, as will be used here, allows managers to use information, or, in our case, models, to make decisions. The manager is able to enter a series of inputs for the marketing mix, competition, costs, and other relevant factors and analyze how the decision criteria (e.g., sales, profits) change. See Chapter 4 for a more detailed discussion of DSS.

the unit cost. The manager could have the optimal price outputted once a and b are estimated.

To be able to use equation (1) to set price, it is necessary to know a and b because the firm usually knows its cost. To estimate a and b, a data set is required, similar to the data given in Table 8-1 which shows prices and sales. Statistical estimation is used based on a fitting criterion (usually minimizing the squared-error difference between actual sales and estimated sales) to estimate the unknown parameters, a and b. To estimate a and b for the data given in Table 8-1, a least-squares regression program was used with the inputs being the natural log of sales as the dependent variable and the natural log of price as the independent variable. The resulting estimates were a = 12.94 and b = −5.29. The pricing manager can now use the estimated values of a and b to set price. (In fact, only b is needed to set the optimal price.)

Price Simulator

To show a more complex example of the use of models in making decisions, a retail pricing decision support system called a price simulator will be briefly discussed. The goal of the pricing simulator is to set price for a complete product category. Currently, retailers set margin goals for each product category and then try to price so that they reach these margin goals. The problem with this approach is that it does not relate price to quantity sold. The goal of the pricing simulator is to determine the optimal (or near-optimal) prices for the category. For simplicity there will be three items in the category, and the specific demand model for each of the three items is given in equation (2).

$$S_{i,t} = \alpha_i(P_{i,t})^{-\beta_i} \, \Pi_{j \neq i}(P_{j,t})^{\beta_{ij}} \text{ for } i = 1, 2, 3 \qquad (2)$$

where $S_{i,t}$ = sales of item i at time t
$P_{i,t}$ = price of item i at time t
β_i = the own price coefficient for item i
β_{ij} = the cross-price coefficient for item i with item j

Notice that there are cross-price elasticities in the model as evidenced by coefficient β_{ij}. Table 8-2 gives the values of β_i and β_{ij} (e.g., own and cross-price elasticities). A solution to the optimal pricing for the three items can only be found through searching over numerous values of the three prices, p_1, p_2, p_3. Alternatively, the manager can try different prices and come close to the optimal prices.

Originally, management at the retail chain required that the pricing manager obtain a 25% gross margin for the category being analyzed. The 25% was set by management based on chain profit goals and their belief about the price sensitivity of the category. To do this the prices given in Table 8-3 were used along with the unit cost to the retailer. The profit margin for each item is given and the weekly profits and sales are also given. Note that item 1 is priced lower than items 2 and 3 because the store manager decided to aggressively price the leading item in the 96 oz subcategory—Tropicana.

Table 8-4 gives an alternative pricing policy in which the prices of items 2 and 3 are lowered and the gross margin percentage for the category is now significantly below the 25% (19.82%) required by management.

TABLE 8-2
Price Simulator—Example

Item Description	Own and Cross-Price Elasticity Matrix		
Minute Maid 96 oz	−8	0.5	0.5
Tropicana 96 oz	0.5	−7	0.5
Citrus Hill 96 oz	0.5	0.5	−7

TABLE 8-3
Price Simulator—Example Prices, Costs, and Profits

Item Description	Prices	Costs	Profit per Unit	Profit Percent	Sales (dollars)	Profit (dollars)
Minute Maid 96 oz	$2.79	$2.09	$0.70	25.09%	$2,272	$570
Tropicana 96 oz	$2.99	$2.09	$0.90	30.10%	$2,021	$608
Citrus Hill 96 oz	$2.99	$2.09	$0.90	30.10%	$2,021	$608
					$6,314	$1,787
Category				28.30%		

TABLE 8-4
Price Simulator—Example Prices, Costs, and Profits Alternate Plan

Item Description	Prices	Costs	Profit per Unit	Profit Percent	Sales (dollars)	Profit (dollars)
Minute Maid 96 oz	$2.49	$2.09	$0.40	16.06%	$4,533	$728
Tropicana 96 oz	$2.69	$2.09	$0.60	22.30%	$3,415	$762
Citrus Hill 96 oz	$2.69	$2.09	$0.60	22.30%	$3,415	$762
					$11,363	$2,252
Category				19.82%		

However, the profits are substantially higher than the retail manager's profits ($2,252 vs. $1,787), even though the margin percentage is below the goal set by the retailer.

This example demonstrates how a decision support system can improve profitability. To do this requires a mathematical model in which the parameters have been statistically estimated. The mathematical model relates prices to sales using the statistically estimated coefficients. Through the model, the retail pricing manager is able to improve performance by trying alternative prices and determining the quantity to be sold for each item and total category profits. Without a mathematical model, the manager must rely on "gut feel," or must match competition, neither of which may be optimal.

The major inhibitor in the use of the type of decision support system just described is the need to obtain coefficient estimates for thousands of statistical models quickly, which must not be counterintuitive or defy economic or marketing theory. If, for example, the price simulator produced a positive coefficient for a given item's own price elasticity, the optimal policy would be to increase the price of that item to infinity. No manager would do that, nor would the manager be willing to use the model for setting other prices. Therefore, sophisticated procedures are needed to ensure that a large number of models can be produced with feasible coefficient estimates. We call this "mass-producing" models.

MASS-PRODUCING MODELS

The last section established the importance of using models within DSSs in order to use information effectively to make decisions. Because of the vast quantities of data now available, in order to use models in conjunction with DSSs, it is necessary to mass-produce them. By mass-producing models, we mean producing thousands of models with little or no human intervention. This is very different from the traditional procedures used to produce statistical models. Most of the current models are used to design generic marketing policies. For example, an advertising-sales model establishes that carryover effects exist, so managers learn to recognize that advertising's effect is not immediate. Their policy becomes one of building advertising awareness and image through a long, concerted advertising campaign. In developing these types of models marketing academics and practioners who develop models often work with small data sets in which five or ten models are created.

Today's decision maker is in a different position. Information must be fed directly into a model. The pricing manager of a retailer or the trade marketing manager of a manufacturer has to make too many decisions too rapidly, which requires thousands of models to make item-specific decisions. Hence, they do not have the luxury of hand-made models. For data and information to be used effectively, models need to be made widely available, which requires producing them cost effectively. The solution is mass-produced models.

Many statisticians, marketing researchers, and academics are opposed to the concept of mass-produced models. Modeling is believed to be an art form, and many activities associated with statistical estimation and model building, such as residual analysis, are difficult to automate. Yet user needs, i.e., managers who need to rely on models, require models to be produced on a scale comparable to the databases available. Nielsen Marketing Research and Information Resources have begun mass-producing models because of the large number of models demanded by their client base. Some direct marketing firms also have devised methods to mass-produce models. The requirements and methods to mass-produce models have not been discussed in the literature, and the methods currently used are very similar to conventional model building. Yet as models are mass-produced, the techniques required to build them must change.

To understand the problems associated with mass-producing models for DSSs, we will return to the price simulator example. As we stated earlier, the purpose of a price simulator is to allow the price manager within a retail chain to evaluate profit and sales effects of proposed retail shelf-price changes. If the simulator is able to predict these effects accurately, then the retailer can price closer to the optimal level.

The category to be analyzed is refrigerated orange juice, and only five items will be used in this example. Table 8-5 gives a sample price and

TABLE 8-5
Sample Decision Support System Category Manager (refrigerated orange juice)

	Own and Cross-Elasticity Matrix					
Item Description	Trop 64 oz	MM 64 oz	Citr Hill 64 oz	Trop 96 oz	MM 96 oz	Priv Lab 96 oz
Tropicana 64 oz	−2.32	0.35	0.44	0.07	−0.05	0.43
Minute Maid 64 oz	0.48	−1.63	0.71	0.14	0.13	0.21
Citrus Hill 64 oz	0.36	0.06	0.98	−0.06	0.02	0.05
Tropicana 96 oz	1.40	0.01	0.38	−2.54	1.45	1.11
Minute Maid 96 oz	−0.31	0.96	0.17	0.41	−3.12	2.56
Private Label 96 oz	0.01	−0.45	0.05	0.06	0.21	−4.35

cross-price elasticity matrix. One should note that all diagonal elements of the table should be *negative*, implying that demand curves slope downward. Similarly, all cross-price elasticities should be *positive* because the items being analyzed are substitutes. Notice that in Table 8-5, not all entries have the correct sign. For example, Citrus Hill 64 oz has a positive price elasticity and MM 96 oz has a negative cross-price elasticity with respect to Tropicana 64 oz.

What are the implications of these incorrect signs? Suppose, as pricing manager for the chain, you decide to use the price simulator to test a reduced price of Citrus Hill, because the profit margin for Citrus Hill is higher than other items in the category and you would like to increase its volume. The current item prices are given in Table 8-6. You decide to reduce the price of Citrus Hill from $1.69 to $1.59 and see what impact it has on the sales of Citrus Hill and the category. The column titled "Item Sales at Regular Prices" shows the weekly sales of each item at the chain, and the one titled "Test Prices" shows that all of the other prices are held constant except for Citrus Hill's price. The sales estimates for the test prices are listed in the column titled "Item Sales at Test Prices." It shows the disturbing result that for the proposed price decrease for Citrus Hill 64 oz, all items, including Citrus Hill 64 oz, lose sales. Part of the decline in item sales is expected because competitive items are likely to lose sales because of a price reduction from Citrus Hill. However, the sales of Citrus Hill should increase and, as important, the sales increase for Citrus Hill should be larger than the loss in sales for the other items in the category.

This simple example shows what happens when the statistical estimates for price elasticities do not meet certain conditions. The decision support system, which relies on these coefficients, produces erroneous recommendations which a manager would quickly reject. It is essential, therefore,

TABLE 8-6
Price Evaluation Using Category Manager

Item Description	Regular Prices	Test Prices	Item Sales at Regular Prices	Item Sales at Test Prices	Difference
Tropicana 64 oz	1.69	1.69	1,710	1,665	−45
Minute Maid 64 oz	1.69	1.69	1,290	1,235	−55
Citrus Hill 64 oz	1.69	1.59	334	315	−19
Tropicana 96 oz	2.39	2.39	1,257	1,228	−29
Minute Maid 96 oz	2.39	2.39	694	687	−7
Private Label 96 oz	1.89	1.89	7,343	7,321	−22

that the price and cross-price elasticities have the correct signs and sensible magnitudes.

The example just described raises the question of how prevalent are coefficients with the wrong signs for price? Obviously, no generalization can be made, but to offer some evidence of the magnitude of the problem, a set of store-level POS data for canned tuna, 6.5 oz size, was analyzed using the following model:

$$\ln S_t = \alpha + \beta \ln P_t + \delta \ln(DD_t + 1) + \gamma \ln RP_t + \Sigma_j \, \tau_j \, \ln X_{j,t} \quad (3)$$

where S_t = the sales of the brand being studied
    P_t = the shelf price of the brand being studied
    DD_t = the deal discount, which is simply the shelf price minus the deal price divided by the shelf price
    RP_t = the relative shelf price of the brand, which is its price divided by the weighted average of all prices in the market with the weight being the long-term market shares of the brand
    $X_{j,t}$ = other explanatory factors such as trend and other adjustments based on the store environment

One might quarrel with the model used but it is a log-log model and will help illustrate the magnitude of the problem encountered by modelers who are producing coefficients for decision support systems.

In the market being analyzed, Chicago, data were available for three chains at the store level for four brands (which account for a high percentage of retail sales and item sales). Table 8-7 summarizes the coefficient estimates for price and deal discount and indicates the number of times the signs were correct. Note that for each chain, there were multiple stores, each with a coefficient estimate. For example, for chain 1—brand 3, there were 28 stores in the sample and 24 had the wrong sign for price. Figure 8-2 presents a bar graph of the estimated price elasticities sorted by magnitude for the largest chain in the market. One can see that about 30% of the estimated price elasticities have the wrong sign (the elasticities should be negative).

Whereas this analysis is for just one category, the problems encountered are commonplace in most modeling of POS data. Blattberg and George (1991) present results for a different category. The problem is that the statistical techniques that are commonly used (e.g., ordinary least squares) cannot ensure correct signs and magnitudes, adjust for outliers, or provide

TABLE 8-7
Price and Deal Coefficient Effects

Chain	Brand	Price Elasticities		Deal Coefficients	
		Mean	Percentage Wrong Signs	Mean	Percentage Wrong Signs
1	1	− 0.094	42.9%	5.047	0.0%
1	2	0.640	28.6	4.984	0.0
1	3	1.341	85.7	6.669	0.0
1	4	− 4.066	0.0	7.153	0.0
2	1	− 1.060	0.0	4.685	0.0
2	2	− 1.430	0.0	5.343	0.0
2	3	− 2.030	0.0	6.018	0.0
2	4	− 0.243	0.0	1.948	25.0
3	1	0.811	33.3	5.775	0.0
3	2	− 0.653	3.7	2.927	0.0
3	3	− 0.537	29.6	6.291	0.0
3	4	− 2.089	0.0	4.844	0.0

time-varying parameter estimates. Because of these limitations, it is necessary to move to a new generation of statistical techniques used in marketing which allows users to mass-produce models while ensuring that they can be used effectively within a decision support system. Below a brief discussion is given of the requirements of the new generation of statistical modeling techniques required to mass-produce models.

REQUIREMENTS FOR MODELS TO BE USED IN DECISION SUPPORT SYSTEMS

For models to be mass-produced and simultaneously used effectively in DSSs, they must meet certain user requirements. Little (1970) described a set of criteria for models, and we will adapt some of these to make them relevant to mass-produced models. The models must

- Predict accurately
- Provide the correct signs and magnitudes for the coefficients
- Adapt to a changing environment
- Incorporate competitive effects within product lines, categories, and across firms
- Require minimal human intervention
- Be updated automatically

FIGURE 8-2
Price Elasticities Across Stores Chain 3 — Brand 1

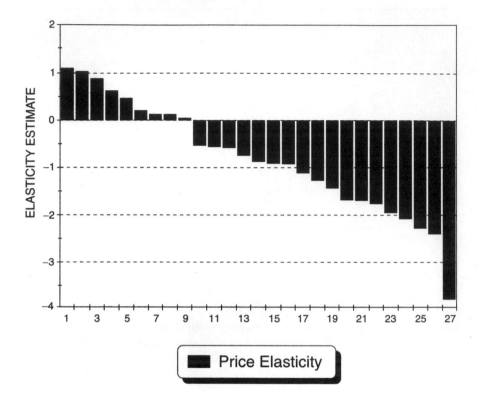

Predicts Accurately

Whereas accurate model prediction does not ensure good models, it is necessary before managers will rely on the model's results. For obvious reasons, if managers see poor predictions, they reject the model. Predictive accuracy serves as an "implicit" validation of the model, though good model predictions must be tempered by correct signs and magnitudes. This often requires a critical trade-off by modelers who might choose less-predictive accuracy in order to maintain correct signs and magnitudes of coefficients.

Correct Signs and Magnitudes

One of the most common uses of models is to conduct "what-if" analyses, as shown above. The basis for "what-if" analyses is the model's coefficients. It is critical to produce coefficient estimates that generate reasonable managerial decisions. Correct signs for coefficients (e.g., negative price elasticities) and reasonably estimated magnitudes for the coefficient estimates are required. This is a major challenge when working with a large number of models.

Adapting to a Changing Environment

The models built must be able to (1) capture changing marketing mix effectiveness and (2) adapt as new information becomes available. A variety of factors cause the changing effectiveness of marketing mix variables such as promotional and price sensitivity changes because of economic conditions, new product introductions, changing consumer behavior, and constantly changing competitive strategies. Below we discuss an example of changing promotional effects and describe alternative procedures to incorporate time-varying effects into statistical models.

Little Human Intervention

It is impossible to analyze 1,000 models manually. Cost to the user is prohibitive, and models must be built in a short time frame, otherwise their value diminishes to the user. This requires modeling procedures that use expert or smart systems with little or no human intervention to estimate and evaluate coefficients and predictions and to provide diagnostic information (see McCann and Gallagher 1990). Users must recognize the trade-off between highly individualized models (more accurate) and mass-produced models created with smart systems (large number of models built quickly). Only if models can be mass-produced will databases be used effectively, because managers and analysts cannot process the vast quantities of data generated by the systems. Thus, a critical requirement is to develop models that require little human intervention.

Automatic Model Recalibration

On a periodic basis, models need to be recalibrated. Coefficients need to be reestimated, variables added or removed, and occasionally the model structure modified. Because of limited staff availability in most companies, it is necessary to update the models automatically. This can be accomplished by the model builder analyzing subsets of data, designing new model structures, and then using smart systems to build the models. The updating procedure must be fast and relatively low cost, because users do not want high variable costs every time their models need to be recalibrated. If the recalibration is slow, firms will not update their models as frequently as required.

Automatic Model Selection

In some situations, there may be competing models or a need to search through data to develop hypotheses by studying the relationship between residuals and other variables. Using some form of automated model selection would be highly advantageous in these cases. McCann and Gallagher (1990) discuss automating the modeling process, but it is also necessary to automate residual analysis and, potentially, model selection.

STATISTICAL PROCEDURES TO MASS-PRODUCE MODELS

In the past 20 years, statistical techniques have been developed that help modelers estimate parameters to be used in decision support systems. This section begins with a description and overview of alternative estimation procedures which can be used separately or in combination to aid in mass-producing models. Advanced techniques are required to ensure parameter estimates that provide sensible decisions from a DSS. The section ends with three examples of techniques that can be used to mass-produce models.

Alternative Estimation Procedures

The requirements listed above provide us with some general direction as to the statistical techniques we should use to model the data. Table 8-8 lists the user requirement and the statistical technique or methodology that can be used to meet the user's needs. This list is not exhaustive, and user

TABLE 8-8
Alternative Modeling Approaches

User and Technical Requirement	Modeling Approach
Fast	Variants of Ordinary Least-Squares Regressions
Not Vulnerable to Extreme Values	Robust Methods
Correct Signs and Magnitudes	Empirical Bayes Methods, Penalty Functions, or Constrained Estimation
Time-Varying Parameters	Kalman Filter or Nonparametric Procedures
Automated Diagnostics	Expert Systems

needs will depend upon the specific application being studied. Below is a brief description of each requirement and methodology that can be used.

Fast. This is one of the most difficult and important issues that need to be addressed, because some of the tools recommended later may decrease speed. However, because of the large number of models being built, it is necessary to use routines that provide estimates as quickly as possible. Traditional regression procedures which require no searching across parameters usually offer the fastest estimation procedure, whereas more sophisticated procedures, explained below, may require several iterations to search for parameter estimates. In the future this will be less of a problem because of the availability of high-powered workstations and other fast scientific computers.

One procedure that can be employed to speed up estimation is pooled regression. Pooled regression is a simple variant of ordinary least-squares (OLS) and can be easily programmed using existing packages. One form of pooled estimation assumes all coefficients are identical across cross-sections (except for the intercepts). This significantly reduces the number of parameters that need to be estimated. For example, in modeling store-level POS data, pooled estimation assumes the same effects across stores. Thus, the price and promotional effects are identical across all stores within a chain or market if data are pooled at the market level. It is generally superior to running OLS on the aggregated data (Wittink, Porter, and Gupta 1991).

Not vulnerable to extreme values. It is commonplace to have outliers caused by data collection errors, incorrect causal data, or a random event. When the outliers significantly influence the model's estimates, incorrect signs and magnitudes can result. Robust methods, which are "less vulnerable" to outliers, deal with these types of data problems and are well established in the statistical literature. These methods either omit points (outliers) or use a different criterion than least-squared errors to select the estimates. Below we discuss robust estimation and show what happens when outliers appear in point-of-sale data.

Correct signs and magnitudes of coefficients. In the price simulator example given above, the primary problem that kept recurring was incorrect signs or incorrect magnitudes. To provide coefficient estimates that have the correct magnitudes and signs, constrained estimation or the use of penalty functions can be used. These are discussed below. An alternative procedure is to use shrinkage estimators, which takes a weighted average of the estimate for a given cross-section (e.g., a store or a market), and the estimate across all the cross-sections (see Blattberg and George 1991 for a more detailed discussion). Thus, shrinkage estimators do not allow a given cross-sectional estimate to be too large or too small in absolute magnitude relative to the overall estimate for the entire data set. In general, this can improve the number of correct signs and can avoid estimates whose magnitudes appear to be out of range.

Time-varying effects or time-adjusted estimates. As stated earlier, it is unlikely that marketing effects are constant because of changing economic conditions and perturbations in the market. Several procedures are available to allow the model's underlying parameters to have their estimates updated as new data become available. We showed an example in which the effects of promotions are changing over time and described one procedure that can be used to estimate this changing effect. Another procedure mentioned below is a Kalman filter, which works like exponential smoothing except that the parameter, not the sales, estimate is updated. Without adjusting for changing parameter estimates, the DSS may under- or overestimate the impact of a given marketing mix variable.

Automated diagnostics. Because it is necessary to identify poor models, it is necessary to automate the diagnostic tests one usually performs visually. For this reason, some type of expert system in combination with various diagnostic tests can be used. McCann and Gallagher (1990) describe the use of expert systems to do this type of analysis. Schmitz (1993) discusses the use of estimates of abnormal points to trigger a written text. Combining diagnostic tests with a written script would aid the researcher in identifying likely problems. For example, if the Durbin-Watson statistic were used for determining whether or not serial correlation was present and its value appeared to be outside the normal bounds of the test, then the test would indicate serial correlation might be present and could recommend specific "fixes" to the model to reduce the level of serial correlation. The modeler is looking at thousands of models, so some type of scenario analysis would be highly beneficial to speed up the diagnosis of modeling problems.

Several Alternative Estimation Procedures to Mass-Produce Models for DSSs

When mass-producing models, the user does not have the luxury of evaluating every model because thousands are being built. Yet serious problems in using the models in a DSS can occur if the modeling techniques do not "guarantee" coefficient estimates that produce sensible decisions. This section shows the need to develop alternative modeling procedures by giving examples from POS data. Several techniques are recommended to overcome some of these problems. Specifically, the problems to be discussed are outliers, incorrect signs, and time-varying effects. In each case, the DSS implications are shown.

Robust regression. Robust regression has been used for many years, being first recognized as a mechanism to avoid weighing large outliers as heavily as OLS. Minimizing the absolute value of the residual (often called MAE regression or, more recently, l_1 regression) is used in order to reduce the influence of certain overly influential data points. By weighting extreme points less (or omitting them), it is hoped that contaminated observations count less.

The theory of robust regression (and robust estimation in general) assumes that there are contaminated (errors in the independent variables or the dependent variable) points that, if identified, should be removed from the analysis. Figure 8-3 shows an example of some data in which

FIGURE 8-3
Sales and Promotions (contaminated points indicated)

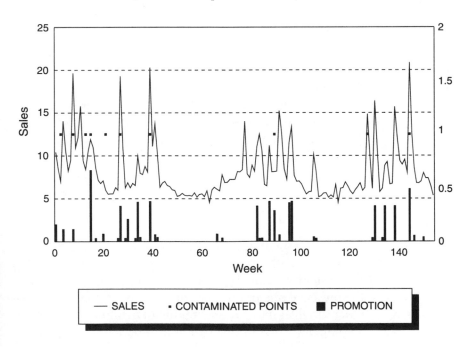

it is fairly clear that there are contaminated points at weeks 38 and 65 as well as weeks 14 and 88. Contaminated points in POS data are often caused by (1) missing causal data (e.g., a promotion occurred and was not recorded), (2) inaccurate causal data (e.g., indicating a promotion when none occurred), and (3) inaccurate sales data (e.g., a week of data does not include all days or it includes more than a week because of inaccurate transmission of the data to the host). There are also likely to be many other causes such as "out-of-stocks," changing competitive activity, and new product introductions which are beyond the control of the firm. The critical issue is identifying the contaminated points and using procedures that are robust to both "X" and "Y" contamination—Y contamination is contaminated data points for the dependent variable and X contamination is for the independent variables. Many robust procedures focus only on contamination of the dependent variables and hence miss problems because of inaccurate causal variables. This problem will be highlighted later with an example.

One method that appears to be robust with respect to both types of contamination (the independent variable and dependent variable) is least median squared estimation (LMS) (see Rousseeuw and Leroy 1987). There is also a related trimmed OLS procedure which determines the observations to remove by using the residuals from LMS, sorting them, and removing the top and bottom k%.

To see how LMS and trimmed OLS work, a data set was used from a consumer product company in which it is likely that there are "contaminated points." The contamination in this data set is caused by (1) omitted causal data and (2) incorrect causal data. The sales and promotional data were plotted in Figure 8-3. In week 38 there is a large sales increase but only a small promotion is indicated, and in week 65 there is no peak but there is an indication of a promotion. There are other contaminated points in the data set.

The first estimates to be presented are OLS. The model used is

$$\ln(S_t) = \alpha + \beta_1 P_t + \beta_2 PD_t + \gamma_1 P_{t-1} + \gamma_2 P_{t-2} \qquad (4)$$
$$+ \gamma_1 P_{t-3} + \Sigma_j \delta_j X_{tj} + \tau CP_t$$

where S_t = sales for the item at time t for the item being analyzed
 P_t = the presence of a promotion (0,1) for the item at time t
 PD_t = the promotional discount in cents for the item at time t
 P_{t-i} = the presence of a promotion for the item at time $t-i$ (0,1)
 X_{tj} = other variables in the model for the item or market at time t
 CP_t = a competitive item's promotion at time t

Table 8-9 displays the parameter estimates from OLS, and it is clear that there are several problems with the OLS estimates. The sign for the dollar magnitude of the promotional effect is negative, which implies that as the promotional allowance offered increases, sales decrease. Clearly this is unlikely to be true. The optimal decision based on this model is to offer zero price discount or even a negative price discount which is clearly wrong.

Two alternative estimation methods are the robust procedure described above. Table 8-9 also shows these parameter estimates. Figure 8-4 shows the predictions from the trimmed OLS procedure and the OLS predictions along with an indicator for the omitted points. By omitting these points, the estimated promotional effect becomes positive. Whereas some researchers may find omitting points to improve estimation to be counterintuitive, it generally results in superior estimates.

We will now compare the implications of four estimation procedures — OLS, LMS, trimmed OLS 3%,[7] trimmed OLS 10% — in a decision support system. The promotional discount was increased from \$.10 to \$.50. (See Figure 8-5.) For the OLS and LMS estimates, sales decreased (the multiplicative coefficient is less than one). Trimmed OLS, on the other hand, resulted in an increase in sales when the promotional discount was increased, which is clearly more plausible. Thus, by using "robust" methods, estimates with the correct sign were produced. OLS, because it uses contaminated points in obtaining its estimates, resulted in poorer estimates, even though the model fits were better.

Constrained regression and penalty functions. One way to guarantee that parameter estimates lie within the correct range is to use some

TABLE 8-9
Comparison of Modeling Procedures Coefficient Estimates

	Promotional Discount	Cannibalization	Presence of Promotion
Ordinary Least-Squares	−0.0699	−3.7447	1.9724
Least Median Squares	−1.0999	6.8298	1.7327
Ordinary Least-Squares Trimmed 10%	0.4022	−5.3270	1.4356
Ordinary Least-Squares Trimmed 3%	0.1449	−4.3677	1.7422

---

[7] Three percent and 10% refer to the percentage of points trimmed. For example, 3% means the highest and lowest percent of the points are deleted from the estimation sample and then OLS is run on the remaining points.

FIGURE 8-4
Trimmed versus OLS Comparison of Fitted Values

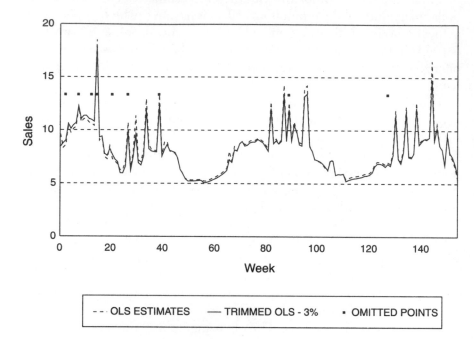

--- OLS ESTIMATES   — TRIMMED OLS - 3%   · OMITTED POINTS

form of constrained regression. The constraint can be of the form that the parameter estimate must be greater than a given value, such as requiring promotional coefficients to be positive or requiring that the price coefficient be negative. A related procedure is to use a criterion function which significantly increases the loss measure (e.g., squared-error loss) when the parameter estimate has the wrong sign or magnitude. For example, if the criterion function is least-squared error, then another penalty can be added to the sum of squared errors, which determines the distance of the parameter estimate from the constraint. As the parameter estimate moves closer to the "constraint," the penalty increases, and since the goal is to minimize the criterion function, the resultant estimate is unlikely to violate the constraint. Let us define β to be a vector of parameter values. Instead of minimizing RSS(β), the method of penalized least-squares estimates β by minimizing

$$P_{LS} = RSS(\beta) + P(\beta) \tag{5}$$

where $P(\beta)$ is a function that penalizes the values of the vector of parameters β and RSS(β) is the sum of squares from the OLS estimate.

FIGURE 8-5
Multiplicative Promotional Effect Deal Increase from 10 to 50 Cents

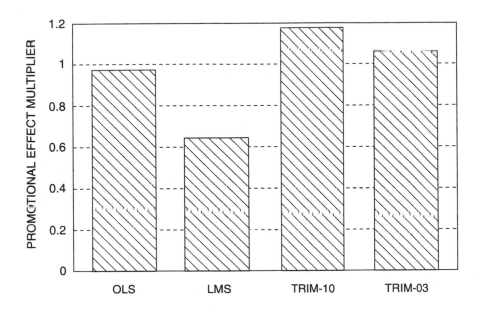

The difference between constrained estimation and the use of a penalty function is that constrained estimates are usually set to the constraint value when the parameter estimate violates the constraint, whereas the penalty function estimate is often away from the constraint. However, it is an empirical issue as to which procedure is superior.

To better understand the penalty function and constrained estimates, it is beneficial to use an example. The data set to be used is POS data for a frequently purchased product category sold through grocery retailers. Four major brands exist in this market, and the goal is to estimate price and cross-price elasticities as well as the promotional effects. Three estimation procedures were used: OLS, constrained OLS (CLS), and penalized least-squares (PLS). The model used in the analysis is

$$\ln(S_{i,k,t}) = \alpha_k + \Sigma_i \ \beta_{i,k,1} \ SP_{i,k,t} + \beta_{i,k,4} \ D_{i,k,t} \qquad (6)$$
$$+ \beta_{i,k,3} \ DISP_{i,k,t} + \beta_{i,k,4} \ F_{i,k,t}$$

where $\ln(S_{i,k,t})$ = Log sales at time t for brand i at store k
$SP_{i,j,t}$ = Shelf price at time t for brand i at store k

$D_{i,k,t}$ = Percentage deal discount at time t for brand i at store i

$DISP_{i,k,t}$ = Indicator variable at time t if brand i at store k is displayed

$F_{i,k,t}$ = Indicator variable at time t if brand i at store k is feature advertised

For the parameters used above the following desirable ranges were identified:

Constant	(0,100)		
Own-price	(−2,−20)	cross-price	(0,10)
Own-deal discount	(0,10)	cross-deal discount	(−10,0)
Own-display	(0,10)	cross-display	(−10,0)
Own-feature advertising	(0,10)	cross-feature advertising	(−10,0)

The parameter ranges above were derived using two key factors: (1) theoretically derived signs for the variables, and (2) likely ranges based on an "optimization" model. Regarding the signs of the variables, the price coefficient must be negative, own promotion positive, cross-elasticities positive, and cross-promotion effects negative. If one assumes a simplistic optimization model such that promotional and price decisions are independent in the semilog formulation given in equation (5), the optimal price is $c - c\{1/(-\beta + 1)\}$. For the item being modeled, the cost (to the retailer) is 1.00, and so if we set $\beta_1 = -2$, then the optimal price is $1.00 - 1.00 (1/(-2 + 1)) = 2.00$ or the price is twice the cost. If the coefficient is -20, then the optimal price is $1.00 - 1.00 (1/(-20 + 1)) = 1.053$ or a 5.3% markup. For the category being considered, a markup smaller than 5% (and hence a larger coefficient) is unlikely to make sense. Similar analyses can be conducted for the other coefficients. To use penalty functions, it is therefore important to set realistic ranges for the coefficients. These ranges can be set using relatively simple optimization models.

Another constraint, not added in this analysis, is that the sum of the cross-elasticities weighted by their sales volume must be less than the own price elasticity multiplied by its volume. If this does not hold, then a price decrease for one brand can actually decrease total category sales in units. Although this could occasionally occur in estimation without restraints, it is unlikely to happen very often in practice.

The specific penalty function used for the price elasticity coefficient is $e^{\lambda(\beta_1 + 2)} + e^{-\lambda(\beta_1 + 20)}$ which implies that when the value of β_1 is greater than -2, the first element of the penalty function becomes large. If, on the other hand, the value of β_1 is less than -20, the second term becomes large. Thus, when the values of β_1 go outside the range of the constraint, the penalty function value, $P(\beta)$, becomes large. Because the goal is to minimize the penalized least-squares function with respect to the parameter β_1, it is likely that the parameter β_1 will lie within the range set by the model builder. The same form of the penalty function is used for the other parameters, but the constant added or subtracted in the exponent is different.

The constrained regression model works roughly the same way. Rather than creating a penalty function, it requires that the coefficient estimate (1) lies within a range, (2) is greater than, or (3) is less than a given value. When that constraint is violated, the estimate is usually set at the constrained value making the constraint the critical point in the estimation procedure. Penalty functions provide greater flexibility because one usually wants the estimated value to be significantly different from the constraint.

To compare how the two procedures work, a set of parameter estimates were computed using both constrained model estimation and penalty function estimation. The data set was available for two brands in three chains. The two brands represent in excess of 80% of the volume within the subcategory they represent. Table 8-10 presents the coefficient estimates for three models at one store: ordinary least-squares (OLS), constrained least-squares (CLS), and penalized least-squares (PLS). Two

TABLE 8-10
Ols vs. Constrained and Penalized Least-Squares Chain 2—Store 5

Procedure		Deal	Feature			Squared Error	
Intercept		Discount	AD	Display	Price	in Sample	81-121
			Brand 1	Own Effects			
OLS	2.06	3.64	0.36	0.99	2.84	18.57	469.26
PLS	1.88	3.20	0.60	1.00	−4.45	21.82	8.18
CLS	1.11	3.35	0.54	1.00	−2.00	19.62	14.96
			Brand 2	Cross Effects			
OLS		0.02	−0.59	0.07	18.27		
PLS		−0.93	−0.21	−0.08	3.60		
CLS		−0.35	−0.48	−0.02	4.22		
			Brand 3	Cross Effects			
OLS		1.93	0.09	−1.12	−18.48		
PLS		0.12	0.13	−0.64	2.06		
CLS		0.00	0.00	−0.44	0.00		
			Brand 4	Cross Effects			
OLS		−0.93	0.51	−0.53	−6.70		
PLS		−0.64	0.20	0.20	0.18		
CLS		0.00	0.00	0.00	0.00		

criteria were reported to evaluate the "quality" of the two models: (1) the objective function value for the fitted sample, which is the sum of squared errors excluding the constraints or penalty functions, and (2) the predictive sum of squared errors between the predicted and actual logged sales. These are also reported in Table 8-10. Approximately 33% (40 out of 121) of the observations were excluded for the hold-out sample. The objective function criterion for the fitted sample shows the degree to which OLS fits the estimation sample better than either CLS or PLS, which one would expect theoretically. However, the prediction results show that OLS performs worse than the other two methods.

If one aggregates across all stores, PLS and CLS perform about the same with respect to predictive sum of squared errors. However, it should be noted that PLS generally results in estimates that imply a much greater effect for marketing variables than CLS. Whereas predictive testing is important, the ultimate goal of these procedures is in a DSS. If one believes that many of the promotional effects are masked because of other factors or because of errors in the causal data, then techniques that estimate higher promotional effects may not fit the data as well but may lead to more profitable decisions. Clearly, more testing of these procedures is necessary and will be the focal point of future research in this area, including determining the effect of different penalty function models.

Time-varying parameters. As was discussed earlier, a serious problem in estimating a model's coefficients using long time-series is that the coefficients can vary over time. Several methods can be used to model data of this type. One typical approach is to segment the data into several subintervals and apply fixed-parameter model estimation to each. Another is to use "moving-window estimation" in which the subinterval is gradually changing. (See Hartie and Tibshirani 1990, Cleveland 1979, and Eubank 1988 for a detailed discussion of the use of moving-window estimation.) It is also possible to model the coefficients as a function which depends upon time. An alternative is to model the parameters in a stochastic fashion. Let X_t be the vector of independent variables and Y_t the dependent variable. We model the data by

$$Y_t = \Sigma_i X_{i,t}\, \beta_{i,t} + \epsilon_t \tag{7a}$$

$$\beta_{i,t} = \beta_{i,t-1} + v_{i,t} \tag{7b}$$

where ϵ_t and $v_{i,t}$ each are normally distributed with mean 0 and variance σ^2_ϵ and δ^2_v, respectively. The coefficient $\beta_{i,t}$ at time t depends upon $\beta_{i,t-1}$ at time $t-1$ with a small variation. This model assumes that the coefficient for promotions, price, and other factors vary over time. If $v_{i,t} = 0$ for a given parameter, then it is assumed to be a fixed parameter. The time-varying coefficients can then be estimated by the popular Kalman filter model, or, in simple cases, by maximum likelihood estimates directly. (See Judge et al. 1980 for a detailed description of how the procedure works and Chui and Chen 1991 for examples of the application of the Kalman filter.)

To illustrate how this method works, we used a data set for bathroom tissue supplied by Dominick's Finer Food Co., a major grocery chain in the Chicago area. The model is applied to sales data for two brands, Charmin and Northern, one of its major competitors:

$$\ln(S_t) = T_t + \beta_t P_{i,1} - \gamma_{t,2} P_{i,t} + \Sigma_j \delta_j X_{j,t} + \epsilon_t^2 \tag{8a}$$

$$T_t = T_{t-1} + \epsilon_t^T \tag{8b}$$

$$\beta_t = \beta_{t-1} + \epsilon_t^\beta \tag{8c}$$

where $\ln(S_t)$ = Log sales at time t
T_t = Trend at time t
$P_{i,1}, P_{i,2}$ = Percent price reduction at time t for Charmin and Northern
$X_{j,t}$ = Non-time varying variables

and ϵ_t^S, ϵ_t^T, ϵ_t^β are normally distributed random noise with unknown variance.

Figure 8-6 shows a plot of β_t, the coefficient for promotion for Charmin, along with the OLS coefficient estimates which assume β_t is constant. One sees that the promotional effect increases in the latter part of the series as the promotional discount decreased and the frequency increased.

Figure 8-7a and Figure 8-7b show the fitted values for the time-varying parameter model compared to the OLS fitted values and to the actual sales (in logs). One sees that OLS produces lower predictions than the time-varying parameter model, partially because it does not pick up the changing effect of the promotion in the latter periods as shown in Figure 8-6. The promotional spikes in the actual data do not show as large a decline in the size of the spikes in the latter part of the data, and the time-varying parameter model produces larger estimates (similar to the actual) in the last part of the data because it "recognizes" this change in promotional effect.

For a marketing manager, it is extremely important to understand that the effects of promotions are actually increasing (or decreasing) because

FIGURE 8-6
Time-Varying Coefficients Estimates OLS versus Time-Varying Estimates

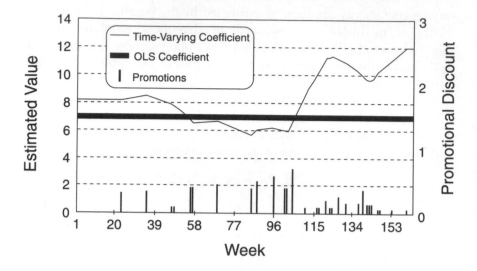

FIGURE 8-7a
Time-Varying Coefficients Comparison of Fitted Values

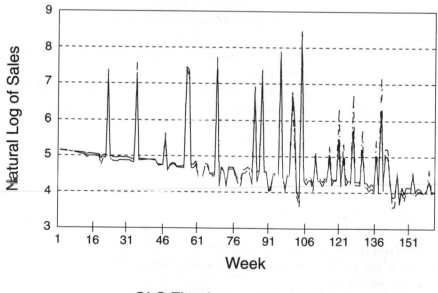

FIGURE 8-7b
Time-Varying Coefficients Comparison of Actual versus Fitted Values

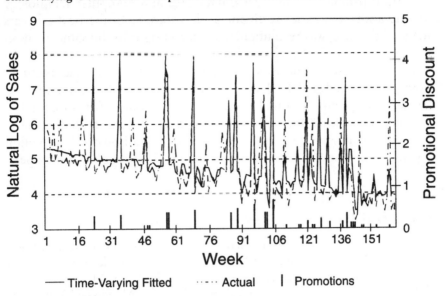

Time-Varying Fitted ···· Actual I Promotions

it affects the willingness of the firm to promote and the amount that the firm must discount when a promotion is offered. In the above example, because the firm knew that the promotions were becoming more effective, they were able to continue to run lower promotional discounts and still obtain volume objectives. A constant coefficient model will not adjust for the change in marketing effectiveness.

CONCLUDING COMMENTS

This chapter has given an overview of the issues and procedures that can be used to model large-scale POS databases. Very few marketing academics or practitioners have identified or directly dealt with the unique problems that result from the type of data being modeled or the needs and requirements of marketing practitioners. We have attempted to focus on these issues and provide some recommendations regarding approaches to "mass-produced" marketing models to be used in DSSs. Clearly, more research is needed on this topic.

Marketing's growth in sophistication will depend upon academics' and practitioners' ability to develop a strong empirical base for managerial decision making in much the same way as finance. Finance offers an interesting parallel. In the 1960s, databases and computer technology became available to analyze financial decisions. Over the next 20 years financial thinking was revolutionized. Marketing is in the same position finance was in the 1960s—powerful databases now exist for the marketing profession to use for decision making. Through the development of more sophisticated analytical tools to understand the information in these databases, marketing can make a major leap forward. Firms that fail to recognize and utilize the power of these databases will be left trying to compete with relatively useless data in a highly sophisticated information environment. These firms will find it tougher and tougher to compete.

REFERENCES

Blattberg, Robert C., and Edward George (1991). "Seemingly Unrelated Equations: Shrinkage Estimation of Price and Promotional Elasticities." *Journal of the American Statistical Association*, vol. 86, June, pp. 304–315.

Blattberg, Robert C., and Steve Hoch (1990). "Database Models and Managerial Intuition: 50% Model + 50% Manager." *Management Science*, vol. 36, pp. 887–889.

Blattberg, Robert C., and Kenneth Wisniewski (1989). "Price-Induced Patterns of Competition." *Marketing Science*, vol. 8, pp. 291–309.

Broemeling, Lyle D., and Tsurumi Hiroki (1987). *Econometrics and Structural Change*. New York: Marcel Dekker.

Chui, C.K., and G. Chen (1991). *Kalman Filter: With Real-Time Applications*, 2d ed. New York: Springer-Verlag.

Cleveland, William S. (1979). "Robust Locally Weighted Regression and Smoothing Scatterplots." *Journal of the American Statistical Association*, vol. 74, pp. 829–836.

Deighton, John, D. Peppers, and M. Rogers (1993). "Consumer Transaction Databases: Present Status and Prospects." Chapter 3, this volume.

Eubank, Randall L. (1988). *Spline Smoothing and Nonparametric Regression*. New York: Marcel Dekker.

Hartie, T.J., and R.J. Tibshirani (1990). *Generalized Additive Models*. London: Chapman and Hall.

Ing, David (1993). "The Evolution of Decision Support Systems and Databases in Consumer Goods Marketing." Chapter 4, this volume.

Judge, George G., William Griffiths, R. Carter Hill, and Tsoung-Chao Lee (1980). *The Theory and Practice of Econometrics*. New York: John Wiley.

Little, John D.C. (1970). "Models and Managers: The Concept of a Decision Calculus." *Management Science*, vol. 16, pp. B466–485.

———— (1979). "Decision Support Systems for Marketing Managers." *Journal of Marketing*, vol. 43, no. 3, Summer, pp. 8–27.

McCann, John M., and John P. Gallagher (1990). *Expert Systems for Scanner Data Environment*. Boston: Kluwer Academic Publishers.

Montgomery, David B., and Glen L. Urban (1969). *Management Science in Marketing*. Englewood Cliffs, N.J.: Prentice-Hall.

Rousseeuw, Peter J., and Annick M. Leroy (1987). *Robust Regression and Outlier Detection*. New York: John Wiley.

Schmitz, John (1993). "Expert Systems for Scanner Data in Practice." Chapter 5, this volume.

Wittink, D., J. Porter, and S. Gupta (1993). "Biases in Parameter Estimates from Linearly Aggregated Data When the Disaggregated Model is Non-Linear." Working Paper, Cornell University.

9

ARTIFICIAL INTELLIGENCE FOR DESIGNING MARKETING DECISION-MAKING TOOLS

Raymond R. Burke

THIS CHAPTER PRESENTS *a third perspective on the emerging use of expert systems for marketing decision making. As in the previous chapters this chapter begins by reviewing the need for useful approaches to meet customer needs. Its focus is on "artificial intelligence" (AI) approaches, which are essentially systems where the knowledge base can be encoded as a set of conditions and actions using "IF/THEN" rules. The chapter discusses the use of AI for both "everyday" and strategic decision making and problem solving. Two important distinctions between the two are that (1) the system requirements for everyday and strategic decisions are different and (2) current methodologies are better suited for the former than the latter. The chapter identifies new techniques that can further the development of AI systems for strategic decisions. As a notable example of this, the chapter briefly describes the ADCAD system, a procedure to assist advertisers with the formulation of advertising objectives, copy strategy, and the selection of communications techniques.*

In conjunction with Chapters 5, 6, 10, and 11, this chapter should be of great value to readers who are considering implementing expert system/ AI methodologies in their strategic and tactical marketing operations.

INTRODUCTION

Marketing decisions are inherently complex and error prone because of the tremendous variety of decision options and the large number of consumer and environmental factors determining the performance of marketing programs. These decisions are likely to become even more difficult in the future (Drucker 1980; Peters 1987). Because of technological changes, consumers are getting information faster, so their knowledge, interests, and lifestyles are changing more quickly. Daily news of the economic and political conditions in the United States, Europe, Asia, and the Middle East affect consumers' perceptions of their own well-being, their expectations of future events and opportunities, and the nature and timing of their purchase decisions. The complexity of the marketplace is also increasing. Marketers have increased the volume of new product introductions, advertising, and promotion activities. In 1988, consumer packaged-goods manufacturers introduced over 10,000 new products, and this number is increasing by about 10% per year (Fannin 1989).

Within this complex environment, marketers are forced to make an increasing number and variety of decisions. There are more creative options, promotion options, and media options than ever before. These decisions are made with greater frequency, as marketing planning shifts from the national to the regional level. Some companies are moving to microsegmentation, using individual-level databases to customize marketing programs to the needs and circumstances of individual consumers (Coogle 1990).

Fortunately, technological developments have provided marketers with more detailed information on consumers and markets. John McCann estimates that product managers are supplied with one billion new numbers each week. There has also been an increase in the amount of published marketing research. Over the past ten years there have been a number of significant new theoretical and empirical findings providing insights on the performance of marketing variables and approaches for meeting customers' needs. However, the data and theory are hard to use. Much of this knowledge is locked up in textbooks and journal articles and is not available at the time of marketing decisions. Other knowledge is poorly developed, and/or is dispersed throughout the organization. Time constraints may limit its use.

The objective behind the development of Artificial Intelligence (AI) systems in marketing is to allow managers to make better use of available information in order to design more effective marketing programs. Academics and practitioners are faced with the job of harnessing data and knowledge to help managers consider more alternatives, sharpen their interpretations, and make decisions quickly. My purpose here is to review recent efforts to develop expert systems in the marketing domain. It is argued that artificial intelligence can support both operational decisions which are made routinely and frequently and strategic decisions which involve extensive planning and reasoning. However, the system requirements for everyday and strategic decisions are different, and current methodologies are better suited for the former than the latter. The chapter identifies new techniques that can further the development of AI systems for assisting strategic decisions.

AI SYSTEMS FOR EVERYDAY DECISIONS

There are a myriad of decisions and procedures involved in the marketing of products and services. Many of these tasks are performed routinely and frequently, including the collation and analysis of marketing research data, the timing of marketing expenditures, the management of inventory, and the adaptation of marketing programs to address the needs of specific customers and the challenges of regional competition. When there is sufficient procedural knowledge available, computer systems can be developed to automate these decisions, saving time and money. As Leonard-Barton and Sviokla (1988) note, "Some of the greatest opportunities for expert systems lie in small everyday tasks" (p. 91). This is evidenced by the increasing number of software systems with "embedded" AI technology.

To illustrate the nature of a system for everyday decisions, let's start with the example of a retail inventory-management system. The goal of the retailer is to carry enough inventory to satisfy customer demand and to avoid stockouts. A simple expert system might consist of a small set of rules triggered by inventory conditions. When stock falls below some predetermined level, an order is placed for more merchandise. A more sophisticated system might dynamically balance predicted customer demand and item profitability against the costs of placing an order and carrying inventory (Kotler 1991, p. 560).

When creating expert systems to assist with everyday decisions, the objective is to automate what is known, and to help managers make decisions *faster and more accurately*. The emphasis is on building a system with a *correct* knowledge base. The knowledge about how to make these decisions is often publicly available and relatively complete and consistent. There is not much debate among experts about the appropriate steps to take in a particular situation. Moreover, the knowledge is generalized and can be applied in a variety of contexts.

There have been a number of recent AI applications of this type (see Table 9-1).[1] The prevalence of UPC scanner data has stimulated the

---

[1]See Wierenga (1990) for a detailed comparison of a number of marketing expert systems developed by academics.

TABLE 9-1
AI Systems for Everyday Decisions

Scanner Data Analysis and Exception Reporting	
CoverStory	Schmitz, Armstrong, and Little 1990
INFER	Rangaswamy, Harlam, and Lodish 1991
PROMOTER	Abraham and Lodish 1987
PROMOTION DETECTIVE	McCann and Gallagher 1990
SCAN*EXPERT	Bayer and Harter 1991
SHANEX	Alpar 1991
Statistical Analysis and Forecasting	
DANEX	Bockenholt, Both, and Gaul 1989
Rule-based Forecasting	Collopy and Armstrong 1989

development of expert systems that perform a variety of routine data analysis tasks, including filtering data, fitting models, identifying what's important or unusual in the data, and explaining the causes. The PRO-MOTER system (Abraham and Lodish 1987) analyzes data on factory shipments, warehouse withdrawals, and store sales to identify weeks during which promotions were run, determine baseline levels of sales, and estimate the impact of trade and consumer promotions. Similarly, McCann and Gallagher's (1990) PROMOTION DETECTIVE identifies promotion weeks and reports the impact of causal factors along with an explanation of abnormalities. Alpar's (1991) SHANEX program locates market share changes and identifies the causes, as does Bayer and Harter's (1991) SCAN*EXPERT program. Rangaswamy, Harlam, and Lodish's (1991) INFER program and Schmitz, Armstrong, and Little's (1990) CoverStory software interpret statistical analyses of scanner data, report noteworthy facts and trends in market activities, and identify causal factors.

Marketers have also developed expert systems to perform other data analysis chores. Bockenholt, Both, and Gaul's (1989) DANEX (Data ANalysis EXpert) software selects multidimensional scaling and cluster analysis techniques for positioning and segmentation. Collopy and Armstrong's (1989) Rule-Based Forecasting System selects methods to produce extrapolation forecasts.[2]

AI systems have a number of characteristics that make them especially effective for everyday decisions. They provide symbolic representation and heuristic reasoning, permitting the manipulation of concepts and relationships as well as figures and formulae. Because the problem-solving

---

[2]Other applications of AI for data analysis are described in Gale (1986).

knowledge for routine decisions is relatively complete, consistent, and generalized, it can be encoded as a set of conditions and actions using "IF/THEN" rules. AI systems are cost effective for repetitive decisions, because the expense of building the system can be spread over a large number of decisions. These systems can be used to filter large volumes of information and summarize the key findings, thereby helping managers cope with the tremendous amount of market data now available.

The users of these systems typically have either low ability (e.g., in the area of data analysis) or low motivation (because the task is too time consuming, or trivial). McCann and Gallagher (1990) report, "[Brand managers] are not great analysts and do not enjoy the time-consuming effort involved in analyzing and understanding data" [p. 79].

In these applications, the information inputs and outputs may change continuously, but the knowledge base is static. Therefore, the user does not need to modify the internal workings of the system. However, the expert system is not simply a "black box." Because knowledge is treated as data, the system can provide explanations to users by reporting the facts, models, and rules that led to particular conclusions. The DANEX program, for example, can report the reasons why a particular data analysis technique was selected and why others were rejected by the system (Bockenholt, Both, and Gaul 1989). Feigenbaum and McCorduck (1983, p. 64), note, "Designers work hard to achieve [this transparency] because they understand that the ultimate use of an expert system will depend upon its credibility to its users, and the credibility will arise because the behavior is transparent, explainable." In a sense, the expert system is a "glass box," where one can observe the internal operation but cannot directly manipulate the contents.

AI SYSTEMS FOR STRATEGIC DECISIONS

Expert systems are often touted as being especially effective when knowledge in a particular domain is scarce and incomplete (e.g., Hayes-Roth, Waterman, and Lenat 1983). These systems can codify the available knowledge, distribute it to decision makers, and assist them with reasoning under uncertainty.[3] The marketing area would therefore seem to be a

---

[3]One of the earliest approaches to reasoning with uncertainty was incorporated in MYCIN, a system for selecting antibiotic therapy for bacteremia (Shortlifte 1976). MYCIN used certainty factors to indicate the strength of heuristic rules. The interested reader should see Shafer and Pearl (1990) for a collection of readings describing the various methods for coping with uncertainty in expert systems.

great opportunity for the application of AI methods. Marketing knowledge is often scarce and incomplete, and many decisions are based on conflicting information, tentative assumptions, and subjective rules of thumb. Examples include decisions about the introduction of new products, product positioning, advertising, promotion, and international negotiations, among others (Rangaswamy et al. 1987).

All of these marketing decisions are "strategic" in the sense that they involve the development of marketing plans that match a firm's objectives and resources with the changing opportunities in the marketplace (Kotler 1991, p. 33). Unlike the routine decisions discussed in the last section, the strategic decisions are individually very important and are made relatively infrequently. The decision makers are themselves "experts," who have both high ability and motivation. However, they have other cognitive limitations such as limited memory, time constraints, selective perception, and attentional capacity. The objective in developing the expert system is to overcome these cognitive limitations and to help the user to reason *broader and deeper*. The goal is to discover what is new and to create insights.

There have been a number of recent applications in the areas of marketing planning and marketing mix decisions (see Table 9-2). In the advertising domain, Burke et al.'s (1990) ADCAD (ADvertising Communication Approach Designer) sets marketing and communication objectives, selects creative strategies, and identifies effective communication

TABLE 9-2
AI Systems for Strategic Decisions

Advertising	
ADCAD	Burke et al. 1990
ADEXPERT	Winter and Rossiter 1992
CAAS	Kroeber-Riel and Esch 1992
ESWA	Neibecker 1987, 1991
Media Planning System	Mitchell 1986, 1988
Product	
INNOVATOR	Ram and Ram 1988, 1989, 1990
New Product Introduction	Gaul and Schaer 1988
The Strategist	Schumann et al. 1987
Promotion	
ESIE	Entemann and Cannon 1987
PEP	Bayer, Lawrence, and Keon 1988
Textbook Promotion Advisor	McCann and Gallagher 1990
Strategy	
PORTER	Walden 1989

approaches. Neibecker's (1987, 1991) ESWA selects between alternative copy proposals by predicting consumers' emotional responses and ad recall. Mitchell's (1986, 1988) Media Planning System provides media planners with decision frames to help in structuring their analyses. Winter and Rossiter's (1992) ADEXPERT assists with the construction and evalua- tion of advertisements. Kroeber-Riel and Esch's (1992) CAAS (Computer- Aided Advertising System) comprises both a diagnostic expert system for evaluating advertising concepts and a planning system which searches for effective emotional concepts, pictures, and pictorial layouts.

In the promotion area, Bayer, Lawrence, and Keon (1988) derived rules from promotion experts and empirical research results to develop the PEP program, a decision support system for planning consumer sales- promotion campaigns for consumer packaged goods. Entemann and Cannon's (1987) ESIE (Expert System Inference Engine) system uses rules derived from published empirical research to provide guidance on sales promotion decisions. McCann and Gallagher's (1990) Textbook Promotion Advisor uses public domain knowledge, adapted from books and magazines, to recommend a list of consumer and trade promotions given a set of objectives and market conditions.

In the new product area, Schumann et al.'s (1987) Strategist software performs product portfolio planning using rules derived from the BCG and GE planning matrices. Ram and Ram's (1988, 1989, 1990) INNOVA- TOR program screens new product concepts in the financial services area with rules generated from expert opinion and secondary sources (e.g., *The Wall Street Journal, Money*). Combining a NEWS-type model and decision heuristics, Gaul and Schaer's (1988) New Product Introduc- tion system analyzes the marketing plans of new products to predict sales and market shares, and to make go/no-go recommendations.

Walden (1989) describes an expert system for strategic market manage- ment based on Porter's (1985) concepts of competitive advantage and value chain analysis. The system is used by marketing managers in the building industry to assess the strength of alternative strategies, such as cost leadership or differentiation, for particular products and customer segments.

An Illustrative Example

To illustrate both the advantages and problems associated with expert systems for strategic decisions, let's examine the ADCAD system (Burke et al. 1990).[4] As noted above, ADCAD was designed to assist advertisers of consumer products with the formulation of advertising objectives, copy strategy, and the selection of communication techniques. This section describes the structure of ADCAD's knowledge base, presents some example rules, and shows a sample consultation.

ADCAD's knowledge base consists of a set of rules derived from existing theories of advertising effectiveness (e.g., the elaboration-likelihood model, Petty and Cacioppo 1983; the Rossiter-Percy communication model, Rossiter and Percy 1985), empirical findings (e.g., Stewart and Furse's 1986 study of TV advertising), and interactions with the creative staff of the Young & Rubicam advertising agency. Table 9-3 lists a selection of rules for deciding on brand positioning, message and presenter characteristics, and the emotional tone of the ad. ADCAD's user interface is question and answer. The computer first asks a series of questions about the communication problem. It then sorts through the knowledge base and picks out the facts, heuristics, and experiences that are relevant to the present situation. The system reasons by deduction, matching user input against the premises of rules to draw inferences. Figure 9-1 presents an overview of the stages in the advertising design process, a subset of the communication variables, and a sample of the factors affecting each of the decisions.

A sample consultation with ADCAD, based on the Suave shampoo case (Albion 1984), is shown in the Appendix.[5] ADCAD first requests the name and product class of the brand to be advertised and the number and names of the market segments (Part A). It then asks a series of questions to identify appropriate marketing and advertising objectives (Parts B and C). At any time during the consultation, the user can ask "What" is the definition of the terminology used in the system's questions, and "Why" a certain piece of information is requested. Next, ADCAD attempts to select a benefit to be featured in the advertisement and determine effective communication approaches (Part D). At the end of the consultation, ADCAD presents its conclusions (Part E) along with the associated confidence factors (not shown). The user can ask how a conclusion was reached, and ADCAD will report the underlying rationale for the recommendation (Part F). The user can also conduct "what if"

---

[4]A version of ADCAD, with a simplified knowledge base and explanatory facilities, is available as part of the ADSTRAT program (Gatignon and Burke 1991).

[5]A more detailed discussion of the Suave consultation is given in Burke et al. (1990).

TABLE 9-3
Example Rules from ADCAD

Positioning
- IF ad objective = convey brand image or reinforce brand image AND brand purchase motivation = social approval AND brand usage visibility = high THEN possible benefit = "status" (cf. Holbrook and Lehmann 1980)
- IF ad objective = convey brand information or change brand beliefs AND perceived differences between brands = small or medium AND perceived relative performance = inferior or parity AND relative performance = superior AND current brand loyalty = competitor loyal THEN message comparison = direct comparison against competition (Gorn and Weinberg 1983)
- IF ad objective = convey brand information or reinforce brand beliefs AND conflicting information = likely AND education = college or graduate AND product knowledge = high AND involvement = high THEN message sidedness = two-sided (McGuire and Papageorgis 1961)

Message Characteristics
- IF ad objective = increase top-of-mind awareness THEN technique = jingle, rhyme, or slogan (MacLachlan 1984)
- IF ad objective = convey brand information or reinforce brand beliefs AND market share > 18.5 AND brand switching = high AND product type = existing THEN technique = sign off (Stewart and Furse 1986)
- IF ad objective = convey brand information or change brand beliefs AND message processing motivation = low AND message processing ability = low THEN ad format = problem solution (Schwerin and Newell 1981)

Presenter Characteristics
- IF ad objective = convey brand information or change brand beliefs AND message processing ability = low THEN presenter expertise = high (Rhine and Severance 1970)
- IF presenter expertise = high THEN time of identification in message = early (Sternthal, Dholakia, and Leavitt 1978)
- IF ad objective = convey brand information or change brand beliefs AND involvement = high THEN presenter objectivity = high (Choo 1964)

Message Emotion
- IF ad objective = convey brand image or reinforce brand image or change brand image THEN emotional direction = positive (Young & Rubicam, Staff Interview)
- IF ad objective = convey brand image or reinforce brand image AND brand purchase motivation = sensory stimulation AND message processing motivation = high THEN emotional tone = elation (Rossiter and Percy 1987)
- IF ad objective = change brand beliefs AND message processing motivation = low AND purchase anxiety = low AND brand use avoids fearful consequences = yes THEN emotional tone = high fear (Ray and Wilkie 1970)

---

analyses, revising the input information and observing the effects on the system's conclusions.

The ADCAD system provides a number of benefits (Burke et al. 1990). It enriches the knowledge environment of the decision maker, expanding the range of creative options. It provides a preliminary evaluation of options by offering supportive reasoning. It allows sensitivity analysis to investigate the impact of alternative assumptions. It assures a link between the advertising execution and the marketing and communication objectives. It provides direction for research by identifying relevant information through the consultation and sensitivity analysis. Finally, it assists with

FIGURE 9-1
Stages in Advertising Design

the training of novice advertising managers and students. The system has been welcomed by advertising and brand managers, who are often looking for a rationale for their current advertising and ideas for new communication approaches.

Problems with Rule-Based Systems

Like other rule-based systems, ADCAD has a number of limitations that are associated with the nature of strategic knowledge and the knowledge engineering process (Burke 1991). For many strategic decisions, there is an enormous problem space and insufficient knowledge in the public domain to build a useful system. For example, McCann and Gallagher (1990, p. 77) report, "The most important [conclusion] was the realization that in the promotion area the marketing literature would not carry one very far towards the development of an operational and useful expert system." Therefore the system builder must tap into the proprietary knowledge of companies. Furthermore, because marketing strategy and the marketing mix are active areas of research, the problem-solving knowledge changes over time. Consequently, it can take years of effort to build a system.

The IF/THEN representation of rule-based systems provides a seemingly flexible method of encoding knowledge. However, the development of rules from marketing theories, experiments, models, heuristics, and cases requires a substantial amount of creative judgment. Rules must be abstracted from the original situation, with consequent loss of context. For example, in the promotion area, one might observe that a luggage manufacturer was able to increase sales by offering a vacation sweepstakes (with hotel and airfare to a tropical destination). The expert system builder might infer that a sweepstakes can increase sales, or perhaps that a vacation sweepstakes can increase sales. However, this rule may not apply to automobiles, because air travel is a complement of luggage, but a substitute for an automobile (cf. Varadarajan 1985). Observed relationships often depend on the context, and these dependencies must be explicitly represented in the rule premises. The knowledge engineer must also resolve inconsistencies between conflicting rules. This is particularly a problem when relying on multiple sources of knowledge. There are often differences of opinion among experts on the appropriate course of action. Furthermore, it is difficult to update the knowledge base as new findings are reported because of implicit rule dependencies.

Because many of these knowledge engineering decisions are hidden from the end-user, it is difficult to evaluate the quality of the knowledge base. The final product is often a patchwork of theory and empirical findings, held together by the expert system. To address the problem of incomplete knowledge, marketers have often attached uncertainty weights to the rules. However, this does not solve the problem, as the rules themselves may be incorrect. The performance of marketing programs may instead depend on complex interrelationships between the brand, the market, consumers, and the environment.

NEW APPROACHES

Rule-based expert systems attempt to transform the various kinds of marketing knowledge into a single, generalized representation. As Carbonell (1986, p. 384) notes, "The tacit assumption that domain knowledge must necessarily be represented as large sets of context-independent rules is proving to be only an early engineering decision, and a very limiting one at that." An alternative approach is to represent knowledge in its original context and to dynamically abstract the relationships to analogous new situations. By computerizing the abstraction process, the process becomes consistent, visible, and subject to evaluation and refinement. The user has direct access to the contextual knowledge supporting the system's conclusions, and can evaluate the relevance of the findings for a particular problem. This approach is used in the ADDUCE program (Burke 1991).

ADDUCE was designed to help advertisers anticipate how consumers might react to new advertising concepts. The sources of knowledge in ADDUCE are the same as ADCAD. However, the information about objects and attributes is encoded in a frame-based representation (Minsky 1975). Theoretical relationships are represented as abstract rules which are used to deduce outcomes in new situations. Empirical knowledge is represented as associations between specific objects which are generalized to analogous new situations. The goal of the analogical reasoning system is to capture complex relationships present in these specific cases and bring them to bear on the problem at hand.[6]

ADDUCE's user interface is question and answer. The system begins

---

[6]These episodic representations contain a considerable amount of irrelevant situational information. However, this is essential for case-based reasoning, as a simplification of abstraction may not retain the important contextual dependencies (cf. McCartney 1990).

the consultation by asking a series of background questions about the brand, the advertising, and the target audience. It then analyzes the problem by applying inheritance and deductive reasoning to theoretical relationships and analogical (lateral) reasoning to empirical relationships. In the first case, ADDUCE operates in basically the same way as ADCAD, matching user input with rule premises to draw conclusions. With respect to empirical relationships, ADDUCE infers how consumers will react to new ads by searching for relevant past advertising experiments and then generalizing research results across similar contexts. When the program accumulates sufficient evidence to predict one or more consumer responses, it presents its conclusions to the user. The user can then compare the past and present cases by examining their shared and distinctive features.[7]

A second system, PREDITAR (PREDicitve Insights Through Analogical Reasoning), was designed by Lee, Burke, and Wind (1990) to answer two key questions: What is the likely performance of a new financial service product, and What changes in the product or situation are required to achieve certain levels of performance? The system uses a knowledge base of past financial products introduced by the new business development division of a major brokerage firm.

The system first asks the user for a description of the product concept to be evaluated. It then searches the database of past cases to identify the set of cases which are most similar in terms of brand, market, consumer, and environmental characteristics. The system abstracts performance information from the past cases and formulates a prediction for the new concept. Upon request, the system can explain its predictions in terms of past examples.

The user can then provide feedback on the accuracy of these predictions, in which case the system modifies its similarity metric to improve its selection of relevant cases. For correct forecasts, the system increases the weighting of attributes shared by the proposed product and the retrieved case and decreases the weighting of distinctive attributes. The learning mechanism is based on research by John Holland on pattern recognition and classification (Holland 1975, 1986). Although the system requires repeated trials to attain efficient performance, it has the advantage of being self-organizing and very flexible. The authors are exploring various other approaches for calculating the similarity between cases,

---

[7]See Burke (1991) for a detailed description of ADDUCE and a sample consultation.

estimating the similarity weights, and updating the weights based on performance feedback. In addition, the analogical reasoning process can be enhanced by adding mechanisms to combine several analogs and to apply transformation operators in order to increase the similarity of past cases to the target problem (Kolodner and Penberthy 1990).

Another approach to improving the representation of knowledge and contextual information in the marketing domain is McCann and Gallagher's (1990) DEALMAKER program for evaluating trade deals. Like AD-DUCE and PREDITAR, this system is object oriented, representing background information about objects (markets, retailers, consumers, and brands) as well as the relations between these objects. However, while ADDUCE and PREDITAR make the transition from rules to frames, DEALMAKER goes an additional step to represent world models. The system attempts to capture a marketing or sales manager's mental model of a market. It combines quantitative knowledge about consumer behavior in local markets with qualitative knowledge of retailer responses to trade promotions. As McCann and Gallagher (1990, p. 177) note, "Model-based reasoning systems are distinguished from strictly rule based systems by attempting to build an explicit model of the entities, structures, principles of operation, and behavior of some system."

DEALMAKER allows the user to devise a promotion plan and explore the consequences of implementing that plan in several different markets. For a given plan, the system predicts the number of chains that accepted the deal and how much revenue was generated for the manufacturer, as well as the price, display size, and advertising size set by individual retailers. Upon request, the system can then explain the retailers' actions.

All three of these systems are designed to simulate how customers might respond to different marketing programs rather than to produce normative strategy recommendations. The system does not replace the decision maker. Instead, the user must play an active role in querying the system, testing alternative scenarios, and exploring different lines of reasoning.

MOVING AHEAD . . .

We have seen a natural progression in the development of expert systems in marketing, where computers were first used to automate existing business routines and are now being applied to decisions requiring extensive analysis and planning. Each type of decision presents unique challenges and opportunities for the system developer. These are discussed below.

Everyday Decisions

There are substantial opportunities for the development of expert systems for everyday decisions. Commercial expert systems have already been created to analyze mailing lists and select the most promising prospects (Persoft's More/2 system), to study buyer profiles and suggest sales proposals (DEC's XSEL program), and to generate price quotes for computer equipment (TI's Pricing Analysis; see Kastiel 1987). In advertising production, systems assist publishers with laying out newspapers (Crosfield's Expert Publishing System) and positioning printing plates on the presses (Rockwell's Press Lineup Advisor; see Cook and Schleede 1988). McCann, Tadlaoui, and Gallagher's (1990) Merchandising Analyst helps grocers lay out weekly feature advertising. In the future, the grocer might automate decisions about setting retail prices, picking assortments of brands and sizes, and allocating shelf space (Phipps 1987).

There are two major challenges for the expert system builder. The first is to assemble knowledge bases that are coherent, correct, and complete. The rule-based architectures currently available are most suitable for problems with a small solution space and reliable, static knowledge (Stefik et al. 1983). These systems are often designed to operate with a minimum of analyst intervention, so it is critical that the knowledge base be thoroughly tested and debugged.

The second challenge is to match the system's I/O with the user's I/O; that is, to match the decision maker's terminology and resources (databases, information systems) with the system's questions and suggestions. Direct links from expert systems to databases will reduce the number of questions asked of users, unambiguously define required input, ensure data currency, and permit individual rather than aggregate-level analysis. The use of expert systems for operational decisions will increase as electronic data interchange between marketers and customers, distributors, and suppliers gains acceptance.

Of course, some users will desire direct access to the knowledge base underlying the system's decisions. However, this becomes less necessary as one gains confidence in the validity of the rules. As one commercial user noted, "I don't care if there's a witch running around in a little black box . . . . I want to see results" (Kastiel 1987, p. 52).

When expert systems communicate directly with users, an important question is how to format information for decision makers. For example, what's the best way to convey the insights from scanner data? CoverStory (Schmitz, Armstrong, and Little 1990) presents written reports whereas Promotion Detective (McCann and Gallagher 1990) uses a graphical display. Behavioral research suggests that the information format may affect decision making. In alpha-numeric displays, information is acquired in correspondence with the importance weights of the attributes, whereas under graphic conditions, the acquisition of information is influenced by its visual salience (Jarvenpaa 1990). Most of the scanner data analysis systems produce explanations of changes in market activities. The content of these explanations can constrain the manager's conclusions, thereby affecting subsequent decisions (cf. Kunda 1990).

Strategic Decisions

The focus in developing expert systems for strategic decisions has been on knowledge refinement: finding the smartest and most verbal experts, and codifying their problem-solving heuristics in a knowledge base. This will continue to be difficult. As Ted Levitt (1989) noted, Babe Ruth knew a lot about hitting home runs, but he couldn't share this wisdom. Many expert decisions are based on the recognition of complex patterns learned through experience, rather than on the application of explicit rules.[8] Feigenbaum and McCorduck (1983, p. 75) argue that "knowledge acquisition is the great research problem that AI laboratories must face and solve in the coming decade."

For future AI systems to gain acceptance, the contents of their knowledge bases must be *accessible*. They must be understandable, properly qualified, and available to the group of individuals involved in the decision. The increasing focus on total quality management implies cross-functional teams (e.g., marketing, engineering, manufacturing, and design) working together to design products (Eisenhart 1990). Networked decision support and AI systems can bring together these business functions. For example, IBM and the University of Arizona have developed the Electronic Meeting System which includes software tools with problem-

---

[8]Wierenga (1990) suggests that neural network models might be used when knowledge is incomplete and decisions are based on pattern recognition (see, e.g., Bayer 1990; Sen, Colombo, and Buchanan 1990). These systems require no a priori specification of the relationships between inputs and outputs. Unfortunately, they lack the explanatory facilities of expert systems, which are particularly important for strategic decisions.

solving techniques such as brainstorming and idea organization, whereas the University of Minnesota has created a Software-Aided Meeting Management program. The knowledge base must also maintain contextual information to substantiate the system's recommendations. The user can then assess the value of a particular piece of knowledge in a given situation, judging whether it is out of date (because of time dependencies) and/or irrelevant (because of context dependencies).

The knowledge representation must be rich, matching the user's mental models, classes, categories, dependencies, constraints, uncertainties, similarities, assumptions, and hypotheses. Lamberti and Wallace (1990) find that certain knowledge organization formats are more conducive to high- versus low-skill employees' performance with expert systems. "Low-skill employees performed significantly faster and more accurately when answering questions requiring concrete knowledge organization. High-skill employees performed faster, although not necessarily more accurately, when responding to questions requiring abstract versus concrete knowledge organization" (p. 298). Pei & Reneau (1990) report, "The results suggest that learning was facilitated only for groups with congruence between the [rule-based expert system's] problem-solving strategy and a subject's memory structure" [p. 263].

For strategic decisions, information *and* knowledge are changing. Therefore, the AI system must be *adaptive*: it must be upgradeable, compliant, and responsive. The system should allow the refinement and addition of rules to the knowledge base. It must be an "open box," where users have free access to its contents.

Moreover, the system must transform existing knowledge to fit the problem and modify the knowledge base in response to feedback. The reasoning process must be rich, going beyond information in the knowledge base by (1) identifying a range of alternatives rather than a single approach, (2) permitting nonmonotonic reasoning (allowing hypotheses to be asserted and retracted), (3) reasoning by analogy (transforming past experience to address new situations), and (4) learning (using feedback about performance to modify the knowledge base).[9] It is not sufficient to simply repeat what has been discovered to work in the past. Riesbeck and Schank (1989, p. 7) note, "In business, each new case changes the

---

[9]It may take a long time to evaluate the quality of strategic decisions. It is therefore a challenging problem to collect this evaluative information and feed it back into the system for learning.

world sufficiently so that the methods that were specifically applied may not work again." As Walt Disney once said, "You can't top pigs with pigs."

While these challenges are daunting, there are also great opportunities for the development of AI systems for strategic decisions, as suggested by the applications described earlier. In contrast to the past applications, the newer open box applications, if properly designed, will increase in value over time, as the knowledge base is amended with new findings (cf. Glazer 1991). These systems will facilitate knowledge accumulation and empirical generalizations within firms, thus allowing companies to leverage their knowledge resources.

Appendix
Sample Consultation with ADCAD

Part A: Market Assessment
What is the name of the brand to be advertised?
>>*suave*

In which product category does Suave belong? Before responding, carefully consider the major brands and products with which Suave competes.
>>*shampoo*

How many distinct segments are you trying to reach with your ad? The segments may be chosen on any suitable criteria. The system will ask you several questions about each segment such as age, education, and brand loyalty.
>>*1*

Give a name to segment-1. Use a maximum of ten characters.
>>*women 18–34*

Part B: Marketing Objectives
At what stage in the life cycle is the product category shampoo?
  1. introduction   3. maturity
  2. growth   4. decline
>>*3*

How often do women 18–34 use products in the category shampoo?
  1. no usage   3. frequently
  2. infrequently
>>*3*

Is the current purchase interval for shampoo short, medium, or long?
>>*short*
What is the market share of Suave in segment women 18–34? Give a number between 0.00 and 100.0.
>>*2.0*

How would you characterize the current loyalty of women 18–34 to Suave?
  1. loyal to brand   4. unfavorable brand switcher
  2. loyal to competitor   5. split-loyalty
  3. favorable brand switcher   6. productive nonuser
>>*what*

The brand loyalty of consumers can range from high loyalty to your brand (i.e., only your brand is regularly purchased) to high loyalty to one of your competitors. Consumers may also be loyal purchasers of your brand and a select group of competing brands (split loyalty), perhaps to satisfy the needs of multiple users in the household or multiple usage situations. Consumers may show very little loyalty, switching between a set of brands which may or may not include your brand. (These are favorable and unfavorable brand switchers, respectively.)

How would you characterize the current loyalty of women 18–34 to Suave?
1. loyal to brand
2. loyal to competitor
3. favorable brand switcher
4. unfavorable brand switcher
5. split loyalty
6. product nonuser
>>4

How would you characterize past usage of Suave in segment women 18–34?
1. none
2. some
>>why

If this segment has tried our brand in the past, but is now using one or more of our competitors' brands, then we should attempt to attract these consumers back to our brand.

How would you characterize past usage of Suave in segment women 18–34?
1. none
2. some
>>1

A possible marketing objective is: stimulate brand trial. Is this a marketing objective that should be considered for further analysis?
>>yes

Part C: Advertising Objectives
What is the primary motivation(s) in segment women 18–34 for the purchase of your brand?
1. problem removal
2. problem avoidance
3. current brand dissatisfaction
4. restocking
5. sensory stimulation
6. intellectual stimulation
7. self-esteem
8. social approval
>>7,8

When do consumers in segment women 18–34 generally make brand choices?
1. prior to purchase
2. at point of purchase
>>2 cf 70

Is the Suave package typically visible at the time of purchase?
>>yes

What is the ability of women 18–34 to recognize the Suave package at the point of purchase?
1. low
2. high
>>1

Are the physical/health risks associated with the use of Suave in segment women 18–34 low or high?
>>low

Do consumers in segment women 18–34 perceive small, medium, or large differences in performance across brands?
>>small

A possible communication objective is: create/increase brand recognition. Is this a communication objective that should be considered for further analysis?
>>y

A possible communication objective is: communicate brand image/mood/lifestyle. Is this a communication objective that should be considered for further analysis?
>>y

Part D: Communication Approaches
Will brand usage be visible in segment women 18–34?
>>*no*

At what retail price is Suave sold in segment women 18–34? Type in dollars and cents for a typical size as in: 110.95.
>>*1.40*

At what retail price are your major competitors' brands sold in segment women 18–34? Type in dollars and cents for a typical size as in: 110.95.
>>*3.60*

How does your brand actually perform relative to major competing brands?
   1. inferior   3. superior
   2. parity
>>*2*

Is the benefit "value" delivered by Suave?
>>*y*

Is the benefit "value" unique to Suave?
>>*y*

Is the benefit "value" important to consumers in segment women 18–34?
>>*y*

A possible benefit to be featured in the ad is: value. Is this a benefit that should be considered for further analysis?
>>*n*

What benefit is to be featured in the ad?
>>*quality*

How would you characterize the level of complexity encountered in the use of Suave? Is it low, moderate, or high?
>>*low*

Is visibility in the ad of benefit "quality" offered by Suave low, moderate, or high?
>>*high cf 60*

Would it be possible to demonstrate the benefit "quality" in the ad?
>>*yes*

Is visibility in use of benefit "quality" offered by Suave low, moderate, or high?
>>*low*

Is this target segment male, female, or both?
>>*female*

How would you characterize the current level of competition in this product category in segment women 18–34? Is it light, moderate, or heavy?
>>*heavy*

Part E: Recommendations
Recommendations for segment women 18–34 are as follows:

No.	Component	Recommended Value
1	featured benefit	quality
2	number of benefits	few
3	benefit claim	extreme positive claim
4	message comparison	no comparison
5	message sidedness	one-sided
6	presenter presence	present
7	presenter sex	female
8	presenter identity	celebrity

Part E: Recommendations *(continued)*

No.	Component	Recommended Value
9	presenter recognizability	high
10	presenter attraction	high
11	presenter likability	high
12	presenter identification	early
13	format	demonstration of product in use
14	format	endorsement by celebrity
15	format	vignette
16	technique	capture consumer emotions
17	technique	closeup
18	technique	color illustration
19	technique	long package display
20	technique	music
21	technique	surrogate indicators of performance
22	technique	visual stimuli/imagery
23	emotional strength	high
24	emotional direction	positive
25	authenticity of portrayal	high
26	emotional tone	apprehension followed by flattery

Part F: Rationale
If you would like an explanation for any of these recommendations, enter the corresponding sequence number followed by <RETURN>, else hit <RETURN>.

8

Just a moment please . . .
The advertising objective is to communicate or reinforce your brand's image, mood, or an associated lifestyle to consumers who are not highly motivated to process your ad message. A celebrity presenter can attract the consumer's attention, enhance your brand's image, and become a memorable cue for brand evaluation (Petty, Cacioppo, and Schumann 1983; Young & Rubicam Staff Interview). Would you like to see an explanation at the next level of detail?

>>y

Explanation at level 2:
The marketing objective is to stimulate brand trial and consumers are interested in purchasing your brand primarily to feel good or to enhance their self-image. Therefore, the advertising should communicate a positive brand image, mood, or lifestyle (Rossiter and Percy 1987; Wells 1981). Continue?

>>n

Would you like an explanation for any other recommendation?

>>n

Would you like to rerun this consultation for segment women 18–34 with different input scenarios?

>> no

Consultation complete. Thank you.

REFERENCES

Abraham, Magid M., and Leonard M. Lodish (1987). "PROMOTER: An Automated Promotion Evaluation System." *Marketing Science,* 6 (2), 101–123.

Albion, Mark S. (1984). *Advertising's Hidden Effects: Manufacturers' Advertising and Retailing Pricing.* Westport, Conn.: Auburn House.

Alpar, P. (1991). "Knowledge-Based Modeling of Marketing Managers' Problem-Solving Behavior." *International Journal of Research in Marketing*, 8 (April), 5–16.

Bayer, Judy (1990). "Neural Networks: Learning to Associate Marketers' Behavior with Consumers' Behavior." Paper presented at the Annual Conference of the Association for Consumer Research, New York (October).

Bayer, Judy, and R. Harter (1991). " 'Miner,' 'Manager,' and 'Researcher': Three Modes of Analysis of Scanner Data." *International Journal of Research in Marketing*, 8 (April), 17–28.

Bayer, Judy, Stephen Lawrence, and John W. Keon (1988). "PEP: An Expert System for Promotion Marketing." In E. Turban and P.R. Watkins (eds.), *Applied Expert Systems*. Amsterdam: North-Holland, 121–141.

Bockenholt, Ingo, Martin Both, and Wolfgang Gaul (1989). "A Knowledge-Based System for Supporting Data Analysis Problems." *Decision Support Systems*, 5, 345–354.

Burke, Raymond R. (1991). "Reasoning with Empirical Marketing Knowledge." *International Journal of Research in Marketing*, 8 (April), 75–90.

Burke, Raymond R., Arvind Rangaswamy, Jerry Wind, and Jehoshua Eliashberg (1990). "A Knowledge-Based System for Advertising Design." *Marketing Science*, 9 (3), 212–229.

Carbonell, Jaime G. (1986). "Derivational Analogy: A Theory of Reconstructive Problem Solving and Expertise Acquisition." In R.S. Michalski, J.G. Carbonell, and T.M. Mitchell (eds.), *Machine Learning: An Artificial Intelligence Approach*, vol. 2. Los Altos, Calif.: Morgan Kaufmann, 371–392.

Choo, Tong-He (1964). "Communicator Credibility and Communication Discrepancy as Determinants of Opinion Change." *Journal of Social Psychology*, 64, 65–76.

Collopy, Fred, and J. Scott Armstrong (1989). "Rule-Based Forecasting." Working paper #89-14, The Weatherhead School of Management, Case Western Reserve University.

Coogle, Joe (1990). "Data-Base Marketing." *Marketing & Media Decisions* (January) 75–76.

Cook, Robert Lorin, and John M. Schleede (1988). "Application of Expert Systems to Advertising." *Journal of Advertising Research*, (June/July), 47–56.

Drucker, Peter F. (1980). *Managing in Turbulent Times*. New York: Harper & Row.

Eisenhart, Tom (1990). "After 10 Years of Marketing Decision Support Systems, Where's the Payoff?" *Business Marketing* (June), 46–51.

Entemann, Carl W., and Hugh Cannon (1987). "A Rule-Based Expert System for Sales Promotion Management." In *Proceedings of the 1987 Conference of the American Academy of Advertising*. Las Vegas, Nev.: American Academy of Advertising.

Fannin, Rebecca (1989). "Where Are the New Brands?" *Marketing & Media Decisions* (July), 22–27.

Feigenbaum, Edward A., and Pamela McCorduck. *The Fifth Generation: Artificial Intelligence and Japan's Computer Challenge to the World.* Reading, Mass.: Addison-Wesley, 1983.

Gale, William A., ed. (1986). *Artificial Intelligence and Statistics.* Reading, Mass.: Addison-Wesley.

Gatignon, Hubert, and Raymond R. Burke (1991). ADSTRAT: *An Advertising Decision Support System.* San Francisco, Calif.: Scientific Press.

Gaul, Wolfgang, and A. Schaer (1988). "A PROLOG-Based PC Implementation for New Product Introduction." In Wolfgang Gaul and M. Schader (eds.), *Data, Expert Knowledge, and Decisions.* Berlin: Springer-Verlag, 67–79.

Glazer, Rashi (1991). "Marketing in an Information-Intensive Environment: Strategic Implications of Knowledge as an Asset." *Journal of Marketing,* 55 (October), 1–19.

Gorn, Gerald J., and Charles B. Weinberg (1983). "Comparative Advertising: Some Positive Results." In Richard P. Bagozzi and Alice M. Tybout (eds.), *Advances in Consumer Research,* vol. 10. Cincinnati: Association for Consumer Research, 377–380.

Hayes-Roth, Frederick, Donald A. Waterman, and Douglas B. Lenat (1983). "An Overview of Expert Systems." In Frederick Hayes-Roth, Donald A. Waterman, and Douglas B. Lenat (eds.), *Building Expert Systems.* Reading, Mass.: Addison-Wesley, 3–29.

Holbrook, Morris B., and Donald R. Lehmann (1980). "Form versus Content in Predicting Starch Scores." *Journal of Advertising Research,* 20 (August), 53–62.

Holland, John H. (1975). *Adaptation in Natural and Artificial Systems.* Ann Arbor: University of Michigan Press.

———— (1986). "Escaping Brittleness: The Possibilities of General Purpose Algorithms Applied to Parallel Rule-Based Systems." In R.S. Michalski, J.G. Carbonell, and T.M. Mitchell (eds.), *Machine Learning: An Artificial Intelligence Approach,* Los Altos, Calif.: Morgan Kaufman, 593–623.

Jarvenpaa, Sirkka L. (1990). "Graphic Displays in Decision Making—The Visual Salience Effect." *Journal of Behavioral Decision Making,* 2, 247–262.

Kuettel, Diane Lynn (1987). "Computerized Consultants." *Business Marketing,* 72 (March), 52–74.

Keon, John W., and Judy Bayer (1986). "An Expert Approach to Sales Promotion Management." *Journal of Advertising Research,* 26 (3), 19–28.

Kolodner, Janet L., and Theresa L. Penberthy (1990). "A Case-Based Approach to Creativity in Problem Solving." In *Proceedings of the Twelfth Annual Conference of the Cognitive Science Society.* Hillsdale, N.J.: Lawrence Erlbaum, 978–985.

Kotler, Philip (1991). *Principles of Marketing,* 5th ed. Englewood Cliffs, N.J.: Prentice-Hall.

Kroeber-Riel, Werner, and Franz-Rudolf Esch (1993). "CAAS: Computer Aided Advertising System." In Werner Kroeber-Riel and Franz-Rudolf Esch (eds.), *Expert Systems in Advertising.* Munich: Vahlen-Verlag, forthcoming.

Kunda, Ziva (1990). "The Case for Motivated Reasoning," *Psychological Bulletin,* 108 (3), 480–498.

Lamberti, Donna M., and William A. Wallace (1990). "Intelligent Interface Design: An Empirical Assessment of Knowledge Presentation in Expert Systems," *MIS Quarterly,* September, 279–311.

Lee, Hoon Young, Raymond R. Burke, and Jerry Wind (1990). "An Analogical Reasoning System for New Product Concept Evaluation." Paper presented at the Marketing Science Conference, University of Illinois, Champaign/ Urbana, Ill. (March).

Leonard-Barton, Dorothy, and John J. Sviokla (1988). "Putting Expert Systems to Work." *Harvard Business Review,* March–April, 91–98.

Levitt, Theodore (1989). "Management and Knowledge." *Harvard Business Review,* reprint #89316, p. 8.

MacLachlan, James (1984). "Making a Message Memorable and Persuasive." *Journal of Advertising Research,* 23 (January), 51–59.

McCann, John M. (1986). *The Marketing Workbench.* Homewood, Ill.: Dow Jones-Irwin.

McCann, John M., and John P. Gallagher (1990). *Expert Systems for Scanner Data Environments: The Marketing Workbench Laboratory Experience.* Boston: Kluwer Academic Publishers.

McCann, John M., A. Tadlaoui, and J.P. Gallagher (1990). "Knowledge Systems in Merchandising: Advertising Design." *Journal of Retailing,* 66 (3), 257–277.

McCartney, Robert (1990). "Reasoning Directly from Cases in a Case-Based Planner." In *Proceedings of the Twelfth Annual Conference of the Cognitive Science Society.* Hillsdale, N.J.: Lawrence Erlbaum, 101–108.

McGuire, William J., and Demetrios Papageorgis (1961). "The Relative Efficacy of Various Types of Prior Belief-Defense in Producing Immunity against Persuasion." *Journal of Abnormal and Social Psychology,* 62, 327–337.

Minsky, Marvin (1975). "A Framework for Representing Knowledge." In Patrick Winston (ed.), *The Psychology of Computer Vision.* New York: McGraw-Hill, 211–277.

Mitchell, Andrew A. (1986). "The Use of Alternative Knowledge Acquisition Procedures in the Development of a Knowledge-Based Media Planning System." *International Journal of Man-Machine Studies,* 26, 399–412.

——— (1988). "The Development of a Knowledge-Based Media Planning System." In Wolfgang Gaul and M. Schader (eds.), *Data, Expert Knowledge, and Decisions.* Berlin: Springer-Verlag, 67–79.

Neibecker, Bruno (1987). "Einsatz von Expertensystemen im Marketing." Universitat des Saarlandes, Institut fur Konsumund Verhaltensforshung, Saabrucken, Germany.

——— (1991). "Concept for Construct Validation of Expert Systems in Marketing." Paper presented at DGOR (Deutsche Gesellschaft fur Operations Research), Stuttgart, Germany.

Pei, Buck K.W., and J. Hal Reneau (1990). "The Effects of Memory Structure on Using Rule-Based Expert Systems for Training: A Framework and an Empirical Test." *Decision Sciences*, 21, 263–286.

Peters, Thomas J. (1987). *Thriving on Chaos: Handbook for a Managerial Revolution*. New York: Alfred A. Knopf.

Petty, Richard E., and John T. Cacioppo (1983). "Central and Peripheral Routes to Persuasion: Application to Advertising." In Larry Percy and Arch G. Woodside (eds.), *Advertising and Consumer Psychology*. Lexington, Mass.: D.C. Heath/Lexington Books, 3–23.

Petty, Richard E., John T. Cacioppo, and David Schumann (1983). "Central and Peripheral Routes to Advertising Effectiveness: The Moderating Role of Involvement." *Journal of Consumer Research*, 10 (September), 135–146.

Phipps, John (1987). "Future Directions in Supermarket Merchandising: The Expert System." Working paper, Touche Ross, San Francisco.

Porter, Michael E. (1985). *Competitive Advantage: Creating and Sustaining Superior Performance*. New York: Free Press.

Ram, Sudha, and Sundaresan Ram (1988). "INNOVATOR: An Expert System for New Product Launch Decisions." *Applied Artificial Intelligence*, 2, 129–148.

——— (1989). "Expert Systems: An Emerging Technology for Selecting New Product Winners." *Journal of Product Innovation Management*, 6, 89–98.

——— (1990). "Screening Financial Innovations, An Expert System Approach." *IEEE Expert*, August, 20–28.

Rangaswamy, Arvind, Raymond R. Burke, Jerry Wind, and Jehoshua Eliashberg (1987). "Expert Systems for Marketing." *MSI Technical Report*, no. 87–107, 1–50.

Rangaswamy, Arvind, Jehoshua Eliashberg, Raymond R. Burke, and Jerry Wind (1989). "Developing Marketing Expert Systems: An Application to International Negotiations." *Journal of Marketing*, 53, 24–39.

Rangaswamy, Arvind, Bari A. Harlam, and Leonard M. Lodish (1991). "INFER: An Expert System for Automatic Analysis of Scanner Data." *International Journal of Research in Marketing*, 8 (April), 29–40.

Ray, Michael L., and William L. Wilkie (1970). "Fear: The Potential of an Appeal Neglected by Marketing." *Journal of Marketing*, 34 (January), 54–62.

Rhine, Ramon J., and Laurence J. Severance (1970). "Ego-Involvement, Discrepancy, Source Credibility, and Attitude Change." *Journal of Personality and Social Psychology*, 16, 175–190.

Riesbeck, Christopher K., and Roger C. Schank (1989). *Inside Case-Based Reasoning*. Hillsdale, N.J.: Lawrence Erlbaum.

Rossiter, John R., and Larry Percy (1985). "Advertising Communication Models." In Elizabeth C. Hirschman and Morris B. Holbrook (eds.), *Advances in Consumer Research*, vol. 12. Provo, Ut.: Association for Consumer Research.

———— (1987). *Advertising and Promotion Management*. New York. McGraw-Hill.

Schmitz, John D., Gordon D. Armstrong, and John D.C. Little (1990). "CoverStory—Automated News Finding in Marketing." *Interfaces*, 20 (6), 29–38.

Schumann, M., Patricia A. Gongla, Kyoung-Sang Lee, and J. Gene Sakamoto (1987). "Business Strategy Advisor: An Expert System Implementation." Paper, IGM Los Angeles Scientific Center.

Schwerin, Horace S., and Henry H. Newell (1981). *Persuasion in Marketing*. New York: John Wiley.

Sen, Shahana, Richard Colombo, and Bruce Buchanan (1990). "Estimation of Choice Models Using Neural Nets." Paper presented at the Annual Conference of the Association for Consumer Research, New York (October).

Shafer, Glenn, and Judea Pearl, eds. (1990). *Readings in Uncertain Reasoning*. San Mateo, Calif.: Morgan Kaufmann Publishers.

Shortliffe, Edward. H. (1976). *Computer-Based Medical Consultations: MYCIN*. New York: American Elsevier.

Stefik, Mark, Janice Aikins, Robert Balzer, John Benoit, Lawrence Birnbaum, Frederick Hayes-Roth, and Earl Sacerdoti (1983). "The Architecture of Expert Systems." In Frederick Hayes-Roth, Donald A. Waterman, and Douglas B. Lenat (eds.), *Building Expert Systems*. Reading, Mass.: Addison-Wesley, 89–126.

Sternthal, Brian, Ruby Dholakia, and Clark Leavitt (1978). "The Persuasive Effect of Source Credibility: Tests of Cognitive Response." *Journal of Consumer Research*, 4 (March), 252–260.

Stewart, David W., and David H. Furse (1986). *Effective Television Advertising: A Study of 1000 Commercials*. Lexington, Mass.: D.C. Heath/Lexington Books.

Varadarajan, P. Rajan (1985). "Joint Sales Promotion: An Emerging Marketing Tool." *Business Horizons*, September–October, 43–49.

Walden, Pirkko (1989). "Expert Systems in Marketing Decision Making." Memostencil nr. 143, preliminara forskningsrapporter 24.8.1989, Foretagsekonomiska Institutionen, Abo Akademi, Abo, Finland.

Wierenga, Berend (1990). "The First Generation of Marketing Expert Systems." Working Paper no. 90-009, Marketing Department, The Wharton School, University of Pennsylvania.

Winter, Franz L., and John R. Rossiter (1993). "ADEXPERT: A New System for Advertisement Construction and Evaluation." In Werner Kroeber-Riel and Franz-Rudolf Esch (eds.). *Expert Systems in Advertising*. Munich: Vahlen-Verlag, forthcoming.

10

MARKETING DECISION SUPPORT SYSTEMS IN TRANSITION

Lakshmi Mohan and William K. Holstein

AMONG THE MOST IMPORTANT *tools of the marketing information revolution have been the marketing decision support systems (MDSS) — whose purpose are the conversion of raw data into managerially useful information. This chapter and the following one by Hoch provide an overview of the general status and prospects of MDSS. Subsequent chapters go into much greater detail about some of the specific issues raised.*

In this chapter, Mohan and Holstein focus on many of the problems facing organizations as they try to implement MDSS so that the systems can realize their full potential. Among the areas discussed are the level of detail in data required for decision making, the integration of data obtained from different sources or heterogeneous databases, issues involved in collecting and processing soft data on topics such as competition and market trends, procedures for storing and handling data, and resolving questions of data ownership and access.

One of the chapter's main points is that the level of MDSS adoption has varied considerably both across and within industries. In particular, industrial (as opposed to consumer) product firms tend to be, in the authors' words, "marketing data poor." Using some specific industrial product contexts as examples and case studies, the authors identify what the sources of the limited application of MDSS have been, and, consequently, what steps must be taken to help rectify the situation.

INTRODUCTION

Marketers use data to support problem finding, problem solving, and decision making. *Marketing decision support systems* (MDSS) are computer systems designed to help them in these tasks. The term MDSS sets these systems apart from traditional management information systems, which generate a great deal of data and reports, but often not enough interpretable information to manage the business. The purpose of an MDSS is, simply stated, to convert raw data into useful marketing information. The key words here are *convert* and *useful*.

Conversion implies the integration of data, models, and analytic tools with supporting software and hardware. Useful implies the production of information that can form a basis for marketing action.

The term MDSS is only one of the labels used in practice for systems of this type. MDSS has taken root under other labels such as marketing management information systems, marketing and sales productivity systems, market analysis and information systems, and sales decision support systems. We use the term quite broadly, but with specific prerequisites — *systems that integrate data, models, and analytic tools to support marketing and sales*. This is consistent with Little's early definition of an MDSS (Little 1979).

MDSS has developed in quite diverse ways in different companies and, particularly, in different industries. Systems range in complexity from an integrated database focusing primarily on data retrieval and simple manipulation, to analysis of data using quite sophisticated and powerful models to, in some recent applications, expert systems technology to extract "knowledge" from the data. This wide variance is because of dissimilar patterns of data availability and different approaches to marketing and decision making. Understanding this diversity is an important part of understanding MDSS as it exists today.

This chapter reflects a strongly held view about the role of MDSS: as organizations become more customer-focused, MDSS systems will expand in scope and sophistication and become an essential component of the company's ability to understand the marketplace and to remain competitive. Yet, many problems will have to be overcome for MDSS to realize its full potential. The acquisition and management of the data that form the foundation for MDSS are particularly key problems. Once the data are available, their analysis, and the generation and delivery of knowledge, become critical.

We look first at how MDSS is used today and why implementation lags in some industries; second, at the problem of data, the key implementation challenge in MDSS; third, at contemporary issues such as empowering and executive information systems and how they are changing the role of MDSS; fourth, at the problems of dealing with the continuing data explosion and the need to support larger user groups. We conclude with a summary of trends that will shape the future of MDSS.

MDSS PRACTICE IS UNEVEN

To understand where MDSS is today, we begin with the frequently purchased consumer packaged goods (CPG) industry which leads in the use of MDSS. We then contrast it with the situation in industrial marketing where progress has been slower, and comment on the factors that may explain the difference.

Consumer Packaged Goods

MDSS can be traced to the early 1970s when companies such as Coca-Cola and Nabisco found that they were *data-rich* but *information-poor*. The earliest MDSS applications occurred in the CPG industry for two reasons: CPG companies had an earlier, clearer focus on the customer and the competitive marketplace, and they had available much more, and much better, data than companies in other industries. For example, beginning in the 1930s with the Nielsen store audit for tracking market shares, a variety of syndicated data services have provided sales measurements at every stage in the distribution pipeline.

Despite the strong lead, MDSS usage has not evolved in a uniform manner across companies in the CPG industry. A study of 13 firms in 1984–1985 found that most MDSS applications involved market status reporting, i.e., "how things are." They did not extend to market *response reporting*, i.e., "how effective specific marketing actions are" (McCann 1986).

The problem was not the lack of a conceptual basis for response analysis. Little provided several examples of market response models more than a decade ago. He also described a full-blown MDSS that had evolved from market status reporting to market response reporting over a multi-year period (Little 1979). Clearly there is an intellectual cost associated with the use of powerful MDSS systems. Not all managers are equally motivated to use such systems, so the unevenness in MDSS practice persists today. For example, some CPG companies are well ahead of others in applying expert systems technology.

Industrial Marketing

Systems for industrial products clearly lag the CPG industry. Until recently, the focus of industrial marketing was on *products*, not customers, because of the dominance of technology over marketing (Lillis and McIvor 1985). Hence, they lacked the strong marketing orientation of the CPG companies. The situation is exacerbated by the difficulty of getting competitive information that, in the CPG industry, is routine. This is because the customer base for industrial products is heterogeneous and products do not go through centralized distribution channels as do most consumer packaged goods.

The academic community has also not given industrial MDSS the same attention as that given to consumer products MDSS. For example, a blueprint for using MDSS at every stage in the product life cycle for consumer products was published in Little's 1979 paper. There is, even today, no counterpart for industrial products in the published literature. But the prime reason for the lag in MDSS practice in industrial products has been lack of data.

Unlike consumer product firms, industrial product companies are typically data-poor, or more, precisely, *marketing-data-poor*.

The problem is frustrating because (1) data needed for the marketing function are usually *not collected*; (2) useful market data that are collected by the sales force in call reports are *not captured* in the computer; and (3) data that are available are *not usable* because they are difficult to access, poorly organized, not reported in a timely fashion, or internally inconsistent.

A case history of MDSS at General Electric speaks to this point, and to the source of the problem as well. GE's information systems have historically been under the control of financial operations and so have focused on financial information systems. Lillis and McIvor (1985) describe the difficulty of extracting marketing information from the GE information system:

> Information on orders, sales and margins . . . are of maximum value when tied to legitimate and meaningful market segments. And segment-based data are of limited use to finance, hence the common misalignment problem between finance and marketing. The source of the problem is that the detail of market information to meet the mission of the finance function is different from the level required to guide market decisions.

The problem of inadequate marketing data is not peculiar to industrial products. The banking industry is awash with computerized data about its customers. Yet Citibank found itself in the same predicament as did many industrial products companies in the mid-1980s. A McKinsey consultant involved in a project to examine information requirements at Citibank noted:

> We found, in the first place, that the management . . . didn't even have a good profile of its markets and its customers. It didn't really know in summary form what [its position was] with respect to discrete market segments. And without that sort of information, it is pretty difficult to manage the business. . . . There was very little account profitability and not even market-segment profitability information. (Urban and Star 1991)

An Industrial MDSS Example

The following example is typical of the situation in technology-driven firms, which often recognize the importance of marketing and the need for an MDSS only when the environment forces them to do so. An MDSS emerged after a crisis and helped change the culture of the organization.

Until recently, this business (belonging to a *Fortune* 20 company) concentrated only on "new units" and had a commanding 70% share of the U.S. market. Spare and renewal parts were viewed as a support function, and the company perceived its strength as leadership in technology. With demand outstripping supply, the business operated more as *order-takers* rather than *order-seekers*.

Then disaster struck when the market for new units literally evaporated because of a sharp decline in domestic consumer demand, combined with government regulatory actions which provided no incentives to customers to install new units. This forced management to change its business focus from new units to spare and renewal parts in the domestic market, and to look beyond the shores of the United States for new business.

When you don't have data, how do you proceed? This company did not limit the MDSS application to existing data. Rather, it examined the critical success factors for the business. This led to a precise definition of the data that had to be captured, and identified some required data that were not available in existing systems.

In both market segments the entrenched competition was stiff—small vendors in the domestic market and international companies in the export market. Price became an important factor. The first priority for this business was obviously to become competitive in price. A dual strategy was adopted to achieve this objective—increase productivity and reduce costs. The end result was a dramatic trimming of the breakeven level by a factor of nine.

The primary aim of the company's business strategy then shifted to *improved customer service*. This entailed a clear definition of what constituted customer service and priorities for achieving it. Initially, two critical success factors were targeted:

Quote performance: to reduce the turnaround time for the response to a request for a quote; and
Shipment performance: to meet the customer's "want date."

Improved customer service implied a need to monitor the responsiveness of the quote and shipment processes. This, in turn, required *new data* to be captured. The existing information systems in the company had a tremendous wealth of financial information but not the type of data needed for tracking customer service. The new data were, interestingly, all from internal data sources but with the spotlight on the customer. A good example is the information needed on dates for determining customer-related "cycle times":

Date of request for quote and date of quote release—this determines the "quote cycle";
Date of order vis-à-vis customer "want" date to determine the "requested cycle"; and
Date of order vis-à-vis date of shipment to determine the "ship cycle."

Cycle times were important for improving service. Tracking these times with other relevant data in an integrated MDSS database provided a management tool for changing the organization culture from technology-driven to market-driven.

This example shows that an MDSS does not have to be large and sophisticated to be effective, but it does have to convert raw data into useful, actionable information. It also demonstrates a valuable approach for getting started with MDSS. The early emphasis on critical success factors is particularly helpful in a marketing-data-poor environment because it focuses attention on what managers *must* know, rather than what is nice to know, or what happens to be available.

DATA ISSUES

The quality of the MDSS is only as good as the quality of the data that drive it. Further, data problems are more difficult to solve than hardware and software problems. Particular issues that we will discuss include the detail required for marketing decision making, integrating data obtained from different sources and residing in different databases, incorporating soft data on things such as competition and market trends, and resolving questions of data ownership and the level of detail for storing data.

Data Gaps

At the outset, there are *gaps* in the available internal data. Some details required for MDSS are lacking because of the accounting and cost orientation of most management information systems.

Here is an example of available, but incomplete, data in a CPG company. An MDSS to evaluate the effectiveness of trade promotions was stalled because the computerized data bank of the company only had data on *how much was spent* on promotions (which was needed for accounting) but not *when the promotion was run*. McCann (1986) observed the same lacuna in his 13-firm study.

To move the development of the MDSS forward, the information on the timing of promotions had to be manually extracted from log books for each brand and trade promotion. Eventually a promotional event calendar system had to be developed to track the dates and types of trade promotions.

The same accounting and cost orientation is responsible for the customer database in many companies not having ancillary information on the type of customer to permit segment analysis of sales data. Even product cost data are not available at the level of actionable detail that is necessary to identify opportunities to cut costs.

The root cause of the data gap is that, when the accounting systems were designed, no one gave any thought to the use of that data for marketing analysis. There is a clear lesson here. Accounting systems, especially those that deal with sales and costs, are an important source of data for MDSS. Hence, the design of these systems must incorporate the requirement of marketing.

Data Integration

Another common data problem deals with *integrating data* in different internal databases. This problem is often compounded by discrepancies in data definitions and coding schemes. We quote a Lockheed executive:

The importance of standard definitions can be illustrated by the use of the word *"sign-up."* In general, the term refers to a customer's agreement to buy an aircraft. However, prior to the establishment of a standard definition, it tended to be used differently by various organizational units. To marketing people, a sign-up was when a *letter of intent* to buy was received. Legal services considered it to be when a *contract* was received. Finance interpreted it as when a *down payment* was made. The standard definition of a sign-up now used is "a signed contract with a non-refundable down payment." (Houdeshel and Watson 1987)

The data integration problem gets worse when external databases are also involved. The experience of the MDSS development team in the U.S. subsidiary of Glaxo, a multinational pharmaceuticals manufacturer, is an example. The MDSS, which was installed in 1989, was the first marketing system in Glaxo to integrate data from different sources—sales and quotas, market shares, call-reporting information, demographics, and prescriptions. The Glaxo team's observation sums up the problem faced by anyone who has had to cope with multiple data sources:

> When the project commenced in mid-1988, the production systems from which the data was extracted were not designed to integrate with other production data. The relationships between the different data sources (e.g., product levels) had to be defined. The integration effort was very resource intensive. (Sands 1991)

Aside from the resource-intensive nature of the data integration problem, the sheer time factor cannot be ignored. A decision support systems manager at Quaker Oats noted that combining internal and external databases with different file formats and data languages requires an "understanding of each barrier—as a result, the project will move slowly, one area at a time" (Francett 1990).

The lesson for both marketing managers and MDSS developers is not to underestimate the hidden costs and the time required to get the MDSS database up and running.

Soft Data

An even more serious issue is that MDSS systems should not be limited to the *hard* data contained in existing internal systems. The *soft* data on buying processes, competitors' activities, and market trends in the call reports of the sales force are important, especially for those industries where the call reports are the only source of such data. In these industries, salespeople have most of the relevant real-time market knowledge based on their frequent contact with customers. These, admittedly soft, data are usually left out of the computer because of the focus of information systems on hard-data-oriented accounting and operations applications.

It is not a trivial matter to incorporate the call report data into a usable database, but the payoff for companies that have done it has been worth the effort. In almost every instance, the format of the call report must be modified so that consistent data are collected in a form that lends itself to computerization. Further, the sales force must be motivated to collect the desired information in the new report format. This can be facilitated by building capabilities into the MDSS for supporting the sales force so that it receives benefits from the system. This is the successful strategy that Frito-Lay adopted in developing an MDSS from the data gathered by the sales force through its hand-held computers (Applegate 1991).

Data Management

The MDSS database should be designed not only to meet today's information needs, but to be flexible enough to handle the needs of the future. This raises the question of the level of detail for *storing* the data. A conceptual solution to this problem has been available for some time — a corporate data architecture composed of three distinct databases. As proposed by Procter & Gamble:

> The current data at the transactional level will be in the *transaction* databases. These databases will feed the *historical* database that will store data at the lowest level of detail deemed necessary for flexible response. The *application* database will contain the data extracted from the historical database and aggregated at the desired level of detail to meet current needs. (Laning, Walla, and Airaghi 1982)

Performance and cost factors also have to be considered and the trade-off is not a simple matter. Each firm must design its own system in light of its specific needs.

Finally, the controversial question of data *ownership* must be addressed. Information is power and the politics of competition within a company is a real obstacle to developing a common, shared MDSS database. As an example, two divisions in the same company are each purchasing their own copy of the same market data from an external vendor! The question of who gets what data thwarts the exploitation of marketing opportunities. In particular, the sharing of customer information to promote *cross-selling* in multidivision organizations tends to be a victim of the politics of data.

Because data is an important issue in MDSS implementation, management attention is required to deal with it. A specific individual, a data administrator, should be given the responsibility and authority for managing the data resource. Database administration is a demanding job and the individuals involved must receive appropriate rewards.

THE IMPACT OF CONTEMPORARY MANAGEMENT ISSUES

Many companies have recognized two imperatives for managing in the 1990s:

1. The *customer* should be central to a market-driven enterprise. This is really a rediscovery of the marketing concept as the cornerstone of a management philosophy. Peter Drucker said it well in 1954:

   > There is only one valid definition of business purpose: to create a satisfied customer. . . . Marketing is so basic . . . that it is not a specialized activity at all . . . it is the whole business seen from the point of view of its final result, that is, from the customer's point of view. (Drucker 1954)

2. The organization should be fast, flexible, and responsive to be competitive in a dynamic and complex business environment. The key to such an organization is the *empowering* of employees all the way down through the organization.

   The CEO of General Electric, a champion of the concept of empowering employees, asserts that the key to GE's sustaining its competitive position in the 1990s is "the individual, not the system." He elaborated his notion of empowering as follows:

   > The distilled essence of competitiveness [is] the reservoir of talent and creativity and energy that can be found in each of our people. That essence is liberated when we make people believe that what they think and do is important . . . and then get out of their way while they do it. (Welch 1988)

We discuss next the implications of these issues and how they will affect the future role and scope of MDSS.

MDSS Has a Role in Performance Evaluation

An organization that is genuinely market-driven and customer-focused should have *market-based measures* for gauging management and business performance:

> Measurement and reward systems are critical in developing a market-oriented business. Just as managers will emphasize those things that top management's statements of values and beliefs focus their attention on, they will also do those things for which they are evaluated and rewarded. (Webster 1988)

A Coopers & Lybrand study of business planning has advocated that traditional indices of customer satisfaction and service levels should be supplemented by *market-based financial measures*. Examples include rates of return by channel of distribution, by type of account, and by type of media expenditure. Such measures facilitate better integration of financial management with marketing, and allow a clear focus on marketing goals rather than cost-control goals (Coopers & Lybrand 1985).

Although measurement and reward systems fall within the purview of top management, the implications for an expanded role for MDSS are significant. In essence, the MDSS should not be limited to supporting only the marketing and sales functions. It should have a broader purpose and, as we note later, be carefully connected to other management support systems in areas such as purchasing, manufacturing, and logistics which precede sales in the business process. Certainly, the MDSS should drive market-based performance evaluation systems for other functional areas that interact with marketing.

To illustrate the broader scope of an MDSS in performance evaluation, we present an example from a food-products company. The company's critical success factor in the face of increasing competition was defined to be *customer service*. This factor was translated into two specific indicators: the *fill ratio* of shipments to orders, and the *freshness* of the product delivered, measured by the remaining shelf life of the shipped product.

These two market-based indicators monitored the performance of all functions involved in delivering the product to the customer — marketing, sales production, and distribution. Previously production decisions were governed by efficiency indicators such as ingredient wastage. This led to long production runs and diminished shelf life. Distribution, on the other hand, watched the order fill rate without concern for the shelf life of the product delivered.

The new performance measures required new data to be captured in the invoicing and inventory control systems. Orders had to be tracked in addition to shipments. Further, information on shipments and on-hand inventory of each product had to be broken down by the code dates stamped on the containers to determine the shelf life of the product. These data requirements were built into the design of the distributed information system that replaced the older (centralized) transaction system.

Here we see a customer-oriented database driving performance measurement across the company, not just in marketing and sales—an excellent example of how MDSS can help improve performance as measured from the perspective of the customer. This example also illustrates the merit of designing transaction systems and the MDSS together to avoid the data gap problem.

Decision Support for the Sales Force

Empowering employees with authority and decision-making responsibilities has a prerequisite: the availability of relevant information to effectively fulfill those responsibilities and leverage their capabilities. Historically, MDSS has supported the product and brand management groups in corporate headquarters. However, one of the most significant benefits of MDSS comes from supporting salespeople and their frontline management.

Support for the sales force began by automating the paperwork that consumed much of the time of salespeople. The microcomputer revolution removed the technological barriers to do this. In the CPG industry, Frito-Lay was a pioneer in automating the sales force. They equipped 10,000 route salespeople with hand-held computers and reported savings of two and a half hours per week per salesperson—enough to justify an investment of $40 million in hardware and software.

The principal value, however, has come from a sales decision-support system that utilizes data from the hand-held computers. The system provides the basis for weekly "one-on-one" meetings between salespeople and managers. It has changed the way the sales force is managed—from a retrospective, implicit *perspective* to a real-time, explicit management *process*.

Several sales productivity applications have been implemented in industrial marketing which go beyond field reporting to other sales support tasks such as tracking leads, checking inventory and order status, managing distributors, and so forth. One study estimates the sales increases arising from the improved efficiency of the sales staff as ranging from 10% to more than 30%, with investment returns often exceeding 100% (Moriarty and Swartz 1989).

The best MDSSs move beyond paperwork automation and productivity applications to support the selling process itself. In industrial marketing, personal selling is usually more prominent than other elements in the marketing mix such as advertising and promotion. One of the early applications was an interactive system for allocating sales force effort to customers by setting call norms for individual accounts. A key feature of the system is the use of judgmental inputs obtained from salespeople. These judgments are used to estimate the amount of business that can be generated from a particular account under different levels of call intensity (Lodish 1974).

Empowering sometimes involves problems of scale. In the financial services and other service industries, which are intrinsically information intensive, one might think that providing information support to the front line dealing with customers would be an established practice. It is not, in part because of the difficulty of building a unified customer information file which tellers and other salespeople can access. Bank of America required more than 5 million lines of code to integrate information on 20 million accounts, information that had been filed in several separate databases. Once the unified customer database was established, a system for branch staffs to sell and service bank products, including a cross-selling program, could be introduced. As a result of the new system, Bank of America reports that market share, revenue, and profit have all rebounded from the setbacks faced by the bank in the mid-1980s (SIM *Special Report* 1991).

CPG companies have started to provide tools to the sales force to prepare fact-based sales presentations. The present market environment is propelling the use of such tools because retailers want convincing arguments based on hard data before they put a product on the shelf. Yet the overwhelming amount of data from scanners and other sources on prices, displays, and features makes it virtually impossible for salespeople to dig into the data and identify selling opportunities. They need an *MDSS with smarts*. Commercial products are now available from data companies—SalesPartner from Information Resources followed by Sales Advisor from Nielsen. These systems sort through the mountain of data and help salespeople craft a presentation based on merchandising (displays and features), pricing, and shelf space management. The newer systems incorporate features such as an easy-to-use interface, fill-in-the-blank screens for data entry, and pop-up windows to create customized sales presentations.

User friendly software does not, by itself, guarantee successful implementation. The organizational and training issues surrounding the delivery of knowledge remain an obstacle. Although expert systems obviate the requirement for a team of expensive MBAs to perform the analysis using conventional MDSS tools, the diffusion of knowledge to the sales force level may still require an intermediary. A senior manager in a large consumer products company noted to one of the authors that it is still necessary to have a key account person *at the local level*. This person should have analytical skills and know local retail market conditions in order to prepare the initial sales presentation.

We observe a similar problem in industrial marketing with the use of services such as Dow Jones News Retrieval, Dialog, and Nexus. These services have vast libraries that salespeople can access to get information about their customers—not just who the executives are but also what is happening with the company, its competitors, and the industry. This knowledge can help them be more effective in their sales presentations, but it is not easy to sort out the relevant information. Here again, some intelligence is needed in the delivery mechanism to assist the users to find the useful information and ignore the rest.

The Link with Executive Information Systems

The contemporary view that executive information systems (EIS) used by top managers should have an external customer focus and empower all levels in the organization makes their linkage with marketing and MDSS crucial.

Executive information systems, sometimes called executive support systems to emphasize a full range of capabilities such as electronic mail and calendaring, are usually designed to support an individual executive or the executive team. This has obvious implications for the database and the user interface. The EIS database has to have a broader span than the databases of systems supporting a function or a department. The interface has to be user friendly and, in best practice, should facilitate navigating through a very large database.

A natural starting point for many EIS systems is monitoring financial performance indicators since they are of immediate concern to top management and the data are readily available. The focus of EIS, however, has expanded with the recognition that financial indicators are the *end result* of the way in which an organization manages its business. To be useful, the EIS should be concerned with the critical success factors, i.e., the specific factors most responsible for the organization to achieve its goals, and the indicators that best track the behavior of each factor (Rockart and DeLong 1988).

With increasing competition, the emphasis in the EIS is changing from an inward perspective to an outward customer orientation. The more progressive, customer-driven companies are now tracking market-oriented performance indicators such as market shares, delivery performance, and quality measures.

An example from an outstanding service competitor with a strong quality orientation, Federal Express, is instructive. The CEO credits the Federal Express service-level measurement system with the achievements that led to the 1990 Malcolm Baldrige National Quality Award. His description of what is measured is noteworthy because it is derived from a combination of internal hard data and soft judgmental data:

> We use what we call service quality indicators. We have 12 things that we know disappoint our customers, and we measure them every single day—how many packages were delivered on the wrong day? on the right day? late? damaged? How many billing corrections we had to make, and things like that. These 12 indicators are weighted in terms of the way they are viewed by the customer. If we lose a package, it's rated 10 times more than if something is a bit late. . . . Every day there is a mathematical measurement of Fedex's service level. (Maglitta 1991)

The empowering concept also has a significant impact on EIS systems. The contemporary view is that EIS should not be limited to supporting only the executive user group as indicated by the *executive* in EIS. The EIS should support all levels in the organization, become *everyone's* information system or an *enterprise intelligence* system driven by a *corporate data warehouse, and be accessed, as appropriate, by all knowledge* workers in the organization.

If EIS is to become an enterprisewide system, information must be pushed down to the front lines of the business. Thus, an MDSS that empowers the sales force must become an important component of the EIS. Furthermore, the customer and market-driven focus that should be embedded in the EIS dictate that the MDSS database, with its external data on customers and markets, is the crux of the corporate data warehouse.

The MDSS-EIS link is also essential to achieve a balanced organization that leverages the benefits of both centralized and decentralized decision-making and control systems. This is an important point. Empowering, as noted earlier, means passing decision-making authority to the front lines. Yet, empowering does not mean the wholesale relinquishing of responsibility to lower levels — there must still be management by higher-level executives.

The president and CEO of Pepsico Worldwide Foods (Frito-Lay's parent) makes the point clear:

> Over the next few years we must decentralize market decisions to enable us to be more responsive and flexible. But senior management cannot abdicate responsibility for understanding and controlling the direction of the business. And, for legal reasons, we must maintain fairly tight control over some activities such as pricing. (Applegate 1991)

Access to detailed data at the top of the organization can actually facilitate the decentralization of decision making. Phillips Petroleum, for example, gave senior executives access to price information from 240 motor fuel terminals. They in turn delegated individual pricing decisions to local terminal managers. This was possible because corporate managers can monitor all price information and maintain the necessary control over this critical business activity (Main 1989).

Therefore, a proper MDSS-EIS link can create *a shared understanding of the business and the direction the company needs to take.*

The shared understanding idea is demonstrated in the Frito-Lay system which started as the hand-held computer project for automating the paperwork of the salespeople. The sales data provided the foundation for "time-synchronizing" the entire business process — from purchasing through manufacture and logistics to sales — and to integrate information throughout the process. To the internal data, with a scope never before available, Frito-Lay added external scanner data on consumer sales, pricing, shares, distribution and displays, and so forth, creating a true corporate-data warehouse.

The Frito-Lay system illustrates integrated management support that delivers timely and consistent information to all levels of management. It is a good example of an *enterprise intelligence system* encompassing an EIS that supports the top 200 executives; a sales decision-support system that supports sales personnel in the field; a market analysis and profitability reporting system for the corporate staff; and additional support systems for manufacturing, logistics, and purchasing. The system has facilitated the move to decentralize Frito-Lay into four geographic business areas with profit and loss responsibility (Applegate 1991).

THE CHALLENGE FOR TODAY'S MDSS

The Frito-Lay case puts into sharp relief the challenge for today's MDSS systems—to convert an explosion of data into useful information and to deliver it to a large and diverse user group.

The data explosion is not really a recent phenomenon—there has always been lots of data, often of the *wrong* kind. A top priority in MDSS is the development of integrated databases containing all relevant marketing data, from both internal and external sources. The database building effort is both resource intensive and time consuming. But the effort can yield excellent results—in many companies the marketing data *are* available, in much larger quantity and of much better quality than ever before. The sheer quantum is striking in the CPG industry where the availability of scanner data has resulted in *two to three orders of magnitude more data*. Advances in information technology will bring even more.

The challenge now is too much data of the *right* kind. This observation applies not only to CPG but to many other industries where customer-specific information can now be tracked in the marketing database.

Supporting larger and more diverse user groups has become necessary because of two important trends in the marketing environment. The first is a shift away from broadbrush national marketing toward *micromarketing* tailored to a regional or local market, to an individual chain or store, or even to a single customer. In the future we will see much more marketing to *segments of one*.

Nowhere is this trend more evident than in the financial services industry. Several firms have closed the loop between providing services to customers and catering to customer needs with customized products. For example, information from automatic tellers and automated interrogation of accounts helps firms better understand customer needs (Braddock 1989).

A second trend is the increasing pace of competition and environmental change, making *timeliness in decision making* a critical success factor.

The MDSS strategy to address these trends calls for a decentralized system through which users in marketing and sales can generate the desired information from a central data warehouse. Running a decentralized system where the users do most of their own retrieval and analysis raises the need for a system design that users can customize. Dealing with the data glut requires intelligence in the system for automating the analysis. Expert systems in marketing is therefore a fertile field for research (see, e.g., McCann and Gallagher 1990; Alpar 1991; and Bayer and Harter 1991)

User-Customizable MDSS Design

Experience has now shown that MDSSs should be user customizable with at least the following features:

Several different *analysis capabilities*, e.g., exception reporting based on user-defined exceptions, ranking based on user-defined variables, custom-designed market segments for market share analysis, customizable reports to handle user-defined measures and aggregation levels, and the ability to view the information in tabular or graphic form.

An extremely *easy-to-learn user interface*. A popular method for entering user specifications for the desired analysis is the fill-in-the-blank screen. Pop-up windows and pull-down menus are useful devices to assist the user to navigate through the database.

An MDSS database may be visualized as a four-dimensional "data cube." The dimensions are products, regions, time, and variables (e.g., volume, market share, price, promotional events, calls). Each of the first three dimensions of the data cube is a hierarchy—for example, region is a hierarchy from the customer, through larger and larger areas, to the national, and even international, levels. The interface must allow the user to slice through the data cube in different ways and select the appropriate hierarchy for analysis.

A *drill down* capability to move from a top-line, aggregated report down to more detailed levels.

A *save selections* feature for regenerating a saved report, possibly with some changes in parameters. An enhancement of this feature allows the user to save a group of selections to create an online slide show.

Error handling procedures in the interface to flag inconsistent or inappropriate selections.

Several DSS software shells and other software products are available for implementing these customizable design concepts. An illustrative application is the Glaxo (pharmaceuticals) MDSS (Sands 1991).

Intelligent Exception Reporting

The data explosion is making it infeasible for users to wade through numerous reports, whether on screen or in hard copy, to find the information they should act upon. Traditional exception reporting and the facility to drill down to the detail behind any number provides a partial solution to this problem but has two limitations: (1) users must still sift through the exception reports to determine the ones they should focus on; (2) the approach of looking at high-level reports and, where called for, drilling down to the detail runs the risk of not spotting lower-level exceptions.

An intelligent exception reporting capability stores the exception specification as a "rule" for the report. The system "intelligently" screens each level of the data and reports only important exceptions. Visual clues in the screen report can be used to indicate that unexpected numbers exist at lower levels.

More intelligence can be embedded in exception reporting. The state-of-the-art draws on rule-based expert systems to find the important events in the data; essentially replicating what an analyst would do in digging through the mass of data.

An expert system that automates this process and presents the findings in the form of a cover memo that an analyst would write is the CoverStory system (Schmitz, Armstrong, and Little 1990). CoverStory automatically sorts through a large database, identifies trends and exceptions as well as the possible causal factors for those events, and then creates a concise memorandum, with text and graphs, to describe the *news* in the data. The application of this expert system to scanner databases by Ocean Spray Cranberries, Inc., has made it possible for a single marketing professional to find the important news in a large database containing about 400 million numbers covering up to 100 data measures, 10,000 products, 125 weeks, and 50 markets; and to get it to the right people in a timely fashion (Schmitz et al. 1990).

Automated Market Response Analysis

Analysis of data to determine market response to various marketing actions requires an analyst to look for relationships in the data. Traditional spreadsheet or statistical methods are time consuming but adequate when the volume of data is manageable. The detail available in scanner data enables measurement of response to nearly every type of marketing stimulus but precludes traditional methods of analysis. The answer again lies in using expert systems techniques to mimic the hands-on processes employed by the analyst. Such methods have been successfully implemented in the areas of promotion evaluation (Abraham and Lodish 1987) and coupon evaluation (Little 1990).

Electronic Marketing Advisers

The conversion of data into useful information can be viewed as a progression: first, status reporting on what happened; then, response reporting to explain why it happened; and, ultimately, action-oriented information on what to do about it.

Much research is under way to develop knowledge-based systems to emulate the planning function. An advanced application to the brand management function is in the development stages (McCann et al. 1991).

Expert systems technology has reached a stage where it is not the bottleneck for knowledge delivery, but creation of marketing knowledge is. To summarize Mitchell, Russo, and Wittink (1991):

Causal structures for understanding market responses are relatively loose compared, for example, to the engineering domain. The marketing environment is complex because it is affected by intelligent human opponents, not well-understood laws of nature.

Marketing knowledge is incomplete, even though there is encouraging progress from nearly two decades of empirical research in marketing science.

Knowledge that humans have, which is not captured in the expert system, affects marketing systems more than other applications.

The role of expert systems in marketing, at least at the present stage of development, is not to replace human beings. The best systems act as collaborators to relieve the human of the simpler, more structured, more repetitive tasks. An example of such a man-machine system is a proposed media-planning system where the problem is decomposed into a number of subproblems, each of which can be solved by a choice of methods: an expert system, an optimization model, or by the decision maker's judgment (Mitchell 1988).

This brings MDSS back to the original role envisaged for it: to support the problem-solving and decision-making function of marketing and sales professionals.

CONCLUSION

The role and scope of MDSS has expanded from its initial objective of supporting product and brand management groups in corporate head-quarters.

Micromarketing and fast response to changes in the marketplace require a decentralized approach to marketing. Many tactical decisions are being shifted to the sales team who is more knowledgeable about local conditions. This empowerment has led to the expansion of the MDSS for providing decision support to the sales force and their frontline management.

The impetus for broadening the scope of MDSS has come from the management imperative of bringing a customer focus to all activities. MDSS is the means for delivery of information on customers and markets to other functional areas. The changing emphasis in executive information systems from financial to market-oriented performance indicators makes the link with MDSS crucial.

The challenge for today's MDSS is to handle the data glut. There is only one solution to the data glut problem—build intelligence into the MDSS to automate the analysis. Expert system ideas have been implemented to scan the data warehouse, diagnose brand and market performance, and generate selling points for presentations to key accounts. There is much research activity taking place in this area, leading us to observe that expert system techniques will become an important component of MDSS.

MDSS has come a long way in the past two decades. MDSS systems are providing high value and have become an integral part of business, but in many companies MDSS is still unfinished business. In companies that are drowning in data, the task is to deliver knowledge synthesized from the analysis of data. In marketing-data-poor companies, the task is to get the data. This is no small task, but once it is accomplished, these companies can reap the rewards that have been demonstrated in the data-rich consumer packaged-goods companies.

In all companies, the sales force has emerged as a prime "customer" for MDSS. MDSS will link with other functional and corporate information systems. Indeed, MDSS will be the key to the conversion of raw data into useful information to support *all* activities that impinge on the *customer*.

REFERENCES

Abraham, Magid, and Leonard Lodish. "PROMOTER: An automated Promotion Evaluation System." *Marketing Science*, vol. 6, no. 2 (1987), 101–123.

Alpar, P. "Knowledge-based Modeling of Marketing Managers' Problem Solving Behavior." *International Journal of Research in Marketing*. vol. 8, no. 1 (April 1991), 5–16.

Applegate, Lynda M. "Frito-Lay Inc.: A Strategic Transition (C)." #9-190-071. Boston: Harvard Business School (1991).

Bayer, J., and R. Harter. " 'Miner,' 'Manager,' and 'Researcher': Three Modes of Analysis of Scanner Data." *International Journal of Research in Marketing*, vol. 8, no. 1 (April 1991), 17–28.

Braddock, Richard S., "Keeping the Customer at the Fore," 1989 Marketing Conference. New York: Conference Board, October 1989.

Coopers & Lybrand/Yankelovich, Skelly and White. "Business Planning in the Eighties: The New Marketing Shape of American Corporations." Internal report (1985).

Drucker, Peter F. *The Practice of Management*. New York: Harper & Row, 1954.

Francett, Barbara, "Marketeers Dig for Openings in a Blizzard of Raw Data." *Computerworld* (October 15, 1990), 93–96.

Houdeshel, George, and Hugh J. Watson. "The Managerial Information and Decision Support (MIDS) System at Lockheed-Georgia," *MIS Quarterly*, vol. 11, no. 1 (March 1987), 132.

Laning, Laurence J., Gary O. Walla, and Larry S. Airaghi. "A DSS Oversight: Historical Databases." *DSS-82 Transactions*. Providence, R.I.: The Institute of Management Sciences (1982), 89.

Lillis, Charles M., and Bonnie J. McIvor. "MDSS at General Electric: Implications for the 1990s from Experiences in the 1970s and 1980s." In Robert D. Buzzell, ed., *Marketing in an Electronic Age*. Boston: Harvard Business School Press, 1985, 89–105.

Little, John D.C. "Decision Support Systems for Marketing Management." *Journal of Marketing*. vol. 43 (1979), 9–27.

————. "Information Technology in Marketing." Working Paper, Sloan School of Management, MIT (September 1990).

Lodish, Leonard M. "Vaguely Right Approach to Sales Force Allocation." *Harvard Business Review* (January–February 1974), 119–124.

McCann, John M. *The Marketing Workbench*. Homewood, Ill.: Dow Jones-Irwin, 1986.

McCann, John M., and John Gallagher. *Expert Systems for Scanner Data Environments: The Marketing Workbench Laboratory Experience*. Boston: Kluwer Academic Publishers, 1990.

McCann, John M., W.G. Lahti, and J. Hill. "The Brand Manager's Assistant: A Knowledge-Based System Approach to Brand Management." *International Journal of Research in Marketing*, vol. 8, no. 1 (April 1991), 51–74.

Maglitta, Joseph. "Being the Best in Business." *Computerworld* (February 25, 1991), 61.

Main, Jeremy. "At Last, Software CEO's Can Use." *Fortune* (March 13, 1989), 80.

Mitchell, A.A. "The Development of a Knowledge-Based Media Planning System." In W. Gaul and M. Schader, eds., *Data, Expert Knowledge and Decisions*. New York: Springer, 1988, 67–79.

Mitchell, A.A., J.E. Russo, and D.R. Wittink. "Issues in the Development and Use of Expert Systems for Marketing Decisions." *International Journal of Research in Marketing*, vol. 8, no. 1 (April 1991), 41–50.

Moriarty, Rowland T. and Gordon S. Swartz. "Automation to Boost Sales and Marketing." *Harvard Business Review* (January–February 1989), 100–109.

Rockart, John F., and David W. DeLong. *Executive Support Systems*. Homewood, Ill.: Dow Jones-Irwin, 1988.

Sands, Sharon. "Glaxo Inc.'s User-Customizable DSS." *DSS-91 Transactions*. Providence, R.I.: The Institute of Management Sciences, 1991, 247–254.

Schmitz, John D., Gordon D. Armstrong, and John D.C. Little. "CoverStory—Automated News Finding in Marketing." *Interfaces*, vol. 20, no. 6 (November–December 1990), 29–38.

SIM *Special Report*. Chicago: Society for Information Management (October 1991).

Urban, Glen L., and Steven H. Star. *Advanced Marketing Strategy*. Englewood Cliffs, N.J.: Prentice-Hall, 1991.

Webster, Frederick E., Jr. "Rediscovering the Marketing Concept." Marketing Science Institute Working Paper, Cambridge, Mass. (January 1988).

Welch, John F., Jr. "Managing for the Nineties." Paper presented at the General Electric Annual Meeting (April 27, 1988).

11

EXPERTS AND MODELS
IN COMBINATION

Stephen J. Hoch

IN THE ABSENCE OF *sufficient data, managers typically make decisions based on their own experience and "intuition." This has been the case historically for most marketing decisions. One of the main consequences of the information revolution—as evidenced by many of the chapters in this volume—is that intuitive decision making is being replaced by model-based decision making. (Of course, faced with too much data, and the ability to use models to process them, managers often fall back on their intuition!) At the same time, as other chapters suggest, model-based decision making is not without problems, and replacing managerial intuition with models may buy certain advantages, but only at the cost of giving up others.*

The solution is to combine the best of both worlds—managers and models—and this chapter describes the issues involved in doing so. In the words of the author,

> *I propose that firms must take advantage of the comprehensiveness and consistency of large-scale database models and at the same time utilize the adaptability and intuition of experts when making routine market forecasts.*

One important issue—which has plagued researchers for years—is the definition of intuition. The chapter begins by describing a way to conceptualize managerial intuition that is both theoretically sound and measurable. The chapter then discusses some specific ways in which managerial judgment can be combined with statistical models and demonstrates how the process is used in an actual application involving sales forecasting. Finally, the chapter concludes by distinguishing the methods described here from those discussed in other chapters in this volume—for example, the expert system and artificial intelligence approaches outlined in Chapters 9, 10, and 11.

INTRODUCTION

The decision environment facing business is more information intensive than ever. Given this data explosion, some observers would argue
that it is no longer tenable for managers to base decisions solely on
intuition. There is general agreement that in order to tap into the benefits
that can accompany enormous databases, businesses have to build models—be they statistical, econometric, or based on artificial intelligence
and other forms of formal decision support. Without the ability to usefully
summarize the data, managers become buried in a sea of facts and
numbers and decision performance can actually decline. The information
revolution has made database models mandatory, but they are not a
problem-free panacea. The wholesale replacement of managers with
models cures some problems but also creates new ones. I offer a partial
solution to resolving the trade-off between model-based versus intuition-
based decision making.

I propose that firms take advantage of the comprehensiveness and
consistency of large-scale database models and at the same time utilize
the adaptability and intuition of experts when making routine marketing
forecasts. I will focus my discussion on recent work examining various
ways of combining expert judgment with statistical models—with the net
result of getting managers to more effectively work *with* rather than
against formal database-oriented decision support systems. The chapter
is partitioned into four sections. First, I describe a way to conceptualize
managerial intuition. Understanding the capabilities and limits of experts
provides a necessary backdrop for thinking about how to jointly utilize
model and expert forecasts. Second, I examine various methods that can
be employed to combine statistical models with expert judgment. Third,
I briefly describe a recent application of the methodology to a sales-
forecasting task. Finally, I identify relevant domains of application for
the methodology and in doing so attempt to distinguish expert-model
combinations from other information-driven decision support systems
based on neural networks, artificial intelligence, or other heuristic-based
production systems.

CONCEPTUALIZING INTUITION

What are the differences between forecasts based on statistical models
and those relying on expert judgment? Both operate on the available
data defining the target event. But whereas models consider the decision-

relevant information in a consistent, mechanical fashion, experts often rely on intuition. Dictionaries define intuition as the act or process of coming to direct knowledge or certainty without reasoning or inferring; it is conceptualized as a keen and quick insight. Noddings and Shore (1981) show that opinion about intuition has varied dramatically over time, from being glorified as the only certain form of knowledge (a view espoused by Descartes and Spinoza) to being castigated for its unreliability. Despite the disagreement over the value of intuition, there is a consensus that decision makers find it difficult to articulate the genesis of their intuition. Intuition is illusive, and because it often defies description it has been difficult to quantify. Moreover, intuition's slippery nature can make it difficult to use in formal business decisions, at least use wisely.

Although evidence on the validity of intuition is equivocal (for reviews see Blattberg and Hoch 1990; Bunn and Wright 1991; Hogarth and Makridakis 1981), for present purposes I assume that many business experts do possess valid intuition. What follows is a brief summary of the strengths and weaknesses of models and expert judgment.

Where Experts Are Weak and Models Are Strong:

- Experts are subject to decision biases of perception and evaluation. Models are unbiased though subject to specification error.
- Experts often suffer from overconfidence and may be influenced by organizational politics that encourage strategic responding. Models take base rates into account and are immune to social pressures for consensus.
- Experts get tired, bored, and emotional. Models do not. Models can process and summarize massive databases. With modern statistical techniques, models can identify useful empirical regularities not observable to the human eye.
- Experts do not consistently integrate the evidence from one occasion to another. Models optimally weight the evidence.

Where Models Are Weak and Experts Are Strong:

- Models know only what the expert has told the model builder. Experts know what questions to ask and can identify new variables that should

be included in the model. Whereas experts can diagnose and predict, most models can only predict.[1]
- Experts are proficient at attribute valuation, providing subjective evaluations of variables that are difficult to measure objectively.
- Models are consistent, but as a consequence are also rigid. Experts are inconsistent but are flexible in adapting to changing conditions.
- Experts have highly organized, domain-specific knowledge. They may have superior pattern-matching skills and may be able to recognize and then interpret abnormal cases containing what Meehl (1954) called "broken leg" cues, cues that are very diagnostic but so rare that they are difficult to anticipate and therefore include in a model.

As decision inputs, experts and models are both substitutes and complements. They are substitutes because both types of predictions take into account much of the same decision-relevant information; they are also substitutes because models derive from the knowledge of the experts. But models and experts are also complements because where one decision input is weak the other is stronger and vice versa. Research usually frames the problem as expert *versus* model, a substitute perspective, rather than as expert *and* model, a complement perspective. In the next section I describe a method for taking advantage of the consistency offered by a model and the intuition that can only come from an expert.

Isolating Intuition

One obstacle to taking advantage of an expert's intuition is finding it. Not only do we not know what intuition looks like, the experts cannot tell us much about it either. Fortunately, in order to engineer higher-quality predictions, we do not have to understand intuition so much as be able to isolate it in a form that can be coupled with a statistical model. Blattberg and Hoch (1990) developed a statistical method for identifying intuition. Assume the following information is available: a set of predictor variables X (an nxk matrix); a criterion variable Y (an nx1 vector); and

---

[1]On the other hand, many artificial intelligence models are specifically designed for diagnosis, such as in the medical arena. More recently, applications such as IRI's CoverStory and SalesPartner are designed to diagnose the cause of a problem (e.g., an outlying observation).

a set of expert predictions P (also an nx1 vector). Begin by building the best-fitting model of Y given the cues (X) using multiple regression,

$$Y = X\beta + \epsilon. \tag{1}$$

Let $M^\wedge - X\beta^\wedge$ be the vector of model predictions. By definition, the expert cannot integrate (linearly) the same information in a more efficient manner; model predictions ($M^\wedge$) represent an upper bound on the linear information that can be extracted from these environmental cues. The key question is whether the expert can add predictive power above and beyond that captured by the model.

Operationally, expert intuition is defined as the residual portion of a decision maker's prediction, controlling for the external variables or predictor variables, X. We isolate intuition by regressing the decision maker's predictions onto the model's predictions,

$$P = \gamma M^\wedge + U, \tag{2}$$

and in standardized form,

$$p = \alpha m^\wedge + (1-\alpha^2)^{1/2} u \tag{3}$$

where α equals the correlation between p and $m^\wedge$, and u represents standardized residuals. u is the "unique" part of the decision maker's prediction containing both valid intuition and error. The valid intuition could result from the decision maker's ability to pick up omitted variables, like broken leg cues, or nonlinearities and interactions not incorporated into the model. u is orthogonal to $m^\wedge$, the correlation between the decision maker's prediction (p) and the criterion (y) can be expressed as,

$$r(y,p) = \alpha r(y,m^\wedge) + (1-\alpha^2)^{1/2} r(y,u). \tag{4}$$

Now that we have a means of isolating expert intuition, the question becomes whether we as modelers can put u to better use than the expert has as expressed through their raw predictions or forecasts. In other words, is it possible to combine the model ($m^\wedge$) and intuition (u) together in a better manner? The answer is obviously yes. Given the assumptions underlying OLS regression, an optimal combination of the model and intuition can be no less accurate than the best of the two decision inputs in isolation; adding any new variable would increase the overall fit, at least on the estimation sample though not necessarily on a holdout sample. Consider first a combination of model predictions with the raw predictions of the expert,

$$y^\wedge = b_1 m^\wedge + b_2 p \qquad (5)$$

where $y^\wedge$ is the prediction from an optimal combination of model and expert. The overall fit of the combination of model and expert can be written as,

$$R^2(y,y^\wedge) = b_1 r(y,m^\wedge) + b_2 r(y,p). \qquad (6)$$

b_1 and b_2 represent the relative weights for the model and the expert. To understand the trade-off between model and intuition, Eq. 6 needs to be rewritten. Substituting Eq. 4 into Eq. 6 and simplifying results in

$$R^2(y,y^\wedge) = r(y,m^\wedge)^2 + r(y,u)^2. \qquad (7)$$

Eq. 7 shows that if experts have no intuition, i.e., $r(y,u) = 0$, then the model should receive full weight. Whenever the expert does have some valid intuition [$r(y,u) = 0$], there exists some combination of the predictions of the model and expert that will be more accurate than either of the single inputs. Two useful statistics fall out of this analysis. The first is the correlation $r(y,u)$ which represents the validity of expert intuition. $r(y,u)$ is the semi-partial correlation (Cohen and Cohen 1975), the correlation between y and p after partialling the model ($m^\wedge$) out of expert predictions (p). Regular partial correlations, where model predictions are controlled for in both the criterion and expert forecasts, can also be calculated [this is equivalent to the correlation between the residuals in Eq. 1 and Eq. 3, i.e., $r(\epsilon,u)$]. When squared, they represent the percent of variance in the outcome unexplained by the model that can be explained by expert intuition.

In summary, we now have an analytic method to separate an expert's intuition from the model parameters of the a priori known variables. It can be used to assess the relative contribution of model and intuition to overall predictive accuracy. Moreover, it helps us determine the emphasis that should be accorded to the model relative to the expert.

COMBINING EXPERT AND MODEL FORECASTS

There are numerous ways to utilize intuition through the combination of expert and model forecasts. My view is that the "best" method should be simple to implement, defensible to other parties, and consistently reproducible from occasion to occasion.

Estimation of "Optimal" Weights

Optimal weights for expert and model can be estimated using OLS regression on a calibration sample. These weights can then be used to form a linear combination of expert and model for prediction purposes. Blattberg and I (1990) studied five real-world forecasting situations. We found that an expert-model combination using optimal regression weights increased overall forecast accuracy in hold-out samples by 16% (R^2 increase of .09). Not only were experts able to pick up over 24% of the variance unexplained by the models, inclusion of expert predictions reduced by over 50% the shrinkage in accuracy that would have been observed if we had relied exclusively on the model. Model shrinkage is inevitable in most forecasting situations. It occurs both because of dynamic changes in the decision environment that are not anticipated during model development and because of overspecification of the original model (e.g., including irrelevant variables).

50:50 Heuristic Weighting

Over the past 20 years an extensive literature has accumulated on the combining of forecasts (Clemen 1989). As a by-product of the search for the "best" combining method, the overriding conclusion is that almost any combination is better than no combination. Moreover, simple averages often do as well and sometimes even better than more sophisticated approaches that take into account the relative accuracy and dependence between forecasts (Bunn 1988). Blattberg and Hoch (1990) found that a simple 50:50 heuristic worked almost as well as optimal regression weights on hold-out samples (a reduction in R^2 of only .01). And in more volatile environments, it is conceivable that a simple average will work better; with estimated weights, one runs the risk of overspecification, i.e., including extra variables that pick up variance due to nonsystematic white noise (Einhorn and Hogarth 1975).

Expert Adjustment of Model Forecasts

Experts can also make adjustments to model forecasts or in some cases completely override the model. Previous research on expert adjustment has produced mixed results. In several laboratory studies, the opportunity for adjustment has led to either no improvement or an actual decrement in performance (e.g., Armstrong 1982; Carbone et al. 1983). Other studies, conducted in their natural decision-making domains, provide a more optimistic picture. Work in the early 1970s on the subjective revision of econometric model forecasts by the forecasting economists (Evans, Haitovsky, and Treyz 1972; Fair 1976) showed that the adjustments reduced prediction errors of ex ante econometric models. Mathews and Diamanthopoulos (1986) found that product managers increased accuracy by modifying sales forecasts of a simple exponential smoothing model. Although the models were based on only eight data points each, the study suggests that experts can at minimum make useful revisions of simple models. Murphy and Brown (1984) show that weather forecasters have learned how to work with statistical inputs, modifying model predictions on the fly when they do not jibe with more subjective bases of information; subjective revisions lead to improved accuracy for shorter lead times (12–24 hours), suggesting that the forecasters are able to factor in information not available to the model. In fact, the atmospheric models now are sophisticated and the relevant data so overwhelming that weather forecasters always base their subjective forecasts on the model forecasts.

Expert adjustments undoubtedly have the potential to increase forecast accuracy, especially if done in a structured manner. If the adjustment task is unstructured, however, judgmental inconsistency could easily cancel out any incremental contribution based on intuition. With inconsistent adjustments, mechanical combination will dominate combination by means of human intervention. In multi-attribute environments characterized by lower predictability ($R^2 < .25$), Hoch and Schkade (1991) found that intuitive predictions are more accurate when people are instructed to anchor on the average and adjust for case-specific differences rather than when they engage in a more natural pattern-matching process. If people anchor on model predictions (which are more sophisticated averages conditioned on case-specific information) and then adjust for intuitions, expert adjustments may have much to offer.

Mechanical Combination Weighted by Subjective Confidence

The first two methods rely on a constant set of weights, either empirically or heuristically determined. In the first method the weights are dependent on the relative validity of model and expert over a large set of cases. When making predictions about new cases, the weights are always applied in the same consistent manner. But what happens when an expert is not equally confident about the accuracy of each forecast? It seems likely that experts will be more confident about some forecasts and less confident about others. There are two interesting questions here: (1) Do experts have any insight (meta-knowledge) about the accuracy of their individual forecasts?; and (2) assuming that they do, can we develop a scheme for differentially weighting model and expert inputs that provides an improvement in predictive accuracy over a constant weighting scheme? No published research has examined the viability of such an approach.

Expert Synthesis of Independent Model and Expert Forecasts

After making their forecasts, experts are shown model forecasts and allowed to adjust their own forecast in any way they wish. Implicitly, we might expect the expert's adjustments to be dependent on their subjective confidence in their forecasts, though not as mechanistically as the previous method. Although the expert has more information here because of access to model prediction, it is not clear how consistently the expert will differentially weight the model and their own predictions. This technique differs from the more standard expert adjustments of model forecasts by allowing the expert to compare subjective to objective inputs, not simply react to the model. Which technique proves best depends on two things. First, how does the presence of a model forecast influence the expert's intuition? Forecasters may be hesitant (or lazy) about adjusting too far from a model forecast even when their intuition would tell them otherwise; the model may inhibit intuition. Second, how do the two methods influence the size of the adjustments that experts make? It is possible that expert synthesis may lead to excessive adjustments from the model if experts anchor on their own forecasts and then insufficiently adjust for model predictions. In contrast, expert adjustment of model forecasts would seem to encourage experts to anchor on the model (which effectively provides a statistical base rate) and then adjust for whatever intuition they may have. Comparative performance of the two techniques then is dependent on whether and how the model influences intuition generation process and the validity of the model relative to intuition.

A RECENT APPLICATION

This section describes a recent application of an expert + model combination in sales forecasting. It extends existing research in two directions. First, it examines the utility of an attempt to partially quantify intuition. Second, it considers whether predictive accuracy can be improved by using experts' confidence judgments to differentially weight expert and model forecasts.

Method

The forecasting task involved estimating sales of fashion apparel through direct mail catalogs. Two years of sales data were available; there were 2,002 observations generated from five catalog mailings in each of the two years. There were eight individual buyers who made sales forecasts for subsets of items. These forecasts were made in the context of ongoing business; all forecasts were made prior to the mailing of a catalog, but after all marketing-decision variables (e.g., price, size of photo, location) had already been established. Besides making sales forecasts, buyers also made two additional judgments. First, they categorized each item into one of two groups: "runners" and "non-runners." In the direct mail business, a runner is the vernacular for an item whose sales can "take off." The runner variable was an attempt to at least partially quantify buyer intuition. These judgments were collected because, after building an initial model on older historical data, I observed the largest residuals on the highest-selling items; a variety of model adjustments did not alleviate the problem. Buyers' residuals did not show the same pattern. For the second judgment, buyers indicated their level of confidence in each of their forecasts using a 1 (unconfident) to 5 (confident) scale. Rather than relying on a single constant set of weights, expert and model forecasts can be differentially weighted by including an interaction term between confidence (c) and the buyer's forecasts (p),

$$y = b_1 m^\wedge + b_2 p + b_3 cp = b_1 m^\wedge + (b_2 + b_3 c)p. \qquad (8)$$

Assuming that the expert's predictions are positively correlated with outcomes (y) and that confidence is positively related to accuracy $[r(y,p)]$, then b_3 will also be positive. This implies that when the experts' confidence in their own predictions is high, more weight will be placed on those predictions (increased by a factor of $b_3 c$).

Results

The model was estimated on about 1,000 observations. Table 11-1 displays the predictive accuracy of the buyers, the model, an "optimal" combination of model + buyer, and a 50% model + 50% buyer combination. Results for the model with and without the "runner" variable are

TABLE 11-1

Type of Forecast	Estimation Sample		Prediction Sample	
	R^2	mse	R^2	mse
Buyer	.483	484	.582	357
Model (+"runners")	.570	410	.588	361
Model (without "runners")	.468	507	.401	524
"Optimal" Combination	.617	380	.617	342
50% Model + 50% Buyer	.594	380	.637	312
50:50—no runners	.567	405	.590	356
"Best" Forecast	.696	285	.748	213

reported. For the "optimal" combination, weights for the buyer and model were determined using OLS regression on the estimation sample. Both percentage of variance (R^2) and mean square errors ([forecasts-actual]^2) are shown. The "best" forecast results represent hypothetical forecast accuracy if one could successfully anticipate which decision input, the buyer or the model, would be more accurate in predicting catalog sales for a particular item. As such, the "best" forecast represents an upper bound on the information content extractable from buyer and models.

If we focus attention on the prediction sample, the results can be summarized as follows:

1. Buyer and model (with runners) attained comparable forecast accuracy. The correlation between buyer and model is high, about .8.
2. A 50:50 combination of model and buyer results in an 8.3% increase in variance explained (R^2) and a 13% decrease in overall forecast error (mse) over the best of the single-decision inputs.
3. The 50:50 combination also outperforms the "optimal" combination based on regression weights determined from the estimation data. The reason for this is that buyers performed differently during the two time periods. Regression weights estimated during the poor-performing period underweight the buyer during the better-performing period. In other words, the 50:50 heuristic helps finesse the problem of unstable weights.
4. Model predictions benefit greatly by incorporating information from buyers about catalog items that were likely to be "big" sellers (runners). Without taking into account the buyer's "runner" picks, the model is much less accurate (a 46% decrease in R^2; a 49% increase in mse). Moreover, a 50:50 combination of buyer predictions with a model not containing runner picks performs no better than the buyer alone.

This suggests that incorporating the buyer's intuition about "big" items into the model reduces potential bias in model forecasts, reducing possible misspecification error. Although the runner variable is highly correlated with buyer estimates, the runner variable does a better job of "correcting" model predictions than simply throwing buyer forecasts into the model. A model was estimated including buyer forecasts rather than the runner variable. Although this increased the model (with buyer) fit, $R^2 = .60$, a 50:50 combination with buyer forecasts could perform no better, $R^2 = .601$.

5. "Best" predictions reduce forecast errors by a third; this suggests that it may be possible to improve accuracy by differentially weighting buyer and model forecasts on a case-by-case basis.

6. A confidence-adjusted weighting scheme was estimated on the first year's data according to Eq. 8. The correlation between buyer confidence and accuracy (mse) was positive, $r = .45$. What we are really interested in, however, is whether the buyer confidence rating provides information concerning the differential accuracy of the model versus the buyer, operationalized as the ratio (mse model)/(mse model + mse buyer). The correlation between buyer confidence and this ratio was also positive but lower, $r = .18$, at least partly because of the high correlation between buyer and model. As a consequence, the attempt at differential weighting based on buyer confidence did not work. The overall fit, $R^2 = .607$, was less than that obtained using the 50:50 mechanical heuristic.

In summary, forecast accuracy can be improved by utilizing a combination of model and expert forecasts rather than by relying on only one of the decision inputs. A 50:50 combination worked best, reinforcing the notion that "simple and parsimonious" often dominates more complicated schemes.

APPROPRIATE APPLICATION DOMAINS FOR EXPERT-MODEL COMBINATIONS

Applications of expert-model combinations have successfully improved marketing decision making in several business applications (Blattberg and Hoch 1990; Bunn and Wright 1991). And, conceptually, taking advantage of the relative strengths of both statistical models and managerial intuition would seem to make sense in many decision-making situations. However, to utilize the basic expert + model methodology, there are a number of preconditions:

1. *The experts must demonstrate actual expertise.* At first glance this point may seem too obvious to mention. There are two polar views of experts. One view, based on research in judgment and decision making, has emphasized a general lack of forecasting expertise by documenting situations where experts show no measurable improvement in performance (e.g., Armstrong 1985; Dawes, Faust, and Meehl 1989; Hogarth and Makridakis 1981). Some of the studies can be questioned because they appear to have placed experts in unfamiliar or unfair tasks where they cannot adequately utilize their knowledge. The other view virtually assumes superior performance on the part of experts (Chi, Glaser, and Farr 1988). One reason for these conflicting views may have to do with the ambiguity of the definition of what constitutes an expert. Not only are experts considered to possess profound knowledge and to be very skillful, they also are highly trained specialists and advisers with much experience. And, although training and experience are often associated with superior performance, there have been and will continue to be cases where experts do not perform well. This can happen because an expert becomes out of date, because the expert certification process is flawed, or because expertise gained in one domain (e.g., consumer packaged-goods marketing) does not transfer to another related domain (durable goods marketing).

2. *A model must be estimable.* A variety of factors can interfere with the model-building process. First, adequate historical data may not always be available. Sometimes data collection is very expensive and other times people forget to keep score. And even when data are available, they may not be representative of likely future conditions. Second, some decision outcomes cannot be put into an easily quantifiable form, or the outcome may be categorical with no apparent underlying continua. Model and expert outputs have to be combinable into a single quantity. But in many situations involving problem diagnosis, for example, predictions and outcomes are discrete events (disease X, Y, Z). And although it is possible to build statistical classification models (e.g., multiple discriminant analysis), it is less obvious how to combine expert and model output. Moreover, in diagnosis, accuracy in predicting the final outcome (the root problem) often may be less important than the speed and cost of the path (e.g., diagnostic tests) to get there.

More important, there are a large class of business decisions where the data available for model building have been influenced and/or contaminated by the decision-making process itself. As Einhorn and Hogarth (1978) point out, most judgments and predictions lead to actions; and, although one can observe outcomes associated with the chosen action, one cannot observe outcomes that might have occurred if different actions had been taken. For instance, imagine that you have scanner data on sales, price, and promotional activity. You then estimate the appropriate elasticities to enable you to calculate an "optimal" everyday price for a product. Although such an analysis in all likelihood would be very informative, the model results clearly would be influenced by the previous pricing promotion decisions which generated the sales data (e.g., adoption of deep discounting strategy for one brand and shallow discounting for another brand may dramatically change the size of the observed coefficients). Marketing experiments with multiple conditions can be run to partially get around this problem, but experiments are too expensive to conduct on an ongoing basis. Therefore, such models probably will be more heuristic than optimal in form, telling us what works better, not what works best.

3. *Experts and models should be moderately redundant.* Holding constant the information content in each decision input, ideally one would prefer uncorrelated expert and model forecasts. However, when experts and models are only loosely unrelated, one has to question whether one or both forecasts have much validity. A more likely scenario is that the two inputs will be reasonably correlated; in the Blattberg and Hoch (1990) study, the average correlation was about .7. If the level of redundancy were to get much higher, the combination may not provide much incremental improvement.

Comparisons with Other Decision Support Systems

Decision support systems (DSS) offer at least three general benefits over human decision making: consistency, scope, and scale. All DSS, be they based on AI, trained neural networks, statistical models, or math programming, are programmatic: provide the same inputs and you are guaranteed the same output. Because DSS are mechanized, they are able to deal with problems of broad scope, i.e., decisions involving multiple inputs. DSS performance normally improves with increases in the number of inputs; human performance can suffer when overloaded with data.[2] DSS also are well suited to problems of large scale. Computers do not tire easily and the variable costs of running them are low. Experts, on the other hand, are expensive and their time is limited.

So how does one decide on which DSS option to pursue for a given problem? As a starting point, I suggest expert + model combinations. There are several reasons for this. First, compared to other approaches, they are faster, easier, and less expensive to develop. To begin all one really needs is an expert, a historical database, and a statistical package. Expert + model combinations are pragmatic; one does not need much of a theory to begin making progress. Second, in my experience they usually work; and even if they do not happen to improve accuracy, the chance of a decrement in accuracy is very low. Third, it is relatively easy to obtain organizational buy-in. Not only do people not need to change current behavior very much, such as would be required in many hands-on decision calculus approaches, decision makers can feel that they have retained a large degree of control because intuition is explicitly incorporated into all forecasts.

There are some limitations to applying expert + model combinations, some alluded to earlier, that may render the approach unworkable:

1. *Model-expert combinations require direct participation by an expert.* Normally, this is not much of a problem. However, in problems of sufficiently large scope and scale, it may be better to have no human intervention at all. For example, Information Resources Inc. processes a total of over 45 million transactions each week from 3,000 different retailers; and the data need to be subjected to quality control. People have excellent pattern-matching skills which can be used to easily detect many of the data problems; however, the large scale of the problem effectively precludes analyst intervention. Instead, IRI relies on a neural network system for quality control.
2. *Combinations of experts and models require data for validation.* With no measure of validity, it is not clear how the inputs should be combined. And without validation, organizational buy-in will be more difficult to achieve. Many AI-based expert systems are developed in data-poor environments where a model cannot be easily estimated.
3. *Expert-model combinations cannot ask questions.* A primary focus of many expert systems is on diagnosis rather than prediction, where the

---

[2]It should be noted that there is also a point of oversaturation of DSS, where adding more variables can hurt the performance of a model.

criterion is expedient and heuristic detective work rather optimization (à la a statistical model).

In summary, the simple-minded combinations of experts and models discussed here are best viewed as a forecasting tool rather than a policy-making tool. The current evidence shows rather conclusively that expert-model combinations can increase predictive accuracy. It is less clear whether they can be used in their current form to set strategy and tactics.

CONCLUSIONS

The amount of data available to business decision makers can only grow. More data only causes headaches if it remains unstructured and is used only to generate accounting reports. There will be lower returns on the rapid advances in data processing technology if we do not start to do a better job of turning data into information. There are a variety of ways to do this as demonstrated throughout the chapters in this book. I will conclude with four pieces of advice for those who have to manage data and use it to make better decisions:

1. If you can build a model, build it. Even a naive model is often better than no model at all (Blattberg and Hoch 1990).
2. If you have experts who can render judgments and opinions, collect them and archive them along with the rest of the data.
3. If you can build a model and have access to expert opinion, try combining them together. Experts are inconsistent but often do have valid intuition. Models show no flashes of inspiration, but they are consistent and tractable. Experts and models are complements, not substitutes.
4. After forecasts and decisions are made, keep score. If you do not monitor outcomes, it will be difficult to improve database models and for that matter increase expert intuition.

REFERENCES

Armstrong, J.S., "The Forecasting Audit." In S. Makridakis and S.C. Wheelwright (eds). *The Handbook of Forecasting.* New York: John Wiley, 1982.
————. *Long-Range Forecasting.* New York: John Wiley, 1985.
Blattberg, R.C., and S.J. Hoch. "Database Models and Expert Intuition: 50% Model + 50% Manager." *Management Science,* 36 (1990), 887–889.
Bunn, D. "Combining Forecasts." *European Journal of Operations Research,* 33 (1988), 223–229.

———— and G. Wright. "Interaction of Judgemental and Statistical Forecasting Methods: Issues and Analysis." *Management Science*, 37 (1991), 501–518.

Carbone, R., A. Andersen, Y. Corriveau, and P.P. Corson. "Comparing for Different Time Series Methods the Value of Technical Expertise, Individualized Analysis, and Judgmental Adjustment." *Management Science*, 29 (1983), 559–566.

Chi, M.T.H., R. Glaser, and M.J. Farr. *The Nature of Expertise*. Hillsdale, N.J.: Lawrence Erlbaum, 1988.

Clemen, R.T. "Combining Forecasts: A Review and Annotated Bibliography." *International Journal of Forecasting*, 4 (1989), 559–584.

Cohen, J., and P. Cohen. *Applied Multiple Regression/Correlation Analysis of the Behavioral Sciences*. Hillsdale, N.J.: Lawrence Earlbaum, 1975.

Dawes, R.M., D. Faust, and P. Meehl. "Clinical versus Actuarial Judgment." *Science*, 243 (1989), 1668–1673.

Einhorn, H.J., and R.M. Hogarth, "Unit Weighting Schemes in Decision Making." *Organizational Behavior and Human Performance*, 13 (1975), 171–192.

————. "Overconfidence in Judgment: Persistence of the Illusion of Validity." *Psychological Review*, 85 (1978), 395–416.

Evans, M.K., Y. Haitovsky, and G.I. Treyz, assisted by V. Su. "An Analysis of the Forecasting Properties of U.S. Econometric Models." In B. Hickman (ed.), *Econometric Models of Cyclical Behavior*. New York: National Bureau of Economic Research, 1972.

Fair, R.C. "An Evaluation of a Short-Run Forecasting Model." In L.R. Klein and E. Burmeister (eds.), *Econometric Model Performance: Comparative Simulation Studies of the U.S. Economy*. Philadelphia: University of Pennsylvania Press, 1976.

Hoch, S.J., and D.A. Schkade. "Anchoring on the Mean versus Pattern Matching in Intuitive Prediction." Center for Decision Research, University of Chicago, Graduate School of Business, 1991.

Hogarth, R.M., and S. Makridakis. "Forecasting and Planning: An Evaluation." *Management Science*, 27 (1981), 115–138.

Mathews, B.P., and A. Diamanthopoulos. "Managerial Intervention in Forecasting: An Empirical Investigation of Forecast Manipulation." *International Journal of Research in Marketing*, 3 (1986), 3–10.

Meehl, P.E. *Clinical versus Statistical Prediction*. Minneapolis: University of Minnesota Press, 1954.

Murphy, A.H., and B.G. Brown. "A Comparative Evaluation of Objective and Subjective Weather Forecasts in the United States." *Journal of Forecasting*, 3 (1984), 369–393.

Noddings, N., and P.J. Shore. *Awakening the Inner Eye: Intuition in Education*. New York: Teacher's College Press, 1984.

12

HARNESSING THE MARKETING INFORMATION REVOLUTION: TOWARD THE MARKET-DRIVEN LEARNING ORGANIZATION

George Day and Rashi Glazer

THE REVOLUTION IN MARKETING *information is putting an enormous stress on the traditional organization. As information grows exponentially, and as its useful half-life shortens, organizations are being challenged to learn faster. This means absorbing more information, making sense of it quickly, and sharing new insights so members can act ahead of the competition.*

Organizations with a superior learning competency *have a deeper understanding of their present markets and are better equipped to take action based on an accurate anticipation of the responses of customers, channels, and competition. It is apparent that traditional organizational structures, systems, processes, and coordinating mechanisms are impeding the development of this learning competency. This chapter describes the feasible organization changes that can overcome these impediments and ensure that a competitive advantage is realized from investment in information systems.*

Fortunately, the developments in information systems that unleashed the data deluge have also enhanced the ability of organizations to learn about their markets. For example, widespread availability of hand-held computers permits salespeople to obtain daily reports on orders' inventories and prices and to speed the information to where it is needed. Electronic data interchange creates a continuous flow of information about customer requirements and usage patterns and enhances two-way communications with customers. Document imaging systems allow widespread access to complete client records. The expert systems described in earlier chapters offer possibilities for quickly extracting meaning from information. Meanwhile organizational memory is enhanced because of the completeness of the transaction data that can be automatically captured, especially when com-

bined with methods that facilitate retrieval, such as case-by-case foresight and smart indexing.

Those who would resolve organizational problems must also recognize that information systems can sometimes impede responsiveness to fast-changing market environments. Although marketing, sales, accounting, and manufacturing may have much more to say to each other, the incompatibilities of databases and software impediments often prevent the timely sharing of knowledge needed for integrated decisions. More information won't be beneficial if it leads to myopic attention to short-term detail at the expense of obscuring long-run trends. For example, there is a legitimate concern that product managers in food companies are overly reliant on the real-time details of microtransaction activity from scanner data, yet overlook more subtle evidence of long-run erosion in customer perceptions of brand superiority. Finally, as companies pursue the potential of information technology to proliferate product variants for specific segments, their decisions are often made in piecemeal fashion without regard to cross-functional implications. The increased complexity results in cost and time burdens that soon offset the benefits of the investments in information systems.

Ultimately, the ability of a business to adapt effectively to its fast-changing environment will depend on its putting into place structures, systems, skills, and processes through which it can learn faster than the competition. But this raises two questions: How do organizations learn?, and How do information systems enhance this learning?

INTRODUCTION

The focus of most of the chapters in this volume has been the impact of the marketing information revolution on the external activities of the firm—in particular, on gaining a strategic competitive advantage through a better understanding of customer behavior. Equally as dramatic, however, is the effect of the revolution on the internal structure and information-processing styles of the firm itself. While many companies have initially tried to embrace the information revolution within the context of their existing organizational structures, it is becoming apparent that this approach will no longer suffice. The enormous increases both in the volume of information and the speed with which it can be transmitted are rendering the traditional forms obsolete. As a number of commentators across many disciplines have noted, for companies that wish to succeed in the information age there is no alternative to the (potentially) radical realignment of the structures, processes, and coordinating mechanisms that have characterized most modern organizations for nearly a century. Without such changes, the huge investments in information systems made by firms in the pursuit of strategic advantage are unlikely to bear fruit.

This chapter presents a framework for thinking about how the marketing information revolution will influence the internal organizational structure and information-processing style of the firm. The authors use the notion of the market-driven learning organization as the core concept—i.e., in the information age, the successful organization is a learning organism. Noting that the traditional organizational structure is inherently biased to impede learning, they describe the issues that need to be addressed to overcome these impediments. Of particular interest is their contention that the processes by which organizations and individuals learn share many features in common. This provides the basis for identifying those characteristics that distinguish the learning organization: open-minded inquiry, synergistic information distribution, information interpretation, and accessible memories.

The chapter also discusses those "architectures" that are most conducive to developing a learning competency. Although information systems are an important part of these structures, the emphasis is less on technology than on the human and social factors that need to change if the firm is to take full advantage of the marketing information revolution and become a market-driven learning organization.

ORGANIZATIONAL LEARNING PROCESSES

The processes of individual and organizational learning have a surface similarity. Information is acquired, given meaning through interpretation, and either acted on immediately or stored in memory for later use (Levitt and March 1988; Fiol and Lyles 1985). However, organizational learning is more than the cumulative results of its members' learning. Employees come and go, but the collective memory preserves the knowledge. Organizations also need processes for sharing information from different sources—and for distributing it to many different parts of the organization.

Learning processes are initiated by the acquisition of knowledge through routine tracking and scanning, continuous experimentation, or directed market inquiries aimed at explaining and resolving problems. However, the extent of learning depends on how well the information is pieced together and distributed widely so that it can be used (Huber 1991). Often it is distributed to a memory repository—data bank—for later use.

Before the information can be acted upon, it has to be interpreted through a process of sorting, classification, and simplification to reveal coherent patterns. This is a function of the mental models of managers that contain decision rules for filtering information and useful heuristics for deciding how to act on the information in light of the anticipated outcomes. Mental models have both an indirect effect on information acquisition by distinguishing critical information from what can safely be ignored and a facilitating effect on decision making by reducing uncertainty. To the extent these individual mental models are accessible, they add to the collective memory of useful lessons about what has worked and why.

Although learning is a continuous process, each separate learning loop shown in Figure 12-1 is completed when the actions and their consequences are lodged in memory and unexpected results or discrepancies trigger further inquiry to help explain what happened.

MARKET-DRIVEN LEARNING PROCESSES

There is a close affinity between the generic organizational learning activities and the definition of a market orientation, which is, "the organizationwide *generation* of market intelligence pertaining to current and future customer needs, *dissemination* of the intelligence across depart-

FIGURE 12-1
Organization Learning Processes

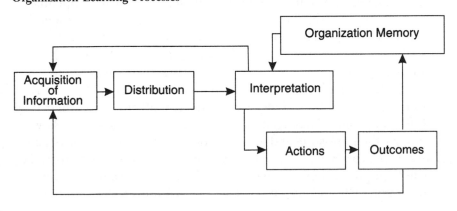

ments, and organizationwide *responsiveness* to it" (Kohli and Jaworski 1990). The similarities should not be surprising. Both deal with organizational adaptation to changing market environments. What is lacking in both our concept of learning and this definition of market orientation is a way to identify the characteristics of those organizations that are obviously superior at learning about, and orienting themselves to, their markets. We propose that these market-driven organizations are distinguished by (1) open-minded inquiry, (2) synergistic information distribution, (3) information interpretation, and (4) accessible memories (Day 1991). Each of these points of superiority is rooted in the culture of the organization and is facilitated by the organizational structure and systems. Thus, these four characteristics provide a template for appraising the contribution of information systems to the learning competency.

Open-Minded Inquiry

All organizations acquire information about trends, events, opportunities, and threats in their market environment in the same basic ways: scanning, direct experience, imitation, or problem-solving inquiries. Market-driven learning organizations excel by approaching these activities in a more thoughtful and systematic fashion, in the belief that all decisions start with the market. The following are the most distinctive features of their approach to inquiry:

Active scanning. All organizations track key market conditions and activities and try to learn from the departures from what is normal and expected. However, often this is only top-down learning, for there is a blockage of information from the frontline employees. In market-driven organizations, these frontline contacts, who hear complaints or requests for new services and see the consequences of competitive activity are motivated to inform management systematically.

Self-critical benchmarking. Most firms do regular tear-down analyses of competitors' products and occasionally study firms for insights into how better to perform discrete functions and activities. Market-driven firms study attitudes, values, and management processes when they study nonpareils. They recognize that they can always learn how to improve their measures and the way individual functions work together.

Continuous experimentation and improvement. All organizations tinker with their procedures and practices and take actions aimed at improving productivity and customer satisfaction. However, most are not very serious about systematically planning and observing the outcomes of these ongoing changes, so those that improve performance are adopted and others are dropped.

Informed imitation. Market-driven firms study their direct competitors so they can emulate successful moves before the competition gets too far ahead. This requires thoughtful efforts to understand why the competitor succeeded, as well as further probes for problems and shortcomings to identify improvements that would be welcomed by customers.

Guided inquiries. Finally, market-driven firms are likely to have something akin to an inquiry center, which Barabba and Zaltman (1991) define as an entity and capability by which the firm is able to anticipate market requirements and resolve problems, as well as provide comprehensive information that can be used by all functions, so they can be creative in responding in an integrated fashion.

Synergistic Information Distribution

As a general rule, organizations do not know what they know (Huber 1991). They may have good systems for storing and locating "hard" routine accounting and sales data, but can't locate a certain piece of information within the organization or assemble all the needed pieces in one place. This is especially true of competitor information. Manufacturing may be aware of certain activity through common equipment suppliers; sales may hear about initiatives from distributors and collect rumors from customers; and the engineering department may hire someone from a competitor.

Market-driven firms don't suffer unduly from organizational chimneys, silos, or smokestacks that bottle up information vertically within functions. Instead, information is widely distributed, its value is mutually appreciated, and those functions with potentially synergistic information know where else it could beneficially be used.

Mutually Informed Interpretations

The simplifications inherent in the mental models used by managers facilitate learning when they are based on undistorted information about important relationships and are widely shared throughout the organization. These mental models impede learning when they are incomplete, unfounded, or seriously distorted—by functioning below the level of awareness—so they are never examined. A market-driven organization avoids these pitfalls by using scenarios and other devices (deGeus 1988). These force managers to articulate, examine, and eventually modify their mental models of how their markets work and how competitors and suppliers will react and the parameters of the response coefficients in their marketing programs.

Problems arise when functional managers have very different mental models and don't appreciate or accept that there are other valid interpretations. Divergent mental models are especially dysfunctional in team activities such as new product development where participants may have very different ideas of the performance criteria, target market, or positioning. The result is an absence of integrity in the final product (Clark and Fujimoto 1991).

The likelihood of realizing uniformity of meaning or consistency of mental models goes up when (1) the information is uniformly framed or labeled as it is distributed, (2) the media of communication provide rich and reinforcing cues, (3) the amount and complexity of information doesn't overload the capacity to extract interpretations (since other managers will simply selectively perceive what they are ready to perceive and ignore the rest (Huber 1991) and (4) managers don't have to discard or unlearn too much obsolete, misleading, or discrepant information (Hedberg 1981).

Accessible Memory

Market-driven inquiry, distribution, and interpretation will not have a lasting effect unless what is learned is lodged in the collective memory. Organizations without practical mechanisms to remember what has worked and why will have to repeat their failures and rediscover their success formulas over and over. Collective recall capabilities are most quickly eroded by turnover through transfer and rapid disbanding of teams and data banks that are inaccessible to the entire organization. Here is where information technology plays an especially significant role. First we need to consider how the systems should be configured.

INFORMATION STRUCTURES FOR LEARNING

Successful learning is a function of effective information acquisition and processing. In this section, we explore the question, What kind of information-processing structures—or "architectures"—are required so that organizations can develop a learning competency characterized by open-minded inquiry, synergistic distribution, informed interpretation, and accessible memory? Whereas these structures are clearly facilitated by information-technology systems, our focus here is less on the technology per se than on the human and "social" factors (departmental boundaries, functional areas of specialization, and so forth) that may need to change if true organizational learning is to be possible.

The notion of the *firm as an information processor* has engaged the attention of theorists for some time (e.g., Galbraith 1977; March and Simon 1958; Williamson 1975); but, in light of the information revolution, it becomes perhaps the central concern of both students of management and practitioners alike. Even casual observation of the way in which the typical firm is designed reveals that information-processing structures have not been developed to make learning an organizational priority. Indeed, quite the contrary. In many instances firms appear to be structured deliberately to restrict the amount or type of learning that takes place.

Upon reflection, this is not surprising. The organizational-contingency perspective (Galbraith and Nathanson 1978; Miles and Snow 1978) demonstrates convincingly the need for a "fit" between strategy, structure, and the demands of the external environment. For a good part of this century—during which the modern corporation has taken shape—the "information environment" has been considerably more capacity constrained than it is today. Most successful large firms got that way by following a high-volume market-share strategy driven by continual cost reductions—through economies of scale and experience effects based on standardized products and processes. These organizations thrive in—and often depend upon—environmental stability and predictability, i.e, a world in which both the amount of information processing and the speed of information transmission are limited. For them, learning tends to be "rote," confined to the specialized area of *efficiency*, primarily through lowering costs (as in the case of the experience curve); but the integration of genuinely new information is to be postponed as long as possible. Successful small organizations, on the other hand, manage to survive profitably by choosing narrow-focused niche strategies—i.e., by finding market needs and fulfilling them. Whereas this approach relies critically on a high level of sensitivity to environmental conditions—an important characteristic of real learning—the relatively scarce resources of these firms nevertheless constrain the scope of learning to rather limited domains.

Traditional Information-Processing Structures

What is the information-processing structure associated with the traditional "limited-learning" organization? This is of interest in its own right, but more important, it helps us understand the attributes required for designing an information-processing structure as the basis of a true learning organization.

In discussing alternative organizational information-processing structures, a not-so-coincidental metaphor is suggested: that of the computer. In this regard, the traditional firm bears a close resemblance to the "Von-Neumann architecture" digital machine that has dominated contemporary computing technology. The conventional computer is characterized by three features: (1) sequential information processing—i.e., no matter how fast the processing, each item of information is reported upon individually in turn; (2) standardized representation of data—i.e., in numerical (digital) form; (3) local, spatially separated memory stores—i.e., each piece of information resides in a specific physical location.

In similar fashion, the traditional firm "moves" products (and even services) in serial, sequential fashion from R&D, through production, to marketing, and then sales (Figure 12-2, adapted from Glazer 1989). The information required to make decisions in these areas is in each localized, spatially separate functional department, which develops its own area of expertise: scientific and engineering data in R&D, cost and operations data in production, customer and competitor data in marketing and sales, and so forth. The language used to represent and thus communicate information both within and among departments is the standardized accounting system and related quantitative measures; information of a

FIGURE 12-2
The Traditional Organization's Information-Processing Structure

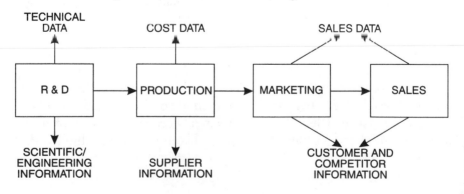

more qualitative nature which cannot be easily coded to conform with the standards is ignored.

Both the digital computer and the traditional firm are remarkable at performing certain tasks. Given a *plan*—i.e., a well-specified set of inputs and precise group of instructions—outputs are produced at extremely high levels of efficiency. At the same time, both the computer and the firm are remarkably deficient at performing other tasks—many of which are associated with what we have defined as "learning." Most notable, perhaps, is that, when confronted with an item of information, the traditional architecture has no conceptual way of determining whether the information is known (i.e., already stored in memory) or unknown (i.e., not stored in memory), in which case it must be "learned." For example, if presented with two customer transaction records—one of which is already in a database, the other which is not—the traditional architecture will perform the same exhaustive search in both instances before making either a positive or a negative identification. Similarly, one of the most prevalent problems faced by the typical (large) firm, when confronted with changing environmental parameters, is deciding whether or not the incoming information represents something genuinely new that calls for a strategic redirection. Sometimes, appropriate identification is not made until it is too late to act.

The inability to "know what it knows" (i.e., meta-knowledge) is a characteristic of an information-processing structure that is sequential and based on localized, spatially separate memory stores. Among other implications, it is associated with (1) a failure to appreciate the degree to which the meaning of information is context dependent, (2) the related difficulties in reasoning by analogy—i.e., noticing similarity relations— which is at the core of pattern recognition, and (3) the inability to easily incorporate complex feedback from the environment. The overall consequence is that such a structure severely limits performance in situations where *adaptability* and *response*—as opposed to planning—are the key determinants of success.

Learning-Oriented Information-Processing Structures

The preceding discussion suggests that, in contrast to localized memory, sequential processing, and standardized digital/numerical data, an information-processing structure designed to promote learning would be based on the opposite: (1) parallel information processing, (2) multiple sources of data representation including analog representation, (3) distributed memory stores, and (4) the integration of individual learning processes. Once again, not so coincidentally, these are among the key attributes of the newer computer architectures being designed in attempts to develop true "thinking" — i.e., learning — machines. What are the implications of these structures (Figure 12-3, Glazer 1989) for information processing in organizations?

Parallel processing. Learning-oriented information structures permit information to be processed in parallel. In parallel information processing, different items of information can be operated upon simultaneously by a single processor and the same item of information can be operated upon simultaneously by different processors. The advantage of having discrete items of information processed together is that their connections and interactions become the focus of attention. This is the foundation for *pattern recognition*, a main characteristic of higher-order learning and a major organizational imperative in light of the information revolution.

The advantage of using multiple processors on a single item of information is that general problems can be broken down into component subproblems which are then handled in tandem. Here, the overriding consideration is *speed*, not just for its own sake, but because many problems can only be solved in real-time (Eisenhardt 1989) — e.g., being ready with the next generation of a product in markets with increasingly ephemeral life cycles. This is why, whereas parallel processing architectures can be simulated sequentially, the attendant loss in speed may

FIGURE 12-3
Learning-Oriented Firm's Information-Processing Structure

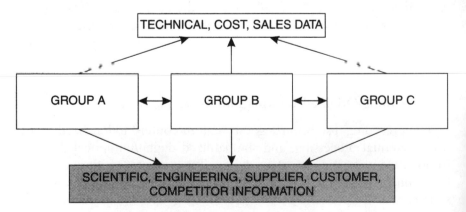

render a solution useless in practice. When the "general problem" is typically the design and implementation of a particular strategy, the gain in speed (e.g., in time to market or reaction to competitive activity) can be enormous when different members in the organization work in parallel on a problem's components. Furthermore, parallel processing structures are inherently redundant, which makes them remarkably *resistant to damage*—in this case, the loss of key managerial talent.

Information technology systems can play a vital role here; information can be organized to permit simultaneous access by different areas or departments within the firm, thus *encouraging* parallel processing. Beyond this, parallel processing depends critically on coordination (who works on which subproblem), and this cannot be achieved without appropriately designed information systems that regulate the information *flows* so that every user has exactly the right information at the precise instant it is needed.

Multiple sources/analog representation of information. A second characteristic of learning-oriented information-processing structures is that they permit data to be represented in a variety of ways. The older architectures—by forcing a standard (numerical/digital) way for information to be represented and thus transmitted—have traded computational efficiency for environmental reality. In the traditional firm, what cannot be measured numerically (in terms of an increasingly restrictive and simplistic set of criteria) does not exist. Yet information comes in a variety of forms, and often the most meaningful information is presented in ways that do not readily lend themselves to precise numerical representation.

An important alternative form is *analog representation*. Technically, an analog measurement system (or computer) is one that uses processes "analogous" to the processes being computed. Analog measurement is most useful for directly comparing the degree to which objects or sets of objects resemble—i.e., are "close to"—each other without the need for intermediate translation through the number system. This is why analog procedures, which are typically correlated with parallel processing and form the basis of pattern recognition, appear to be intimately connected to learning—in both novices and experts alike. For example, is it reasonable to expect that the digital clock will ever replace the analog "when-the-big-hand-is-on-the-twelve-and-the-little-hand-is-on-the-three" method of teaching children to "tell" time? If in doubt, peer into the cockpit of an airplane and count the ratio of analog to digital instruments. What little children know, so apparently do those responsible for making split-second decisions on which many lives may depend: analog processing mechanisms are absolutely critical whenever real-time performance is required. Although analog representation may often be "fuzzy" and imprecise, the loss in precision is more than compensated for by the efficiency gained in focusing on the pattern, or "gestalt," and not the detail.

Within the organization, the acceptance of analog representation (and the associated growth in analogical reasoning capability) begins with the admittance of richer and more flexible modes of presentation into the data system. Clearly, the information technology, which is still far too bandwidth limited, is not yet perfected. Alternative presentation modes cannot yet be fully integrated into the standard data structures, though recent developments in multimedia (voice, video, and so forth) integration are encouraging. However, although technologists do their part, the really hard work falls to management—whose task it is to create measurement and performance systems that incorporate the new forms. In many cases, the data themselves are already there, "collected" as a consequence of open-minded inquiry, as noted above: customer loyalty and satisfaction, service performance, quality, and so forth. Yet these are exactly the sorts of data that are best represented in nontraditional ways (e.g., a taped interview with a customer talking about the firm's level of satisfaction). A good deal of effort has gone into developing methodologies for representing these data in forms appropriate for the current accounting system, but efforts might better be spent at reforming the accounting systems to admit a wider class of information.

The integration of voice, video, and other multimedia with standard text and data (numbers) is of practical consequence, but it is also an important metaphor for the transition to a learning organization. From the standpoint of an information-processing "organism," multimedia information is *sensory* in nature—associated with what has (perhaps unfortunately) been called the "peripheral nervous system" and "bottom-up" processing. This has traditionally been viewed as the domain of communications activity, both between the organism and the outside world and within the organism itself. By contrast, text and data tend to belong to so-called higher-order, or top-down, processing—associated with (again unfortunately perhaps) what has been called the "central nervous system."

One of the great mistakes in information technology is that the communications and central processing systems have grown up independently of each other. (Rectifying this mistake appears to be the top priority of the information industries—computers, telecommunications, and so forth—in this decade). We now know, from the study of living information-processing organisms, that the sharp distinction between central and peripheral, and the separation between sensory and higher-order processing, is essentially misleading. Intelligent information processors—learners—employ, indeed require, a sophisticated interaction between the two systems. Both top-down and bottom-up processing modes rely heavily on mechanisms traditionally associated with the other.

Distributed memory stores. At its most fundamental, a distributed memory is one in which an item of information is stored at multiple locations—in the extreme case, everywhere! From a technical standpoint, in many distributed architectures, an item of information has no independent existence but is actually represented only through the interactions or pattern of connections among several "nodes." More generally, however, as it applies to the firm, a distributed structure is characterized by the capability for individuals throughout the organization to *access* the same pool of information instantaneously as needed. In such a climate, issues over the ownership or appropriateness of the information are far less important than ensuring that there are opportunities for it to be shared and used.

Information technology systems are crucial in developing a meaningful distributed memory structure. At least networks need to be established so that everyone in the organization can effectively transmit information to and receive information from everyone else. This involves adopting corporatewide standards (or translation capability) in protocols, computer operating systems, application languages, and file-management procedures. Beyond this, however, data files have to be organized so that the inherent associations or relations among different items of information (e.g., customer transaction records and production data) are made transparent.

Often, the nature of these associations may not become clear until managers actually discover them in the course of accessing and using the information. If so, then a primary function of the information technology system is to record these usage patterns so they can serve as a guide to organizing the file structures themselves. The goal is to endow the firm's memory with sufficient "plasticity" so that it is continuously evolving—not only by incorporating new items of information but, more fundamentally, changing with respect to the way information is organized. The traditional architectures begin with fixed, static structures and then force-fit new data into them. Users—i.e., managers—then adapt their decision-making behavior to these preexisting structures. By contrast, in dynamic, living memories—which are the basis for learning—the way information is structured is determined by the way it is used. As usage patterns change, so too does the way information is structured. Systems adapt to managerial behavior rather than the reverse.

Integration of individual learning processes. The information technology systems within most organizations reflect the separation between sensory/communications and central information-processing functions. More troublesome, however, is that this separation also underlies the model of the traditional organization as an information processor, independent of its technological infrastructure. By contrast, a learning organization is one whose architecture—based on analog parallel distributed processes—allows for the integration of top-down and bottom-up procedures. Consequently, open-minded inquiry (typically a bottom-up function), informed interpretation, and accessible memory (both typically top-down functions) are inherently interconnected. "Informed interpretation" *guides* the inquiry procedure, even as it *receives* the output for further processing. Accessible memory stores are not passive "dumping grounds" but active, dynamic structures that change as they are used and thus, in turn, influence both the direction of inquiry and the scope of interpretation.

The true test of the extent of *coordination* among the three components is whether or not the organization uses *feedback*. From the standpoint of the firm, the question of feedback is simple: Does the organization use new information—either incoming from the external environment or as a consequence of a shift in its own internal state—to *change its behavior* within a time frame during which the information is still relevant? This, of course, is what is meant by learning. The notion of an information revolution, as expressed in this book, suggests that the time frame during which information stays relevant or meaningful is shortening all the time. If so, then the required feedback mechanisms are increasingly instantaneous and the organization must "learn how to learn" in real time. Our hypothesis is that the information-processing structure described provides a means of achieving this objective.

MANAGING THE TRANSITION TO A MARKET-DRIVEN LEARNING ORGANIZATION

The management of information plays a pivotal role in the transition of the traditional organization with limited learning potential to the market-driven organization where a flexible and responsive learning competency is a source of competitive advantage. However, this transition will not happen unless the transformation of the information-processing structure, described in the previous section, is supported by an equivalent transformation of the organization's structures, systems, and processes.

The principal organizational innovations are summarized in Table 12-1 and elaborated in the next section. Both the learning-oriented organization and its information-processing infrastructure serve as a platform for specific applications of information technology which can enhance the ability of the organization to learn about its markets. We conclude with some specific possibilities drawn from innovative firms as an incentive to those who would consider making the wrenching changes needed to capitalize on the information revolution.

Organizational Transitions

Leading thinkers about organizations (e.g., Savage 1990; Senge 1990) have identified four related dimensions on which high-potential learning organizations differ from traditional limited learning organizations. Associated changes along each of these dimensions are needed to extract the full value from the concomitant changes in information-processing structures.

Organizational structures. The traditional "steep" hierarchy has a "command and control" structure with orders originating at the top. Strategies are devised by a few "visionary" thinkers at the top and handed

TABLE 12-1
Tandem Transitions of the Organization and Information-Processing Structure

	Traditional Organizations	*Learning Organizations*
Organizational Environment		
Structures	Centralized with Steep Hierarchies	Decentralized and Flatter
Processes	Sequential	Parallel
Coordination	Functional	Multiple
	"Chimneys" with Localized Expertise	Task-focused Teams
Communications	Vertical	Horizontal
Information-Processing Structure		
Processing	Sequential	Parallel
Representation of Data	Standardized	Multiple Sources
	Numerical/Digital	Analog
Memory	Local	Distributed
	Spatially Separate	
Integration of Processes	Separated	Interconnected

down to lower echelons for implementation. This model assumes that the leaders have the necessary knowledge (i.e., information!) and wisdom, that there is adequate time for exhaustive analysis before taking action, and that the lower echelons are waiting for their orders. Now the emphasis has shifted to empowerment of the people closest to the point of decision making, in recognition of their superior knowledge (access to information) of the fast-changing circumstances. The new challenge is to motivate and coordinate these individual initiatives so they support the overall strategic thrust. This requires flatter hierarchies and decentralized structures.

Organizational processes. Just as information processes need to be in parallel to achieve rapid gains in speed, so are organizational activities speeded up by shifting from sequential to parallel processes. The problem with sequential modes of decision making is the isolation of activities. Each function has a role to play, but lacks an appreciation of the constraints the other functions live under. When conflicts arise or problems need to be resolved, a complete functional process has to be recycled with consequent loss of time and the inevitable blame shifting. Parallel processing means more than having the functions operate concurrently — they must work together. This is best achieved through spatial proximity, but may be less essential with new developments in information systems' networking and common windowing formats.

Coordination. Traditional, limited learning organizations have strong functional lines of authority, with specialized knowledge and capability lodged within the functional partitions ("smokestacks"), but not readily available elsewhere. This model is being challenged by the desirability of parallel decision making, which puts a premium on cross-functional communication and integrated problem solving. Indeed, successful parallel processing depends ultimately, of course, on a coordinating mechanism. There must be some efficient means of deciding how the problem should be broken down, i.e., which are the relevant subcomponents, and who should be assigned to work on which part(s).

Traditional functional separation is also less feasible when information flows into the organization through many channels, with no function having a monopoly. This is most apparent with customer information, where marketing was once the sole listening point. However, in an era of comprehensive relationships between customers and suppliers that embrace all functions, there are multiple listening points. The information is best acquired and used by task-focused teams, which are becoming the new locus of learning. These teams may focus on either products or markets, but their role is embedded into the daily operations of the organization. There is nothing temporary or ad hoc about it. Influence within a team is more a function of individual knowledge—and capacity for learning—than formal position or seniority.

Communication. As Savage (1991) notes, the shift from vertical to horizontal communication is inevitable when people come to be seen not as turf owners but as knowledge resources within a team or network. Vertical communications still has its place in the organization, but the balance of top-down versus bottom-up information flows is shifting.

SUMMARY: THE NEED FOR A RESEARCH AGENDA

In this chapter we argue that a major imperative emerging from the marketing information revolution is the need to develop a superior learning competency. At the same time, the very information systems that motivate the transition toward a learning organization also provide the means for its realization. What is required now, it would appear, is a concerted effort by both practitioners and academics to investigate those principles and methods that will prove most useful in guiding the transition with as little disruption as possible. Such a research agenda would, among its highest priorities, attempt to identify both the *operational procedures* that firms use to implement the information-processing structures associated with superior learning and the *operational measures* they can use to assess whether or not an organization has indeed achieved a learning competency.

REFERENCES

Barabba, Vincent P., and Gerald Zaltman (1991). *Hearing the Voice of the Market: Competitive Advantage through Creative Use of Market Information.* Boston: Harvard Business School Press.

Clark, Kim B., and Takahiro Fujimoto (1991). *Product Development Performance: Strategy, Organization, and Management in the World Auto Industry.* Boston: Harvard Business School Press.

Day, George S. (1991). *Learning About Markets.* Cambridge, Mass: Marketing Science Institute.

de Geus, Arie P. (1988). "Planning As Learning." *Harvard Business Review,* March–April, 70–74.

Eisenhardt, Kathleen (1989). "Making Fast Strategic Decisions in High-Velocity Environments." *Academy of Management Journal*, 32, 543–576.

Fiol, C. Marlene, and Marjorie A. Lyles (1985). "Organizational Learning." *Academy of Management Review*, 10, 803–813.

Galbraith, Jay (1977). *Organizational Design*. Reading, Mass.: Addison-Wesley.

Galbraith, Jay, and D.A. Nathanson (1978). *Strategy Implementation: The Role of Structure and Process*. St. Paul: West Publishing.

Glazer, Rashi (1989). *Marketing and the Changing Information Environment: Implications for Strategy, Structure, and the Marketing Mix*. Cambridge, Mass.: Marketing Science Institute.

Hedberg, Bo (1981). "How Organizations Learn and Unlearn." In *Handbook of Organizational Design*, P.C. Nystrom and W.H. Starbuck (eds.). London: Oxford University Press, 8–27.

Huber, George (1991). "Organizational Learning: The Contributing Processes and Literatures." *Organization Science*, 2, 88–115.

Kohli, Ajay K., and Bernard J. Jaworski (1990). "Market Orientation: The Construct, Research Propositions and Managerial Implications." *Journal of Marketing*, 54, 1–18.

Levitt, Barbara, and James March (1988). "Organizational Learning." In *Annual Review of Sociology*, Richard Scott and Judith Blake (eds.). 14, 319–340.

March, James, and Herbert Simon (1958). *Organization*. New York: John Wiley.

Miles, Raymond E., and Charles C. Snow (1978). *Organizational Strategy, Structure and Process*. New York: McGraw-Hill.

Savage, Charles M. (1990). *Fifth Generation Management*. Maynard, Mass.: Digital Equipment Corporation.

Senge, Peter M. (1990). *The Fifth Discipline: The Art and Practice of the Learning Organization*. New York: Doubleday.

Williamson, Oliver E. (1975). *Markets and Hierarchies: Analysis and Antitrust Implications*. New York: The Free Press.

13

IDENTIFYING THE LEGAL AND ETHICAL RISKS AND COSTS OF USING NEW INFORMATION TECHNOLOGIES TO SUPPORT MARKETING PROGRAMS

Paul N. Bloom, Robert Adler, and George R. Milne

THE CHAPTERS IN THIS *volume have taken a purely market orientation to the onset of the information revolution. This, of course, is somewhat unrealistic, since the adoption of new information technologies and the emergence of the information economy take place in a broader social context. In particular, the information revolution raises a series of legal and ethical issues that are among the most important faced by society in many generations. In recent years, several well-publicized information technology initiatives have either been abandoned or delayed because the companies involved did not pay sufficient attention to the concerns over individual rights expressed by those most likely to be affected by the adoption of the new technologies.*

Whether the information revolution ultimately turns out to be a force for individual freedom or for coercion is an issue that is sure to be debated for many years to come. At the same time, the outcome of that debate, as well as the timing and extent of a truly information intensive economy, is likely to be influenced by the actions now taken by organizations in the vanguard of the revolution.

This chapter describes an approach to help marketers avoid legal and ethical problems when using new information technologies. The approach explores both the legal and ethical ramifications of using new information technologies for the general strategic and tactical purposes described in the other chapters—i.e., (1) to improve new market knowledge, (2) to improve response capabilities, (3) to improve persuasive communications, and (4) to improve strategy selection. For each application, and for each of the relevant information technologies, there are potential harms to customers, channel members, competitors, and employees. Privacy concerns and antitrust issues are highlighted as two of the most likely to occur. The chapter discusses the possible legal actions that might result from the harms and threats of new information technologies, as well as how self-regulation and advocacy efforts might mitigate the risks and costs.

INTRODUCTION

New information technologies clearly are changing the way marketers think and behave. Information can be acquired today in more extensive, timely, and usable forms than ever before, and this has given marketers a whole new range of capabilities. Marketers can now instantaneously access enormous amounts of information about customers and competitors; they can respond to customer inquiries and orders at breakneck speeds; they can employ technologically sophisticated communications tools to enhance the persuasiveness of their selling efforts; and they can use sophisticated computer models and artificial intelligence systems to help guide them to better strategic and tactical decisions. Effective use of new information technologies is allowing marketers to gain distinct and profitable competitive advantages in several industries.

Incorporating new and more powerful information technologies into a firm's marketing program cannot be done without some risks and costs (Capon and Glazer 1987; Marx 1988). Problems can arise with hardware, software, support systems, security, and personnel. Moreover, the use of new information technologies can also generate legal and ethical problems for a marketer. The potential for inflicting serious harm on customers, competitors, channel members, or even one's own employees exists when using some technologies, and marketers should recognize that if harm does occur they may find themselves under attack from these parties.

This chapter presents an approach (see Figure 13-1) that marketers can adopt to help them avoid legal and ethical problems when using new information technologies. The approach consists of a systematic series of questions that a marketer could address with the goal of identifying the risks and costs of using a particular new technology. Questions are framed about the potential for harm to affected individuals and groups (customers, employees, channel members, and competitors) to occur, as well as legal action resulting from this harm and other threats such as boycotts and negative publicity. In addition, a question is included that asks how self-regulation and advocacy efforts might mitigate the risks and costs.

The approach suggested here is intended to be relevant for examining

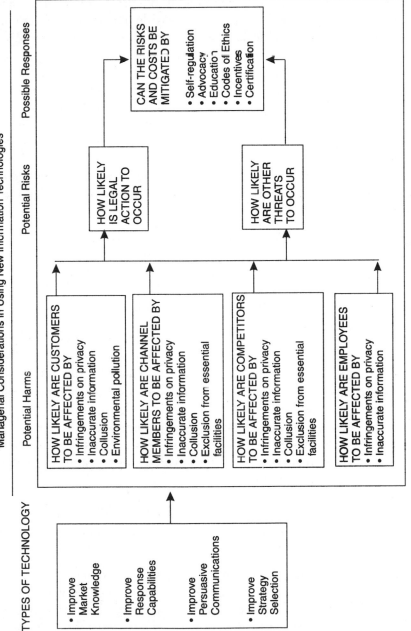

FIGURE 13-1
An Approach for Assessing Legal and Ethical Risks and Costs of Using New Information Technologies
Managerial Considerations in Using New Information Technologies

problems that can develop for marketing managers or marketing researchers in the use of new information technologies to support the marketing
of conventional products and services. We do not explicitly cover problems
that could emerge in the development and marketing of the new information technologies themselves, although certainly the marketers of these
technologies are affected when their customers/users have legal and ethical problems. Hence, topics like patent and copyright law for new software
or communications systems are not addressed directly. Instead, we treat
the problems that can arise in areas like privacy protection and antitrust
when a marketer is not cautious enough in the way new information
technologies are employed.

The types of new information technologies we are concerned about
can be classified into four categories. These cover technologies that can
be used for improving

1. **market knowledge.** This includes technologies that can be used to
   obtain detailed information about customers, competitors, employees,
   and so forth to help enhance, for example, segmentation, targeting,
   product design, service features, and promotion. Technologies such
   as computer matching, electronic eavesdropping, and "people meters"
   are examples.
2. **response capabilities.** This includes technologies that can be used to
   improve the accuracy and response times for order-taking, bidding,
   delivery, and so forth. Technologies such as "Caller ID," large-scale
   computerized reservation systems, and automatic order-entry systems
   are examples.
3. **persuasive communications.** This includes technologies that can be
   used to improve the efficiency and effectiveness of promotional approaches. Technologies such as "video carts," automatic dialers, and
   videotext are examples.
4. **strategy selection.** This includes technologies that can be used to
   help marketers sort through information and select strategies and
   tactics that will be more effective. Artificial intelligence systems such
   as IRI's SalesPartner and CoverStory are examples.

Some technologies, such as Caller ID, can fit into more than one
category (e.g., it can enhance market knowledge as well as improve
response capabilities). Recognizing this, we nevertheless suggest that these
categories provide a useful way of identifying critical points during the
marketing process at which careful attention should be paid to problems
associated with the new technologies.

It is also important to note that one type of problem may arise for a marketer when using these technologies individually, and other problems can arise when two or more of these technologies are used in conjunction with one another. The use of Caller ID raises more serious legal and ethical issues when it is combined with some type of computer matching (Carnevale and Lopez 1989).

Each of the identified technology categories is discussed further in the sections which follow. We attempt to highlight ideas and issues to consider when trying to use the approach found in Figure 13-1 to assess the risks and costs of using each category of information technologies. The discussion is much more extensive for technologies used to improve market knowledge and response capabilities, since fewer controversial outcomes appear likely to arise from using technologies to improve persuasive communications and strategy selection. Our overriding goal is to stimulate thinking about the best approach for identifying risks and costs, not to provide accurate assessments of the risks and costs faced by specific types of marketers. Such assessments will require additional research.

TECHNOLOGIES FOR IMPROVING MARKET KNOWLEDGE

Information technologies such as computer matching (McCrohan 1989), electronic eavesdropping (Marcus 1989; Rothfeder et al. 1990), scanner technologies (Sun 1989), and other tools that provide large amounts of easily accessed information about people and institutions have the potential of leading to harm, legal actions, and other threats in a variety of ways. The following sections treat the issues that should be considered in assessing the risks and costs of using technologies that might harm others through (1) invading their privacy, (2) disseminating *inaccurate* information about them, (3) facilitating collusive behavior on the part of sellers, and (4) contributing to environmental pollution. We recognize that other adverse consequences, such as physical harm, may arise from using new technologies, but we have chosen to focus on the consequences most likely to occur.

As a starting point, we note that by far the greatest number of issues arise in considering the privacy area.

Privacy Concerns

Privacy, the so-called right to be let alone, is an evolving and not easily defined concept. In its broadest sense, it refers to the right of an individual or company to be protected against unwarranted intrusions into and unwarranted publicity about their lives (Trubow 1981). New technologies obviously present the potential for serious harm to people (or institutions) under conditions where information about their behaviors, intentions, or interests is used without their knowledge and/or consent, leading them to be *excluded from* or *included in* activities in such a way that they are harmed economically, psychologically, or physically.

In some cases, the act of *acquiring* information can be improper. The mere act of unauthorized electronic eavesdropping strikes many of us as so offensive that we would judge it to be wrong irrespective of whether or not the eavesdropper acquired embarrassing information.

In other instances, privacy concerns would not be triggered merely by the gathering of information. Once information is gathered, however, improper *disclosure* of it would raise privacy concerns. For example, credit bureaus are generally free to collect financial data about consumers, yet they face substantial penalties for revealing this data to unauthorized persons.

In still other instances, information disclosure is not the improper act—the problem is the wrongful *use* of the information. When computer matching or electronic eavesdropping is used to "check up" on people without their knowledge and/or consent, and they are then prevented from getting access to certain products or services (e.g., medical care, educational opportunities) or denied employment or job advancements, serious consequences can occur. Hidden check-ups on people's medical backgrounds, purchasing habits, telephone answering styles, and service-provision skills—ostensibly done to ensure that customers will not create problems or to keep employees "on their toes"—can be interpreted as facilitating discrimination and unfair business practices.

In addition to creating exclusionary outcomes, hidden computer matching and monitoring can also lead to undesirable illusionary outcomes, where people are put on "target" lists for direct mail and telemarketing efforts against their wishes. Being an unwanted target can produce psychological and economic harm. People are annoyed, and they feel that "Big Brother" is manipulating them or using up their valuable time. A by-product can be the harm brought to the marketing research community, which must deal with the lower cooperation and response rates from consumers who feel distrustful of *any* marketing activities.

To say that privacy law is evolving is not to say that marketers face anything like a privacy litigation crisis. In fact, privacy as a *legal* right is not as extensive or established as one might think. For example, most citizens think of the

Fourth and Fifth Amendments in the U.S. Constitution as containing protection against abusive searches and seizures or against self-incrimination. Most, however, do not realize that these protections apply only to *governmental*, not private, abuses. In fact, most of the federal legislation relating to privacy in recent years—e.g., the Privacy Act of 1974, the Right to Financial Privacy Act of 1978, the Electronic Communications Act of 1986, and the Computer Matching and Privacy Protection Act of 1988—has placed limits on the ability of the government, not private citizens or groups, to examine and use information about Americans.

Although privacy law is still evolving, a variety of legal actions could face a company or organization that violates privacy concerns. For example, a company that uses hidden technology tools to facilitate actions that have exclusionary results faces a variety of negative possibilities that start with privacy transgressions but end up provoking other types of lawsuits, including nonprivacy types. The following are among the variety of lawsuits that face marketers raising privacy concerns:

1. Lawsuits charging discrimination of various types (e.g., racial, sex, age) or unfair labor practices (e.g., wrongful discharge).
2. Lawsuits filed under statutes aimed at limiting privacy abuses in particular industries. For example, the Fair Credit Reporting Act prohibits information dissemination by credit bureaus without a "legitimate business reason." Similarly, the Video Privacy Act of 1988—passed on the heels of disclosures about Supreme Court nominee Robert Bork's video rental habits—prohibits disclosure of a person's video rentals. In the same vein, the State of California requires companies that compile and sell "bad tenants" lists to notify the people that they are on the lists and provide them with an opportunity to correct the information in their files.
3. Lawsuits filed under antiwiretap laws. This has happened in Pennsylvania in a challenge to the introduction of Caller ID.
4. Lawsuits filed under common law, claiming application of the tort of "unreasonable intrusion into the seclusion of another." Historically, the courts have tended to assess damages for this tort only for intentional actions like unauthorized eavesdropping, wiretapping, rifling through another's papers, or entry onto another's property.
5. Lawsuits filed by channel members under the antitrust laws, claiming that they have been victimized by unwarranted "refusals to deal."
6. Lawsuits filed by competitors and others claiming that copyrighted information about themselves has been illegally acquired.

Consistent with the limited role currently occupied by privacy law, most targeting methods used for direct mail and telemarketing efforts are generally not regulated. Few statutes expressly prohibit specific targeting methods. For example, using credit information has generally been viewed as within the "legitimate business reasons" provisions of the Fair Credit Reporting Act.

To say that current marketing methods are not regulated is not to say that the law is unlikely to change soon. To the contrary, consumer groups and others have been pressuring strongly for privacy protection measures in recent years, and congressional hearings have been held on these matters (Direct Marketing Association 1990). Public policy makers have noted the results of several recent public opinion polls showing strong citizen concern about privacy matters. For example, according to a 1990 Harris poll, 79% of Americans express concern about threats to personal privacy—an increase of 15% since 1978. Of those surveyed, 46% stated they were "very concerned" (Equifax 1990).

This strong public concern has triggered a number of legislative and regulatory initiatives. Hundreds of initiatives have been introduced in state legislatures throughout the United States, and numerous bills are under consideration in Congress. Although it is difficult to forecast precisely which bills will be enacted, the following proposed legislation is under consideration:

Fair Credit Reporting Act: Bills have been introduced that would strengthen consumer privacy rights under the FCRA in a variety of ways. One approach would eliminate the practices of "prescreening" (doing a credit check on a consumer before making a marketing solicitation) and target marketing based on credit data. Another approach would not eliminate these practices, but would provide greater notice to consumers of the possibility of such practices and an opportunity for consumers to "opt out" of these practices.

Restrictions on Certain Types of Matching: Several states have recently passed laws prohibiting matching of information about individuals from certain sources. For example, California has a law forthcoming that prevents the commercial use of personal information created from state-agency transactions (e.g., automobile registrations, property transfers). Additionally, Maryland has a new law prohibiting retailers from (1) requiring phone numbers from people when they sign credit card slips or (2) requiring credit card numbers from people when they pay by personal check.

FTC Marketing Rules: In the post-Reagan years, the Federal Trade Commission has become more active in regulating the marketplace. In particular, the FTC has focused on a variety of telemarketing activities.

"No Call" Laws: A number of states are considering legislation that would enable consumers to place a mark next to their names in telephone books indicating their desire not to be solicited via the telephone. Telemarketers would be prohibited from soliciting these individuals.

Restrictions on Hours for Soliciting: Several states are considering limits on the hours within which telemarketers would be able to solicit consumer business.

"Caller ID" Restrictions: A significant number of states have pending legislation to regulate Caller ID services. Most would permit consumers to "block" their numbers from appearing on Caller ID phones (Toth 1990). Additionally, at least one state has banned the reselling of names and numbers acquired through Caller ID technology.

Additional statutes clearly could be passed that (1) give consumers the right to prevent data about them from entering data bases or lists, or that (2) prohibit the resale of customer names and related data to others. Several European countries already have laws that accomplish these objectives.

Marketers in the direct mail industry have responded to privacy concerns by becoming more aggressive about developing and publicizing self-regulation programs that will allow people to remove their names from mailing lists or prevent their names and related data from being sold to other lists. Association and company codes of ethics have been strengthened recently and given more visibility (e.g., the Direct Mail Association's "Mail Protection Service"). Perhaps the most extreme act of self-regulation thus far was Lotus Development's decision not to introduce its previously announced "Marketplace" software, which would have given businesses inexpensive access to data on millions of households. Lotus cited the public outcry about this product's threat to privacy rights as a reason for its decision (Miller 1991; Wilke 1991).

Some associations and companies, however, have mounted a serious lobbying effort to prevent more controlling legislation in the privacy area. Among those who are most concerned about putting on more controls are the members of the marketing research community. Although they recognize that people's privacy fears have contributed to a reduction in willingness to cooperate with marketing research studies, they fear that putting too many controls on the content and availability of databases and lists could make their jobs even more difficult.With more restrictions, marketing researchers may be put in the position of only being able to obtain data from previously recruited panels, which could reduce the representativeness of samples.

Inaccurate Information Concerns

Information about people can be entered or transmitted inaccurately, and this can lead to the same types of harm discussed above. Even people who are aware that they are being "checked" can be injured—if the data about them are wrong. One statute that is designed to prevent the dissemination of inaccurate information is the Fair Credit Reporting Act. People can gain access to their credit records and make needed corrections. Additional legislation that requires all list managers to give people on their lists the ability to make corrections could clearly become a reality. Of course, marketers have the option of allowing people to correct files on themselves—and of publicizing this self-regulation mechanism. Or they can wait to see that type of legislation gets passed in this area.

Collusion Concerns

New information technologies will clearly make it easier and cheaper to obtain accurate and timely data about the actions of competitors. For example, trade associations should be able to maintain more extensive and current databases about the behavior of their members, relying on tie-ins with the computer systems of members to automatically accumulate desired information. Lengthy association surveys of members could become a thing of the past. Additionally, timely information about competitors could be obtained from syndicated services or from agreements between competitors to share the cost of establishing and managing high-technology data collection systems or databases. Sharing data on "who bought what from whom at what terms and at what time" could reveal valuable information about both customers and competitors. Still other information about competitors could be obtained by using technologies like real-time scanners of news reports or wire services, which a firm could use to set off "alarms" whenever a competitor took certain actions.

Having accurate and timely information about the prices, marketing tactics, and customers of competitors can certainly make it easier to implement a collusive agreement. Such information allows a firm to be more effective at "policing," or monitoring competitors to make sure the agreement is not being violated. Prices can be more readily fixed or markets more readily allocated as a consequence. Moreover, even if an explicit collusive agreement does not exist, having accurate and timely information about competitors can facilitate "tacit" collusion, where firms can parallel each other's pricing and marketing behavior and avoid aggressive competition.

The antitrust enforcement agencies have had a long history of looking carefully at the data collection and reporting activities of trade associations. Several classic cases have found certain variations of such activities to be part of a pattern of behavior that demonstrates the existence of a collusive agreement (Stern and Eovaldi 1984). Moreover, the direct exchange of current pricing data between competitors, without going through an association, has also been found to be partial evidence of the existence of a collusive agreement (see *U.S.* v. *United States Gypsum Co.*, 438 U.S. 422[1978]). To rule that a Sherman Act, Section 1, restraint of trade exists, the courts have generally required that the existence of a collusive agreement be demonstrated, and findings of "tacit collusion" or illegal parallel behavior have been rare in recent times (Stern and Eovaldi 1984). However, the courts have vacillated through the years on what they view as constituting the existence of a collusive agreement.

According to one antitrust observer:

> Exchanges of many types of information, especially concerning historical, rather than current, economic activity, have been upheld as permissible where a third party collects the data and participants are not individually identifiable. However, the exchange of very recent or current prices or customer information may be dangerous and violate the Sherman Act if it can be found to have potentially anticompetitive effects. (Givens 1989, pp. 141-142)

Further, if the data are withheld from buyers, then the courts will view the information exchange more suspiciously.

Thus, it appears that data collection and reporting systems could draw attention from the antitrust enforcement agencies if (1) the data is too current, (2) no third party like a trade association is involved in its collection, (3) it is easy to identify who reported what, and (4) buyers do not have access to the data (Wilcox 1971; Stern and Eovaldi 1984). For example, the airline industry is currently under investigation by the Justice Department for using its Airline Tariff Publishing information system and a complex signalling scheme to collude on prices (Nomani 1990).

A firm may want to avoid establishing information systems with suspicious characteristics, especially if anything else about its interactions with its competitors can be construed as suggesting that a collusive agreement exists. It is interesting to note that the widely referenced PIMS program avoided these dangers when it was established. They use historical data, are an entity separate from their member firms, do not permit identification of firms, and allow others (including academics) access to the data.

Environmental Pollution Concerns

The use of computer matching to generate mailing lists could be seen as facilitating the distribution of tons of unwanted and unnecessary "junk mail." Because much of the paper used is difficult to recycle, information technologies can be viewed as indirectly contributing to the solid-waste disposal problems facing many communities. To date, environmental groups have been reluctant to lobby for more restrictions on junk mail because they are such heavy users of it themselves when they do fund raising. However, it seems plausible that some activist groups will support restrictions on the creation of lists in the hope of reducing the tide of junk mail.

Eventually, the combination of privacy and environmental concerns could lead to a situation where the only lists that could be used would be of persons who explicitly consented to have their names included. Whether legislation that requires this could be written in such a way that First Amendment free-speech rights were not infringed upon is hard to predict. Certainly, members of the direct mail industry are likely to raise First Amendment arguments in defending their practices. These marketers can be expected to promote self-regulation of the type discussed above as an alternative to formal restrictions on list content.

TECHNOLOGIES THAT ENHANCE RESPONSE CAPABILITIES

New information technologies are providing more efficient and effective ways of communicating with and serving customers. Ordering a part, making a reservation, paying bills, and arranging for a service call can all be done electronically, with little need for human intervention. Either people or computers can talk to computers, providing more timely, just-in-time delivery, and saving on sales force expenses. As more and more companies set up sophisticated systems to take orders and arrange deliveries, we can foresee situations developing where buyers purchase all of their needs through these systems. The cost and inconvenience of ordering outside the system will keep them loyal. In those cases, sellers who are not part of the systems will have difficulty gaining access to buyers and could be harmed financially. The "essential facilities" needed to do business with major customers will have been denied to them, and they may want to use the antitrust laws to gain access. This antitrust concern represents the major issue that should be considered by users of information technologies that enhance response capabilities.

A series of cases has established an "essential facilities" doctrine under the Sherman Act. The seminal case was *U.S. v. Terminal Railroad* (224 U.S. 383 [1912]). In this case, a group of railroads gained control of a bridge over the Mississippi River near St. Louis. The bridge and accompanying terminal were located at a critical junction, and practical alternatives for competitors did not exist. The Supreme Court ruled that the group owning the bridge would be required to allow competitors to become part of the ownership consortium. This case established the principle and allowed for plaintiffs to sue groups of firms that monopolistically controlled an essential resource. Since this case, the doctrine has been applied to permit excluded competitors to gain access to the Associated Press wire service (*Associated Press* v. *U.S.*, 326 U.S. 1 [1945]), the multiday ski-lift ticket in Aspen, Colorado (*Aspen Skiing* v. *Aspen Highlands*, 472 U.S. 585 [1985]), electric transmission lines (*Otter Tail Power* v. *U.S.*, 410 U.S. 366 [1973]), and natural gas pipelines (*Consolidated Gas* v. *City Gas*, 665 F. Supp. 1493 (S.D. Fla. [1987]).

The Seventh Circuit Court recently summarized what seems to be the prevailing view among courts for establishing an "essential-facilities" violation of the Sherman Act (under either Section 1 or 2). Requirements were set out in an Appeals Court Decision in *MCI Communications* v. *AT&T*, 708 F.2d 1081 (7th Cir., [1983], cert. denied, 464 U.S. 891 [1983]). In allowing MCI access to AT&T's local telephone lines, the Seventh Circuit Court outlined four elements necessary to establish liability under the doctrine:

1. control of the essential facility by a monopolist;
2. a competitor's inability practically or reasonably to duplicate the essential facility;
3. the denial of the use of the facility to a competitor; and
4. the feasibility of providing the facility.

Additionally, the doctrine can only be applied when allowing access to the facility would result in improved competition (Areeda and Hovenkamp 1989).

We can envision situations where users of automatic order entry systems, reservation systems, credit-checking systems, automatic teller systems, and the like could be sued by a competitor or one of the antitrust enforcement agencies for failing to provide access to their essential facilities. The outcome of these cases is difficult to predict, since the court decisions involving firms that are not utilities (which clearly *are* monopolies) are somewhat limited. The *Aspen* case was decided on slightly different grounds at the Supreme Court level—although the Circuit Court ruled that Aspen Ski denied the use of its essential multiday ski-lift ticket—and the *Associated Press* case involved an illegal combination of firms, making it suitable for a Sherman Act, Section 1 violation. There have been no Supreme Court decisions that have treated whether the essential facilities doctrine should apply to individual monopolizing firms under Section 2 of the Sherman Act (although several lower court decisions have done so) (Podell 1989). Nevertheless, given the recent Justice Department decision blocking the American-Delta Reservation System merger because of concerns about access to the system (*News and Observer* 1989), we believe that substantial sentiment exists for opening up essential facilities. We think it would be difficult for a company that possesses a monopoly over a technology that provides access to important customers to defend the denial of its use. Thus, companies should avoid creating bottlenecks that could limit competitor access to customers.

TECHNOLOGIES USED FOR PERSUASIVE COMMUNICATIONS

Technologies such as video carts (Therrien and Konrad 1988), automatic dialers (Barnett 1990), and videotext (Fahey 1990; Mayer 1988) are being used to actually sell offerings for marketers. As long as the information presented using these technologies is honest and accurate, they should not produce high levels of severe harm. Nevertheless, they carry a high potential for annoyance to consumers. Anyone who has received a phone call from a computer dialer in which the phone message continues despite the phone being hung up knows how disturbing such intrusions can be. Just as billboards' aesthetic intrusions have often triggered restrictive legislation, technologies used for persuasive communications appear likely to provoke various controls to the extent that they disturb consumers' tranquility. For example, many states are considering limits on machines that automatically dial and play a recorded message to solicit consumer business. Among the approaches under consideration: prohibitions on such calls without advance permission for such calls, prohibitions on computer dialers that continue playing even after a consumer has hung up, and requirements that a live operator obtain a consumer's permission to play a recording prior to playing such recordings (Farhi 1989). Similarly, the recent explosion in the use of facsimile machines has led to a number of "fax attacks," in which advertisements have tied up fax machines at a time when consumers or businesses wished to transmit important materials. A number of states have under consideration limits on such advertisements.

In addition, people could be harmed by making purchasing decisions in too rushed or too thoughtless a manner because of these technologies. The reaction could be public pressure for (1) "cooling-off" laws to allow people a few days to get their money back after purchase or (2) laws that restrict certain uses of the technologies (e.g., JunkFax). Marketers should do careful research to determine customer acceptance of a technology and to clarify its legal status before building a major marketing effort around that technology.

TECHNOLOGIES TO SUPPORT STRATEGIC DECISIONS

Artificial intelligence systems and similar models are able, in some cases, to make important decisions for managers, or at least to dramatically reduce the effort necessary to make a good decision. Naturally, with some of these systems, it is tempting to have the systems or models make certain decisions on their own, without human intervention or with only minimal surveillance of the system. If the system either makes a decision that harms people — or recommends such a decision — the company could be liable for damages. A recent example of technology "run wild" occurred in a so-called program-trading computer program which apparently deepened the stock market losses in 1989 when the market dropped over 500 points on Black Friday. Laws that could come into play cover product liability, consumer protection, and antitrust. To avoid legal difficulties, companies should probably limit how much decision-making responsibility is delegated to these systems or models.

CONCLUSION

A variety of legal and ethical problems confront marketers who use new information technologies to support their marketing programs. Identifying situations where using a new information technology could harm various groups is not straightforward; for each technology there are many uses and many ways it can be combined with other technologies. The approach outlined in this chapter attempts to provide a broad framework that systematically maps the uses of the various technologies to the groups harmed by the technologies, the type of harm, the legal and ethical risks of using the technologies, and the possible managerial responses to potential legal and ethical problems. Currently, problems likely to be most bothersome to marketing managers stem from public concern over privacy infringements when new technologies are used. However, in the future, once legislation clearly defines where privacy rights begin and end, antitrust problems may come to the forefront. Adopting the kind of careful approach to assessing risks and costs suggested in this chapter should allow marketers to avoid and mitigate problems in all areas and to make more effective and efficient use of new information technologies.

REFERENCES

Areeda, Phillip E., and Herbert Hovenkamp (1989). *Antitrust Law: 1989 Supplement*. Boston: Little, Brown.

Barnett, Jim (1990). "Random Calls Elicit Outcry." *Raleigh News and Observer* (August 7), D1.

Capon, Noel, and Rashi Glazer (1987). "Marketing and Technology: A Strategic Coalignment," *Journal of Marketing*, 51 (July), 1–14.

Carnevale, Mary Lu, and Julie Amparano Lopez (1989). "Making a Phone Call Might Mean Telling the World about You," *The Wall Street Journal* (November 28), A1.

Direct Marketing Association (1990). *Code of Ethics*.

Equifax Report on Consumers in the Information Age (1990).

Fahey, Alison (1990). "Videotex Hard-sell." *Advertising Age* (August 30).

Farhi, Paul (1989). "Some Machines Won't Take No for an Answer." *Washington Post National Weekly Magazine* (October 16–22), 34, at col. 4.

Givens, Richard A. (1989). *Antitrust: An Economic Approach*. New York: Law Journals Seminars-Press.

Marcus, Amy Dockser (1989). "Callers on Cordless Phones Surrender Privacy Rights." *The Wall Street Journal* (November 29), B1, B5.

Marx, Peter (1988). "The Legal Risks of Using Information as a Competitive Weapon." *Software Law Journal*, 2, 185–201.

Mayer, Robert N. (1988). "The Growth of the French Videotex System and Its Implications for Consumers." *Journal of Consumer Policy*, 11 (March), 55–83.

McCrohan, Kevin F. (1989). "Information Technology, Privacy, and the Public Good." *Journal of Public Policy and Marketing*.

Miller, Michael W. (1991). "Lotus Is Likely to Abandon Consumer Data Project." *The Wall Street Journal* (January 23), B1.

News and Observer (1989). "American, Delta Drop Reservation System Merger." June 23, 5B.

Nomani, Asra Q. (1990). "Fare Warning: How Airline Trade Price Plans." *The Wall Street Journal* (October 9), 1, B10.

Podell, David M. (1989). "The Evolution of the Essential Facilities Doctrine and Its Application to the Deregulation of the Natural Gas Industry." *Tulsa Law Journal*, 24, 605–625.

Rothfeder, Jeffrey, Michele Galen, and Lisa Driscoll (1990). "Is Your Boss Spying on You?" *Business Week* (January 15), 74–75.

Stern, Louis W., and Thomas L. Eovaldi (1984). *Legal Aspects of Marketing Strategy: Antitrust and Consumer Protection Issues*. Englewood Cliffs, N.J.: Prentice-Hall.

Sun, Lena H. (1989). "Checking Out the Customer." *Washington Post* (July 9), H1, col. 3.

Therrien, Lois, and Walecia Konrad (1988). "Coming to a Shopping Cart Near You: TV Commercials." *Business Week* (May 30), 61–62.

Toth, Victor J. (1990). "Calling Line ID vs. Privacy: A Regulatory Update." *Business Communications Review*, 20 (March), 62–66.

Trubow, George (1981). "The Development and Status of Information Privacy Law and Policy in the United States." Paper presented at the American Bar Association's National Symposium on Personal Privacy and Information Technology (October 4–7).

Wilcox, Clair (1971). *Public Policy toward Business*. Homewood, Ill.: Richard D. Irwin.

Wilke, John R. (1991). "Lotus Product Spurs Fears about Privacy." *The Wall Street Journal* (January 15), B1, B5.

14

MARKETING INFORMATION TECHNOLOGIES IN JAPAN

Hotaka Katahira and Shigeru Yagi

IT MAY STILL BE THE CASE *that the marketing information revolution is most developed in the United States, but this is unlikely to remain so for long. With the internalization and globalization of business—phenomena that themselves are a function of the spread of information technologies on a worldwide scale—changes anywhere are rapidly adopted everywhere. This book primarily describes the activities of U.S. organizations and markets, but no volume such as this would be complete without a discussion of the impact of the marketing information revolution on other economies and cultures. Of greatest interest perhaps is what is happening in this area in Japan.*

This chapter presents an overview of the state-of-the-art in point-of-sale marketing systems in Japan. An electronic point-of-sale system represents, of course, only one aspect of the marketing information revolution, but as described in this chapter, it is an instructive example because it illustrates how differing market conditions across cultures lead to the use of essentially the same technology in somewhat different ways. This should be of value not only to those interested in how the information revolution is influencing marketing in Japan, but also to those concerned with the more general question of how alternative consumer behavior patterns (whether in the same or different culture) may require different technology adoption patterns.

An additional feature of the chapter is that the authors, who are among the leading proponents of information technology in Japan, are, respectively, an academic and a practitioner. The chapter reflects this dual perspective by presenting both concrete, real-world examples as well as an example of how data are used to build a more formal, analytical POS model.

INTRODUCTION

It may be surprising that Japan is the second largest user/supplier of point-of-purchase "scanner" data yet only second to the United States in introducing a single-source data system. This chapter presents an overview of the state-of-the-art in the use of electronic point-of-sale marketing data systems in Japan. At the same time, it gives the non-Japanese audience some insights into how the various hardware and software associated with marketing data systems might be different under different market and cultural conditions.

The first section of the chapter describes the general characteristics of the Japanese market and the practice of marketing. Next, an overview of Japanese scanner data systems is provided. There are described the uses of the data by Japanese marketing management, while two specific applications (one industrial, the other academic) are discussed next. Finally, there are some brief observations about some remaining issues that need to be resolved before marketing information technologies can be truly integrated into the Japanese marketing infrastructure.

THE JAPANESE MARKET AND MARKETING IN JAPAN

Japan is a country where the people of a single ethnic origin live on a group of isolated islands in the northwestern end of the Pacific Ocean. Culturally homogeneous and economically relatively wealthy, Japan would appear to present an "easy" case for marketers in the textbook sense. This, however, is not the case. Japanese experience shows that homogeneity in an advanced economy could be as much a liability as an asset to marketers. It is instructive to note some of the factors accounting for this phenomenon. This also helps one understand both the similarities and the differences in the needs and uses of scanner data technologies between Japan and the United States.

Three factors are particularly relevant in making marketing in Japan a "difficult" task: the importance of the emotional dimension to buying behavior, the influence of others, and decisions at the point-of-purchase. These factors are reviewed, in turn, below.

Importance of the Emotional Dimension to Buying Behavior

Consumer needs with respect to the physical attributes of products are relatively homogeneous, and competing brands in a product class

are all equally satisfactory in terms of these attributes. Naturally, marketers are interested in further differentiation of their brands to gain competitive advantage. They look to nonphysical dimensions like image and
"personal touch." Nonessential and intangible differences between offerings do matter and work in Japan.

Empirical evidence of this abounds. In the automobile market, for
example, Toyota Soarer sells far better than its sister brand, Toyota Supra,
even though both are identical except for the outer "skins" and the brand
images. In the cosmetics market, Kao's Sophina lipsticks do not sell well,
even though in blind tests they are rated higher than the French prestige
brand names like Chanel and Christian Dior.

Marketers realize the importance of image and engage in a "soft sell"
approach significantly more often than in the United States (Tanaka
1991). Brand competition seems to be in an "image space" in most
markets. Even a noodle soup emphasizes image appeals in its commercials. Consequently, it is far more difficult to explain the successes and
failures of brands than in the case of physical attribute-based differentiation, and overall demand is not "logically" predictable.

Influence of Others

Most Japanese consumers are not autonomous utility maximizers. They
base their decisions not only on what a product is to them individually
but on what *others* think it is and what others think about their buying
it. The dynamic process of one influencing another is seemingly initiated
with a limited number of fashion and/or opinion leaders as well as the
fashion or trend-conscious magazines. However, because these media
inherently promote "variety-seeking" behavior, this gives rise to highly
unstable and volatile market conditions. By way of example, this is reflected in the striking figures of market share changes in the detergent
and shampoo markets, as shown in Table 14-1. Nine of the top ten
detergent brands and five of the top ten shampoo brands in April–Septem
ber 1987 disappeared from the top ten list in the period April–September
1991. Markets change quickly in an unpredictable direction.

Decision at the Point-of-Purchase

The final purchase/brand choice decision is usually made at the point-
of-purchase, rather than prior to shopping. This is significantly more so
in Japan than in the United States, where consumers typically decide to

TABLE 14-1
Market Shares of Yen Sales, 1987 and 1991

	1987 April–September		1991 April–September	
	Brand (manuf.)	Share	Brand (manuf.)	Share
Detergent				
1.	Attack (Kao)	23.1	Attack (Kao)	31.0
2.	Top (Lion)	17.0	Hitop (Lion)*	13.5
3.	New Beads (Kao)	11.3	Ultra Arier (P&G)*	12.6
4.	Cheer Ace (P&G)	9.4	Lemon Cheer (P&G)*	8.8
5.	Zab (Kao)	8.3	Lion Spark (Lion)*	5.6
6.	Coop P. Soap (Coop)	4.7	Kao Just (Kao)*	5.6
7.	Liquid Top (Lion)	3.9	Lion Dash (Lion)*	4.6
8.	Alpha (Lion)	3.6	Biobeads (Kao)*	2.2
9.	Liquid Cheer Ace (P&G)	3.4	Lever Surf (Lever)*	1.8
10.	Liquid Zab (Kao)	2.3	Surf 1-Pak (Lever)*	1.7
Shampoo				
1.	Kao Merit (Kao)	16.3	Kao Merit (Kao)	13.2
2.	Timotei (Lever)	11.9	Super Mild (Shisedo)*	9.3
3.	Snstr Tonic (Snstr)	7.5	P&G Rejoy (P&C)*	7.7
4.	Haircologn (Shisedo)	6.4	Soft in One (Lion)*	6.4
5.	Kao Essential (Kao)	6.3	Snstr Tonic (Snstr)	4.4
6.	Kao Pure (Kao)	6.1	Kao Merit (Kao)*	4.4
7.	Lion Aquame (Lion)	4.3	Salon Selective (H. Cts)*	4.1
8.	Lion Hairist (Lion)	3.3	Kao Essential (Kao)	3.9
9.	GNYU Showeran (Gyunyu)	2.4	Lion Aquame (Lion)	3.6
10.	Morning Fresh (Shisedo)	2.0	Lux Super Rich (Lever)*	3.3

*denotes those not on the 1987 lists.

buy before shopping (Tanaka 1991). This implies the following format or structure to the purchase decision: the factors of image orientation and others' influence play an important role in the formation of the *choice set*; the final buying decision is determined by POP factors such as price deals, displays, and so forth. This suggests that market share can easily erode unless the marketer carefully monitors what is happening at the retail point-of-sale and responds quickly and appropriately to changes.

When taken together, the three factors contribute to the Japanese manufacturers' perceptions of the market that

- Consumers' tastes are difficult to measure and correctly satisfy;
- Consumers' tastes change very quickly and unpredictably over time; and
- A large number of consumers are sensitive to in-store displays and the price deals of their favorite brands.

These perceptions, in turn, lead to the following general observations about the Japanese marketplace:

- An enormous number of new products/brands are introduced;
- Physically similar products are sold under different brand names with different images;
- Brands are relatively short lived;
- Advertising emphasizes emotional appeals; and
- Competition among brands is fierce at the store level in the form of displays and price deals.

Manufacturers engage in "machine gun" trial-and-error marketing rather than try to pinpoint their marketing through solid planning. Under such circumstances, what is more important is to act and then see the results as quickly as possible. In this context, the following quote is of interest: "When Kozo Osone, the executive in charge of developing Sony's compact Discman, heard that the company's marketing people were thinking about commissioning a research study, he told them not to waste their money" (Johansson and Nonaka 1987).

The focus of marketing research in Japan is on the post-introduction rather than the pre-introduction phase. It involves

- Continuous monitoring of brand sales/shares movements;
- Tracking of new brand shares;
- Tracking of incumbents' shares after a new brand introduction; and
- Measurement of the effects of in-store promotions.

Though these factors are, of course, salient for U.S. marketers as well, they would appear to be of relatively greater importance to Japanese companies, given the characteristics of Japanese consumer behavior. Demand for these items of information is very strong, particularly among the major packaged-goods manufacturers, and is being increasingly met by advances in marketing data technologies, as reviewed next.

THE DEVELOPMENT OF POINT-OF-SALE AND SCANNER DATA IN JAPAN

POS Data

POS systems were first introduced in Japan on an experimental basis in 1978. The JAN (Japanese Article Number) code, a "source-marking" standard for consumer packaged goods corresponding to the UPC in the United States, was established, as was the marking of bar codes on packages at the same time. That year might therefore be called the start of the marketing information revolution in Japan.

In 1983, 7-Eleven Japan Co., the largest convenience store chain, started using a POS system in all of its stores. This accelerated the penetration of POS systems in Japan (Table 14-2). Today, almost all consumer packaged goods have bar code markings, and almost 100% of the supermarkets and major convenience chains have POS systems installed. The systems are beginning to penetrate smaller, independent stores but are still relatively rare in "mom and pop" stores and drugstores. However, beer brewers and pharmaceutical firms are particularly keen on building their own POS networks through liquor stores and drugstores.

The increase in the use of the JAN code has been remarkable, and it has been applied to a wide range of products–not only packaged goods but clothes, books, and even some consumer durables. As a result, it has been reported that the code is in danger of not being able to cover all products in the near future.

For the first several years of use, individual retail chains collected and analyzed POS data within their own organizations. The first large-scale interorganizational supply of data began in 1985 when the Distribution Code Center of Japan, a subsidiary of MITI (Ministry of International Trade and Industry), started its service. It collected data from over 100 supermarkets around the nation and supplied them to its member companies, including major retailers and manufacturers. Its intent was to promote the diffusion of POS usage.

Today, there are several companies offering POS data services (Table 14-3). Their backgrounds vary and they may roughly be classified as marketing research firms, newspaper publishers, trading houses, and hard-

TABLE 14-2
Penetration of POS

Year	No. of JAN Users	No. of POS Stores	No. of POS Registers
1979	27	1	3
1980	53	2	17
1981	86	25	154
1982	217	91	406
1983	1,744	1,909	4,740
1984	5,231	2,725	7,255
1985	11,016	4,212	12,196
1986	19,250	7,930	29,769
1987	26,440	11,711	40,691
1988	32,537	21,348	63,981
1989	38,449	42,880	119,137
1990	44,723	70,061	183,497

TABLE 14-3
Organizations Offering POS Data Services

Marketing Data Services
  Nihon Keizai Shinbun
  Shakai Chosa Institute
  Nielsen Japan
  Fuji Research Institute
Printing
  Dai-Nihon Printing
  Toppan Printing
Trading
  Mitsubishi Corp.
Computer Hardware
  NEC
  Hitachi
  Unisys Japan
  Fujitsu FIP
  TEC Electronics

ware manufacturers. They offer services either as a stand-alone (commercial) venture or as a complementary service to their traditional customers.

Scanner panel single-source data. The first scanner panel started in Japan in 1983. Presently, there are six major panels, which are evenly divided into two groups based on their scanning methods: store scanning and home scanning (Table 14-4). The former is a typical American-style panel, where a member uses an ID card when checking at the store POS register. The latter is specifically designed for the Japanese shopping climate (described below), where a panel member scans whatever he or she has bought on a given day past a scanner installed in the home.

The following are among the characteristics of the Japanese shopping climate that favor the use of the home-scanning method:

- The geographical density of the retail stores is very high and consumers patronize various kinds of stores. For example, there are 63 supermarkets/convenience stores and 961 smaller stores in 4.8 square miles of the target area used by the VR scanner panel.
- The supermarket chains are not cooperative in the installation of external scanner terminals.
- Shoppers are mobile and make a substantial portion of their purchases at stores outside the "designated" panel area, e.g., malls and department stores in downtown Tokyo.

Consequently, the store-scanning method works only if (1) the target panel area is geographically and commercially isolated and (2) scanners are installed in the majority of the stores located in the area. In most

TABLE 14-4
Japanese Scanner Panels

(A) Store Scanning			
Name	*Since . . .*	*Samples*	*Area/No. of Stores*
RSD Scan Panel	1983	10,000	Kanto, Kansai, Chukyo, Chugoku (14 stores)
Nikkei NEEDS-SCAN Panel	1986	1,200	Metropolitan area (2 stores)
MARIONET/RMS Panel	1989	22,000	Metropolitan area, Shizuoka, Kansai (46 stores)

(B) Home Scanning			
Name	*Since . . .*	*Samples (Households)*	*Area*	*Characteristics*
VR HomeScan	1987	1,000	2-km radius area in the metropolitan area	A sole single-source data in Japan DATA • Purchase data • TVCMs exposure • Store promotion • Newspaper insertion ad • Weather and temperature
Quick Purchase Report	1987	2,500	Metropolitan area	(without marketing variables)
SCI Scanning System	(1992)	(9,968)	Nationwide (Japan)	(without marketing variables)

metropolitan areas neither condition is likely to be true, so store scanning covers a relatively low percentage of household purchases. Home scanning naturally avoids this coverage problem but nevertheless has its own limitations, for example,

- Causal data (in-store information such as displays, price promotions, and so forth) must be collected from the majority of the stores patronized by panel members;
- Panel members' task of recording all relevant data is by no means easy, and errors of omission as well as input may be considerable.

Significant efforts have been made by the POS data service firms to increase the coverage of the causal data from stores in terms of the share of purchases made. At the same time, validation studies have shown that measurement errors from home-scanner panel member reporting have been surprisingly small. Thus, the home-scanner approach would appear to be the preferable of the two methods. In the next section, we review one notable example of this approach.

Japanese home-scanning single-source data. The leading edge of Japanese marketing-information technologies is a home-scanner panel coupled with a TV audience research system—the first and so far only single-source data service available in Japan. The system is the VR HomeScan System, run by Video Research Ltd. The system was started in 1987 and employs a panel of 1,000 households living in a 1.3 mile radius in a typical Tokyo suburban residential area.

The typical panel member is a relatively high-income, well-educated, white-collar household with husband commuting to downtown Tokyo. Although the panel is by no means representative of the average, or mass Japanese market, it does serve the needs of manufacturers as a "lead user" market. The data provided from the panel consist of purchase behavior and TV viewing/audience patterns, in-store causal data, and environmental data (Figure 14-1).

FIGURE 14-1
VR HomeScan System

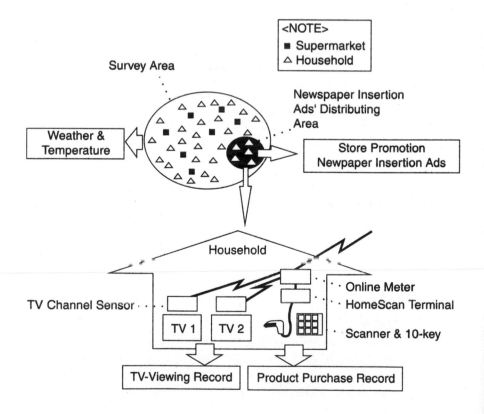

1. *Purchase Data*. The purchases made by all members of the household are input daily through a scanner installed in the home. The input items are as follows:
   - household code;
   - store code (pre-coded)
     (a) supermarkets, by store
     (b) convenience stores, by chain
     (c) department stores, by category
     (d) all other stores, by category
     (e) gift
     (f) sample;
   - JAN code;
   - purchase units; and
   - purchase price per unit.

   JAN codes are input by a scanner. All other items are input through a 10-key board or pre-coded keys.
2. *TV Audience Data*. TV channel sensors are installed at the TV sets in the home and connected online to the host computer. They record the time each channel was on and off. These data are then matched with the area TV schedule and the household's exposure to television programming is measured. (Cable TV is not available in the area comprising the panel, and television programming consists of five major VHF channels and a few UHF or satellite channels.)
3. *Store Causal Data*. Major supermarkets in the panel area are monitored daily for in-store promotion activities and newspaper ad insertions ("features"). The coverage of supermarkets has been increasing and, as of fall 1991, was 80% of supermarkets in the area.
4. *Environmental Data*. The weather, temperature, and so forth, of the area is monitored and recorded daily, along with information about special local events (such as athletic meetings of area schools) that are likely to affect the purchase behavior of households in the area.

From a data management perspective, input error checks and the maintenance of the JAN code dictionary are among the most important concerns. For the former, the following steps are followed: first, questionable inputs are automatically checked by the host computer in terms of purchase units and purchase prices. Next, those purchases where the number of units exceeds 10 and/or where the prices are outside of the manufacturer's specified range are examined by the database manager. He or she qualitatively judges the validity of the entry using past data from the household, contemporaneous data from other households, and the causal data from the stores. The percentage of "discarded" purchases is .1–.3% of the total records.

Households with poor reporting performance are identified by low-input frequencies and/or low total expenditures. After a number of follow-ups, these households are eliminated from the panel. The overall dropout rate per year, including those eliminated from the panel for low performance, is less than 10%. Most of the dropouts are movers; elimination accounts for only 2–3%.

The maintenance of the JAN code dictionary is also essential to the effective operation of the panel. The dictionary is updated daily, using both external information services and in-house inquiries. When a code is found unidentified, an inquiry is made at the store of purchase by a VR representative, using price and purchase data information. The newly identified JAN code is then edited and added to the code dictionary along with information about product attributes.

THE USE OF MARKETING INFORMATION

POS Data

Because POS data are store specific they are naturally used most extensively by retailers at the store level. Their greatest use comes from what is called "ABC analysis." The store manager classifies all items in order of yen sales volume into A, B, and C categories and then drops those in the C category from the assortment carried. The data are also used for inventory management, in-store promotion decisions, and shelf space allocations. As can be seen, these uses are relatively unsophisticated in terms of the state-of-the-art, and storewide experiments, such as those reported by Wilkinson et al. (1982), have not yet been undertaken.

POS data are also used by manufacturers to assist in their marketing decisions, but not nearly as extensively as by retailers. Typical applications involve obtaining information about what is happening on the "retail front," in particular, changes in selling price and other marketing variables of their own as well as rivals' brands. This information is especially helpful in new product introductions, and some companies use it systematically for tracking new brand sales (Kuga 1990). A major concern is the representativeness of the data, of course, and so most users supplement it with nationwide store audit data such as the Nielsen Retail Index.

POS data are also used by manufacturers to provide merchandising support for their retailers. Such support is in general an important function of Japanese consumer packaged-goods manufacturers (Masuda 1988). It should be noted, however, that (in Little's 1979 terminology) use of data in this way is primarily to provide "status" information, rather than "response" information in the form of price or in-store promotion elasticities. These more sophisticated applications have yet to be implemented in any major way.

Scanner Panel/Single-Source Data

The advantages of scanner panel data are that they are household based, that all purchases by a household are captured on a category-by-date basis, and that the household characteristics are known. Consequently, one can obtain much richer information on household purchase behavior as well as on brands' sales performance from panel data than from aggregate POS data. Consumer goods manufacturers have begun to be aware of these advantages, and the interest in and usage of panel data among various types of institutions is as high as for POS data (Kobayashi and Draper 1990).

The VR panel offers the following "menu" on a regular basis:

1. Basic time-series tables: brand × week time series of purchased household percentage (this is equal to the purchase rate), total yen and unit sales, shares, and so forth;
2. Shares of the store types by category or brand;
3. Frequency distributions of the interpurchase time × category;
4. Brand switching matrices among the specified set of brands in a category;
5. Market penetration data of new brands: weekly or monthly time series of purchase rates, trial rates, penetration rates, and purchase frequency distributions;

(nos. 1–5 may be classified based on household characteristics)

6. GRP by brand;
7. TV program audience rate by household purchase characteristics (e.g., heavy vs. light users) of a category; and
8. Household purchase rate of brand or category by the number of exposures to a TV spot.

The VR system also provides a customized summary and analysis of the following tables:

1. Cross-classification of households by purchase characteristics: heavy/light, brand loyal/switcher, deal prone or not, innovator/early adopter. and so forth;
2. Brand competition switching matrices;
3. Distribution of selling prices;
4. Correlation between purchase rates and TV GRP and/or promotion frequencies;
5. Speed of penetration of new brands (see, e.g., Figure 14-2); and
6. The number of TV exposures and trial purchase rates for new brands (see, e.g., Figure 14-3).

From the users' point of view, the advantages of the home-scanning system over the store-scanning method are several: first, because of the wider coverage of stores, statistics such as the distribution of selling prices

FIGURE 14-2
Penetration of New Detergent Brands

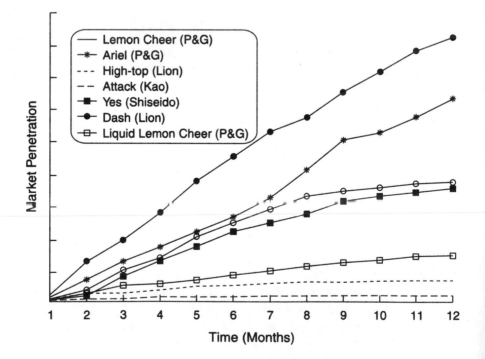

FIGURE 14-3
TV-CM Exposure and Purchase Rate of New Beer Brand

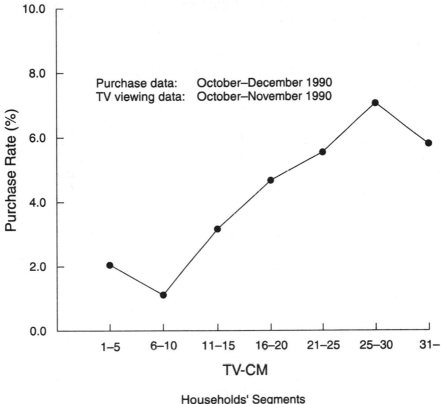

Households' Segments
by TV-CM Exposure Level

across outlets and the purchase shares by store type can be calculated. Second, for a given purchase history, missing observations are minimized. Third, brand managers particularly like having a household's total purchase history in conjunction with information about a new product introduction. It gives a clear picture of how many, and who, have tried the brand (in terms of demographics, brand loyalty, and so forth).

Furthermore, the single-source aspect is attracting the attention of more advanced marketers who can measure the effects of their own advertising and promotion at the household level and get information about competitive advertising and promotion activities. In this regard, manufacturers have shown an increasing interest in measuring the effectiveness of TV advertising and in the fact that projects are beginning to be implemented that involve weight tests, tests of temporal insertion patterns, and analyses of advertising wearout.

Marketing Information and the "Japanese Management Style"

Much has been written about the general differences in "style" between Japanese and U.S. managers. In this section, some brief observations are made as to the influence of the Japanese management style on the use of marketing information such as that from POS scanner systems.

Management by consensus has often been identified as a major characteristic of Japanese management. In most cases decisions are initiated by middle management, then passed on to the various organization members involved in the decision, including top management, before being finalized. It is assumed that all parties share information relevant to a decision, which is often qualitative in nature, based on their hands-on experience with the marketplace. Quantitative data, such as that from POS scanners, are typically too detailed and complex in their raw form to be shared — even though in many cases all parties have access through the organization's internal information system. Consequently,

- In their raw form, scanner data are perceived as not directly relevant to marketing decision making.
- There are a small number of managers (often at the middle level) in charge of handling, editing, and interpreting the data.
- Since, as noted above, scanner data are typically used (at least by manufacturers) to support the "tactics" of marketing (as opposed to strategy), the information thus processed is used by actual decision makers insofar as it backs up and justifies their existing beliefs or helps them find out about anomalies in the marketplace.

Of course, there are exceptions. A few leading manufacturers, for example, use a brand management system wherein brand managers are fully responsible for all brand marketing decisions and make very sophisticated use of scanner data.

From the interorganizational point of view, long-term trade relationships are another characteristic of Japanese management. Traditionally, in distribution, large manufacturers are organized into keiretsu consisting of a hierarchy of wholesalers and retailers under their control. On the other hand, the rise of supermarkets has challenged the manufacturers' dominant position in the value chain. This has been fueled by the marketing information revolution and the influence of scanner technology in giving the supermarkets an informational advantage.

Recently, however, the opposite trend has begun to be observed in Japanese markets. The increasingly extensive availability of the various sources of scanner data to the manufacturers has started to give the manufacturers a potential information advantage, even over large supermarkets. Manufacturers now know what is happening in their product categories across all supermarket chains and can use this information in their negotiations with a given chain.

As noted above, manufacturers are using POS data to provide merchandising support for their retailers. An emerging trend is that of manufacturers beginning to organize their own in-house POS networks, collecting data on sales, prices, margins, and inventories of all items carried by each independent retailer. The manufacturers give merchandising advice to the individual member retailers based on the data accumulated across all retailers. This has strengthened the dominant keiretsu structures.

Thus, the balance of power along the distribution chain has been affected by the advent of marketing information technologies. As is true in the United States, what is critical now is no longer how much data one or the other party has relative to another, but how "good" a use the party makes of the data. The players in the game—both manufacturer and retailer—are experimenting through trial and error for the most efficient and effective formats for using scanner-based information.

AN APPLICATION: A NEW BRAND PREDICTION MODEL

A recent successful example of using single-source data is a model developed by VR to predict the purchase rate of a new brand before and/ or shortly after its introduction. The model represents a first step toward integrating the rich data collected from the single-source scanner system with a relatively simple model, giving rise to strong results. Drawing on the structure of new product–tracking models developed in the United States (e.g., LITMUS, Blackburn and Clancy 1982), the model has been simplified and adapted for using the single-source data. The model has so far been applied to two dozen new brands in a variety of consumer packaged-goods categories. The results from these applications have, in turn, been accumulated and used to improve the accuracy and reliability of new applications.

Model

The purchase rate of a new brand is decomposed into a trial rate and a repeat rate, as follows:

$$Z(t) = T(t) + R(t),$$

where $Z(t)$ is the purchase rate at time t and $T(t)$ and $R(t)$ are the trial and repeat rates, respectively. These three rates are relative to the total number of households. The trial rate, in turn, is specified as follows:

$$T(t) = PEN(t) - PEN(t-1),$$

where $PEN(t)$ is the percentage of households that have purchased the new brand at least once until time t. $PEN(t)$, in turn, is specified to be a function of a saturation parameter and a number of marketing variables, including distribution coverage, cumulated advertising GRP (measured within the single-source data), reach of features, price promotion percentage, special displays (number of stores × days), and sampling intensity.

In similar fashion, the repeat rate is specified to be a function of the price promotion percentage, the reach of features, and a seasonality factor.

Prediction Method and Examples

To obtain the predicted time series of $Z(t)$'s from $t = 0$ or some time after $t = 0$, one has to determine the values of the marketing variables as well as a variety of parameters set by the model. For the former, if the brand has already been launched, the marketing programs used for the introductory months are used as inputs. The model's parameters (including the saturation parameter $PEN(t)$) are basically determined by judgment, using data estimated from previous applications. VR has approximately 200 sets of parameters estimated from previous cases of new product introductions. For applications where the new brand has not yet been introduced, there are no data yet from the marketplace, so parameter values must be determined by using estimates from cases similar to the target one and making judgmental adjustments.

Figures 14-4, 14-5, 14-6, and 14-7 show the results of the model for four applications. Figure 14-4 shows the estimates for the purchase rate $Z(t)$ and the values of some marketing variables. Figures 14-5, 14-6, and 14-7 show the fit of the trial, repeat, and purchase rates' models, respectively. As can be seen, the fit is good in all cases. To date, the

FIGURE 14-4
Purchase Rate and Marketing Variables

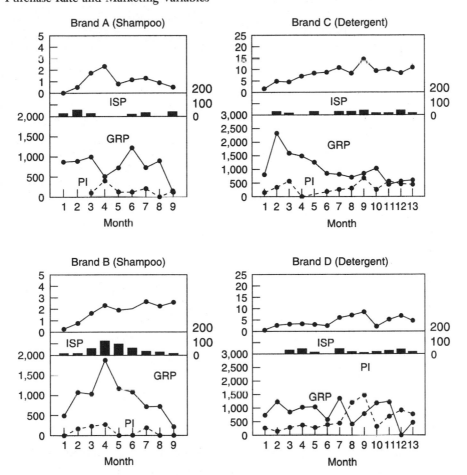

ISP: In-Store Promotion
GRP: Gross Rating Points
PI: Price Index

model has been applied in over 20 cases. Its attractions are its accuracy, relative simplicity, and evolutionary nature. Given the characteristics of the Japanese marketing environment, in particular the rapid pace of new product introduction and the need for early detection of success and failure rates, this type of model should continue to gain wide acceptance.

FIGURE 14-5
Fit of Trial Rate Model

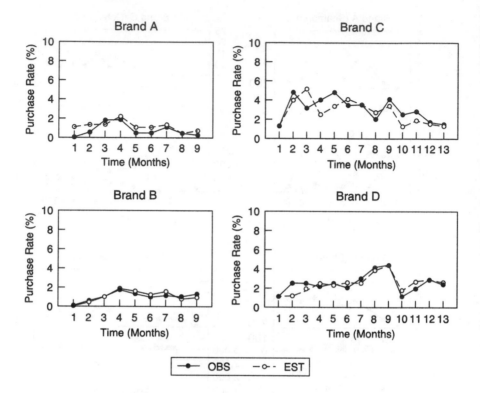

CONCLUSION

Although perhaps not to the same extent as in the United States, the development and penetration of marketing information technologies in Japan have been noteworthy and have become an important part of the marketing infrastructure. At the same time, several problems are still quite apparent. In "hardware," an increase in geographical coverage of POS data, more extensive and detailed supply of in-store causal data, and the standardization of the data format across differences are among the most pressing. The last point is particularly critical, since the parallel use of different POS and scanner panel services is both desirable and very likely to continue in actual applications contexts. The standardization process would produce enormous economies in this respect.

Perhaps more serious in terms of "software," the perceptual gap between the users and the actual technological capability is still very large. The

FIGURE 14-6
Fit of Repeat Rate Model

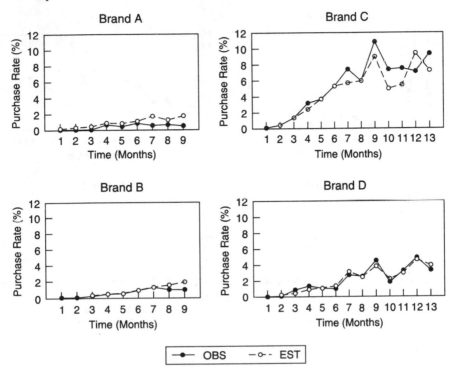

advantages of using the technologies—especially at strategic levels—are appreciated by only a few of the leading, "advanced" manufacturers. For example, even of Kao, a firm known for the extensive use of cutting-edge marketing technologies (Kuga 1990), it was said, "Kao executives analyze point-of-sale data weekly and wholesale inventory and sales statistics monthly. The company occasionally uses consumer surveys and other quantitative research tools, but executives never base marketing decisions primarily on the information from them" (Johansson and Nonaka 1987).

Progress is thus required on both sides. From the standpoint of the technology, user friendliness is absolutely essential—in particular, the development of a user friendly interface on top of the increasingly efficient and effective information-processing/analysis capabilities. From the point of view of users, the situation is not as straightforward. As with the diffusion of any real innovation, success is dependent ultimately on an uncertain and gradual penetration process based on favorable word of mouth, if

FIGURE 14-7
Fit of Purchase Rate Model

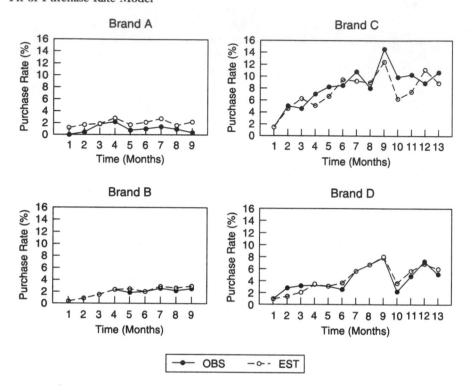

any, from a limited number of "lucky" satisfied lead users. Although the prospect looks promising, the process has just begun.

REFERENCES

Blackburn, J.D., and K.J. Clancy (1982). "LITMUS: A New Product Planning Model." In A.A. Zoltners (ed.), *Marketing Planning Models*. New York: North-Holland.

Johansson, J.K., and I. Nonaka (1987). "Market Research the Japanese Way." *Harvard Business Review*, May–June, 16–22.

Katahira, H. (1987). "Preference Heterogeneity in Discrete Choice Modeling." *Journal of Economics* (University of Tokyo) 50 (in Japanese).

Katahira, H., and S. Yagi (1989). "A Latent Cluster Logit Model of Promotional Effects: An Application of the Single-Source Data." *Marketing Science* (Japan Institute of Marketing Science) 33 (in Japanese).

Kobayashi, K., and P. Draper (1990). "Reviews of Marketing Research in Japan." *Journal of Advertising Research*.

Kuga, T. (1990). "Kao's Marketing Strategy." *Journal of Advertising Research*.

Little, J.D.C. (1979). "Decision Support Systems for Marketing Managers." *Journal of Marketing* 43, 9–27.

Masuda, Y. (1988). "The Use of Marketing Information in Japanese Consumer Packaged Goods Manufacturers." *Japanese Marketing Journal* (in Japanese).

Tanaka, H. (1991). "Brand-Building in Japan: Analysis from Consumer and Corporate Behavior Perspectives." Paper presented at the Tenth Advertising and Consumer Psychology Conference, San Francisco.

Wilkinson, J.B., J.B. Mason, and C.H. Paksoy (1982). "Assessing the Short-term Supermarket Strategy Variables." *Journal of Marketing Research* 19.

15

MANAGING THE INFORMATION-INTENSIVE FIRM OF 2001

Stephan H. Haeckel

ALTHOUGH THE FULL RANGE *of consequences associated with the marketing information revolution will probably not be understood for many years, a number of visions of what the "information-intensive" firm of the future will look like are beginning to appear. One such view was presented in Chapter 1 of this volume, which focuses on the ways in which the management of information and information technology will transform the marketing function. In this concluding chapter, another perspective is presented— one that goes beyond a consideration of marketing activities to the broader question of how the information revolution will transform the basic function of the firm itself.*

Placing himself at the beginning of the next decade (and millennium!), the author assumes as a matter of course that the variety of information value-chain processes described in the other chapters have been put in place and are well integrated into the daily operations of the firm. If so, he envisions a world in which "Big M" marketing has fundamentally refocused the entire purpose of the organization away from product offerings and toward responses, with all the changes in business activity and structure that this entails. Of course, this prescription is not particularly surprising and echoes the thoughts of other "information age" writers (both in this book and elsewhere). However, what distinguishes the thesis put forth in this chapter from others is the notion of "management by wire"—the ability to manipulate the business by manipulating information. The results is the development of "enterprise models"—the institutionalizing of the firm's know-how and decision making into a formal (if not entirely mathematical) representation. This is a truly "radical" view of the role of information in transforming the firm of the future—at once the culmination of information value-chain processes and perhaps the ultimate legacy of the marketing information revolution.

INTRODUCTION

Marketing is the process by which an organization relates itself creatively and productively to its environment. This formulation by E. Raymond Corey is particularly useful in thinking about the future. His characterization suggests that marketing abides, but is in constant flux—changing at a pace, amplitude, and frequency dictated by the environment. It positions *responsiveness* as its essential function, rather than one of its objectives, and implies the need for a tight coupling of "how we do things around here" to "what's going on out there"—which is to say, the need to be market driven. Accordingly, the following discussion assumes that the marketing process incorporates the entire cycle of sensing, interpreting, and responding to environmental conditions.

We know that the pace of change is accelerating, reducing the time available for fashioning responses. As available response time diminishes toward "reflex," technological and organizational developments of the next decade will make necessary new marketing skills and tools—some, like "enterprise modeling," not yet even in the marketing lexicon. A noteworthy consequence of accepting a "response process" definition of marketing in an information-intensive, technology-rich environment is the implication that important aspects of marketing management will be not only very different but downright unfamiliar. Indeed, the degree to which the scenario discussed below "doesn't sound like marketing" may well be an indicator of how much change confronts us.

The central thesis of this chapter—of this book, in fact—is that business in general, and marketing in particular, will be an (even more) information-intensive process in 2001. It will be focused on strategies for exploiting information to create personalized responses for individual customers and clients, strategies that will be made both necessary and possible by technology, and which will be carried out in institutional structures whose fluid form makes "organization" an increasingly quaint descriptor.

INFORMATION AS ACTION AGENT

If there is such a thing as a sustainable advantage, it is based on consistently superior information and knowledge. This is why the first priority of Desert Storm was information deprivation. Keeping Iraqi command and control systems ignorant of troop movements was the centerpiece of allied strategy and its dramatic success. Knowing what works and what doesn't, how the players are positioned, and what's-going-on-out-there is prerequisite to good strategy and effective tactical execution, whether you are dropping bombs or coupons.

Although war as a metaphor for marketing is overdrawn, and increasingly inappropriate, the parallel is apt in terms of the strategically determinant role played by information. Information is a strange asset: its value typically increases when it is (selectively) shared; it doesn't obsolesce or depreciate with use, though it may with time; and you can give it away without giving it up.

Reducing uncertainty is its defined function. The director of market research for a leading packaged-goods firm, asked to value his department's information system, answered immediately, "three points of share." He explained that after the system was installed, management was able to make promotion and advertising decisions in days, rather than weeks, because they were more confident they knew what was happening in the marketplace. Faster decisions were immediately and unambiguously accompanied by share improvement. Time is money.

Information as action-agent, rather than symbolic record of the results of action, is the concept behind recently emerging business strategies aimed at enhancing organizational responsiveness to market change. Getting information off the bench and onto the playing field transforms it from an expense of doing business to an asset for doing business. And the transforming agent is, of course, technology.

Information technology can enhance the potential economic value of information by *processing* it faster; *connecting* more of it together; *integrating* it for shared use; and *structuring* it for meaning. Largely by automating manual tasks and processes, computers have already transformed information into a wealth-producing asset comparable to capital and energy. As we learn to structure information in such a way that it codifies desirable institutional behavior, properly architected technology infrastructures will permit us to *manipulate businesses by manipulating information*. I call this "managing by wire" because information systems mediate other mechanisms to interpret management input (decisions) and initiate appropriate changes. It is analogous to "fly by wire" systems in the latest generation of aircraft, in which pilots manipulate software, rather than hydraulics, when they pull back on the stick. With the functionality and scope described later in this chapter, management by wire becomes a logical culmination of the transition to an information economy.

THE MARKETING CHALLENGE: REORIENTING THE BUSINESS

By driving things so much faster, technology increases the premium awarded responsiveness and the importance of marketing. Evidence of this comes from the pervasiveness of the market-driven movement and the increasing focus on services, not to mention *Harvard Business Review* articles with titles like "Marketing is Everything."[1] An ironic by-product could be "the de-functionalization of marketing"[2]—which by 2001 may be the vestigial title of a group of people who specialize in persuading external constituencies. But "Big M" marketing, as it is sometimes called, will be dealing with the task of reorienting businesses from offerings to responses. As used here, "response" means more than giving customers what they say they want; it includes searching for and interpreting signals from the marketplace in order to anticipate and define customer needs.

It is difficult to overstate the trauma that premiums on responsiveness can occasion in a traditional, product-centered company—particularly a successful one—whose natural reaction will be to try to do better what they have always done. But there are limits to driving an old business faster, and so "re-engineering" is necessary. Among the things that may need re-engineering is the fundamental orientation of the business.

Product-Centered versus Service-Centered Orientation

Every business is defined by the offerings it makes, and the requests to which it responds. Product-centered companies tend to major on the former, service-centered companies on the latter, but no business is purely one or the other. Product-centered companies try to make their products as responsive to market needs and wants as possible, and service-centered companies try to define customer needs in terms of their particular range of competence. Knowing on which side of the product-services continuum a company wants to be is strategically important, however, because the objectives, measurements, investments, and opportunities

---

[1]Regis McKenna, "Marketing Is Everything," *Harvard Business Review*, January–February, 1991 65–79.

[2]Frederick E. Webster, Jr., "It's 1990—Do You Know Where Your Marketing Is?" White Paper, Marketing Science Institute, 1989.

appropriate for one side are generally inappropriate for the other (Figure 15-1).

The fundamental disposition of a product-centered company is to pre-package and shrink-wrap as much as possible in the plant to take advantage of economies of scale, and then to offer what has been made. Its metrics of organizational effectiveness are *efficiency and predictability.*

A service-centered company, on the other hand, will major on assembling a customized offering from modular elements (including product and service components) in response to a customer request. It measures organizational effectiveness in terms of *responsiveness and flexibility.*

Many firms in each category have concluded that they must become "solutions companies," i.e., package product and service elements into offerings/responses which solve larger chunks of their customer/client needs. Their common premise is that the value of a solution is greater than the sum of the values of its elements, and that this leads to differentiation and the ability to command premiums. But product-centered companies think of solutions as complicated products—comprehensive offerings applicable to the most important collection of common market requirements; service-centered companies think of solutions as complete responses to a specific customer's specific need. Solutions may be product-

FIGURE 15-1
Organizational Orientation

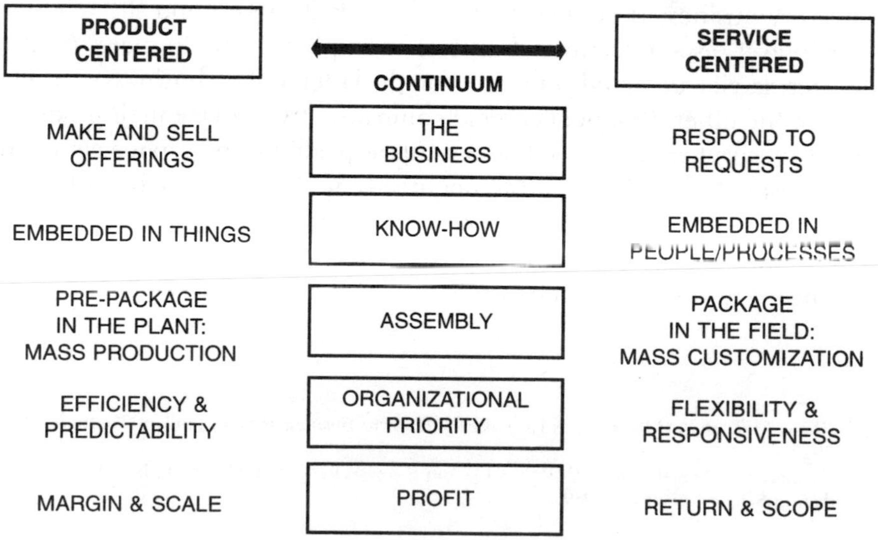

PRODUCT CENTERED	CONTINUUM	SERVICE CENTERED
MAKE AND SELL OFFERINGS	THE BUSINESS	RESPOND TO REQUESTS
EMBEDDED IN THINGS	KNOW-HOW	EMBEDDED IN PEOPLE/PROCESSES
PRE-PACKAGE IN THE PLANT: MASS PRODUCTION	ASSEMBLY	PACKAGE IN THE FIELD: MASS CUSTOMIZATION
EFFICIENCY & PREDICTABILITY	ORGANIZATIONAL PRIORITY	FLEXIBILITY & RESPONSIVENESS
MARGIN & SCALE	PROFIT	RETURN & SCOPE

or service-centric depending on the nature of their constituent parts, and the degree to which they are pre-packaged.

Forces that drive companies toward one side or the other of the continuum include the following:

1. Their view of the values most important to the markets they serve, or wish to enter.
2. Which of the components they make, and which they buy.
3. The length of their product cycles, and the uniqueness of their offerings.
4. Their heritage of success, assets, and competencies.
   Companies offering truly innovative products and services for which markets must be created tend to be product centered, but need not be. (Note that there are successful examples of "service-centered product companies," like Milliken; and "product-centered service companies," like McDonald's or Lawn Doctor.)
5. How they measure success.

Product-centered companies that find that their customers are spending more and more on services, and that declare an intent to become a solutions company, face tactical choices about which services to include in their solutions, which of these to make or buy, and how to recover the cost/expense of producing them. The *strategic* choice they face is whether or not to become service-centric, changing their orientation from producing offerings with a high degree of commonality and pre-packaging, to a focus on mass customization of modular components and responding to customer requests.

Many will undoubtedly opt for a hybrid strategy, and do both of the above—but they must settle on a center of gravity. While product-centered orientation will continue to make sense for many companies, the technology/speed/responsiveness logic makes it plausible that a trend toward service-centric behavior will predominate. This means profound changes in the way businesses are structured, measured, and managed— and how they relate to their customers.

Shifting the center of gravity from offerings to responses modifies the way one thinks about marketing and markets. An offerings mind-set segments customers by buying habits or offering specification: the "PC market," the "generic aspirin market," the "fast-food market." Products and services are designed for, and sold into, these segments. Relationships with customers are defined in terms of transactions, and managed by salespeople or "manufacturer's reps." Marketing management worries about the marketing mix and the "Four Ps" by offering category.

The response-oriented organization does not sell products or services. It sells its relevant competencies, and bills for products and services at a rate dictated by the value of the response to the customer. The assumption is that every response will be unique, and segmentation is by common need for a given set of competencies.

Marketing management is concerned with strategies for establishing and building client relationships, and with institutionalizing competencies so that they can be leveraged by infrastructure. *The essence of the relationship is collaboration and risk/reward sharing.* There are many other important changes that information and technology will inflict upon marketing. In a thought-provoking analysis, Rashi Glazer has developed a series of propositions about what can be expected to occur with increasing information intensity, based on the nature of information as an economic commodity. Among them:

- Shorter and less predictable product life cycles.
- Relative power shifts from sellers to buyers.
- More focus on product profitability, less on share.
- More, and less formal, alliances.
- More focus on cooperation, less on competition.
- More reliance on decision teams that simultaneously process shared information.[3]

It is a truism that change can only be observed against a (relatively) unchanging background, but it is becoming more and more difficult to locate such a background. Marketing people, traditionally concerned with competition, products, and customers, face a future in which competition will become situational rather than institutional; products will become components of responses; and customers and know-how will replace plants and equipment as an organization's primary assets. This, of course, in addition to such matters as globalizing the company; managing multiple, simultaneous, conflicting relationships with other firms; and dealing with all these issues in an environment of greater uncertainty about unformed public policies.

---

[3]Rashi Glazer, "Marketing in an Information-Intensive Environment: Strategic Implications of Knowledge as an Asset," *Journal of Marketing*, vol. 55, October 1991, 1–19.

THE MARKETING IMPLICATIONS OF
TECHNOLOGICAL PROGRESS

In 1991, it took one billion atoms to store a bit of information. That is 100 billion times fewer than it took in 1950, and 10,000 times more than it will take in 2001. This progress at the atomic level is but one index of the inexorable and historically unprecedented rate of improvement in the cost/performance of information technology we are experiencing in the last half of the twentieth century. (See Appendix.) Figure 15-2 depicts the relative cost/performance changes expected in the decade of the 1990s.

Technology has become an economic juggernaut, making itself indispensable by driving things so fast that only technology can keep up. Continuous technological change over decades at the rates we have experienced—and will continue to experience—is driving a need for virtually continuous re-engineering of work, processes, and software. Coming as it does on the heels of 40 years of a rate of change of 25% per year, the order of magnitude of further improvement projected for

FIGURE 15-2
Relative Technological Improvements 1991–2001

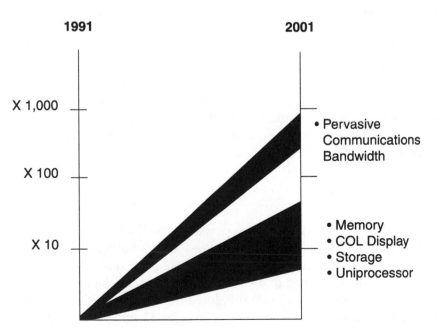

the next decade is a staggering amount. Some of the implications for marketing follow.

More Probes

Ubiquitous and mobile, technology will broadly extend the number of places where a business can capture and process information, and thus be effectively present. It will make economic sense to equip virtually ALL route salespeople, insurance adjustors, delivery trucks, repairpersons, grocery carts, and so forth with portable intelligence and wireless connection to an information infrastructure—enhancing the value of a firm's information assets by making them more comprehensive. Not only will technology become pervasive, people will be more likely to use it, because of more natural human interfaces such as the stylus, the voice, and the finger.

The "intelligent shopping cart," for example, is being tested in several retail stores. Infrared sensors installed throughout the store get location data from a video display/computer mounted on the push-bar of each cart, so that the computer in the back office knows the precise location of every cart at all times. Every shopper's route through the store is recorded, and the information can be used to isolate "dead spots" and change layouts. Ads appear on the video display as the cart nears a given product. In the case of a promotion, the ad may offer the consumer a discount by inviting him or her to push a button on the cart. Since the back-office computer knows when the cart has reached a specific checkout counter, the discount can be applied as the product is scanned, redeeming the "electronic coupon" on the spot. Other buttons allow the shopper to see a map of the store, and the location of any product category. By adding a card scanner to the computer on the cart, an information profile of the shopper could be related to actual in-store activity.

More Detail

Storage, memory, and processing capacities will allow more detail to be captured, structured, and re-used. Previously hidden components of a transaction can be made visible and related to other data. Banks, which have been severely limited in their marketing efforts by the fact that their customer databases are typically structured by account, are beginning to use ATM data on the name, time, place, type, and amount of each transaction, enabling better identification of product usage, customer loyalty, and fund-flow cycles.

Some retailers are already demonstrating the advantages of pushing transaction detail deeper than their competitors—tuning stores to a highly customized profile of local demographics, brand preferences, and shopping patterns. Similarly, airlines that keep track of the individual flying habits of their passengers are able to structure prices by seat and flight for maximum profitability—and selectively reschedule flights at reduced prices for departure times minutes ahead of a discounted competitive flight.

Greater Sampling Rates

With more technological probes on the pulse points of the market, and with substantially reduced communications costs, sampling rates can increase dramatically, so that it will become possible to know, virtually as it happens, "What's going on out there?" Firms that act on this information—such as 7-Eleven in Japan—can use current knowledge of what is being bought by age, sex, day, and hour to make more frequent deliveries of a smaller number of items that fit the buying profile of a particular store as it changes—in effect, putting their warehouses on wheels and implementing "just-in-time shelf management."

Personalization

As it becomes economically feasible to log every sale of everything, each consumer and customer's informational spoor becomes a potential marketing asset. Marui Department Store in Tokyo now has over seven years of purchase history on 8 million customers, and has used relational database technology to integrate information from their customer and credit files. As a result, they can target offers to individual customers for specific products based on actual purchase patterns: for example, designer watches offered to males who fit the following profile: self-employed or executive rank in specified companies; age 30–40; own a house; have purchased (or wife has purchased) a diamond or a fur coat within the previous two years; make current monthly payment of 5,000 yen or more; and have sufficient additional credit available. Similar profiles exist for such items as imported hand-bags, air conditioners, and men's suits.

This kind of strategy will become widespread as the technological cost curve continues its exponential drop. We can expect to see smaller and smaller batches of product delivered just in time to individual customers by online people in intelligent vehicles. Individual customization will become increasingly important as a differentiator, because anything from personalized, interactive advertising to nutritionally "designer Cheerios" will be economically feasible.

Market fragmentation, already under way in most industries, will continue toward its logical endpoint: unitary markets consisting of the individual buyer/client/customer. Out of a wealth of detail will emerge patterns that characterize individual buyers such as "frequent," "heavy user," "store loyal"/"brand loyal"/"competitor loyal," "gourmet," "health conscious," "early adaptor," "price sensitive," "promotion sensitive,"—each a potential target for personalized marketing initiatives.

Of course, there is another aspect of this trend: the potential for abuse of the power that comes with integrated information. The prospect of having multiple parts of our individual information trail integrated into a composite picture is rightfully worrisome. Furthermore, as consumers become more aware of the economic value of the data they generate, how much equity in them will they claim and be entitled to—and how should the cost of keeping track of them be apportioned? Current and prospective public policy is woefully inadequate to deal with these issues, and it is not yet even clear whether the focus will be on regulating the conditions of integration, or on integration itself.

Although public policy uncertainties may dampen the rate of investment in them, customized profiles tracked over time will become an indispensable marketing asset, because they enable a firm to distinguish "good" from "bad" customers. "Customer portfolio management," measuring and ensuring the quality of a firm's customer base, will become a primary marketing responsibility. Indeed, for many companies the customer base will be formally recognized as the single most valuable asset— as it is today with professional practices.

Design by Iteration

Design processes will evolve toward rough-prototype/rapid iteration. More variables will be incorporated in the design, including market, distribution, service, and promotion factors. Start-to-finish multifunctional teams will be enabled by integrative information infrastructures that make modular data and application logic a common, shareable asset. Design results will be represented with such completeness and accuracy that physical prototyping can be greatly reduced, or completely eliminated—as is the case with the next generation of airframes. "Visually initiative displays" will enable better designs by rendering visually explicit what was formerly implicit, allowing the incorporation of better and earlier customer feedback in the design cycle. Almost everything, from buildings to surgical procedures to MBA courses, will be designed on workstations.

Exploitation of Sound and Images

Integrating noncoded information in the form of speech, music, pictures, film clips, and so forth will sweep one more human sense, as well as additional subconscious and emotional responses, into the collection of information technology impacts. Variables such as affect and modality preference will become important design criteria for applications that involve human response, such as electronic shopping, education, consumer panels, and group design.

Managing the Application of Technology Productively

Forty years of 25% per annum improvement in the productivity of processing information has had, assert the authors of *The Corporation of the 1990s*, no measurable productivity impact at the macroeconomic level.[1] And only a limited number of companies claim confidence that they are getting value-received for their investment in information technology. How can this be?

Setting aside the fact that hardware now accounts for substantially less than 50% of the typical IS budget, and ignoring measurement and learning-curve problems, the answer has to lie with the *application* of the technology, not the technology itself. Poor implementation of a good idea and efficient execution of a bad idea are equally nonproductive. As technology speeds things up over the next decade, the latter effect will become increasingly noticeable when it occurs.

Whether or not the potential of information technology is realized in a given business, or by the economy as a whole, is a management issue. As it becomes increasingly clear that efficiency and predictability must yield to responsiveness and flexibility, management must change its priori-

---

[1] Michael S. Scott Morton and Lester Thurow, eds., *The Corporation of the 1990s: Information Technology and Organizational Transformation* (New York: Oxford University Press, 1991).

ties for technology investment from operating the present business more productively to enabling more rapid adaptation. This has major implications for organizational structure and marketing strategy.

ORGANIZATIONAL IMPACT: IT'S NOT EASY BEING FLAT

The scale and scope of institutional change implicit in the scale of technological advance are dramatic; change must be assimilated without capsizing the ship. The internal dynamics of Schumpeter's "creative destruction" may be even more disruptive than those of the external world. Successful institutions must manage transition as well as innovation—must get there from here without prematurely destroying "here."

The slow pace at which large organizations implement change is not usually because of management lethargy. It arises from the exceptional complexity of redesigning processes, management systems, and measurement systems "on the fly." Impelled to action, but daunted by the time, effort, and understanding required to re-engineer the business from an industrial age to a service age institution, many managers focus on that which is easiest to change quickly: organization. The idea is straightforward: create new responsibilities that are better aligned to the issues confronting us, put people in charge, make them accountable, and empower them to sort things out. That used to be a pretty good formula. Why isn't it working so well today? Why is execution so poor, so often? Two reasons stand out: the issues to be dealt with are changing too fast to keep up with; and accountability— "having someone in charge"—is a less important contributor to organizational effectiveness than it was.

Because it seems more tractable, organizational thinking often precedes procedural thinking—as though behavior should accommodate organization, rather than form following function. The concept of changing the organization to change the business is a legacy of the industrial age. But, in jettisoning this baggage, some seem to be ejecting organization itself, and even discipline, which seems extreme.

What Is an "Organization"?

But how extreme? After all, an "organization" is an *arrangement* of constituent elements. It is composed of entities (in human institutions, people and clusters of people) and their relationships. The term *organiza-*

tional change used to mean change from one arrangement to another, but over the past two decades it has increasingly come to mean a move from relatively static arrangements to "more fluid social structures."

"Organization," by definition, appears an inappropriate term to use when the arrangement itself becomes dynamic—a variable responding to changes in other variables. The emerging concept is one of a purposeful system, populated with processes, sensors, skills, roles, assets, and an information infrastructure. It has no commonly accepted name, so we can either use the old label for something new, or invent a new term, like "protean socioeconomic organism"—in either case contributing yet another dollop of confusion to an already difficult subject. I will use "organization," but with the caveat that it doesn't mean what it used to.

The consensus emerging about the organization of the year 2000 is that it will be flat, team-centered, networked, and dynamic. *Fortune* describes it as "a vertiginous pattern of constantly changing teams, task forces, partnerships and other informal structures. . . . teams variously composed of shop-floor workers, managers, technical experts, suppliers and customers will join together to do a job and then disband, with everyone going off to the next assignment.[5]

This need not be as bad as it sounds. First, to the extent it is interpreted as "management-by-letting-go-of-the-reins," it is not likely to happen at all. Responsible managers will not let go of the reins unless they have secured a firm grip on another part of the horse; and if this makes the horse run less efficiently, what's the point? Unsurprisingly, a recent study of large organizations—including some enthusiastic endorsers of the new model—encountered self-directed teams in only a very few, highly specialized circumstances.

Second, the "network of empowered teams" scenario can be very effective, but only if the teams operate in a common context. Organizational context is rendered partly explicit in the hierarchical industrial age company by mission statements, corporate policy letters, job descriptions and so forth. The role of the "office of the vice president of manufacturing" is knowable to anyone, and does not change radically as incumbents come and go. This worked well enough in the relatively static environment of industrial-age marketing. It is proving itself inadequate in the dynamics of today's service-centered economy.

---

[5]"The Bureaucracy Busters," *Fortune*, June 17, 1991.

Needed: An Institutional DNA

The flat(ter) organization will certainly happen, because the benefits in terms of responsiveness and flexibility are too determinant for it not to. But it will not happen successfully as the ad hocracy often depicted: spontaneously formed groups empowered to "do their thing," including deciding what their "thing" is. It will happen successfully when the behavior of these teams is governed (but not dictated) by something which codifies the essential nature of the institution, and the "way we do things around here"—most particularly and importantly, the way we *change* the way we do things around here. This "something" can be thought of as a kind of institutional DNA, because it establishes the potentiality and limits of behavior by the constituent parts of an organism. It governs, but does not dictate, the responses of the organization to external stimuli. Without this, terminal suboptimization occurs.

Suboptimization is the major risk of decentralization. It has traditionally been a built-in feature of interenterprise relationships, which can be thought of as an extreme case of decentralization. But over the past decade, the benefits of coordinated activity demonstrated by just-in-time systems in the manufacturing sector have begun to spread to other industries and functions. Just-in-time systems are possible only through sharing information, which enhances its economic value.

Sharing information about logistics, customer preferences, sales transactions, promotions, and new product introduction plans, consumer goods manufacturers and retailers are helping each other reduce distribution costs, inventories, and out-of-stock occurrences. Kraft's "micromerchandising" program puts massive amounts of structured data in the hands of its sales force, enabling it to develop detailed views of "what's going on out there" in a retailer's stores, and recommend ways of improving sales and profits.[6] Shared information dissolves boundaries and permits higher-level optimization between, as well as within, organizations.

The Organization of 2001

The new organizational structure will differ from its industrial-age predecessor by its *modular character*, its *focus on process*, its *information*

---

[6]"Moving the Pampers Faster Cuts Everyone's Costs," *New York Times*, July 14, 1991.

intensity, and its *explicit rendering.* Because it is enabled by information technology, it will require specification and codification of

- The game being played.
- The conditions under which it makes sense to play.
- The way we plan to play.
- The way in which we will change the way we play.
- How successful play is defined.
- How the status of play is determined.

This institutional mind-set must be explicit and codified in order to form the shared context necessary for focus and coordination of "empowered team networks." To stretch our analogy even further, it expresses purpose and intent to guide the functioning of "institutional DNA."

Anyone who has tried to translate a presentation into prose has a sense of how excruciatingly difficult it can be to make the implicit explicit. We now must contemplate the task of describing the environment, objective, and behavior potential of complex structures with a rigor sufficient to enable them to function as purposeful systems. (A likely candidate for help is the field of linguistics, which is concerned with the question of how reality is mapped into semantic space. Computer science has long used linguistic terms such as "entities," "attributes," "relations," and "syntax." It seems certain that a great deal of research into methodologies and tools for codifying organizational behavior will be undertaken in the coming decade. As this occurs, linguistics will join psychology, economics, cognitive science, and anthropology as instruments of marketing theory development.)[7]

Enterprise Modeling: Creating Institutional DNA

With the exception of interesting, but still essentially trivial, examples of image interpretation by computers, it requires human beings to recognize

---

[7]See Terry Winograd and Fernando Flores, *Understanding Computers and Cognition* (Reading, Mass.: Addison-Wesley, 1991) (originally published in 1984 by Ablex Corp., Norwood, N.J.) for a discussion of how information technology operates in the domain of language and "mediates linguistic action as the essential human activity." Flores has operationalized these concepts in a software program, and has developed a generalized schema for representing processes unambiguously and exhaustively.

See Derek Bickerton, *Language and Species* (Chicago: University of Chicago Press, 1990) for an interesting and accessible discussion of linguistic theory. Bickerton describes the mechanisms by which humans map species-specific perceptions of "reality" into neural space, and then into patterns and assign meaning to them. Computers, however, can leverage speed, and the ability to keep millions of things "in mind," to reveal and present patterns for human consideration.

For example, using mathematics which model the physics of the Red Shift and the spectral analysis of chemical elements, a computer can process digitized signals from a remote galaxy to calculate the distance and size of its constituent parts. The results can be displayed in the form of a three-dimensional picture and rotated in accordance with the rules of descriptive geometry. This permits people to see the galaxy from the back or side, and to discover—as happened recently—a huge void passing laterally through it. The pattern was always implicit in the data, but not until a computer made it manifest could humans recognize and be startled by it.

Using models to structure information can be just as helpful to the brand manager confronted with reams of scanner data as to the scientist inundated with telemetry data. Companies such as Frito-Lay have built "data warehouses" which contain massive amounts of information linked by data models in ways likely to reveal patterns of interest to analysts or executives. This is necessary in order to turn "data glut" into "news," and requires explicit specification of the most important factors, the way they relate to other factors, and which of their attributes should be captured. If the model is extended to describe and relate business processes and the rules by which these processes can be legally and logically combined in accordance with company policy, it is called an Enterprise Model.

Creating such a model is a major undertaking. In the case of one large bank, it required 18 months of heavy executive involvement to represent its retail and wholesale functions in an enterprise model— followed by five years to design and build an information infrastructure that contains the information, business processes, and "DNA code" about how these processes can be combined in a way that conforms to the model. These assets are kept in a systems repository as modular, reusable data and logic elements. The model institutionalizes the bank's know-how and makes it sharable by all in accordance with their authorization to know and act.

Managers can use such a model-driven infrastructure to create and modify financial products with confidence that their actions are consistent

---

semantic space. The structuring disciplines of language (prediction, grammar, and syntax) establish the permissible paths (phrases and sentences) through semantic space. These disciplines offer the potential for rigorous representation of enterprise models in technology.

with the objectives and policies of the bank. The implications of this type of strategy are profound. First, modularizing functions, data, and policy builds flexibility into any organizational structure. It greatly facilitates the problem of designing a change management process, and avoids "hard-wiring" the past, present, or a particular future into institutional behavior. Both the business and the information infrastructure require this kind of "snap-together" architecture. A crucial parameter is the level of granularity—determining the point at which the additional degrees of freedom associated with a finer breakdown of business function and data are outweighed by the cost of maintaining the information asset at this level.

Second, modeling methodologies can be used as a discipline that forces management to get its collective mind around the way the business should be run, and to express it explicitly. Transferring know-how from the "seat-of-the-pants" to the "front-of-the-brain" requires a trial-and-error approach, and relies heavily on methodologies and tools that highlight redundancies and contradictions in the model.

Breakthrough: Continuous Re-engineering

Systems that can generate software directly from an enterprise model's representation of data flows, processes, and human responsibilities appear imminent. To achieve the rigor required for this, the representational schema of a modeling methodology must be able to: unambiguously and consistently characterize any process, at any scale; exhaustively account for the possible outcomes of every process; and show the roles and accountabilities of the human beings involved in carrying them out. At this writing, at least one schema has been empirically verified to have these properties, offering the prospect that within the next few years it will become possible to change the way a business operates by changing the model that represents it.[8] The Enterprise Model would thus become a vehicle for re-engineering the business on a continuing basis, and for ensuring that change is consistently implemented throughout the organization.

The difficulties associated with mapping a model into computer code has been a significant deterrent to the use of enterprise models for the past 15 years. Overcoming them would create a management tool for

---

[8]Ibid.

manipulating the business by manipulating information, i.e., "managing by wire" a significant spectrum of a firm's activities (in the same sense that the pilot of an Airbus or a Boeing 757 "flies by wire").

Of course, even an elaborate model that accurately specifies the parameters of organizational response to environmental stimuli and management intent will not guarantee predictable outcomes—much less success. DNA maps do not, after all, predict golf scores. Management's collective understanding of the business and its environment will remain the major determinant of business success, but that understanding will have to be rendered explicit. The quality of management's abstraction; the accuracy with which it is mapped into the information infrastructure; decisions about the placement of sampling rates of information probes; and the skill with which the model is manipulated and modified will become critical success factors by the end of the decade.

SUMMARY OF KEY CHANGES

*Technology, processing information faster, is increasing the pace of things to an extent that only technology, managing and structuring information better, can enable us to react fast and well enough.

*The costs of processing and communicating data will decrease substantially. Networks, connecting more people, places, and things together, will make it possible to capture and communicate information from and between more sources and destinations. This enhances the value of an organization's information asset by increasing its comprehensiveness, and thus its potential to know and understand more about what is going on inside and outside the organization.

*Sampling rates from these sources can be greater, driven by the same cost/performance curve, making possible reduced reaction time, lower inventories, and additional just-in-time activities. It will be economical to capture greater levels of detail about transactions and business process results. The availability of previously hidden data will allow marketing management to relate them in a larger number of ways, creating additional patterns and shedding more light on the behavior of the firm and its environment.

*Technology platforms and architectures will become more modular and integrative, enabling the sharing of more information and logic. This increases the potential for coordination and collaboration among groups that cross disciplinary, organizational, and institutional boundaries. However, only a small part of the cost of implementing these systems is the technology itself. Re-engineering the applications and data structures that represent a legacy of decades will have to be done at a pace that is both financially and operationally digestible.

*Software tools for managing information about information will mature and expand in functionality. They will increase the amount of context, and therefore meaning and relevance in the data, and will be essential in rescuing us from the "data glut" and "information overload" that would otherwise be the major outcome of more frequently sampling a greater number of probes at deeper levels of detail.

*Methodologies that assist humans in abstracting reality will be applied to model increasingly large and complex chunks of institutional behavior. They may soon become rigorous enough representations of information flow, process flow, and work flow to generate computer code directly from these representations. This opens up the prospect of re-engineering the business by manipulating the model, and of "managing by wire."

*Flatter, networked, empowered teams seem to be a structural imperative in a world where customers value flexibility and responsiveness over efficiency and predictability as the premiere characteristic of organizations they want to deal with. Coherent behavior by the enterprise will require an explicit rendering of much that was previously tacit. The rendering will have to be sufficiently exhaustive, detailed, and accurate to codify presently desirable behavior.

There remains the need to manage change, a management task that itself is changing. "Change management" is often thought of as transition management: we are This; we need to be That; we must manage the change from This to That without going under in the process. The implicit assumption is that the problem is to get, in an orderly way, from one relatively steady state to another. But That, and increasingly This, are less and less likely to exhibit the characteristics of a system in equilibrium.

Therefore, the model will have to include the process by which the need for subsequent change is identified and implemented in accordance with parameters specified by policy makers. It is unclear how long it will take to develop the understanding and techniques for mapping complex human institutions with the precision required, nor what the limits of complexity might be. But there is already evidence that this approach is feasible for sizable domains of corporate activity, given the requisite information and technology infrastructure.

Information Strategies: A Missing Link

If this is a plausible projection of the forces that will shape the environment of the year 2001, and if marketing is to be viewed as the process by which an organization adapts to its environment, then the marketing discipline will encompass responsibility for important elements of the information strategy of a business:

- Deciding how many probes to place, where to place them, how much detail to capture, and how often to sample.
- Acquiring and integrating information from external sources that conform to and supplement internal information structures and applications.
- Establishing when and how the firm should share market information with others.
- Building the information map of the firm, creating relevance criteria for sifting and filtering the data acquired, deciding which patterns are potentially important, and specifying the elements, attributes, and relationships most likely to reveal them.
- Deciding on which elements of "how we do things around here" should be "hard-wired" into computer code, and which should be represented in the model as parameters which govern, but do not dictate, action.
- Using information profiles to manage the firm's customer/client portfolio.
- Managing an increasing portion of the business by wire, that is, by manipulating the information systems' representation of it.

Many businesses are struggling to align their business and information technology strategies. This is very difficult to do without an information strategy to bridge the gap. Marketing is the likely candidate to give responsibility for developing this "missing link" in response-oriented firms.

MARKETING AT THE MILLENNIUM: A SCENARIO

We have considered some of the changes to be expected in the power of technology and information management tools, and in institutional structure. By the end of the twentieth century their cumulative magnitude and scope will have made obsolete many basic concepts about the nature and behavior of businesses—concepts which were givens as recently as 20 years ago.

Of these, perhaps most fundamental is the transformation from product to service-centered behavior. As discussed above, this reorientation leads directly to different optimizing parameters for the business: from efficiency and predictability to flexibility and responsiveness. Taken one step further, it implies a change in the primary managerial function from resource allocation to value management, and suggests the following scenario (Figure 15-3).

Beginning with much better and more elaborate representations of customer/client activity and direction, an inventory is made of the institutional competencies required to make an important and distinctive contribution to client success. Such competencies will be less product and more process/methodology centered. This inventory is assessed in terms of sustainable uniqueness, and availability in-house or by acquisition. Choices can then be made about the core values-added that will always come out "make" in make-buy analyses, and that are the bases of differentiation.

The other values-added required to provide complete responses to customer requests are subject to outsourcing based on make-buy econom-

FIGURE 15-3
Scenario: The Modular, Service-Centered Firm

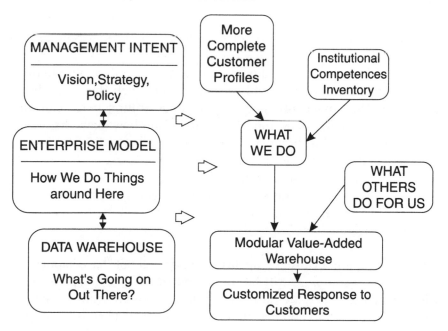

ics. The value chain is thus "unlinked," and becomes a warehouse of modularized values that can combine just-in-time into client responses with an economic lot size of one. "Value modules" common to multiple clients and derived from common institutional competencies are managed to realize economies of scope internally, and across institutional borders.

Such a scenario is made feasible by an equally modular information infrastructure that makes a "manage by wire" enterprise asset out of technology, data, process logic, and policy by relating them through an enterprise model. This explicit rendering of "how we do things around here" is driven by management decisions regarding the firm's purpose, objectives, and policies, and is supported by a data warehouse which contains, in context, up-to-date information about "what's going on out there."

In this context, an "enterprise" is the highest level at which coherent and globally optimized behavior is required in combining values-added for a sufficiently large number of clients. It is a dynamic organism whose purpose and behavior options are codified by the model, and realized through networked teams of intellectual and capital assets. In the service-centered enterprise of Figure 15-3, a new set of marketing decisions will contend for primacy with the famous "Four Ps" of price, product, place, and promotion. Likely candidates are

- Competencies: Which world-class processes and know-how do we have and/or should we develop?
- Values-Added: What should be the value components of our offerings and responses? Which should we make, and which should we buy?
- Models: How much of "how we do things around here" can and should be codified? How much granularity and how many degrees of freedom should we build into the model? What is the process for changing the way we do things?
- Collaborations: Which customers should we invest in? What kind of cooperative arrangements should we make with customers and partners? How much of what kinds of risk are we willing to share with and manage for them?

Previous verbs notwithstanding, this scenario will not "have happened" by 2001. The technology will be there, and many specific applications will have demonstrated the value of capturing, communicating, sharing, and structuring information. Enterprise models will have been implemented for increasingly substantial business domains, but few—if any—large companies will be "managed by wire" across the entire business.

The assertion made here is that by the beginning of the next century there will be unambiguous evidence that this scenario is indeed unfolding, and that "managing by wire" represents a logical culmination of the marketing information revolution.

APPENDIX*
Open Questions

To be useful as a foil for strategic thinking, a scenario must be constructed before the data exist to confirm its validity. But to become a basis for strategic investment, it must be converted from "plausible" to "likely."

Academicians can make important contributions to this conversion. Among the questions needing research are

1. What are the limitations imposed by complexity on the ability to codify an organization's environment, purpose, behavior, and change processes with sufficient accuracy and completeness? How fast are these limitations changing?
2. What can be learned from small-scale prototypes of management by wire? Are they successful prototypes?
3. What methodologies, tools, and techniques are most useful in rendering explicit an organization's nature and function? Which show most promise in relaxing the constraints imposed by complexity?
4. How can "organizational orientation" be operationalized? What parameters most effectively position a given organization on the product-centered/service-centered continuum? Is an orientation profile a useful variable in predicting success?
5. Where are information-based "personalization" strategies emerging? What are the attributes of successful ones?
6. What kind of information and technology infrastructures best support coordinated activity by networks of teams?
7. How much could be learned by creating an enterprise model of a complex business and using it as the basis of a simulated management

These projections of technology are based on work done by IBM Research. This section has benefited from the ideas and suggestions of Dr. John A. Armstrong, IBM vice president of Science and Technology, and those of Dr. Abraham Peled and Douglas J. Wright of IBM Research.

exercise in which information intensity is a key variable, and information investments a management option?

The Technology Juggernaut: Smaller and Fasted Bits, Processed in Parallel by Reusable Modules of Software

HARDWARE

By 2001, the unit cost of uniprocessor logic operations, dynamic RAM memory, optical storage, and color LCD displays will decrease by factors of 6 to 30. The cost of communicating a unit of information, taking into account not only the technology involved but the relative pervasiveness of its deployment will drop by a factor of 100 to 1000. (Figure 15-2).

Photons can carry the mail roughly 100,000 times faster than electrons. The replacement of digital-electrical by digital-optical communication technology gives rise to a technological discontinuity: suddenly we can communicate information orders of magnitude faster than we can process it, inverting a relationship that has existed for 40 years. Today's information systems are designed with trade-offs to accommodate relatively noisy, slow, and expensive communications, which all of a sudden are becoming fast, cheap, and clean. But the huge investment required to replace the old infrastructure will slow the dispersion of optical technology (except in countries where the government edicts it), which is why "pervasiveness" is factored in to the productivity improvement of communications in Figure 15-2. In addition to asset replacement, changes in tariffs, routing, and switching will be required, and the "last mile" problem (e.g., getting gigabit bandwidth economically from the street to the house) is unlikely to be solved by optical fiber in the next ten years.

After the new technology is introduced into new products, and the products into new systems, individual users should experience a composite improvement of one order of magnitude.

Translated into systems capabilities and hardware costs, a system costing roughly $10 million in 2001 could include the following components:

- An optical or magnetic TAPE LIBRARY storage large enough to store a photo of everyone on the planet, or 250,000 hours of high-definition television, or 40 copies of everything in the 1991 Library of Congress;
- An optical DISK LIBRARY storage large enough to hold 3–5 years of transactions of the largest banks in the world;
- Enough DASD to hold 2 billion pages of text, or months of sales transactions for large retail chains;

- One trillion characters of semiconductor MEMORY (enough to process all active airline reservations, or all credit card transactions in main memory); and
- A 500-way, 200 billion instructions per second parallel PROCESSOR.

For an investment of about $50,000 in hardware, a small company could have a system that would provide online storage of its sales catalog; service library; all journals in a given field for the past five years; years of sales transactions; multimedia processing, and real-time natural language queries of data and text. Some of the dramatic technologies that are receiving a great deal of attention in the popular press, such as optical computing (as opposed to optical communications) and superconductivity, are not expected to be commercially important by 2001. Nor will HAL make an appearance by then, because the algorithms that underlie his behavior won't exist.

SOFTWARE

Largely because of techniques for producing reusable software, software development productivity should improve substantially — significantly less than the increase in performance for uniprocessors, but quite respectable compared to other people-intensive activity. There will be more commercial packages available, and these will be designed to facilitate customization by adherence to a growing body of interface standards.

Encapsulation of function in modular software elements such as "objects" will greatly enhance the prospects for building flexibility and responsiveness into applications and their underlying systems software. Integrative systems architectures will provide increasing degrees of connectivity, data and logic sharing, and information structuring tools. These will appear as an additional layer of software, called application frameworks or architectures, which are tailored to the requirements of a specific segment of applications, e.g., reservation systems, insurance systems, and computer-integrated manufacturing systems. If they are well designed, they can dramatically shorten the time to get new applications up and running, as well as provide access to older "legacy" applications and data structures.

It is likely that these application frameworks will trigger the development of a new layer of standards as the need to support alliances and interenterprise transactions increases. Although still a subject of intense debate, it is probable that "open systems" will not be implemented as common software, but as common standards that ensure the interoperability of different systems and application software.

Another class of software, crucial to the scenario described in this chapter, is a collection of software tools and disciplines that generalize new ways of organizing, structuring, searching for, representing, and accessing information. Object-oriented programming, semantic networks and databases, hypertext, and neural networks are a sample of still fairly immature technologies with great promise. They underlie important "information engineering" functionalities such as information retrieval, cross-referencing, keyword extraction, pattern searches, natural language processing, relevance filtering—and exotica such as Knowbots, Software Agents, and Knowledge Navigators. Important progress on a number of these fronts can be anticipated, but their integration into systems will be governed by the tectonic pace of standards definition.

ABOUT THE CONTRIBUTORS

Robert Adler is an associate professor of legal studies in the Kenan-Flagler School of Business at the University of North Carolina. He teaches courses in Business Law, Business Ethics, and Business-Government Relations. He is a graduate of the University of Pennsylvania and the University of Michigan Law School. He has previously worked in Washington, D.C. as counsel to the Subcommittee on Health and the Environment of the Energy and Commerce Committee of the House of Representatives and as an attorney adviser to two commissioners at the U.S. Consumer Product Safety Commission. He currently serves on the board of directors of Consumers Union.

Robert C. Blattberg is the Polk Brothers Distinguished Professor of Retailing and director of the Center for Retail Management in the Kellogg Graduate School of Management at Northwestern University. Prior to this he was the Charles H. Kellstadt Professor of Marketing and director of the Center of Marketing Information Technology in the Graduate School of Business at the University of Chicago. He received his B.A. in mathematics from Northwestern University and an M.S. and Ph.D. in Industrial Administration from Carnegie-Mellon University. His primary research is in database marketing, in particular the development of statistical models to improve managerial marketing decision making. His monograph, "Assessing and Capturing the Soft Benefits of Scanning," has served as a guide for numerous retailers and his book, *Sales Promotion* (Prentice Hall, 1990), is widely recognized as the authoritative publication on the subject.

Paul N. Bloom is professor of Marketing in the Kenan-Flagler School of Business at the University of North Carolina. Prior to this, he served on the faculty of the University of Maryland and was a visiting research professor at the Marketing Science Institute. His B.S. is from Lehigh University, his M.B.A. from the Wharton School at the University of Pennsylvania, and his Ph.D. in marketing from Northwestern University. His research on public policy toward marketing, social marketing, and professional services marketing has appeared in numerous articles and books. He is the author of *Knowledge Development in Marketing: The MSI Experience* and the co-author of *Marketing Professional Services*. He has been active in both the American Marketing Association and the Association for Consumer Research.

Raymond R. Burke is associate professor of Marketing at the Harvard Business School. Prior to this, he was assistant professor of Marketing at the University of Pennsylvania's Wharton School. He earned both his Ph.D. and M.S. in psychology and marketing, respectively, from the University of Florida and his B.A. summa cumma laude from the University of Miami. His research interests focus on advertising communication, consumer decision making, and knowledge-based decision support systems. He is currently working on a series of real and computer-simulated test market experiments to understand better how consumers respond to marketing factors at the point of purchase. His articles have appeared in various journals, including the *Journal of Consumer Research*, the *Journal of Marketing and Marketing Science*. He is the co-author of *ADSTRAT: An Advertising Decision Support System*.

George S. Day is the Geoffrey T. Boisi Professor and Director of the Hunstman Center for Global Competition and Innovation at the Wharton School at the University of Pennsylvania. He received his Ph.D. from Columbia University and has taught at Stanford University, IMD in Lausanne, Switzerland, and the University of Toronto. He served as the executive director of the Marketing Science Institute between 1989 and 1991. His research interests include competitive strategies in global markets, managing new product development, strategic planning processes, and methods and marketing management.

John Deighton is associate professor of Marketing at the University of Chicago's Graduate School of Business. His research in marketing communications, direct response marketing, and financial services marketing is published in the *Journal of Marketing*, the *Journal of Marketing Research*, the *Journal of Consumer Research*, *Organizational Behavior and Human Decision Processes*, *Sloan Management Review*, and *Psychology and Marketing*. He received the 1990 Alpha Kappa Psi award of the *Journal of Marketing*. His early work experience was in brand management at Unilever and as a management consultant specializing in retailing and real estate economics.

Rashi Glazer is chairman of the Marketing Group and associate professor at the Haas School of Business of the University of California at Berkeley. His M.B.A. and Ph.D. are from Stanford University and he has been on the faculty of Columbia University. He has published extensively in leading academic journals in the areas of behavioral and managerial decision making, the relationship between markeing and technology strategy, and the strategic use of information and information technology; he is the co-author of the book *Cable TV Advertising*. He developed the INFOVALUE® program for measuring the value of a firm's information and SUITS®, an interactive computer simulation for teaching the strategic use of information and the integration of information technology strategy with business strategy.

Stephan H. Haeckel is director of Strategic Studies at IBM's Advanced Business Institute. His area of concentration is the impact of information and information technology on business and their implications for corporate strategy development. He speaks internationally on this subject to senior executives in business, government, and education, and has been published by the Harvard Business School Press, the Marketing Science Institute, and the *Harvard Business Review*. During his career at IBM he has served as the director of Advanced Market Development and was one of the authors of IBM's corporate services strategy. He is chairman of the Research Policy Committee of the Marketing Science Institute and vice chairman of its Executive Committee. He has engineering and M.B.A. degrees from Washington University in St. Louis.

Stephen J. Hoch is the Robert P. Gwinn Professor of Marketing and Behavioral Science and a member of the Center for Decision Research in the Graduate School of Business at the University of Chicago. He received his B.A. in Human Biology from Stanford University, an M.B.A. from UCLA, and a Ph.D. from Northwestern University. Prior to his academic appointments, he worked at Walt Disney Productions in various marketing positions. His research interests range from understanding retail strategy and consumer behavior to the psychology of prediction and forecasting. He is particularly interested in how experts should interact with new information technologies and decision support systems. Currently he is directing a project on micromarketing that is a collaboration between the University of Chicago, Dominick's Finer Foods, and 18 consumer packaged-goods companies. His research has been published in journals such as the *Journal of Marketing, Journal of Consumer Research, Management Science,* and the *Sloan Management Review.*

William K. Holstein is Distinguished Service Professor and former dean of the School of Business at the State University of New York at Albany. He received his Ph.D. at Purdue University and previously taught at the Harvard Business School. He is interested in strategic issues in information systems and is the co-author of three books and several articles in the areas of production management, information systems, and BASIC programming.

David Ing is an industry specialist for IBM Canada Ltd. He was a doctoral student at the Faculty of Commerce at the University of British Columbia and received a Master of Management degree from Northwestern's Kellogg School and a Bachelor of Commerce from the University of Toronto. He is a marketing scientist experienced in applying analytical methods with advanced information technologies in the analysis of large point-of-sale and customer databases. He has led projects designing suites of marketing applications in category management, frequent shopper programs, and brand management with clients in the retail and consumer packaged-goods segments in Canada and the United States. He was a founder of the Canadian Centre for Marketing Information Technologies at the Faculty of Management, University of Toronto and has acted as a technical adviser to the Centre.

Hotaka Katahira is professor of Marketing Science, Faculty of Economics, University of Tokyo. He graduated from the Graduate School of Economics at the University of Tokyo. He has been a visiting professor at the Haas School of Business, University of California at Berkeley and the Wharton School of the University of Pennsylvania. His current research interests include choice modeling, analysis of scanner data and international comparisons of consumer behavior. Among his numerous publications are *Marketing Science,* an advanced Japanese textbook on marketing science, and the monograph, "A New Approach to Consumer Choice Analysis." He is currently a director of the Japan Institute of Marketing Science and the editor of the *Journal of Marketing Science,* the first international journal in marketing in Japan.

Byung-Do Kim is currently a visiting assistant professor of Marketing in the Graduate School of Industrial Administration at Carnegie-Mellon

University. He holds a B.B.A. in management from Seoul National University, an M.B.A. from New York University and a Ph.D. in marketing from the University of Chicago. His current research interests include issues associated with econometric modeling of household choice behavior and the implications on retailers' pricing decisions and various statistical problems associated with the analysis of scanner panel data and aggregate store-level data.

John D.C. Little is Institute Professor and Professor of Management Science at the Sloan School of Management, Massachusetts Institute of Technology. He specializes in marketing models and their use in solving business problems. Currently he is particularly interested in the implications for marketing theory and practice of the large databases being collected by bar code readers in supermarkets. He was co-founder and chairman of Management Decision Systems of Waltham, Massachusetts, a marketing consulting and software company that merged into Information Resources, Inc. of Chicago in 1985; he is now a director of IRI. Professor Little received his S.B. and Ph.D. from MIT in physics. He is a member of the National Academy of Engineering.

John M. McCann is professor of Marketing in the Fuqua School of Business at Duke University. His Ph.D. is from Purdue University and he has taught at Cornell University and the University of California at Berkeley. He founded and directs the Marketing Workbench Laboratory, a research center at Fuqua dedicated to research and education into methods for dealing with marketing information. The laboratory has been sponsored by IBM and 25 large consumer packaged-goods manufacturers, retailers, and data vendors. Its research program has produced over 20 knowledge-based systems, which are described in two books: *Expert Systems for a Scanner Data Environment* and *Databases and Knowledge Systems in Merchandising*.

George R. Milne is assistant professor of Marketing at the University of Massachusetts at Amherst. His research interests are in competitive marketing strategy and marketing public-policy areas. He has published in journals such as the *Journal of Marketing*, the *Journal of Public Policy* and *Marketing and Marketing Letters*, as well as several national and international conference proceedings.

Andrew A. Mitchell is the Patricia Ellison Professor of Marketing in the Faculty of Management at the University of Toronto and the executive director of the Canadian Centre for Marketing Information Technologies. He received his Ph.D. from the University of California at Berkeley and has been on the faculties of Carnegie-Mellon University and Pennsylvania State University. He is widely published in such journals as the *Journal of Consumer Research*, the *Journal of Marketing Research*, and *Management Science* and serves on several editorial review boards. He has edited two books, *Psychological Processes and Advertising Effects* and *Advertising, Exposure, Memory and Choice*. His current research includes the development of micro-level behavioral models of advertising and the development of marketing decision support systems combining artificial intelligence and operations research technologies.

Lakshmi Mohan has extensive experience in designing and implementing marketing decision support systems and executive information systems. Prior to joining the management science and information systems faculty of the School of Business at the State University of New York at Albany, she taught at MIT's Sloan School of Management and the Indian Institute of Management in Calcutta. She received her Ph.D. from Columbia University.

Don Peppers is president of Marketing 1:1, an independent consulting firm in Weston, Connecticut, with clients in business development and marketing technology, including MCI, Harley Davidson, Chase Manhattan Bank, and Barry Blau and Partners. He was formerly with Lintas: USA and Chiat/Day. He and Martha Rogers have published a book about the technology of marketing and the future of business competition titled, *The One-To-One Future: Building Relationships One Customer at a Time* (Doubleday/Currency).

Martha Rogers is associate professor of Marketing at Bowling Green State University in Ohio. Formerly a copywriter and advertising executive, she has served on the National Advertising Review Board. Her research has been published in such journals as the *Journal of Advertising Research* and *Current Issues and Research in Advertising*. With Don Peppers she is the co-author of *The One-To-One Future: Building Relationships One Customer at a Time* (Doubleday/Currency).

John D. Schmitz is vice president of Special Projects at Information Resources Inc. in Waltham, Massachusetts. His formal education was in Economics and Operations Research at MIT. He has worked as a consultant, statistician, programmer, and manager. His current interest is in integrating multiple technologies, including expert systems, in marketing decision support systems. He enjoys mountain climbing and triathlons.

Shigeru Yagi is the general manager of the Home Scan System Department, Video Research Ltd., a firm he has been with for more than 20 years. He holds a B.A. in law from Kansai University. He has published a number of papers in the leading marketing journals in Japan and is currently an area editor of the *Journal of Marketing Science*, in charge of industrial applications. He was once a professional popular music singer and is still a karaoke star.

Jianming Ye is an assistant professor of Statistics at the Graduate School of Business, University of Chicago. He received his Ph.D. from the University of Chicago, Department of Statistics in 1992 and a B.S. in mathematics from Xiamen University in 1985. His research interests include modeling marketing effects using point-of-sale retail data and designing new methodologies for the analysis of both scanner and electronic panel data.

INDEX